The Student's Guide to VHDL
Second Edition

The Student's Guide
to VHDL
Second Edition

Peter J. Ashenden

EDA CONSULTANT, ASHENDEN DESIGNS PTY. LTD.

ADJUNCT ASSOCIATE PROFESSOR, ADELAIDE UNIVERSITY

ELSEVIER

AMSTERDAM • BOSTON • HEIDELBERG • LONDON
NEW YORK • OXFORD • PARIS • SAN DIEGO
SAN FRANCISCO • SINGAPORE • SYDNEY • TOKYO
Morgan Kaufmann Publishers is an imprint of Elsevier

MORGAN KAUFMANN PUBLISHERS

Morgan Kaufmann Publishers is an imprint of Elsevier.
30 Corporate Drive, Suite 400, Burlington, MA 01803, USA

∞ This book is printed on acid-free paper.

Library of Congress Cataloging-in-Publication Data
Ashenden, Peter J.
  The student's guide to VHDL / Peter J. Ashenden. -- 2nd ed.
      p. cm.
  Abridged version of the author's Designer's guide to VHDL.
  Includes bibliographical references and index.
  ISBN 978-1-55860-865-8 (pbk. : alk. paper) 1. VHDL (Computer hardware description language)
2. Electronic digital computers--Computer simulation. I. Title.

  TK7888.3.A8632 2008
  621.39'2--dc22

                                          2008011064

ISBN: 978-1-55860-865-8

For information on all Morgan Kaufmann publications,
visit our Web site at *www.mkp.com* or *www.books.elsevier.com*

Printed in the United States.
08 09 10   5 4 3 2 1

To my son Alexander

Contents

Preface

VHDL is a language for describing digital electronic systems. It arose out of the United States government's Very High Speed Integrated Circuits (VHSIC) program. In the course of this program, it became clear that there was a need for a standard language for describing the structure and function of integrated circuits (ICs). Hence the VHSIC Hardware Description Language (VHDL) was developed. It was subsequently developed further under the auspices of the Institute of Electrical and Electronic Engineers (IEEE) and adopted in the form of the IEEE Standard 1076, Standard VHDL Language Reference Manual, in 1987. This first standard version of the language is often referred to as VHDL-87.

Like all IEEE standards, the VHDL standard is subject to review from time to time. Comments and suggestions from users of the 1987 standard were analyzed by the IEEE working group responsible for VHDL, and in 1992 a revised version of the standard was proposed. This was eventually adopted in 1993, giving us VHDL-93. A second round of revision of the standard was started in 1998. That process was completed in 2001, giving us VHDL-2002. After that, further development took place in the IEEE working group and in a technical committee of an organization, Accellera, whose charter is to promote standards for electronics design. These efforts led to the current version of the language, VHDL-2008, described in this book.

VHDL is designed to fill a number of needs in the design process. First, it allows description of the structure of a system, that is, how it is decomposed into subsystems and how those subsystems are interconnected. Second, it allows the specification of the function of a system using familiar programming language forms. Third, as a result, it allows the design of a system to be simulated before being manufactured, so that designers can quickly compare alternatives and test for correctness without the delay and expense of hardware prototyping. Fourth, it allows the detailed structure of a design to be synthesized from a more abstract specification, allowing designers to concentrate on more strategic design decisions and reducing time to market.

This book presents a structured guide to the modeling facilities offered by the VHDL language, showing how they can be used for the design of digital systems. The book does not purport to teach digital design, since that topic is large enough by itself to warrant several textbooks covering its various aspects. Instead, the book assumes that the reader has at least a basic grasp of digital design concepts, such as might be gained from a first course in digital design in an engineering degree program. Some exposure to computer programming and to concepts of computer organization will also be beneficial. *The Student's Guide to VHDL* is a condensed edition of *The Designer's Guide to VHDL*, which is a complete reference describing all of the features in the language. In *The Student's Guide*, we have selected those features that are most commonly used in the educational context, making the book suitable for use in an introductory or intermediate-level course in digital or computer design. Those who need a complete language reference for use in advanced courses or professional practice may prefer to use *The Designer's Guide*.

One pervasive theme running through the presentation in this book is that modeling a system using a hardware description language is essentially a software design exercise. This implies that good software engineering practice should be applied. Hence the treatment in this book draws directly from experience in software engineering. There are numerous hints and techniques from small-scale and large-scale software engineering presented throughout the book, with the sincere intention that they might be of use to readers.

Structure of the Book

The Student's Guide to VHDL is organized so that it can be read linearly from front to back. This path offers a graduated development, with each chapter building on ideas introduced in the preceding chapters. Each chapter introduces a number of related concepts or language facilities and illustrates each one with examples.

Chapter 1 introduces the idea of a hardware description language and outlines the reasons for its use and the benefits that ensue. It then proceeds to introduce the basic concepts underlying VHDL, so that they can serve as a basis for examples in subsequent chapters. The next three chapters cover the aspects of VHDL that are most like conventional programming languages. These may be used to describe the behavior of a system in algorithmic terms. Chapter 2 explains the basic type system of the language and introduces the scalar data types. Chapter 3 describes the sequential control structures, and Chapter 4 covers composite data structures used to represent collections of data elements. In Chapter 5, the main facilities of VHDL used for modeling hardware are covered in detail. These include facilities for modeling the basic behavioral elements in a design, the signals that interconnect them and the hierarchical structure of the design.

The next group of chapters extends this basic set of facilities with language features that make modeling of large systems more tractable. Chapter 6 introduces procedures and functions, which can be used to encapsulate behavioral aspects of a design. Chapter 7 introduces the package as a means of collecting together related parts of a design or of creating modules that can be reused in a number of designs. Chapter 8 deals with the important topic of resolved signals, and Chapter 9 describes a number of predefined and standard packages for use in VHDL designs.

The third group of chapters covers advanced modeling features in VHDL. Chapter 10 covers aliases as a way of managing the large number of names that arise in a large model. Chapter 11 describes generic constants as a means of parameterizing the behavior and structure of a design. Chapter 12 deals with the topics of component instantiation and configuration. These features are important in large real-world models, but they can be difficult to understand. Hence this book introduces structural modeling through the mechanism of direct instantiation in earlier chapters and leaves the more general case of component instantiation and configuration until this later chapter. In Chapter 13, generated regular structures are covered.

In the last two chapters, we focus on synthesis. Chapter 14 covers guidelines for writing synthesizable models. Then Chapter 15 is a case study, showing development of a synthesizable processor core and its use in a small embedded system, a digital alarm clock.

Each chapter in the book is followed by a set of exercises designed to help the reader develop understanding of the material. Where an exercise relates to a particular topic described in the chapter, the section number is included in square brackets. An approximate "difficulty" rating is also provided, expressed using the following symbols:

❶   quiz-style exercise, testing basic understanding

❷   basic modeling exercise—10 minutes to half an hour effort

❸   advanced modeling exercise—one half to two hours effort

❹   modeling project—half a day or more effort

Answers for the first category of exercises are provided in Appendix C. The remaining categories involve developing VHDL models. Readers are encouraged to test correctness of their models by running them on a VHDL simulator. This is a much more effective learning exercise than comparing paper models with paper solutions.

Changes in the Second Edition

The first edition of this book was published in 1998, not long after VHDL-93 had gained acceptance. The latest revision of the language, VHDL-2008, adds a number of significant new language features, making this edition of *The Student's Guide to VHDL* significantly bigger than its predecessor. VHDL-2008 also specifies numerous minor new features and changes to existing features to enhance the usability of the language. This edition integrates descriptions of several of the new and revised features into the text. The differences between the various versions are highlighted in call-outs within the text, headed with "VHDL-2002," "VHDL-93," or "VHDL-87," as appropriate. In addition, some of the material has been removed or rearranged. There is a greater emphasis on synthesis in this edition. What was an appendix on the topic in previous editions of *The Designer's Guide to VHDL* has been substantially revised and promoted to full chapter status in this book. Finally, this edition includes a listing of the main VHDL standard packages as an appendix for reference.

Resources for Help and Information

Although this book covers many of the features of VHDL, there will no doubt be questions that it does not answer. For these, the reader will need to seek other resources.

Accellera is one of a number of organizations that sponsors the EDA Industry Working Groups Web server (www.eda.org). The server has links to Web pages and repositories of several VHDL standards groups and user groups.

Readers who have access to the Usenet electronic news network will find the news group comp.lang.vhdl a valuable resource. This discussion group is a source of announcements, sample models, questions and answers and useful software. Participants include VHDL users and people actively involved in the language standard working group and in VHDL tool development. The "frequently asked questions" (FAQ) file for this group is a mine of useful pointers to books, products and other information. It is archived at www.eda.org.

This book contains numerous examples of VHDL models that may also serve as a resource for resolving questions. The VHDL source code for these examples and the case studies, as well as other related information, is available on the companion website for the book at *books.elsevier.com/companions/9781558608658*.

Although I have been careful to avoid errors in the example code, there are no doubt some that I have missed. I would be pleased to hear about them, so that I can correct them in the on-line code and in future printings of this book. Errata and general comments can be e-mailed to me at *vhdl-book@ashenden.com.au*.

Acknowledgments

The seeds for this book go back to 1990 when I developed a brief set of notes, *The VHDL Cookbook*, for my computer architecture class at the University of Adelaide. At the time, there were few books on VHDL available, so I made my booklet available for on-line access. News of its availability spread quickly around the world, and within days, my e-mail in-box was bursting. At the time of writing this, nearly 20 years later, I still regularly receive messages about the *Cookbook*. Many of the respondents urged me to write a full textbook version. With that encouragement, I embarked upon the exercise that led to the first edition of *The Designer's Guide to VHDL*. Two years after publication of *The Designer's Guide*, the need for a book specifically for students became evident. That led to publication of the first edition of *The Student's Guide to VHDL*. I am grateful to the many engineers, students and teachers around the world who gave me the impetus to write these books and who made them such a success. I hope this new edition will continue to meet the need for a VHDL reference for student use.

In the previous editions of *The Designer's Guide* and *The Student's Guide*, I had the opportunity to extend thanks to the many people who assisted in development of the books. They included my colleagues at the University of Adelaide; my research collaborators, Phil Wilsey at the University of Cincinnati and Perry Alexander at the University of Kansas; the staff at Morgan Kaufmann Publishers, including, in particular, Denise Penrose; the reviewers of the manuscript for the first edition, namely, Poras Balsara of the University of Texas, Paul Menchini of Menchini & Associates, David Pitts of GTE Labs and the University of Lowell and Philip Wilsey of the University of Cincinnati; David Bishop for his contribution to the material on synthesis in the first edition of *The Designer's Guide*; and Mentor Graphics Corporation, for use of their ModelSim simulator to check the example models. I remain grateful to all of these people and organizations for their valuable contributions to the earlier editions and to this edition.

For the current edition, I would also like to thank Jim Lewis, who collaborated on a recent book, *VHDL-2008: Just the New Stuff*. Much of the material from that book has found its way into this book in one form or another. Thanks also to Mentor Graphics Corporation for continued use of the ModelSim simulator to check the example code. I continue to enjoy an excellent working relationship with the staff at Morgan Kaufmann Publishers and their parent company, Elsevier. Thanks to Chuck Glaser, Senior Acquisitions Editor, for his support in the continued development of these VHDL books; to Dawnmarie Simpson, Senior Project Manager in the Production Department, for her meticulous attention to detail; and to Denise Penrose, Publisher, for her longstanding support of my writing endeavors.

I have dedicated *The Designer's Guide to VHDL* to my wife Katrina, in appreciation of her understanding, encouragement, and support during the writing and revising of that book. The first edition of *The Student's Guide to VHDL* I dedicated to our son, Alexander, who was very young at that time. Since then, he has maintained his keen interest in learning and intellectual inquiry, as well as a great sense of humor. It is fitting that I dedicate this second edition to my young scholar also.

Chapter 1

Fundamental Concepts

In this introductory chapter, we describe what we mean by digital system modeling and see why modeling and simulation are an important part of the design process. We see how the hardware description language VHDL can be used to model digital systems and introduce some of the basic concepts underlying the language. We complete this chapter with a description of the basic lexical and syntactic elements of the language, to form a basis for the detailed descriptions of language features that follow in later chapters.

1.1 Modeling Digital Systems

If we are to discuss the topic of modeling digital systems, we first need to agree on what a digital system is. Different engineers would come up with different definitions, depending on their background and the field in which they were working. Some may consider a single VLSI circuit to be a self-contained digital system. Others might take a larger view and think of a complete computer, packaged in a cabinet with peripheral controllers and other interfaces.

For the purposes of this book, we include any digital circuit that processes or stores information as a digital system. We thus consider both the system as a whole and the various parts from which it is constructed. Therefore, our discussions cover a range of systems from the low-level gates that make up the components to the top-level functional units.

If we are to encompass this range of views of digital systems, we must recognize the complexity with which we are dealing. It is not humanly possible to comprehend such complex systems in their entirety. We need to find methods of dealing with the complexity, so that we can, with some degree of confidence, design components and systems that meet their requirements.

The most important way of meeting this challenge is to adopt a systematic methodology of design. If we start with a requirements document for the system, we can design an abstract structure that meets the requirements. We can then decompose this structure into a collection of components that interact to perform the same function. Each of these components can in turn be decomposed until we get to a level where we have some ready-made, primitive components that perform a required function. The result of this process is a hierarchically composed system, built from the primitive elements.

The advantage of this methodology is that each subsystem can be designed independently of others. When we use a subsystem, we can think of it as an abstraction rather than having to consider its detailed composition. So at any particular stage in the design process, we only need to pay attention to the small amount of information relevant to the current focus of design. We are saved from being overwhelmed by masses of detail.

We use the term *model* to mean our understanding of a system. The model represents that information which is relevant and abstracts away from irrelevant detail. The implication of this is that there may be several models of the same system, since different information is relevant in different contexts. One kind of model might concentrate on representing the function of the system, whereas another kind might represent the way in which the system is composed of subsystems. We will come back to this idea in more detail in the next section.

There are a number of important motivations for formalizing this idea of a model. First, when a digital system is needed, the requirements of the system must be specified. The job of the engineers is to design a system that meets these requirements. To do that, they must be given an understanding of the requirements, hopefully in a way that leaves them free to explore alternative implementations and to choose the best according to some criteria. One of the problems that often arises is that requirements are incompletely and ambiguously spelled out, and the customer and the design engineers disagree on what is meant by the requirements document. This problem can be avoided by using a formal model to communicate requirements.

A second reason for using formal models is to communicate understanding of the function of a system to a user. The designer cannot always predict every possible way in which a system may be used, and so is not able to enumerate all possible behaviors. If the designer provides a model, the user can check it against any given set of inputs and determine how the system behaves in that context. Thus a formal model is an invaluable tool for documenting a system.

A third motivation for modeling is to allow testing and verification of a design using simulation. If we start with a requirements model that defines the behavior of a system, we can simulate the behavior using test inputs and note the resultant outputs of the system. According to our design methodology, we can then design a circuit from subsystems, each with its own model of behavior. We can simulate this composite system with the same test inputs and compare the outputs with those of the previous simulation. If they are the same, we know that the composite system meets the requirements for the cases tested. Otherwise we know that some revision of the design is needed. We can continue this process until we reach the bottom level in our design hierarchy, where the components are real devices whose behavior we know. Subsequently, when the design is manufactured, the test inputs and outputs from simulation can be used to verify that the physical circuit functions correctly. This approach to testing and verification of course assumes that the test inputs cover all of the circumstances in which the final circuit will be used. The issue of test coverage is a complex problem in itself and is an active area of research.

A fourth motivation for modeling is to allow formal verification of the correctness of a design. Formal verification requires a mathematical statement of the required function of a system. This statement may be expressed in the notation of a formal logic system, such as temporal logic. Formal verification also requires a mathematical definition of the meaning of the modeling language or notation used to describe a design. The process of verification involves application of the rules of inference of the logic system to prove that the design implies the required function. While formal verification is not yet in everyday use, it is steadily becoming a more important part of the design process. There have already been significant demonstrations of formal verification techniques in real design projects, and the promise for the future is bright.

One final, but equally important, motivation for modeling is to allow automatic synthesis of circuits. If we can formally specify the function required of a system, it is in theory possible to translate that specification into a circuit that performs the function. The advantage of this approach is that the human cost of design is reduced, and engineers are free to explore alternatives rather than being bogged down in design detail. Also, there is less scope for errors being introduced into a design and not being detected. If we automate the translation from specification to implementation, we can be more confident that the resulting circuit is correct.

The unifying factor behind all of these arguments is that we want to achieve maximum reliability in the design process for minimum cost and design time. We need to ensure that requirements are clearly specified and understood, that subsystems are used correctly and that designs meet the requirements. A major contributor to excessive cost is having to revise a design after manufacture to correct errors. By avoiding errors, and by providing better tools for the design process, costs and delays can be contained.

1.2 Domains and Levels of Modeling

In the previous section, we mentioned that there may be different models of a system, each focusing on different aspects. We can classify these models into three domains: *function*, *structure* and *geometry*. The functional domain is concerned with the operations performed by the system. In a sense, this is the most abstract domain of description, since it does not indicate how the function is implemented. The structural domain deals with how the system is composed of interconnected subsystems. The geometric domain deals with how the system is laid out in physical space.

Each of these domains can also be divided into levels of abstraction. At the top level, we consider an overview of function, structure or geometry, and at lower levels we introduce successively finer detail. Figure 1.1 (devised by Gajski and Kuhn, see reference [4]) represents the domains for digital systems on three independent axes and represents the levels of abstraction by the concentric circles crossing each of the axes.

Let us look at this classification in more detail, showing how at each level we can create models in each domain. As an example, we consider a single-chip microcontroller system used as the controller for some measurement instrument, with data input connections and some form of display outputs.

1.2.1 Modeling Example

At the most abstract level, the function of the entire system may be described in terms of an algorithm, much like an algorithm for a computer program. This level of functional modeling is often called *behavioral modeling*, a term we shall adopt when presenting abstract descriptions of a system's function. A possible algorithm for our instrument control-

FIGURE 1.1

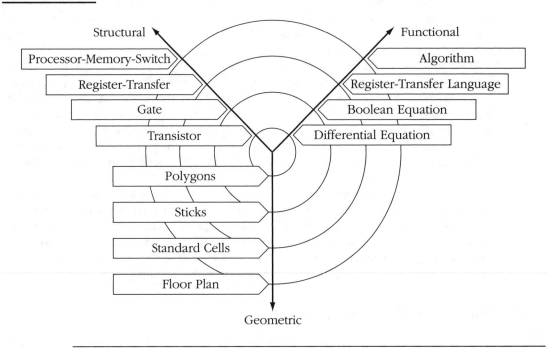

Domains and levels of abstraction. The radial axes show the three different domains of modeling. The concentric rings show the levels of abstraction, with the more abstract levels on the outside and more detailed levels toward the center.

ler is shown below. This model describes how the controller repeatedly scans each data input and writes a scaled display of the input value.

```
loop
  for each data input loop
    read the value on this input;
    scale the value using the current scale factor
      for this input;
    convert the scaled value to a decimal string;
    write the string to the display output corresponding
      to this input;
  end loop;
  wait for 10 ms;
end loop;
```

At this top level of abstraction, the structure of a system may be described as an interconnection of such components as processors, memories and input/output devices. This level is sometimes called the Processor Memory Switch (PMS) level, named after the notation used by Bell and Newell (see reference [3]). Figure 1.2 shows a structural model of the instrument controller drawn using this notation. It consists of a processor connected

FIGURE 1.2

A PMS model of the controller structure. It is constructed from a processor (P), a memory (M), an interconnection switch (S) and two input/output controllers (Kio).

via a switch to a memory component and to controllers for the data inputs and display outputs.

In the geometric domain at this top level of abstraction, a system to be implemented as a VLSI circuit may be modeled using a floor plan. This shows how the components described in the structural model are arranged on the silicon die. Figure 1.3 shows a possible floor plan for the instrument controller chip. There are analogous geometric descriptions for systems integrated in other media. For example, a personal computer system might be modeled at the top level in the geometric domain by an assembly diagram showing the positions of the motherboard and plug-in expansion boards in the desktop cabinet.

The next level of abstraction in modeling, depicted by the second ring in Figure 1.1, describes the system in terms of units of data storage and transformation. In the structural domain, this is often called the register-transfer level (RTL), composed of a data path and a control section. The data path contains data storage registers, and data is transferred between them through transformation units. The control section sequences operation of the data path components. For example, a register-transfer-level structural model of the processor in our controller is shown in Figure 1.4.

FIGURE 1.3

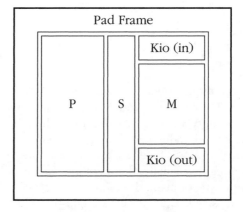

A floor plan model of the controller geometry.

FIGURE 1.4

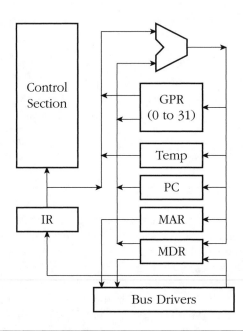

A register-transfer-level structural model of the controller processor. It consists of a general-purpose register (GPR) file; registers for the program counter (PC), memory address (MAR), memory data (MDR), temporary values (Temp) and fetched instructions (IR); an arithmetic unit; bus drivers and the control section.

In the functional domain, a register-transfer language is often used to specify the operation of a system at this level. Storage of data is represented using register variables, and transformations are represented by arithmetic and logical operators. For example, an RTL model for the processor in our example controller might include the following description:

```
MAR ← PC,  memory_read ← 1
PC ← PC + 1
wait until ready = 1
IR ← memory_data
memory_read ← 0
```

This section of the model describes the operations involved in fetching an instruction from memory. The contents of the PC register are transferred to the memory address register, and the **memory_read** signal is asserted. Then the value from the PC register is transformed (incremented in this case) and transferred back to the PC register. When the **ready** input from the memory is asserted, the value on the memory data input is transferred to the instruction register. Finally, the **memory_read** signal is negated.

In the geometric domain, the kind of model used depends on the physical medium. In our example, standard library cells might be used to implement the registers and data transformation units, and these must be placed in the areas allocated in the chip floor plan.

The third level of abstraction shown in Figure 1.1 is the conventional logic level. At this level, structure is modeled using interconnections of gates, and function is modeled by Boolean equations or truth tables. In the physical medium of a custom integrated circuit, geometry may be modeled using a virtual grid, or "sticks," notation.

At the most detailed level of abstraction, we can model structure using individual transistors, function using the differential equations that relate voltage and current in the circuit, and geometry using polygons for each mask layer of an integrated circuit. Most designers do not need to work at this detailed level, as design tools are available to automate translation from a higher level.

1.3 Modeling Languages

In the previous section, we saw that different kinds of models can be devised to represent the various levels of function, structure and physical arrangement of a system. There are also different ways of expressing these models, depending on the use made of the model.

As an example, consider the ways in which a structural model may be expressed. One common form is a circuit schematic. Graphical symbols are used to represent subsystems, and instances of these are connected using lines that represent wires. This graphical form is generally the one preferred by designers. However, the same structural information can be represented textually in the form of a net list.

When we move into the functional domain, we usually see textual notations used for modeling. Some of these are intended for use as specification languages, to meet the need for describing the operation of a system without indicating how it might be implemented. These notations are usually based on formal mathematical methods, such as temporal logic or abstract state machines. Other notations are intended for simulating the system for test and verification purposes and are typically based on conventional programming languages. Yet other notations are oriented toward hardware synthesis and usually have a more restricted set of modeling facilities, since some programming language constructs are difficult to translate into hardware.

The purpose of this book is to describe the modeling language VHDL. VHDL includes facilities for describing structure and function at a number of levels, from the most abstract down to the gate level. It also provides an attribute mechanism that can be used to annotate a model with information in the geometric domain. VHDL is intended, among other things, as a modeling language for specification and simulation. We can also use it for hardware synthesis if we restrict ourselves to a subset that can be automatically translated into hardware.

1.4 VHDL Modeling Concepts

In Section 1.2, we looked at the three domains of modeling: function, structure and geometry. In this section, we look at the basic modeling concepts in each of these domains and introduce the corresponding VHDL elements for describing them. This will provide a feel for VHDL and a basis from which to work in later chapters.

EXAMPLE 1.1   *A four-bit register design*

Figure 1.5 shows a schematic symbol for a four-bit register. Using VHDL terminology, we call the module **reg4** a design *entity*, and the inputs and outputs are *ports*.

FIGURE 1.5

A four-bit register module. The register is named **reg4** *and has six inputs,* **d0**, **d1**, **d2**, **d3**, **en** *and* **clk**, *and four outputs,* **q0**, **q1**, **q2** *and* **q3**.

We write a VHDL description of the interface to this entity as follows:

```
entity reg4 is
  port ( d0, d1, d2, d3, en, clk : in bit;
         q0, q1, q2, q3 : out  bit );
end entity reg4;
```

This is an example of an *entity declaration*. It introduces a name for the entity and lists the input and output ports, specifying that they carry bit values ('0' or '1') into and out of the entity. From this we see that an entity declaration describes the external view of the entity.

1.4.1   Elements of Behavior

In VHDL, a description of the internal implementation of an entity is called an *architecture body* of the entity. There may be a number of different architecture bodies of the one interface to an entity, corresponding to alternative implementations that perform the same function. We can write a *behavioral* architecture body of an entity, which describes the function in an abstract way. Such an architecture body includes only *process statements*, which are collections of actions to be executed in sequence. These actions are called *sequential statements* and are much like the kinds of statements we see in a conventional programming language. The types of actions that can be performed include evaluating expressions, assigning values to variables, conditional execution, repeated execution and subprogram calls. In addition, there is a sequential statement that is unique to hardware modeling languages, the *signal assignment* statement. This is similar to variable assignment, except that it causes the value on a signal to be updated at some future time.

EXAMPLE 1.2   *Behavioral architecture for the four-bit register*

To illustrate these ideas, let us look at a behavioral architecture body for the **reg4** entity of Example 1.1:

```
architecture behav of reg4 is
begin

  storage : process is
    variable stored_d0, stored_d1, stored_d2, stored_d3 : bit;
  begin
    wait until clk;
    if en then
      stored_d0 := d0;
      stored_d1 := d1;
      stored_d2 := d2;
      stored_d3 := d3;
    end if;
    q0 <= stored_d0 after 5 ns;
    q1 <= stored_d1 after 5 ns;
    q2 <= stored_d2 after 5 ns;
    q3 <= stored_d3 after 5 ns;
  end process storage;

end architecture behav;
```

In this architecture body, the part after the first **begin** keyword includes one process statement, which describes how the register behaves. It starts with the process name, **storage**, and finishes with the keywords **end process**.

The process statement defines a sequence of actions that are to take place when the system is simulated. These actions control how the values on the entity's ports change over time; that is, they control the behavior of the entity. This process can modify the values of the entity's ports using signal assignment statements.

The way this process works is as follows. When the simulation is started, the signal values are set to '0', and the process is activated. The process's variables (listed after the keyword **variable**) are initialized to '0', then the statements are executed in order. The first statement is a *wait statement* that causes the process to *suspend*, that is, to become inactive. It stays suspended until one of the signals to which it is *sensitive* changes value. In this case, the process is sensitive only to the signal clk, since that is the only one named in the wait statement. When that signal changes value, the process is resumed and continues executing statements. The next statement is a condition that tests whether the value of the **en** signal is '1'. If it is, the statements between the keywords **then** and **end if** are executed, updating the process's variables using the values on the input signals. After the conditional if statement, there are four signal assignment statements that cause the output signals to be updated 5 ns later.

When all of these statements in the process have been executed, the process starts again from the keyword **begin**, and the cycle repeats. Notice that while the process is suspended, the values in the process's variables are not lost. This is how the process can represent the state of a system.

1.4.2   Elements of Structure

An alternative way of describing the implementation of an entity is to specify how it is composed of subsystems. We can give a structural description of the entity's implementation. An architecture body that is composed only of interconnected subsystems is called a structural architecture body.

EXAMPLE 1.3   *Structural architecture for the four-bit register*

Figure 1.6 shows how the **reg4** entity might be composed of flipflops and gates.

FIGURE 1.6

A structural composition of the reg4 entity.

If we are to describe this in VHDL, we will need entity declarations and architecture bodies for the subsystems. For the flipflops, the entity and architecture are

```vhdl
entity d_ff is
  port ( d, clk : in bit;  q : out bit );
end d_ff;

architecture basic of d_ff is
begin

  ff_behavior : process is
  begin
    wait until clk;
    q <= d after 2 ns;
  end process ff_behavior;

end architecture basic;
```

For the two-input and gate, the entity and architecture are

```vhdl
entity and2 is
  port ( a, b : in bit;  y : out bit );
end and2;

architecture basic of and2 is
begin

  and2_behavior : process is
  begin
    y <= a and b after 2 ns;
    wait on a, b;
  end process and2_behavior;

end architecture basic;
```

We can now proceed to a VHDL architecture body declaration that describes the **reg4** structure shown in Figure 1.6:

```vhdl
architecture struct of reg4 is

  signal int_clk : bit;

begin

  bit0 : entity work.d_ff(basic)
    port map (d0, int_clk, q0);
  bit1 : entity work.d_ff(basic)
    port map (d1, int_clk, q1);
  bit2 : entity work.d_ff(basic)
    port map (d2, int_clk, q2);
  bit3 : entity work.d_ff(basic)
    port map (d3, int_clk, q3);
```

```
gate : entity work.and2(basic)
    port map (en, clk, int_clk);

end architecture struct;
```

The *signal declaration*, before the keyword **begin**, defines the internal signals of the architecture. In this example, the signal int_clk is declared to carry a bit value ('0' or '1'). In general, VHDL signals can be declared to carry arbitrarily complex values. Within the architecture body the ports of the entity are also treated as signals.

In the second part of the architecture body, a number of *component instances* are created, representing the subsystems from which the **reg4** entity is composed. Each component instance is a copy of the entity representing the subsystem, using the corresponding **basic** architecture body. (The name **work** refers to the current working library, in which all of the entity and architecture body descriptions are assumed to be held.)

The *port map* specifies the connection of the ports of each component instance to signals within the enclosing architecture body. For example, bit0, an instance of the d_ff entity, has its port d connected to the signal d0, its port clk connected to the signal int_clk and its port q connected to the signal q0.

1.4.3   Mixed Structural and Behavioral Models

Models need not be purely structural or purely behavioral. Often it is useful to specify a model with some parts composed of interconnected component instances, and other parts described using processes. We use signals as the means of joining component instances and processes. A signal can be associated with a port of a component instance and can also be assigned to or read in a process.

We can write such a hybrid model by including both component instance and process statements in the body of an architecture. These statements are collectively called *concurrent statements*, since the corresponding processes all execute concurrently when the model is simulated.

EXAMPLE 1.4   *A mixed structural and behavioral model for a multiplier*

A sequential multiplier consists of a data path and a control section. An outline of a mixed structural and behavioral model for the multiplier is:

```
entity multiplier is
  port ( clk, reset : in bit;
         multiplicand, multiplier : in integer;
         product : out integer );
end entity multiplier;

-------------------------------------------------

architecture mixed of multiplier is
```

```
        signal partial_product, full_product : integer;
        signal arith_control, result_en, mult_bit, mult_load : bit;
    begin -- mixed

      arith_unit : entity work.shift_adder(behavior)
        port map ( addend => multiplicand, augend => full_product,
                   sum => partial_product,
                   add_control => arith_control);

      result : entity work.reg(behavior)
        port map ( d => partial_product, q => full_product,
                   en => result_en, reset => reset);

      multiplier_sr : entity work.shift_reg(behavior)
        port map ( d => multiplier, q => mult_bit,
                   load => mult_load, clk => clk);

      product <= full_product;

      control_section : process is
        -- variable declarations for control_section
        -- ...
      begin -- control section
        -- sequential statements to assign values to control signals
        -- ...
        wait on clk, reset;
      end process control_section;

    end architecture mixed;
```

The data path is described structurally, using a number of component instances.
The control section is described behaviorally, using a process that assigns to the control signals for the data path.

1.4.4   Test Benches

In our introductory discussion, we mentioned testing through simulation as an important
motivation for modeling. We often test a VHDL model using an enclosing model called a
test bench. The name comes from the analogy with a real hardware test bench, on which
a device under test is stimulated with signal generators and observed with signal probes.
A VHDL test bench consists of an architecture body containing an instance of the component to be tested and processes that generate sequences of values on signals connected
to the component instance. The architecture body may also contain processes that test that
the component instance produces the expected values on its output signals. Alternatively,
we may use the monitoring facilities of a simulator to observe the outputs.

EXAMPLE 1.5   *Test bench for the four-bit register*

A test bench model for the behavioral implementation of the **reg4** register is:

```
entity test_bench is
end entity test_bench;

architecture test_reg4 of test_bench is

  signal d0, d1, d2, d3, en, clk, q0, q1, q2, q3 : bit;

begin

  dut : entity work.reg4(behav)
    port map ( d0, d1, d2, d3, en, clk, q0, q1, q2, q3 );

  stimulus : process is
  begin
    d0 <= '1';  d1 <= '1';  d2 <= '1';  d3 <= '1';
    en <= '0';  clk <= '0';
    wait for 20 ns;
    en <= '1';  wait for 20 ns;
    clk <= '1';  wait for 20 ns;
    d0 <= '0';  d1 <= '0';  d2 <= '0';  d3 <= '0';  wait for 20 ns;
    en <= '0';  wait for 20 ns;
    ...
    wait;
  end process stimulus;

end architecture test_reg4;
```

The entity declaration has no port list, since the test bench is entirely self-contained. The architecture body contains signals that are connected to the input and output ports of the component instance **dut**, the device under test. The process labeled **stimulus** provides a sequence of test values on the input signals by performing signal assignment statements, interspersed with wait statements. Each wait statement specifies a 20 ns pause during which the register device determines its output values. We can use a simulator to observe the values on the signals **q0** to **q3** to verify that the register operates correctly. When all of the stimulus values have been applied, the stimulus process waits indefinitely, thus completing the simulation.

1.4.5   Analysis, Elaboration and Execution

One of the main reasons for writing a model of a system is to enable us to simulate it. This involves three stages: *analysis*, *elaboration* and *execution*. Analysis and elaboration are also required in preparation for other uses of the model, such as logic synthesis.

In the first stage, analysis, the VHDL description of a system is checked for various kinds of errors. Like most programming languages, VHDL has rigidly defined *syntax* and *semantics*. The syntax is the set of grammatical rules that govern how a model is written.

The rules of semantics govern the meaning of a program. For example, it makes sense to perform an addition operation on two numbers but not on two processes.

During the analysis phase, the VHDL description is examined, and syntactic and static semantic errors are located. The whole model of a system need not be analyzed at once. Instead, it is possible to analyze *design units*, such as entity and architecture body declarations, separately. If the analyzer finds no errors in a design unit, it creates an intermediate representation of the unit and stores it in a library. The exact mechanism varies between VHDL tools.

The second stage in simulating a model, elaboration, is the act of working through the design hierarchy and creating all of the objects defined in declarations. The ultimate product of design elaboration is a collection of signals and processes, with each process possibly containing variables. A model must be reducible to a collection of signals and processes in order to simulate it.

We can see how elaboration achieves this reduction by starting at the top level of a model, namely, an entity, and choosing an architecture of the entity to simulate. The architecture comprises signals, processes and component instances. Each component instance is a copy of an entity and an architecture that also comprises signals, processes and component instances. Instances of those signals and processes are created, corresponding to the component instance, and then the elaboration operation is repeated for the subcomponent instances. Ultimately, a component instance is reached that is a copy of an entity with a purely behavioral architecture, containing only processes. This corresponds to a primitive component for the level of design being simulated. Figure 1.7 shows how elaboration proceeds for the structural architecture body of the **reg4** entity from Example 1.3. As each instance of a process is created, its variables are created and given initial values. We can think of each process instance as corresponding to one instance of a component.

The third stage of simulation is the execution of the model. The passage of time is simulated in discrete steps, depending on when events occur. Hence the term *discrete event simulation* is used. At some simulation time, a process may be stimulated by changing the value on a signal to which it is sensitive. The process is resumed and may schedule new values to be given to signals at some later simulated time. This is called *scheduling a transaction* on that signal. If the new value is different from the previous value on the signal, an *event* occurs, and other processes sensitive to the signal may be resumed.

The simulation starts with an *initialization phase*, followed by repetitive execution of a *simulation cycle*. During the initialization phase, each signal is given an initial value, depending on its type. The simulation time is set to zero, then each process instance is activated and its sequential statements executed. Usually, a process will include a signal assignment statement to schedule a transaction on a signal at some later simulation time. Execution of a process continues until it reaches a wait statement, which causes the process to be suspended.

During the simulation cycle, the simulation time is first advanced to the next time at which a transaction on a signal has been scheduled. Second, all the transactions scheduled for that time are performed. This may cause some events to occur on some signals. Third, all processes that are sensitive to those events are resumed and are allowed to continue until they reach a wait statement and suspend. Again, the processes usually execute signal assignments to schedule further transactions on signals. When all the processes have suspended again, the simulation cycle is repeated. When the simulation gets to the stage

FIGURE 1.7

The elaboration of the **reg4** *entity using the structural architecture body. Each instance of the* **d_ff** *and* **and2** *entities is replaced with the contents of the corresponding* **basic** *architecture. These each consist of a process with its variables and statements.*

where there are no further transactions scheduled, it stops, since the simulation is then complete.

1.5 Learning a New Language: Lexical Elements and Syntax

When we learn a new natural language, such as Greek, Chinese or English, we start by learning the alphabet of symbols used in the language, then form these symbols into words. Next, we learn the way to put the words together to form sentences and learn the meaning of these combinations of words. We reach fluency in a language when we can easily express what we need to say using correctly formed sentences.

The same ideas apply when we need to learn a new special-purpose language, such as VHDL for describing digital systems. We can borrow a few terms from language theory to describe what we need to learn. First, we need to learn the alphabet with which the language is written. The VHDL alphabet consists of all of the characters in the ISO 8859 Latin-1 8-bit character set. This includes uppercase and lowercase letters (including letters with diacritical marks, such as "à", "ä" and so forth), digits 0 to 9, punctuation and other special characters. Second, we need to learn the *lexical elements* of the language. In VHDL, these are the identifiers, reserved words, special symbols and literals. Third, we need to learn the *syntax* of the language. This is the grammar that determines what combinations of lexical elements make up legal VHDL descriptions. Fourth, we need to learn the *semantics*, or meaning, of VHDL descriptions. It is the semantics that allow a collection of symbols to describe a digital design. Fifth, we need to learn how to develop our own VHDL descriptions to describe a design we are working with. This is the creative part of modeling, and fluency in this part will greatly enhance our design skills.

In the remainder of this chapter, we describe the lexical elements used in VHDL and introduce the notation we use to describe the syntax rules. Then in subsequent chapters, we introduce the different facilities available in the language. For each of these, we show the syntax rules, describe the corresponding semantics and give examples of how they are used to model particular parts of a digital system. We also include some exercises at the end of each chapter to provide practice in the fifth stage of learning described above.

VHDL-87

VHDL-87 uses the ASCII character set, rather than the full ISO character set. ASCII is a subset of the ISO character set, consisting of just the first 128 characters. This includes all of the unaccented letters, but excludes letters with diacritical marks.

1.5.1 Lexical Elements

In the following section, we discuss the lexical elements of VHDL: *comments, identifiers, reserved words, special symbols, numbers, characters, strings* and *bit strings*.

Comments

When we are writing a hardware model in VHDL, it is important to annotate the code with comments. The reason for doing this is to help readers understand the structure and logic behind the model. It is important to realize that although we only write a model once, it may subsequently be read and modified many times, both by its author and by other engineers. Any assistance we can give to understanding the model is worth the effort. In this book, we set comments in slanted text to make them visually distinct.

A VHDL model consists of a number of lines of text. One form of comment, called a single-line comment, can be added to a line by writing two hypens together, followed by the comment text. For example:

```
... a line of VHDL code ...    -- a descriptive comment
```

The comment extends from the two hyphens to the end of the line and may include any text we wish, since it is not formally part of the VHDL model. The code of a model can include blank lines and lines that only contain comments, starting with two hyphens. We can write long comments on successive lines, each line starting with two hyphens, for example:

```
-- The following code models
-- the control section of the system
... some VHDL code ...
```

Another form of comment, called a delimited comment, starts with the characters "/*" and extends to the closing characters "*/". The opening and closing characters can be on different lines, or can be on the same line. Moreover, there can be further VHDL code on the line after the closing characters. Some examples are:

```
/* This is a comment header that describes
   the purpose of the design unit. It contains
   all you ever wanted to know, plus more.
*/

entity thingumy is
  port ( clk   : in bit; -- keeps it going
         reset : in bit /* start over */
         /* other ports to be added later */ );
end entity thingumy;
```

Since the text in comments is ignored, it may contain comment delimiters. Mixing comment styles can be quite useful. For example, if we use delimited comments in a section of code, and we want to "comment out" the section, we can use single-line comments:

```
-- This section commented out because it doesn't work
-- /* Process to do a complicated computation
-- involving lots of digital signal processing.
-- */
-- dsp_stuff : process is
-- begin
--   ...
-- end process dsp_stuff;
```

However, we should be aware that comments do not nest. For example, the following is ill-formed:

```
-- Here is the start of the comment: /* A comment extending
                                 over two lines */
```

The opening "/*" characters occur in a single-line comment, and so are ignored. Similarly, we cannot reliably use delimited comments to comment out a section of code, since the section might already contain a delimited comment:

```
/* Comment out the following code:
signal count_en : bit; /* counter enable */
*/
```

In this case, the occurrence of the characters "*/" on the second line closes the comment started on the first line, making the orphaned delimiter "*/" on the third line illegal. Provided we avoid pitfalls such as these, single-line and delimited comments are useful language features.

VHDL-87, -93, and -2002

These versions of VHDL only allow single-line comments, not delimited comments.

Identifiers

Identifiers are used to name items in a VHDL model. It is good practice to use names that indicate the purpose of the item, so VHDL allows names to be arbitrarily long. However, there are some rules about how identifiers may be formed. A basic identifier

- may only contain alphabetic letters ('A' to 'Z' and 'a' to 'z'), decimal digits ('0' to '9') and the underline character ('_');

- must start with an alphabetic letter;

- may not end with an underline character; and

- may not include two successive underline characters.

Some examples of valid basic identifiers are

```
A X0 counter Next_Value generate_read_cycle
```

Some examples of invalid basic identifiers are

```
last@value     -- contains an illegal character for an identifier
5bit_counter   -- starts with a non-alphabetic character
_A0            -- starts with an underline
A0_            -- ends with an underline
clock__pulse   -- two successive underlines
```

Note that the case of letters is not considered significant, so the identifiers **cat** and **Cat** are the same. Underline characters in identifiers are significant, so **This_Name** and **This-Name** are different identifiers.

In addition to the basic identifiers, VHDL allows *extended identifiers*, which can contain any sequence of characters. Extended identifiers are included to allow communication between computer-aided engineering tools for processing VHDL descriptions and other tools that use different rules for identifiers. An extended identifier is written by enclosing the characters of the identifier between '\' characters. For example:

```
\data bus\ \global.clock\ \923\ \d#1\ \start__\
```

If we need to include a '\' character in an extended identifier, we do so by doubling the character, for example:

```
\A:\\name\    -- contains a '\' between the ':' and the 'n'
```

Note that the case of letters is significant in extended identifiers and that all extended identifiers are distinct from all basic identifiers. So the following are all distinct identifiers:

```
name \name\ \Name\ \NAME\
```

VHDL-87

VHDL-87 only allows basic identifiers, not extended identifiers. The rules for forming basic identifiers are the same as those for VHDL-93 and VHDL-2002.

Reserved Words

Some identifiers, called reserved words or keywords, are reserved for special use in VHDL. They are used to denote specific constructs that form a model, so we cannot use them as identifiers for items we define. The full list of reserved words is shown in Table 1.1. Often, when a VHDL program is typeset, reserved words are printed in boldface. This convention is followed in this book.

VHDL-2002

The following identifiers are not used as reserved words in VHDL-2002. They may be used as identifiers for other purposes, although it is not advisable to do so, as this may cause difficulties in porting the models to VHDL-2008.

assert	fairness	restrict_guarantee
assume	force	sequence
assume_guarantee	parameter	strong
context	property	vmode
cover	release	vprop
default	restrict	vunit

TABLE 1.1   *VHDL reserved words*

abs	default	label	package	sla
access	disconnect	library	parameter	sll
after	downto	linkage	port	sra
alias		literal	postponed	srl
all	else	loop	procedure	strong
and	elsif		process	subtype
architecture	end	map	property	
array	entity	mod	protected	then
assert	exit		pure	to
assume		nand		transport
assume_guarantee	fairness	new	range	type
attribute	file	next	record	
	for	nor	register	unaffected
begin	force	not	reject	units
block	function	null	release	until
body			rem	use
buffer	generate	of	report	
bus	generic	on	restrict	variable
	group	open	restrict_guarantee	vmode
case	guarded	or	return	vprop
component		others	rol	vunit
configuration	if	out	ror	
constant	impure			wait
context	in		select	when
cover	inertial		sequence	while
	inout		severity	with
	is		shared	
			signal	xnor
				xor

VHDL-93

In addition to those listed for VHDL-2002, the identifier **protected** is not used as a reserved word in VHDL-93.

VHDL-87

In addition to those listed for VHDL-2002 and VHDL-93, the following identifiers are not used as reserved words in VHDL-87:

group	protected	ror	sra
impure	pure	shared	srl
inertial	reject	sla	unaffected
literal	rol	sll	xnor
postponed			

Special Symbols

VHDL uses a number of special symbols to denote operators, to delimit parts of language constructs and as punctuation. Some of these special symbols consist of just one character. They are

```
"  #  &  '  (  )  *  +  -  ,  .  /  :  ;  <  =  >  ?  @  [  ]  `  |
```

Other special symbols consist of pairs of characters. The two characters must be typed next to each other, with no intervening space. These symbols are

```
=>  **  :=  /=  >=  <=  <>  ??  ?=  ?/=  ?>  ?<  ?>=  ?<=  <<  >>
```

Numbers

There are two forms of numbers that can be written in VHDL code: *integer literals* and *real literals*. An integer literal simply represents a whole number and consists of digits without a decimal point. Real literals, on the other hand, can represent fractional numbers. They always include a decimal point, which is preceded by at least one digit and followed by at least one digit. Real literals represent an approximation to real numbers.

Some examples of decimal integer literals are

```
23  0  146
```

Note that –10, for example, is not an integer literal. It is actually a combination of a negation operator and the integer literal 10.

Some examples of real literals are

```
23.1  0.0  3.14159
```

Both integer and real literals can also use exponential notation, in which the number is followed by the letter 'E' or 'e', and an exponent value. This indicates a power of 10 by which the number is multiplied. For integer literals, the exponent must not be negative, whereas for real literals, it may be either positive or negative. Some examples of integer literals using exponential notation are

```
46E5  1E+12  19e00
```

Some examples of real literals using exponential notation are

```
1.234E09  98.6E+21  34.0e-08
```

Integer and real literals may also be expressed in a base other than base 10. In fact, the base can be any integer between 2 and 16. To do this, we write the number surrounded by sharp characters ('#'), preceded by the base. For bases greater than 10, the letters 'A' through 'F' (or 'a' through 'f') are used to represent the digits 10 through 15. For example, several ways of writing the value 253 are as follows:

```
2#11111101#  16#FD#  16#0fd#  8#0375#
```

Similarly, the value 0.5 can be represented as

```
2#0.100#   8#0.4#   12#0.6#
```

Note that in all these cases, the base itself is expressed in *decimal*.

Based literals can also use exponential notation. In this case, the exponent, expressed in decimal, is appended to the based number after the closing sharp character. The exponent represents the power of the base by which the number is multiplied. For example, the number 1024 could be represented by the integer literals:

```
2#1#E10   16#4#E2   10#1024#E+00
```

Finally, as an aid to readability of long numbers, we can include underline characters as separators between digits. The rules for including underline characters are similar to those for identifiers; that is, they may not appear at the beginning or end of a number, nor may two appear in succession. Some examples are

```
123_456   3.141_592_6   2#1111_1100_0000_0000#
```

Characters

A character literal can be written in VHDL code by enclosing it in single quotation marks. Any of the printable characters in the standard character set (including a space character) can be written in this way. Some examples are

```
'A'   -- uppercase letter
'z'   -- lowercase letter
','   -- the punctuation character comma
'''   -- the punctuation character single quote
' '   -- the separator character space
```

Strings

A string literal represents a sequence of characters and is written by enclosing the characters in double quotation marks. The string may include any number of characters (including zero), but it must fit entirely on one line. Some examples are

```
"A string"
"A string can include any printing characters (e.g., &%@^*)."
"00001111ZZZZ"
""   -- empty string
```

If we need to include a double quotation mark character in a string, we write two double quotation mark characters together. The pair is interpreted as just one character in the string. For example:

```
"A string in a string: ""A string"". "
```

If we need to write a string that is longer than will fit on one line, we can use the concatenation operator ("&") to join two substrings together. (This operator is discussed in Chapter 4.) For example:

```
"If a string will not fit on one line, "
& "then we can break it into parts on separate lines."
```

Bit Strings

VHDL includes values that represent bits (binary digits), which can be either '0' or '1'. A bit-string literal represents a string of these bit values. It is represented by a string of digits, enclosed by double quotation marks and preceded by a character that specifies the base of the digits. The base specifier can be one of the following:

- B for binary,

- O for octal (base 8) and

- X for hexadecimal (base 16).

- D for decimal (base 10).

For example, some bit-string literals specified in binary are

```
B"0100011"  B"10"  b"1111_0010_0001"  B""
```

Notice that we can include underline characters in bit-string literals to separate adjacent digits. The underline characters do not affect the meaning of the literal; they simply make the literal more readable. The base specifier can be in uppercase or lowercase. The last of the examples above denotes an empty bit string.

If the base specifier is octal, the digits '0' through '7' can be used. Each digit represents exactly three bits in the bit string. Some examples are

```
O"372"   -- equivalent to B"011_111_010"
o"00"    -- equivalent to B"000_000"
```

If the base specifier is hexadecimal, the digits '0' through '9' and 'A' through 'F' or 'a' through 'f' (representing 10 through 15) can be used. In hexadecimal, each digit represents exactly four bits. Some examples are

```
X"FA"    -- equivalent to B"1111_1010"
x"0d"    -- equivalent to B"0000_1101"
```

Notice that O"372" is not the same as X"FA", since the former is a string of nine bits, whereas the latter is a string of eight bits.

If the base specifier is decimal, the digits '0' through '9' can be used. The digits in the literal are interpreted as a decimal number and are converted to the equivalent binary value. The number of bits in the string is the minimal number needed to represent the value. Some examples are

```
D"23"       -- equivalent to B"10111"
D"64"       -- equivalent to B"1000000"
D"0003"     -- equivalent to B"11"
```

In some cases, it is convenient to include characters other than digits in bit string literals. As we will see later, many VHDL models use characters such as 'Z', 'X', and '–' to represent high-impedance states, unknown values, and don't-care conditions. Models may use other characters for similar purposes. We can include such non-binary characters in bit-string literals. In an octal literal, any non-octal-digit character is expanded to three occurrences of that character in the bit string. Similarly, in a hexadecimal literal any non-hexadecimal-digit character is expanded to four occurrences of the character. In a binary literal, any non-bit character just represents itself in the vector. Some examples are:

```
O"3XZ4"     -- equivalent to B"011XXXZZZ100"
X"A3--"     -- equivalent to B"10100011--------"
X"0#?F"     -- equivalent to B"0000####????1111"
B"00UU"     -- equivalent to B"00UU"
```

While allowing this for binary literals might seem vacuous at first, the benefit will become clear shortly. Note that expansion of non-digit characters does not extend to embedded underscores, which we might add for readability. Thus, O"3_X" represents "011XXX", not "011___XXX". Also, non-digit characters are not allowed in decimal literals, since it would be unclear which bits of the resulting string correspond to the non-digit characters. Thus, the literal D"23Z9" is illegal.

In all of the preceding cases, the number of bits in the string is determined from the base specifier and the number of characters in the literal. We can, however, specify the exact length of bit string that we require from a literal. This allows us to specify strings whose length is not a multiple or three (for octal) or four (for hexadecimal). We do so by writing the length immediately before the base specifier, with no intervening space. Some examples are:

```
7X"3C"      -- equivalent to B"0111100"
8O"5"       -- equivalent to B"00000101"
10B"X"      -- equivalent to B"000000000X"
```

If the final length of the string is longer than that implied by the digits, the string is padded on the left with '0' bits. If the final length is less than that implied by the digits, the left-most elements of the string are truncated, provided they are all '0'. An error occurs if any non-'0' bits are truncated, as they would be in the literal 8X"90F".

A further feature of bit-string literals is provision for specifying whether the literal represents an unsigned or signed number. We represent an unsigned number using one of the base specifiers UB, UO, or UX. These are the same as the ordinary base specifiers B, O, and X. When a sized unsigned literal is extended, it is padded with '0' bits, and when bits are truncated, they must be all '0'. Decimal literals are always interpreted as unsigned, so D is the only base specifier for decimal. We can extend a decimal literal by padding with '0' bits. However, we cannot truncate a decimal literal from its default size, since the default size always gives a '1' as the leftmost bit, which must not be truncated.

We represent a signed number using one of the base specifiers SB, SO, or SX. The rules for extension and truncation are based on those for sign extension and truncation of 2s-complement binary numbers. When a sized signed literal is extended, each bit of padding on the left is a replication of the leftmost bit prior to padding. For example:

```
10SX"71"    -- equivalent to B"0001110001"
10SX"88"    -- equivalent to B"1110001000"
10SX"W0"    -- equivalent to B"WWWWWW0000"
```

When a sized signed literal is truncated, all of the bits removed at the left must be the same as the leftmost remaining bit. For example:

```
6SX"16"    -- equivalent to B"010110"
6SX"E8"    -- equivalent to B"101000"
6SX"H3"    -- equivalent to B"HH0011"
```

However, 6SX"28" is invalid, since, prior to truncation, the bit string would be "00101000". The two leftmost bits removed are each '0', which differ from the leftmost remaining '1' bit. The literal would have to be written as 6SX"E8" for this reason. The rationale for this rule is that it prevents the signed numeric value represented by the literal being inadvertently changed by the truncation.

VHDL-87, -93, and -2002

These versions of VHDL only allow the base specifiers B, O, and X. They do not allow unsigned and signed specifiers UB, UO, UX, SB, SO, and SX; nor do they allow the decimal specifier D. They do not allow the size to be specified; thus, octal literals are always a multiple of three in length, and hexidecimal literals are always a multiple of four in length. Finally, non-digit characters, other than underlines for readability, are not allowed.

1.5.2   Syntax Descriptions

In the remainder of this book, we describe rules of syntax using a notation based on the Extended Backus-Naur Form (EBNF). These rules govern how we may combine lexical elements to form valid VHDL descriptions. It is useful to have a good working knowledge of the syntax rules, since VHDL analyzers expect valid VHDL descriptions as input. The error messages they otherwise produce may in some cases appear cryptic if we are unaware of the syntax rules.

The idea behind EBNF is to divide the language into *syntactic categories*. For each syntactic category we write a rule that describes how to build a VHDL clause of that category by combining lexical elements and clauses of other categories. These rules are analogous to the rules of English grammar. For example, there are rules that describe a sentence in terms of a subject and a predicate, and that describe a predicate in terms of a verb and an object phrase. In the rules for English grammar, "sentence", "subject", "predicate", and so on, are the syntactic categories.

In EBNF, we write a rule with the syntactic category we are defining on the left of a "⇐" sign (read as "is defined to be"), and a pattern on the right. The simplest kind of pattern is a collection of items in sequence, for example:

variable_assignment ⇐ target := expression ;

This rule indicates that a VHDL clause in the category "variable_assignment" is defined to be a clause in the category "target", followed by the symbol ":=", followed by a clause in the category "expression", followed by the symbol ";". To find out whether the VHDL clause

```
d0 := 25 + 6;
```

is syntactically valid, we would have to check the rules for "target" and "expression". As it happens, "d0" and "25+6" are valid subclauses, so the whole clause conforms to the pattern in the rule and is thus a valid variable assignment. On the other hand, the clause

```
25 fred := x if := .
```

cannot possibly be a valid variable assignment, since it doesn't match the pattern on the right side of the rule.

The next kind of rule to consider is one that allows for an optional component in a clause. We indicate the optional part by enclosing it between the symbols "⟦" and "⟧". For example:

function_call ⇐ name ⟦ (association_list) ⟧

This indicates that a function call consists of a name that may be followed by an association list in parentheses. Note the use of the outline symbols for writing the pattern in the rule, as opposed to the normal solid symbols that are lexical elements of VHDL.

In many rules, we need to specify that a clause is optional, but if present, it may be repeated as many times as needed. For example, in this simplified rule for a process statement:

process_statement ⇐
    process is
       ⦃ process_declarative_item ⦄
    begin
       ⦃ sequential_statement ⦄
    end process ;

the curly braces specify that a process may include zero or more process declarative items and zero or more sequential statements. A case that arises frequently in the rules of VHDL is a pattern consisting of some category followed by zero or more repetitions of that category. In this case, we use dots within the braces to represent the repeated category, rather than writing it out again in full. For example, the rule

case_statement ⇐
    case expression **is**

case_statement_alternative

{ ... }

end case ;

indicates that a case statement must contain at least one case statement alternative, but may contain an arbitrary number of additional case statement alternatives as required. If there is a sequence of categories and symbols preceding the braces, the dots represent only the last element of the sequence. Thus, in the example above, the dots represent only the case statement alternative, not the sequence "**case** expression **is** case_statement_alternative".

We also use the dots notation where a list of one or more repetitions of a clause is required, but some delimiter symbol is needed between repetitions. For example, the rule

identifier_list ⇐ identifier { , ... }

specifies that an identifier list consists of one or more identifiers, and that if there is more than one, they are separated by comma symbols. Note that the dots always represent a repetition of the category immediately preceding the left brace symbol. Thus, in the above rule, it is the identifier that is repeated with comma delimiters; it is not just the comma that is repeated.

Many syntax rules allow a category to be composed of one of a number of alternatives. One way to represent this is to have a number of separate rules for the category, one for each alternative. However, it is often more convenient to combine alternatives using the "|" symbol. For example, the rule

mode ⇐ **in** | **out** | **inout**

specifies that the category "mode" can be formed from a clause consisting of one of the reserved words chosen from the alternatives listed.

The final notation we use in our syntax rules is parenthetic grouping, using the symbols "(" and ")". These simply serve to group part of a pattern, so that we can avoid any ambiguity that might otherwise arise. For example, the inclusion of parentheses in the rule

term ⇐ factor { (* | / | **mod** | **rem**) factor }

makes it clear that a factor may be followed by one of the operator symbols, and then another factor. Without the parentheses, the rule would be

term ⇐ factor { * | / | **mod** | **rem** factor }

indicating that a factor may be followed by one of the operators "*", "/" or **mod** alone, or by the operator **rem** and then another factor. This is certainly not what is intended. The reason for this incorrect interpretation is that there is a *precedence*, or order of priority, in the EBNF notation we are using. In the absence of parentheses, a sequence of pattern components following one after the other is considered as a group with higher precedence than components separated by "|" symbols.

This EBNF notation is sufficient to describe the complete grammar of VHDL. However, there are often further constraints on a VHDL description that relate to the meaning of the lexical elements used. For example, a description specifying connection of a signal to a named object that identifies a component instead of a port is incorrect, even though it may conform to the syntax rules. To avoid such problems, many rules include additional information relating to the meaning of a language feature. For example, the rule shown above describing how a function call is formed is augmented thus:

function_call ⇐ function_name 〚 (*parameter*_association_list) 〛

The italicized prefix on a syntactic category in the pattern simply provides semantic information. This rule indicates that the name cannot be just any name, but must be the name of a function. Similarly, the association list must describe the parameters supplied to the function. (We will describe the meaning of functions and parameters in a later chapter.) The semantic information is for our benefit as designers reading the rule, to help us understand the intended semantics. So far as the syntax is concerned, the rule is equivalent to the original rule without the italicized parts.

In the following chapters, we will introduce each new feature of VHDL by describing its syntax using EBNF rules, and then we will describe the meaning and use of the feature through examples. In many cases, we will start with a simplified version of the syntax to make the description easier to learn and come back to the full details in a later chapter. For reference, Appendix B contains a complete listing of VHDL syntax in EBNF notation.

Exercises

1. [❶ 1.4] Briefly outline the purposes of the following VHDL modeling constructs: entity declaration, behavioral architecture body, structural architecture body, process statement, signal assignment statement and port map.

2. [❶ 1.5] Single-line comment symbols are often used to make lines of a model temporarily ineffective. The symbol is added at the front of the line, turning the line into a comment. The comment symbol can be simply removed to reactivate the statement. The following process statement includes a line to assign a value to a test signal, to help debug the model. Modify the process to make the assignment ineffective.

   ```
   apply_transform : process is
   begin
     d_out <= transform(d_in) after 200 ps;
     debug_test <= transform(d_in);
     wait on enable, d_in;
   end process apply_transform;
   ```

3. [❶ 1.5] Which of the following are valid VHDL basic identifiers? Which are reserved words? Of the invalid identifiers, why are they invalid?

last_item	prev item	value-1	buffer
element#5	_control	93_999	entry_

4. [❶ 1.5] Rewrite the following decimal literals as hexadecimal literals.

   1   34   256.0   0.5

5. [❶ 1.5] What decimal numbers are represented by the following literals?

    8#14#   2#1000_0100#   16#2C#

    2.5E5   2#1#E15   2#0.101#

6. [❶ 1.5] What is the difference between the literals 16#23DF# and X"23DF"?

7. [❶ 1.5] Express the following octal and hexadecimal bit strings as binary bit-string literals.

    O"747"   O"377"   O"1_345"

    X"F2"   X"0014"   X"0000_0001"

8. [❶ 1.5] Express the following octal and hexadecimal bit strings as binary bit-string literals, or, if they are illegal, say why.

    10UO"747"   10UO"377"   10UO"1_345"

    10SO"747"   10SO"377"   10SO"1_345"

    12UX"F2"   12SX"F2"   10UX"F2"   10SX"F2"

9. [❶ 1.5] Express the following decimal bit strings as binary bit-string literals, or, if they are illegal, say why.

    D"24"   12D"24"   4D"24"

10. [❷ 1.4] Write an entity declaration and a behavioral architecture body for a two-input multiplexer, with input ports **a**, **b** and **sel** and an output port **z**. If the **sel** input is '0', the value of **a** should be copied to **z**, otherwise the value of **b** should be copied to **z**. Write a test bench for the multiplexer model, and test it using a VHDL simulator.

11. [❷ 1.4] Write an entity declaration and a structural architecture body for a 4-bit-wide multiplexer, using instances of the 2-bit multiplexer from Exercise 10. The input ports are **a0**, **a1**, **a2**, **a3**, **b0**, **b1**, **b2**, **b3** and **sel**, and the output ports are **z0**, **z1**, **z2** and **z3**. When **sel** is '0', the inputs **a0** to **a3** are copied to the outputs, otherwise the inputs **b0** to **b3** are copied to the outputs. Write a test bench for the multiplexer model, and test it using a VHDL simulator.

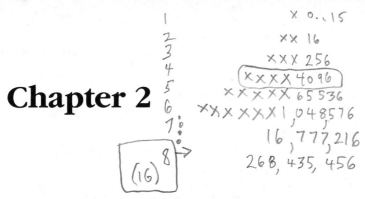

Chapter 2

Scalar Data Types
and Operations

The concept of type is very important when describing data in a VHDL model. The type of a data object defines the set of values that the object can assume, as well as the set of operations that can be performed on those values. A scalar type consists of single, indivisible values. In this chapter we look at the basic scalar types provided by VHDL and see how they can be used to define data objects that model the internal state of a module.

2.1   Constants and Variables

An object is a named item in a VHDL model that has a value of a specified type. There are four classes of objects: constants, variables, signals and files. In this chapter, we look at constants and variables; signals are described fully in Chapter 5. Files are considered an advanced topic and are not discussed in this book. Constants and variables are objects in which data can be stored for use in a model. The difference between them is that the value of a constant cannot be changed after it is created, whereas a variable's value can be changed as many times as necessary using variable assignment statements.

2.1.1   Constant and Variable Declarations

Both constants and variables need to be declared before they can be used in a model. A declaration simply introduces the name of the object, defines its type and may give it an initial value. The syntax rule for a constant declaration is

    constant_declaration ⇐
        constant identifier 〖 , ₒₒₒ 〗 : subtype_indication 〖 := expression 〗 ;

The identifiers listed are the names of the constants being defined (one per name), and the subtype indication specifies the type of all of the constants. We look at ways of specifying the type in detail in subsequent sections of this chapter. The optional part shown in the syntax rule is an expression that specifies the value that each constant assumes. This part can only be omitted in certain cases that we discuss in Chapter 7. Until then, we always include it in examples. Here are some examples of constant declarations:

```
constant number_of_bytes : integer := 4;
constant number_of_bits : integer := 8 * number_of_bytes;
constant e : real := 2.718281828;
constant prop_delay : time := 3 ns;
constant size_limit, count_limit : integer := 255;
```

The reason for using a constant is to have a name and an explicitly defined type for a value, rather than just writing the value as a literal. This makes the model more intelligible to the reader, since the name and type convey much more information about the intended use of the object than the literal value alone. Furthermore, if we need to change the value as the model evolves, we only need to update the declaration. This is much easier and more reliable than trying to find and update all instances of a literal value throughout a model. It is good practice to use constants rather than writing literal values within a model.

The form of a variable declaration is similar to a constant declaration. The syntax rule is

variable_declaration ⇐
    variable identifier ⟦ , ₀₀₀ ⟧ : subtype_indication ⟦ := expression ⟧ ;

Here also the initialization expression is optional. If we omit it, the default initial value assumed by the variable when it is created depends on the type. For scalar types, the default initial value is the leftmost value of the type. For example, for integers it is the smallest representable integer. Some examples of variable declarations are

```
variable index : integer := 0;
variable sum, average, largest : real;
variable start, finish : time := 0 ns;
```

If we include more than one identifier in a variable declaration, it is the same as having separate declarations for each identifier. For example, the last declaration above is the same as the two declarations

```
variable start : time := 0 ns;
variable finish : time := 0 ns;
```

This is not normally significant unless the initialization expression is such that it potentially produces different values on two successive evaluations. The only time this may occur is if the initialization expression contains a call to a function with side effects (see Chapter 6). Constant and variable declarations can appear in a number of places in a VHDL model, including in the declaration parts of processes. In this case, the declared object can be used only within the process. One restriction on where a variable declaration may occur is that it may not be placed so that the variable would be accessible to more than one process. This is to prevent the strange effects that might otherwise occur if the processes were to modify the variable in indeterminate order. The exception to this rule is if a variable is declared specially as a *shared* variable. We discuss shared variables in the full edition of this book.

EXAMPLE 2.1 *Constants and variables in an architecture*

The following outline of an architecture body shows how constant and variable declarations may be included in a VHDL model. It includes declarations of a constant **pi** and a variable **counter**.

```
entity ent is
end entity ent;
architecture sample of ent is
  constant pi : real := 3.14159;
begin
  process is
    variable counter : integer;
  begin
    -- ...              --  statements using pi and counter
  end process;
end architecture sample;
```

2.1.2 Variable Assignment

Once a variable has been declared, its value can be modified by an assignment statement. The syntax of a variable assignment statement is given by the rule

variable_assignment_statement ⇐ ⟦ label : ⟧ name := expression ;

The optional label provides a means of identifying the assignment statement. The name in a variable assignment statement identifies the variable to be changed, and the expression is evaluated to produce the new value. The type of this value must match the type of the variable. The full details of how an expression is formed are covered in the rest of this chapter. For now, just think of expressions as the usual combinations of identifiers and literals with operators. Here are some examples of assignment statements:

```
program_counter := 0;
index := index + 1;
```

The first assignment sets the value of the variable **program_counter** to zero, overwriting any previous value. The second example increments the value of **index** by one.

It is important to note the difference between a variable assignment statement, shown here, and a signal assignment statement, introduced in Chapter 1. A variable assignment immediately overwrites the variable with a new value. A signal assignment, on the other hand, schedules a new value to be applied to a signal at some later time. We will return to signal assignments in Chapter 5. Because of the significant difference between the two kinds of assignment, VHDL uses distinct symbols: ":=" for variable assignment and "<=" for signal assignment.

VHDL-87

Variable assignment statements may not be labeled in VHDL-87.

2.2   Scalar Types

The notion of *type* is very important in VHDL. We say that VHDL is a *strongly typed* language, meaning that every object may only assume values of its nominated type. Furthermore, the definition of each operation includes the types of values to which the operation may be applied. The aim of strong typing is to allow detection of errors at an early stage of the design process, namely, when a model is analyzed.

In this section, we show how a new type is declared. We then show how to define different scalar types. A *scalar* type is one whose values are indivisible. In Chapter 4 we will show how to declare types whose values are composed of collections of element values.

2.2.1   Type Declarations

We introduce new types into a VHDL model by using type declarations. The declaration names a type and specifies which values may be stored in objects of the type. The syntax rule for a type declaration is

type_declaration ⇐ **type** identifier **is** type_definition ;

One important point to note is that if two types are declared separately with identical type definitions, they are nevertheless distinct and incompatible types. For example, if we have two type declarations:

```
type apples is range 0 to 100;
type oranges is range 0 to 100;
```

we may not assign a value of type **apples** to a variable of type **oranges**, since they are of different types.

An important use of types is to specify the allowed values for ports of an entity. In the examples in Chapter 1, we saw the type name bit used to specify that ports may take only the values '0' and '1'. If we define our own types for ports, the type names must be declared in a *package*, so that they are visible in the entity declaration. We will describe packages in more detail in Chapter 7; we introduce them here to enable us to write entity declarations using types of our own devising. For example, suppose we wish to define an adder entity that adds small integers in the range 0 to 255. We write a package containing the type declaration, as follows:

```
package int_types is

  type small_int is range 0 to 255;

end package int_types;
```

This defines a package named **int_types**, which provides the type named **small_int**. The package is a separate design unit and is analyzed before any entity declaration that needs to use the type it provides. We can use the type by preceding an entity declaration with a *use clause*, for example:

```
use work.int_types.all;

entity small_adder is
  port ( a, b : in small_int;  s : out small_int );
end entity small_adder;
```

When we discuss packages in Chapter 7, we will explain the precise meaning of use clauses such as this. For now, we treat it as "magic" needed to declare types for use in entity declarations.

2.2.2 Integer Types

In VHDL, integer types have values that are whole numbers. An example of an integer type is the predefined type **integer**, which includes all the whole numbers representable on a particular host computer. The language standard requires that the type **integer** include at least the numbers $-2,147,483,647$ to $+2,147,483,647$ ($-2^{31} + 1$ to $+2^{31} - 1$), but VHDL implementations may extend the range.

We can define a new integer type using a range-constraint type definition. The simplified syntax rule for an integer type definition is

integer_type_definition ⇐
    range simple_expression 〖 **to** ▯ **downto** 〗 simple_expression

which defines the set of integers between (and including) the values given by the two expressions. The expressions must evaluate to integer values. If we use the keyword **to**, we are defining an *ascending range*, in which values are ordered from the smallest on the left to the largest on the right. On the other hand, using the keyword **downto** defines a *descending range*, in which values are ordered left to right from largest to smallest. The reasons for distinguishing between ascending and descending ranges will become clear later.

An an example, here are two integer type declarations:

```
type day_of_month is range 0 to 31;
type year is range 0 to 2100;
```

These two types are quite distinct, even though they include some values in common. Thus if we declare variables of these types:

```
variable today : day_of_month := 9;
variable start_year : year := 1987;
```

it would be illegal to make the assignment

```
start_year := today;
```

Even though the number 9 is a member of the type **year**, in context it is treated as being of type **day_of_month**, which is incompatible with type **year**. This type rule helps us to avoid inadvertently mixing numbers that represent different kinds of things.

If we wish to use an arithmetic expression to specify the bounds of the range, the values used in the expression must be *locally static*; that is, they must be known when the model is analyzed. For example, we can use constant values in an expression as part of a range definition:

```
constant number_of_bits : integer := 32;
type bit_index is range 0 to number_of_bits - 1;
```

The operations that can be performed on values of integer types include the familiar arithmetic operations:

+	addition, or identity
–	subtraction, or negation
*	multiplication
/	division
mod	modulo
rem	remainder
abs	absolute value
**	exponentiation

The result of an operation is an integer of the same type as the operand or operands. For the binary operators (those that take two operands), the operands must be of the same type. The right operand of the exponentiation operator must be a non-negative integer.

The identity and negation operators are unary, meaning that they only take a single, right operand. The result of the identity operator is its operand unchanged, while the negation operator produces zero minus the operand. So, for example, the following all produce the same result:

```
A + (-B)    A - (+B)    A - B
```

The division operator produces an integer that is the result of dividing, with any fractional part truncated toward zero. The remainder operator is defined such that the relation

```
A  =  (A / B) * B + (A rem B)
```

is satisfied. The result of **A rem B** is the remainder left over from division of A by B. It has the same sign as A and has absolute value less than the absolute value of B. For example:

```
5 rem 3   = 2    (-5) rem 3   = -2
5 rem (-3) = 2    (-5) rem (-3) = -2
```

Note that in these expressions, the parentheses are required by the grammar of VHDL. The two operators, rem and negation, may not be written side by side. The modulo operator conforms to the mathematical definition satisfying the relation

```
A = B * N + (A mod B)    -- for some integer N
```

The result of **A mod B** has the same sign as B and has absolute value less than the absolute value of B. For example:

```
5 mod 3   = 2    (-5) mod 3   = 1
5 mod (-3) = -1   (-5) mod (-3) = -2
```

In addition to these operations, VHDL defines operations to find the larger (**maximum**) and the smaller (**minimum**) of two integers. For example

```
maximum(3, 20) = 20    minimum(3, 20) = 3
```

While we could use an if statement for this purpose, such as the following:

```
if A > B then
  greater := A;
else
  greater := B;
end if;
```

using the **maximum** or **minimum** operation is much more convenient:

```
greater := maximum(A, B);
```

When a variable is declared to be of an integer type, the default initial value is the leftmost value in the range of the type. For ascending ranges, this will be the least value, and for descending ranges, it will be the greatest value. If we have these declarations:

```
type set_index_range is range 21 downto 11;
type mode_pos_range is range 5 to 7;
variable set_index : set_index_range;
variable mode_pos : mode_pos_range;
```

the initial value of **set_index** is 21, and that of **mode_pos** is 5. The initial value of a variable of type **integer** is −2,147,483,647 or less, since this type is predefined as an ascending range that must include −2,147,483,647.

VHDL-87, -93, and -2002

The **maximum** and **minimum** operations are not predefined in these versions of VHDL.

2.2.3 Floating-Point Types

Floating-point types in VHDL are used to represent real numbers. Mathematically speaking, there is an infinite number of real numbers within any interval, so it is not possible to represent real numbers exactly on a computer. Hence floating-point types are only an approximation to real numbers. The term "floating point" refers to the fact that they are represented using a mantissa part and an exponent part. This is similar to the way in which we represent numbers in scientific notation.

Floating-point types in VHDL conform to IEEE Standard 754 or 854 for floating-point computation and are represented using at least 64 bits. This gives approximately 15 decimal digits of precision, and a range of approximately $-1.8E+308$ to $+1.8E+308$. An implementation may choose to use a larger representation, providing correspondingly greater precision or range. There is a predefined floating-point type called **real**, which includes the greatest range allowed by the implementation's floating-point representation. In most implementations, this will be the range of the IEEE 64-bit double-precision representation.

We define a new floating-point type using a range-constraint type definition. The simplified syntax rule for a floating-point type definition is

floating_type_definition ⇐
    range simple_expression 〖 **to** ▯ **downto** 〗 simple_expression

This is similar to the way in which an integer type is declared, except that the bounds must evaluate to floating-point numbers. Some examples of floating-point type declarations are

```
type input_level is range -10.0 to +10.0;
type probability is range 0.0 to 1.0;
```

The operations that can be performed on floating-point values include the arithmetic operations addition and identity ("+"), subtraction and negation ("−"), multiplication ("*"), division ("/"), absolute value (**abs**), exponentiation ("**"), **maximum**, and **minimum**. The result of an operation is of the same floating-point type as the operand or operands. For the binary operators (those that take two operands), the operands must be of the same type. The exception is that the right operand of the exponentiation operator must be an integer. The identity and negation operators are unary (meaning that they only take a single, right operand).

Variables that are declared to be of a floating-point type have a default initial value that is the leftmost value in the range of the type. So if we declare a variable to be of the type **input_level** shown above:

```
variable input_A : input_level;
```

its initial value is −10.0.

VHDL-87, -93, and -2002

The **maximum** and **minimum** operations are not predefined in these versions of VHDL.

VHDL-87 and VHDL-93

In VHDL-87 and VHDL-93, the precision of floating-point types is only guaranteed to be at least six decimal digits, and the range at least −1.0E+38 to +1.0E+38. This corresponds to IEEE 32-bit single-precision representation. Implementations are allowed to use larger representations. The predefined type **real** is only guaranteed to have at least six digits precision and a range of at least −1.0E+38 to +1.0E+38, regardless of the size of the representation chosen by the implementation.

2.2.4   Physical Types

The remaining numeric types in VHDL are physical types. They are used to represent real-world physical quantities, such as length, mass, time and current. The definition of a physical type includes the *primary unit* of measure and may also include some *secondary units*, which are integral multiples of the primary unit. The simplified syntax rule for a physical type definition is

physical_type_definition ⇐
    range simple_expression ⟨ **to** ⫶ **downto** ⟩ simple_expression
       units
           identifier ;
           ⟨ identifier = physical_literal ; ⟩
       end units ⟦ identifier ⟧

physical_literal ⇐ ⟦ decimal_literal ⫶ based_literal ⟧ *unit*_name

A physical type definition is like an integer type definition, but with the units definition part added. The primary unit (the first identifier after the **units** keyword) is the smallest unit that is represented. We may then define a number of secondary units, as we shall see in a moment. The range specifies the multiples of the primary unit that are included in the type. If the identifier is included at the end of the units definition part, it must repeat the name of the type being defined.

To illustrate, here is a declaration of a physical type representing electrical resistance:

```
type resistance is range 0 to 1E9
  units
    ohm;
  end units resistance;
```

Literal values of this type are written as a numeric literal followed by the unit name, for example:

```
5 ohm     22 ohm     471_000 ohm
```

Notice that we must include a space before the unit name. Also, if the number is the literal 1, it can be omitted, leaving just the unit name. So the following two literals represent the same value:

```
ohm     1 ohm
```

Note that values such as **–5 ohm** and **1E16 ohm** are not included in the type **resistance**, since the values **–5** and **1E16** lie outside of the range of the type.

Now that we have seen how to write physical literals, we can look at how to specify secondary units in a physical type declaration. We do this by indicating how many primary units comprise a secondary unit. Our declaration for the resistance type can now be extended:

```
type resistance is range 0 to 1E9
  units
    ohm;
    kohm = 1000 ohm;
    Mohm = 1000 kohm;
  end units resistance;
```

Notice that once one secondary unit is defined, it can be used to specify further secondary units. Of course, the secondary units do not have to be powers of 10 times the primary unit; however, the multiplier must be an integer. For example, a physical type for length might be declared as

```
type length is range 0 to 1E9
  units
    um;                  -- primary unit: micron
    mm = 1000 um;        -- metric units
    m = 1000 mm;
    inch = 25400 um;     -- imperial units
    foot = 12 inch;
  end units length;
```

We can write physical literals of this type using the secondary units, for example:

```
23 mm     2 foot     9 inch
```

When we write physical literals, we can write non-integral multiples of primary or secondary units. If the value we write is not an exact multiple of the primary unit, it is rounded down to the nearest multiple. For example, we might write the following literals of type length, each of which represents the same value:

```
0.1 inch     2.54 mm     2.540528 mm
```

The last of these is rounded down to **2540 um**, since the primary unit for length is **um**. If we write the physical literal **6.8 um**, it is rounded down to the value **6 um**.

Many of the arithmetic operators can be applied to physical types, but with some restrictions. The addition, subtraction, identity, negation, **abs**, **mod**, **rem**, maximum, and minimum operations can be applied to values of physical types, in which case they yield results that are of the same type as the operand or operands. In the case of **mod** and **rem**, the operations are based on the number of primary units in each of the operand values, for example:

```
20 mm rem   6 mm  =    2 mm
 1 m  rem 300 mm  =  100 mm
```

A value of a physical type can be multiplied by a number of type **integer** or **real** to yield a value of the same physical type, for example:

```
5 mm * 6  =   30 mm
```

A value of a physical type can be divided by a number of type **integer** or **real** to yield a value of the same physical type. Furthermore, two values of the same physical type can be divided to yield an integer, for example:

```
18 kohm / 2.0     =  9 kohm
33 kohm / 22 ohm  =  1500
```

Also, the **abs** operator may be applied to a value of a physical type to yield a value of the same type, for example:

```
abs 2 foot     =  2 foot
abs (-2 foot)  =  2 foot
```

The restrictions make sense when we consider that physical types represent actual physical quantities, and arithmetic should be done so as to produce results of the correct dimensions. It doesn't make sense to multiply two lengths together to yield a length; the result should logically be an area. So VHDL does not allow direct multiplication of two physical types. Instead, we must convert the values to abstract integers to do the calculation, then convert the result back to the final physical type. (See the discussion of the **'pos** and **'val** attributes in Section 2.4.)

A variable that is declared to be of a physical type has a default initial value that is the leftmost value in the range of the type. For example, the default initial values for the types declared above are **0 ohm** for **resistance** and **0 um** for **length**.

VHDL-87, -93, and -2002

The **maximum** and **minimum** operations are not predefined in these versions of VHDL. Moreover, the **mod** and **rem** operations are not applicable to values of physical types in these versions.

VHDL-87

A physical type definition in VHDL-87 may not repeat the type name after the keywords **end units**.

Time

The predefined physical type **time** is very important in VHDL, as it is used extensively to specify delays. Its definition is

```
type time is range implementation defined
  units
    fs;
    ps = 1000 fs;
    ns = 1000 ps;
    us = 1000 ns;
    ms = 1000 us;
    sec = 1000 ms;
    min = 60 sec;
    hr = 60 min;
  end units;
```

EXAMPLE 2.2 *Waveform generation*

We can use the **mod** operator on values of type **time** to simplify generation of a periodic waveform. For example, the following process creates a triangle wave on the real signal **triangle_wave**. The constant **t_period_wave** defines the period of the output wave, **t_offset** defines the offset within the triangle wave, and **t_period_sample** defines how many points are in the waveform. The value **now** defines the current time as simulation progresses.

```
signal triangle_wave : real;
...

wave_proc : process is
  variable phase : time;
begin
  phase := (now + t_offset) mod t_period_wave;
  if phase <= t_period_wave/2 then
    triangle_wave <= 4.0 * real(phase/t_period_wave) - 1.0;
  else
    triangle_wave <= 3.0 - 4.0 * real(phase/t_period_wave);
  end if;
  wait for tperiod_sample;
end process wave_proc;
```

By default, the primary unit **fs** is the *resolution limit* used when a model is simulated. Time values smaller than the resolution limit are rounded down to zero units. A simulator may allow us to select a secondary unit of **time** as the resolution limit. In this case, the unit of all physical literals of type **time** in the model must not be less than the resolution limit. When the model is executed, the resolution limit is used to determine the precision with which time values are represented. The reason for allowing reduced precision in this way is to allow a greater range of time values to be represented. This may allow a model to be simulated for a longer period of simulation time.

2.2.5 Enumeration Types

Often when writing models of hardware at an abstract level, it is useful to use a set of names for the encoded values of some signals, rather than committing to a bit-level encoding straightaway. VHDL *enumeration types* allow us to do this. For example, suppose we are modeling a processor, and we want to define names for the function codes for the arithmetic unit. A suitable type declaration is

```
type alu_function is
  (disable, pass, add, subtract, multiply, divide);
```

Such a type is called an enumeration, because the literal values used are enumerated in a list. The syntax rule for enumeration type definitions in general is

enumeration_type_definition ⇐ (⟦ identifier ⟧ character_literal ⟧ ⟦ , ₀₀₀ ⟧)

There must be at least one value in the type, and each value may be either an identifier, as in the above example, or a character literal. An example of this latter case is

```
type octal_digit is ('0', '1', '2', '3', '4', '5', '6', '7');
```

Given the above two type declarations, we could declare variables:

```
variable alu_op : alu_function;
variable last_digit : octal_digit := '0';
```

and make assignments to them:

```
alu_op := subtract;
last_digit := '7';
```

Different enumeration types may include the same identifier as a literal (called *overloading*), so the context of use must make it clear which type is meant. To illustrate this, consider the following declarations:

```
type logic_level is (unknown, low, undriven, high);
variable control : logic_level;
type water_level is (dangerously_low, low, ok);
variable water_sensor : water_level;
```

Here, the literal **low** is overloaded, since it is a member of both types. However, the assignments

```
control := low;
water_sensor := low;
```

are both acceptable, since the types of the variables are sufficient to determine which **low** is being referred to.

When a variable of an enumeration type is declared, the default initial value is the leftmost element in the enumeration list. So **unknown** is the default initial value for type **logic_level**, and **dangerously_low** is that for type **water_level**.

There are three predefined enumeration types defined as

```
type severity_level is
  (note, warning, error, failure);
type file_open_status is
  (open_ok, status_error, name_error, mode_error);
type file_open_kind is
  (read_mode, write_mode, append_mode);
```

The type **severity_level** is used in assertion statements, which we will discuss in Chapter 3, and the types **file_open_status** and **file_open_kind** are used for file operations. (File operations are considered an advanced topic and not described in this book.) For the remainder of this section, we look at the other predefined enumeration types and the operations applicable to them.

VHDL-87

The types **file_open_status** and **file_open_kind** are not predefined in VHDL-87.

Characters

In Chapter 1 we saw how to write literal character values. These values are members of the predefined enumeration type **character**, which includes all of the characters in the ISO 8859 Latin-1 8-bit character set. The type definition is shown below. Note that this type is an example of an enumeration type containing a mixture of identifiers and character literals as elements.

```
type character is (
  nul,  soh,  stx,  etx,  eot,  enq,  ack,  bel,
  bs,   ht,   lf,   vt,   ff,   cr,   so,   si,
  dle,  dc1,  dc2,  dc3,  dc4,  nak,  syn,  etb,
  can,  em,   sub,  esc,  fsp,  gsp,  rsp,  usp,
  ' ',  '!',  '"',  '#',  '$',  '%',  '&',  ''',
  '(',  ')',  '*',  '+',  ',',  '-',  '.',  '/',
  '0',  '1',  '2',  '3',  '4',  '5',  '6',  '7',
  '8',  '9',  ':',  ';',  '<',  '=',  '>',  '?',
```

```
'@',   'A',   'B',   'C',   'D',   'E',   'F',   'G',
'H',   'I',   'J',   'K',   'L',   'M',   'N',   'O',
'P',   'Q',   'R',   'S',   'T',   'U',   'V',   'W',
'X',   'Y',   'Z',   '[',   '\',   ']',   '^',   '_',
'`',   'a',   'b',   'c',   'd',   'e',   'f',   'g',
'h',   'i',   'j',   'k',   'l',   'm',   'n',   'o',
'p',   'q',   'r',   's',   't',   'u',   'v',   'w',
'x',   'y',   'z',   '{',   '|',   '}',   '~',   del,
c128,  c129,  c130,  c131,  c132,  c133,  c134,  c135,
c136,  c137,  c138,  c139,  c140,  c141,  c142,  c143,
c144,  c145,  c146,  c147,  c148,  c149,  c150,  c151,
c152,  c153,  c154,  c155,  c156,  c157,  c158,  c159,
' ',   '¡',   '¢',   '£',   '¤',   '¥',   '¦',   '§',
'¨',   '©',   'ª',   '«',   '¬',   '',   '®',   '¯',
'°',   '±',   '²',   '³',   '´',   'µ',   '¶',   '·',
'¸',   '¹',   'º',   '»',   '¼',   '½',   '¾',   '¿',
'À',   'Á',   'Â',   'Ã',   'Ä',   'Å',   'Æ',   'Ç',
'È',   'É',   'Ê',   'Ë',   'Ì',   'Í',   'Î',   'Ï',
'Ð',   'Ñ',   'Ò',   'Ó',   'Ô',   'Õ',   'Ö',   '×',
'Ø',   'Ù',   'Ú',   'Û',   'Ü',   'Ý',   'Þ',   'ß',
'à',   'á',   'â',   'ã',   'ä',   'å',   'æ',   'ç',
'è',   'é',   'ê',   'ë',   'ì',   'í',   'î',   'ï',
'ð',   'ñ',   'ò',   'ó',   'ô',   'õ',   'ö',   '÷',
'ø',   'ù',   'ú',   'û',   'ü',   'ý',   'þ',   'ÿ');
```

The first 128 characters in this enumeration are the ASCII characters, which form a subset of the Latin-1 character set. The identifiers from **nul** to **usp** and **del** are the non-printable ASCII control characters. Characters c128 to c159 do not have any standard names, so VHDL just gives them nondescript names based on their position in the character set. The character at position 160 is a non-breaking space character, distinct from the ordinary space character, and the character at position 173 is a soft hyphen.

To illustrate the use of the **character** type, we declare variables as follows:

```
variable cmd_char, terminator : character;
```

and then make the assignments

```
cmd_char := 'P';
terminator := cr;
```

VHDL-87

Since VHDL-87 uses the ASCII character set, the predefined type **character** includes only the first 128 characters shown above.

Booleans

One of the most important predefined enumeration types in VHDL is the type **boolean**, defined as

```
type boolean is (false, true);
```

This type is used to represent condition values, which can control execution of a behavioral model. There are a number of operators that we can apply to values of different types to yield Boolean values, namely, the relational and logical operators. The relational operators equality ("=") and inequality ("/=") can be applied to operands of any type (except files), including the composite types that we will see later in this chapter. The operands must both be of the same type, and the result is a Boolean value. For example, the expressions

```
123 = 123    'A' = 'A'    7 ns = 7 ns
```

all yield the value **true**, and the expressions

```
123 = 456    'A' = 'z'    7 ns = 2 us
```

yield the value **false**.

The relational operators that test ordering are the less-than ("<"), less-than-or-equal-to ("<="), greater-than (">") and greater-than-or-equal-to (">=") operators. These can only be applied to values of types that are ordered, including all of the scalar types described in this chapter. As with the equality and inequality operators, the operands must be of the same type, and the result is a Boolean value. For example, the expressions

```
123 < 456    789 ps <= 789 ps    '1' > '0'
```

all result in **true**, and the expressions

```
96 >= 102    2 us < 4 ns    'X' < 'X'
```

all result in **false**.

The logical operators **and**, **or**, **nand**, **nor**, **xor**, **xnor** and **not** take operands that are Boolean values and produce Boolean results. Table 2.1 shows the results produced by the binary logical operators. The result of the unary **not** operator is **true** if the operand is **false**, and **false** if the operand is **true**. The operators **and**, **or**, **nand** and **nor** are called "short-

TABLE 2.1 *The truth table for binary logical operators*

A	B	A **and** B	A **nand** B	A **or** B	A **nor** B	A **xor** B	A **xnor** B
false	false	false	true	false	true	false	true
false	true	false	true	true	false	true	false
true	false	false	true	true	false	true	false
true	true	true	false	true	false	false	true

circuit" operators, as they only evaluate the right operand if the left operand does not determine the result. For example, if the left operand of the **and** operator is false, we know that the result is false, so we do not need to consider the other operand. This is useful where the left operand is a test that guards against the right operand causing an error. Consider the expression

```
(b /= 0) and (a/b > 1)
```

If **b** were zero and we evaluated the right-hand operand, we would cause an error due to dividing by zero. However, because and is a short-circuit operator, if **b** were zero, the left-hand operand would evaluate to false, so the right-hand operand would not be evaluated. For the **nand** operator, the right-hand operand is similarly not evaluated if the left-hand is false. For **or** and **nor**, the right-hand operand is not evaluated if the left-hand is true.

VHDL-87

The logical operator **xnor** is not provided in VHDL-87.

Bits

Since VHDL is used to model digital systems, it is useful to have a data type to represent bit values. The predefined enumeration type **bit** serves this purpose. It is defined as

```
type bit is ('0', '1');
```

Notice that the characters '0' and '1' are overloaded, since they are members of both **bit** and **character**. Where '0' or '1' occurs in a model, the context is used to determine which type is being used.

The logical operators that we mentioned for Boolean values can also be applied to values of type **bit**, and they produce results of type **bit**. The value '0' corresponds to false, and '1' corresponds to true. So, for example:

```
'0' and '1' = '0',  '1' xor '1' = '0'
```

The operands must still be of the same type as each other. Thus it is not legal to write

```
'0' and true
```

The difference between the types **boolean** and **bit** is that **boolean** values are used to model abstract conditions, whereas **bit** values are used to model hardware logic levels. Thus, '0' represents a low logic level and '1' represents a high logic level. The logical operators, when applied to **bit** values, are defined in terms of positive logic, with '0' representing the negated state and '1' representing the asserted state. If we need to deal with negative logic, we need to take care when writing logical expressions to get the correct logic sense. For example, if write_enable_n, select_reg_n and write_reg_n are negative logic bit variables, we perform the assignment

```
write_reg_n := not ( not write_enable_n and not select_reg_n );
```

The variable **write_reg_n** is asserted ('0') only if **write_enable_n** is asserted and **select_reg_n** is asserted. Otherwise it is negated ('1').

Standard Logic

Since VHDL is designed for modeling digital hardware, it is necessary to include types to represent digitally encoded values. The predefined type bit shown above can be used for this in more abstract models, where we are not concerned about the details of electrical signals. However, as we refine our models to include more detail, we need to take account of the electrical properties when representing signals. There are many ways we can define data types to do this, but the IEEE has standardized one way in a package called **std_logic_1164**. The full details of the package are included in Appendix A. One of the types defined in this package is an enumeration type called **std_ulogic**, defined as

```
type std_ulogic is ( 'U',        -- Uninitialized
                     'X',        -- Forcing Unknown
                     '0',        -- Forcing zero
                     '1',        -- Forcing one
                     'Z',        -- High Impedance
                     'W',        -- Weak Unknown
                     'L',        -- Weak zero
                     'H',        -- Weak one
                     '-' );      -- Don't care
```

This type can be used to represent signals driven by active drivers (forcing strength), resistive drivers such as pull-ups and pull-downs (weak strength) or three-state drivers including a high-impedance state. Each kind of driver may drive a "zero," "one" or "unknown" value. An "unknown" value is driven by a model when it is unable to determine whether the signal should be "zero" or "one." For example, the output of an and gate is unknown when its inputs are driven by high-impedance drivers. In addition to these values, the leftmost value in the type represents an "uninitialized" value. If we declare signals of **std_ulogic** type, by default they take on 'U' as their initial value. If a model tries to operate on this value instead of a real logic value, we have detected a design error in that the system being modeled does not start up properly. The final value in **std_ulogic** is a "don't care" value. This is sometimes used by logic synthesis tools and may also be used when defining test vectors, to denote that the value of a signal to be compared with a test vector is not important.

Even though the type **std_ulogic** and the other types defined in the **std_logic_1164** package are not actually built into the VHDL language, we can write models as though they were, with a little bit of preparation. For now, we describe some "magic" to include at the beginning of a model that uses the package; we explain the details in Chapter 7. If we include the line

```
library ieee;  use ieee.std_logic_1164.all;
```

preceding each entity or architecture body that uses the package, we can write models as though the types were built into the language.

With this preparation in hand, we can now create constants, variables and signals of type **std_ulogic**. As well as assigning values of the type, we can also use the logical operators **and**, **or**, **not** and so on. Each of these operates on **std_ulogic** values and returns a **std_ulogic** result of '0', 'X', '0' or '1'. The operators are "optimistic," in that if they can determine a '0' or '1' result despite inputs being unknown, they do so. Otherwise they return 'X' or 'U'. For example '0' **and** 'Z' returns '0', since one input to an and gate being '0' always causes the output to be '0', regardless of the other input.

One important point to note about comparing **std_ulogic** values using the "=" and "/=" operations is that it is not the logic levels that are compared, but the enumeration literals. Thus, the expression '0' = 'L' yields false, even though both values represent low logic levels. If we want to compare logic levels without taking account of drive strength, we should use the matching operators "?=" and "?/=". These operators perform logical equivalence and unequivalence comparisons, respectively. If both operands are '0', '1', 'L', or 'H', the operations yield a '0' or '1' result. For example:

```
'1' ?= 'H'  =  '1'     '1' ?/= 'H'  =  '0'
'0' ?= 'H'  =  '0'     '0' ?/= 'H'  =  '1'
```

The "?=" and "?/=" operators yield 'X' when either operand is 'X', 'Z', or 'W'. However, if either operand is 'U', the result is 'U'. The final exception is for don't care ('–') operands. For these, "?=" always yeilds '1' and "?/=" always yields '0'. Some examples are:

```
'Z' ?= 'H'  =  'X'     'W' ?/= 'H'  =  'X'
'0' ?= 'U'  =  'U'     '0' ?/= 'U'  =  'U'
'1' ?= '–'  =  '1'     '–' ?/= '–'  =  '0'
```

We note briefly here, for completeness, that VHDL also defines the matching operators "?<", "?<=", "?>" and "?=>" for comparing **std_ulogic** values. They treat a logic low level ('0' or 'L') as being less than a logic high level ('1' or 'H'), yield 'X' for comparison with a non-logic-level value other than 'U', and yield 'U' for comparison with 'U'. Comparison with '–' is not allowed. We also note that all of the matching operators are defined for operands of type **bit**, yielding '0' or '1' where an ordinary comparison would yield **false** or **true**, respectively. We will return to the way in which these operators are used in later chapters.

Condition Conversion

We mentioned above that Boolean values are used as condition values to control execution in VHDL models. We have seen this in if statements in previous examples, where Boolean conditions control whether groups of statements are executed or not. When we are modeling digital systems, we often use signals and variables of type **bit** or **std_ulogic** to represent logical conditions. It would seem reasonable to want to use such values in conditions controlling execution. VHDL allows us to do this, as it implicitly converts **bit** and **std_ulogic** values to **boolean** values when they occur as conditions. For example, if we have control signals declared as

```
signal cs1, ncs2, cs3 : std_ulogic;
```

then we can write an if statement as follows:

```
if cs1 and not cs2 and cs3 then
  ...
end if;
```

The logical **and** and **not** operators applied to the signals yield a result of type std_ulogic. However, VHDL implicitly converts this to **boolean**, treating '1' and 'H' as true, and all other values as false. Had we declared the signals to be of type **bit**, the implicit conversion would also occur, with '1' treated as true and '0' as false. Implicit conversion occurs in this way in any place where a Boolean condition is required. Another example of such a place that we have seen is a wait statement, for example:

```
wait until clk;
```

If **clk** is of type **std_ulogic**, the wait statement suspends until **clk** changes to '1' or 'H'.

One final point to note is that implicit conversions don't allow us to write a condition that mixes **bit** or **std_ulogic** operands with **boolean** operands for logical operators. For example, the following is illegal:

```
if cs1 and cs3 and alu_op = pass then ... -- illegal
```

The result of the "=" comparison is of type **boolean**, which cannot be mixed with the std_ulogic operand for the **and** operator. The conversion is only applied to the overall condition. We would have to write the condition as:

```
if cs1 = '1' and cs3 = '1' and alu_op = pass then ...
```

VHDL-87, -93, and -2002

These versions of VHDL do not perform implicit conversion of conditions to **boolean**. Conditions must yield **boolean** results without conversion. Hence, we must write conditions such as:

```
if cs1 = '1' and ncs2 = '0' and cs3 = '1' then
  ...
end if;
```

2.3   Type Classification

In the preceding sections we have looked at the scalar types provided in VHDL. Figure 2.1 illustrates the relationships between these types, the predefined scalar types and the types we look at in later chapters.

The scalar types are all those composed of individual values that are ordered. Integer and floating-point types are ordered on the number line. Physical types are ordered by the number of primary units in each value. Enumeration types are ordered by their decla-

FIGURE 2.1

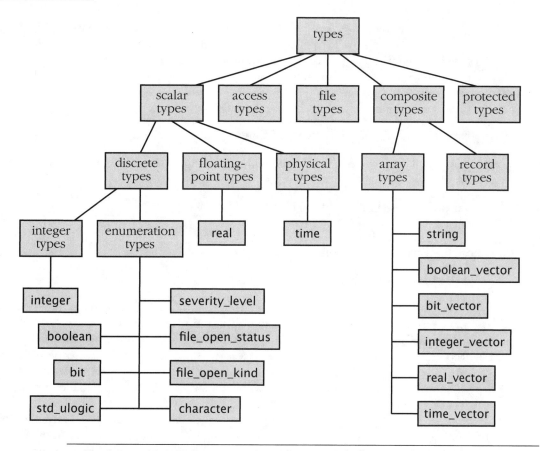

A classification of VHDL types.

ration. The discrete types are those that represent discrete sets of values and comprise the integer types and enumeration types. Floating-point and physical types are not discrete, as they approximate a continuum of values.

2.3.1 Subtypes

In Section 2.2 we saw how to declare a type, which defines a set of values. Often a model contains objects that should only take on a restricted range of the complete set of values. We can represent such objects by declaring a *subtype*, which defines a restricted set of values from a *base type*. The condition that determines which values are in the subtype is called a *constraint*. Using a subtype declaration makes clear our intention about which values are valid and makes it possible to check that invalid values are not used. The simplified syntax rules for a subtype declaration are

subtype_declaration ⇐ **subtype** identifier **is** subtype_indication ;

subtype_indication ⇐
    type_mark 〚 **range** simple_expression 〘 **to** 〛 **downto** 〙 simple_expression 〛

We will look at more advanced forms of subtype indications in later chapters. The subtype declaration defines the identifier as a subtype of the base type specified by the type mark, with the range constraint restricting the values for the subtype. The constraint is optional, which means that it is possible to have a subtype that includes all of the values of the base type.

Here is an example of a declaration that defines a subtype of integer:

subtype small_int **is** integer **range** -128 **to** 127;

Values of small_int are constrained to be within the range –128 to 127. If we declare some variables:

variable deviation : small_int;
variable adjustment : integer;

we can use them in calculations:

deviation := deviation + adjustment;

Note that in this case, we can mix the subtype and base type values in the addition to produce a value of type integer, but the result must be within the range –128 to 127 for the assignment to succeed. If it is not, an error will be signaled when the variable is assigned. All of the operations that are applicable to the base type can also be used on values of a subtype. The operations produce values of the base type rather than the subtype. However, the assignment operation will not assign a value to a variable of a subtype if the value does not meet the constraint.

Another point to note is that if a base type is a range of one direction (ascending or descending), and a subtype is specified with a range constraint of the opposite direction, it is the subtype specification that counts. For example, the predefined type integer is an ascending range. If we declare a subtype as

subtype bit_index **is** integer **range** 31 **downto** 0;

this subtype is a descending range.

The VHDL standard includes two predefined integer subtypes, defined as

subtype natural **is** integer **range** 0 **to** *highest_integer*;
subtype positive **is** integer **range** 1 **to** *highest_integer*;

Where the logic of a design indicates that a number should not be negative, it is good style to use one of these subtypes rather than the base type integer. In this way, we can detect any design errors that incorrectly cause negative numbers to be produced. There is also a predefined subtype of the physical type time, defined as

subtype delay_length **is** time **range** 0 fs **to** *highest_time*;

This subtype should be used wherever a non-negative time delay is required.

VHDL-87

The subtype **delay_length** is not predefined in VHDL-87.

2.3.2 Type Qualification

Sometimes it is not clear from the context what the type of a particular value is. In the case of overloaded enumeration literals, it may be necessary to specify explicitly which type is meant. We can do this using *type qualification*, which consists of writing the type name followed by a single quote character, then an expression enclosed in parentheses. For example, given the enumeration types

```
type logic_level is (unknown, low, undriven, high);
type system_state is (unknown, ready, busy);
```

we can distinguish between the common literal values by writing

```
logic_level'(unknown)    system_state'(unknown)
```

Type qualification can also be used to narrow a value down to a particular subtype of a base type. For example, if we define a subtype of **logic_level**

```
subtype valid_level is logic_level range low to high;
```

we can explicitly specify a value of either the type or the subtype

```
logic_level'(high)    valid_level'(high)
```

Of course, it is an error if the expression being qualified is not of the type specified.

VHDL-87, -93, and -2002

In these earlier versions of VHDL, if a type qualification specified a subtype, the value qualified had to be of that specific subtype. It was not sufficient for it just to be of the base type of the specified subtype. In VHDL-2008, the value is converted to be of the subtype. While there is no distinction in the case of scalar types, when we come to composite types, the distinction can be significant.

2.3.3 Type Conversion

When we introduced the arithmetic operators in previous sections, we stated that the operands must be of the same type. This precludes mixing integer and floating-point values in arithmetic expressions. Where we need to do mixed arithmetic, we can use *type conversions* to convert between integer and floating-point values. The form of a type conversion is the name of the type we want to convert to, followed by a value in parentheses. For example, to convert between the types **integer** and **real**, we could write

```
real(123)    integer(3.6)
```

Converting an integer to a floating-point value is simply a change in representation, although some loss of precision may occur. Converting from a floating-point value to an integer involves rounding to the nearest integer. Numeric type conversions are not the only conversion allowed. In general, we can convert between any closely related types. Other examples of closely related types are certain array types, discussed in Chapter 4.

One thing to watch out for is the distinction between type qualification and type conversion. The former simply states the type of a value, whereas the latter changes the value, possibly to a different type. One way to remember this distinction is to think of "*qu*ote for *qu*alification."

2.4   Attributes of Scalar Types

A type defines a set of values and a set of applicable operations. There is also a predefined set of *attributes* that are used to give information about the values included in the type. Attributes are written by following the type name with a quote mark (') and the attribute name. The value of an attribute can be used in calculations in a model. We now look at some of the attributes defined for the types we have discussed in this chapter.

First, there are a number of attributes that are applicable to all scalar types and provide information about the range of values in the type. If we let T stand for any scalar type or subtype, x stand for a value of that type and s stand for a string value, the attributes are

T'left	first (leftmost) value in T
T'right	last (rightmost) value in T
T'low	least value in T
T'high	greatest value in T
T'ascending	**true** if T is an ascending range, **false** otherwise
T'image(x)	a string representing the value of x
T'value(s)	the value in T that is represented by s

The string produced by the 'image attribute is a correctly formed literal according to the rules shown in Chapter 1. The strings allowed in the 'value attribute must follow those rules and may include leading or trailing spaces. These two attributes are useful for input and output in a model, as we will see when we come to that topic.

To illustrate the attributes listed above, recall the following declarations from previous examples:

```
type resistance is range 0 to 1E9
  units
    ohm;
    kohm = 1000 ohm;
    Mohm = 1000 kohm;
  end units resistance;
```

```
type set_index_range is range 21 downto 11;

type logic_level is (unknown, low, undriven, high);
```

For these types:

```
resistance'left = 0 ohm
resistance'right = 1E9 ohm
resistance'low = 0 ohm
resistance'high = 1E9 ohm
resistance'ascending = true
resistance'image(2 kohm) = "2000 ohm"
resistance'value("5 Mohm") = 5_000_000 ohm

set_index_range'left = 21
set_index_range'right = 11
set_index_range'low = 11
set_index_range'high = 21
set_index_range'ascending = false
set_index_range'image(14) = "14"
set_index_range'value("20") = 20

logic_level'left = unknown
logic_level'right = high
logic_level'low = unknown
logic_level'high = high
logic_level'ascending = true
logic_level'image(undriven) = "undriven"
logic_level'value("Low") = low
```

Next, there are attributes that are applicable to just discrete and physical types. For any such type T, a value x of that type and an integer n, the attributes are

T'pos(x)	position number of x in T
T'val(n)	value in T at position n
T'succ(x)	value in T at position one greater than that of x
T'pred(x)	value in T at position one less than that of x
T'leftof(x)	value in T at position one to the left of x
T'rightof(x)	value in T at position one to the right of x

For enumeration types, the position numbers start at zero for the first element listed and increase by one for each element to the right. So, for the type **logic_level** shown above, some attribute values are

```
logic_level'pos(unknown) = 0
logic_level'val(3) = high
```

```
logic_level'succ(unknown) = low
logic_level'pred(undriven) = low
```

For integer types, the position number is the same as the integer value, but the type of the position number is a special anonymous type called *universal integer*. This is the same type as that of integer literals and, where necessary, is implicitly converted to any other declared integer type. For physical types, the position number is the integer number of base units in the physical value. For example:

```
time'pos(4 ns) = 4_000_000
```

since the base unit is fs.

We can use the **'pos** and **'val** attributes in combination to perform mixed-dimensional arithmetic with physical types, producing a result of the correct dimensionality. Suppose we define physical types to represent length and area, as follows:

```
type length is range integer'low to integer'high
  units
    mm;
  end units length;

type area is range integer'low to integer'high
  units
    square_mm;
  end units area;
```

and variables of these types:

```
variable L1, L2 : length;
variable A : area;
```

The restrictions on multiplying values of physical types prevents us from writing something like

```
A := L1 * L2;    -- this is incorrect
```

To achieve the correct result, we can convert the length values to abstract integers using the **'pos** attribute, then convert the result of the multiplication to an area value using **'val**, as follows:

```
A := area'val( length'pos(L1) * length'pos(L2) );
```

Note that in this example, we do not need to include a scale factor in the multiplication, since the base unit of **area** is the square of the base unit of **length**.

For ascending ranges, T'succ(x) and T'rightof(x) produce the same value, and T'pred(x) and T'leftof(x) produce the same value. For descending ranges, T'pred(x) and T'rightof(x) produce the same value, and T'succ(x) and T'leftof(x) produce the same value. For all ranges, T'succ(T'high), T'pred(T'low), T'rightof(T'right) and T'leftof(T'left) cause an error to occur.

The last attribute we introduce here is T'base. For any subtype T, this attribute produces the base type of T. The only context in which this attribute may be used is as the prefix of another attribute. For example, if we have the declarations

```
type opcode is
   (nop, load, store, add, subtract, negate, branch, halt);
subtype arith_op is opcode range add to negate;
```

then

```
arith_op'base'left = nop
arith_op'base'succ(negate) = branch
```

VHDL-87

The attributes 'ascending, 'image and 'value are not provided in VHDL-87.

2.5 Expressions and Predefined Operations

In Section 2.1 we showed how the value resulting from evaluation of an expression can be assigned to a variable. In this section, we summarize the rules governing expressions. We can think of an expression as being a formula that specifies how to compute a value. As such, it consists of primary values combined with operators and other operations. The precise syntax rules for writing expressions are shown in Appendix B. The primary values that can be used in expressions include

- literal values,

- identifiers representing data objects (constants, variables and so on),

- attributes that yield values,

- qualified expressions,

- type-converted expressions,

- operation functions, and

- expressions in parentheses.

We have seen examples of these in this chapter and in Chapter 1. For reference, all of the predefined operators and the types they can be applied to are summarized in Table 2.2. We will discuss array operators in Chapter 4. The operators in this table are grouped by precedence, with "**", **abs**, and the unary logical reduction operators having highest precedence and the binary logical operators lowest. The precedence rules mean that if an expression contains a combination of operators, those with highest precedence are applied first. Parentheses can be used to alter the order of evaluation, or for clarity.

TABLE 2.2 *VHDL operators in order of precedence, from most binding to least binding*

Operator	Operation	Left operand type	Right operand type	Result type
**	exponentiation	integer or floating-point	integer	same as left operand
abs	absolute value		numeric	same as operand
not	logical negation		boolean, bit, std_ulogic, 1-D array of **boolean** or bit, std_ulogic_vector	same as operand
and	logical and reduction		1-D array of **boolean** or bit, std_ulogic_vector	element type of operand
or	logical or reduction			
nand	negated logical and reduction			
nor	negated logical or reduction			
xor	exclusive or reduction			
xnor	negated exclusive or reduction			
*	multiplication	integer or floating-point	same as left operand	same as operands
		physical	**integer** or **real**	same as left operand
		integer or **real**	physical	same as right operand
/	division	integer or floating-point	same as left operand	same as operands
		physical	integer or real	same as left operand
		physical	same as left operand	universal integer
mod	modulo	integer or physical	same as left operand	same as operands
rem	remainder			
+	identity		numeric	same as operand
−	negation			
+	addition	numeric	same as left operand	same as operands
−	subtraction			
&	concatenation	1-D array	same as left operand	same as operands
		1-D array	element type of left operand	same as left operand
		element type of right operand	1-D array	same as right operand
		element type of result	element type of result	1-D array

Operator	Operation	Left operand type	Right operand type	Result type
sll	shift-left logical	1-D array of **boolean** or bit, std_ulogic_vector	integer	same as left operand
srl	shift-right logical			
rol	rotate left			
ror	rotate right			
sla	shift-left arithmetic	1-D array of **boolean** or bit	integer	same as left operand
sra	shift-right arithmetic			
=	equality	any except file or protected type	same as left operand	boolean
/=	inequality			
<	less than	scalar or 1-D array of any discrete type	same as left operand	boolean
<=	less than or equal to			
>	greater than			
>=	greater than or equal to			
?=	matching equality	bit, std_ulogic or 1-D array of bit or std_ulogic	same as left operand	bit or std_ulogic
?/=	matching inequality			
?<	matching less than	bit or std_ulogic	same as left operand	bit or std_ulogic
?<=	matching less than or equal to			
?>	matching greater than			
?>=	matching greater than or equal to			
and	logical and	boolean, bit, std_ulogic, 1-D array of **boolean** or bit, std_ulogic_vector	same as left operand	same as operands
or	logical or			
nand	negated logical and			
nor	negated logical or			
xor	exclusive or			
xnor	negated exclusive or			

In Section 2.2, we described the **maximum** and **minimum** operations for numeric types. These are examples of function operations that can form primary values in expressions. In fact, these operations are defined for all scalar types, as are the relational operators "<", "<=", ">", and ">=". For numeric types, the **maximum** and **minimum** operations compare the numeric values to determine the result. For enumeration types, the operations compare the position numbers. Thus, enumeration values declared earlier in the list of an enumeration type declaration are considered to be less than those declared later in the list. For example, in the **character** type, 'A' < 'Z', and the minimum of 'c' and 'q' is 'c'.

Another function operation that can be applied to any scalar value is the **to_string** operation. It yields a character-string representation of the value that can be used in any place where we can use a string literal. For example:

```
to_string(123)      = "123"
to_string(456.78)   = "4.5678e+2"
to_string(warning)  = "warning"
```

For floating-point types, **to_string** represents the value using exponential notation, with the number of digits depending on the particular VHDL tool being used. There are, however, two alternate forms of **to_string** for floating-point values that give us more control over the formatting. First, we can specify that the value be represented with a given number of post-decimal digits rather than in exponential form. For example:

```
to_string(456.78, 4) = "456.7800"
to_string(456.78, 1) = "456.8"
```

Second, we can provide a format specification string of the same form as that used in the C **printf** function. For example:

```
to_string(456.78, "%10.3f")  = "   456.780"
to_string(456.78, "%-12.3E") = "4.568E+02   "
```

For physical types, **to_string** represents the value using the primary unit of the type. For example, given the declaration of type **resistance** on page 39:

```
to_string(2.2 kohm) = "2200 ohm"
```

The exception is the physical type **time**, for which **to_string** represents the value as a multiple of the resolution limit. So, for example, if the resolution limit for a simulation is set to **ns**:

```
to_string(29.5 us) = "29500 ns"
```

There is also an alternate form of **to_string** for **time** that allows us to control the unit used to represent the value. For example, even if the resolution limit is set to **ns**, we can represent a time value in microseconds as follows:

```
to_string(29500 ns, us) = "29.5 us"
```

The final predefined function operations on scalar types are the **rising_edge** and **falling_edge** operations, which can be applied to signals of type **boolean**, **bit**, or **std_ulogic**. These allow us to describe edge-triggered behavior in a natural manner. For example, we can write a process describing a D-flipflop as follows:

```
signal clk, d, q : bit;
. . .

dff : process is
begin
  if rising_edge(clk) then
```

```
        q <= d;
    end if;
    wait on clk;
end process dff;
```

For a **boolean** signal s, rising_edge(s) is **true** when s changes from **false** to **true** and **false** at other times (including when s changes from **true** to **false** and when s is not changing). Similarly, falling_edge(s) is **true** when s changes from **true** to **false** and **false** at other times. For a **bit** signal s, rising_edge(s) is **true** when s changes from '0' to '1' and **false** at other times; and falling_edge(s) is **true** when s changes from '1' to '0', and **false** at other times. Finally, for a **std_ulogic** signal s, rising_edge(s) is **true** when s changes from '0' or 'L' to '1' or 'H' and **false** at other times (including changes from or to 'U', 'X', 'W', 'Z', or '–'); and falling_edge(s) is **true** when s changes from '1' or 'H' to '0' or 'L' and **false** at other times.

VHDL-87, -93, and -2002

The unary logical operators (**and**, **or**, **nand**, **nor**, **xor** and **xnor**), the matching relational operators ("?=", "?/=", "?<","?<=", "?>", and "?>="), and the function operations maximum, minimum, to_string, rising_edge, and falling_edge are not provided in earlier versions of VHDL. Also, the **mod** and **rem** operators are not applicable to physical types in earlier versions.

VHDL-87

The shift operators (**sll**, **srl**, **sla**, **sra**, **rol** and **ror**) and the binary **xnor** operator are not provided in VHDL-87.

Exercises

1. [❶ 2.1] Write constant declarations for the number of bits in a 32-bit word and for the number π (3.14159).

2. [❶ 2.1] Write variable declarations for a counter, initialized to 0; a status flag used to indicate whether a module is busy; and a standard-logic value used to store a temporary result.

3. [❶ 2.1] Given the declarations in Exercise 2, write variable assignment statements to increment the counter, to set the status flag to indicate the module is busy and to indicate a weak unknown temporary result.

4. [❶ 2.2] Write a package declaration containing type declarations for small non-negative integers representable in eight bits; fractional numbers between −1.0 and +1.0; electrical currents, with units of nA, μA, mA and A; and traffic light colors.

5. [❶ 2.2] Given the following declarations:

```
signal a, b, c : std_ulogic;
type state_type is (idle, req, ack);
signal state : state_type;
```

indicate whether each of the following expressions is legal as a Boolean condition, and if not, correct it:

a.   a **and not** b **and** c

b.   a **and not** b **and** state = idle

c.   a = '0' **and** b **and** state = idle

d.   a = '1' **and** b = '0' **and** state = idle

6. [❶ 2.4] Given the subtype declarations

    ```
    subtype pulse_range is time range 1 ms to 100 ms;
    subtype word_index is integer range 31 downto 0;
    ```

    what are the values of 'left, 'right, 'low, 'high and 'ascending attributes of each of these subtypes?

7. [❶ 2.4] Given the type declaration

    ```
    type state is (off, standby, active1, active2);
    ```

    what are the values of

    ```
    state'pos(standby)      state'val(2)
    state'succ(active2)     state'pred(active1)
    state'leftof(off)       state'rightof(off)
    ```

8. [❶ 2.5] For each of the following expressions, indicate whether they are syntactically correct, and if so, determine the resulting value.

    ```
    2 * 3 + 6 / 4            3 + -4
    "cat" & character'('0')  true and x and not y or z
    B"101110" sll 3          (B"100010" sra 2) & X"2C"
    ```

9. [❷ 2.1] Write a counter model with a clock input **clk** of type **bit**, and an output **q** of type **integer**. The behavioral architecture body should contain a process that declares a count variable initialized to zero. The process should wait for changes on **clk**. When **clk** changes to '1', the process should increment the count and assign its value to the output port.

10. [❷ 2.2] Write a model that represents a simple ALU with integer inputs and output, and a function select input of type **bit**. If the function select is '0', the ALU output should be the sum of the inputs; otherwise the output should be the difference of the inputs.

11. [❷ 2.2] Write a model for a digital integrator that has a clock input of type **bit** and data input and output each of type **real**. The integrator maintains the sum of successive

data input values. When the clock input changes from '0' to '1', the integrator should add the current data input to the sum and provide the new sum on the output.

12. [❷ 2.2] Following is a process that generates a regular clock signal.

```
clock_gen : process is
begin
  clk <= '1';  wait for 10 ns;
  clk <= '0';  wait for 10 ns;
end process clock_gen;
```

Use this as the basis for experiments to determine how your simulator behaves with different settings for the resolution limit. Try setting the resolution limit to 1 ns (the default for many simulators), 1 ps and 1 µs.

13. [❷ 2.2] Write a model for a tristate buffer using the standard-logic type for its data and enable inputs and its data output. If the enable input is '0' or 'L', the output should be 'Z'. If the enable input is '1' or 'H' and the data input is '0' or 'L', the output should be '0'. If the enable input is '1' or 'H' and the data input is '1' or 'H', the output should be '1'. In all other cases, the output should be 'X'.

Chapter 3

Sequential Statements

In the previous chapter we saw how to represent the internal state of models using VHDL data types. In this chapter we look at how that data may be manipulated within processes. This is done using *sequential statements*, so called because they are executed in sequence. We have already seen one of the basic sequential statements, the variable assignment statement, when we were looking at data types and objects. The statements we look at in this chapter deal with controlling actions within a model; hence they are often called *control structures*. They allow selection between alternative courses of action as well as repetition of actions.

3.1 If Statements

In many models, the behavior depends on a set of conditions that may or may not hold true during the course of simulation. We can use an *if statement* to express this behavior. The syntax rule for an if statement is

> if_statement ⇐
>   ⟦ *if*_label : ⟧
>   **if** condition **then**
>   { sequential_statement }
>   ⦃ **elsif** condition **then**
>   { sequential_statement } ⦄
>   ⟦ **else**
>   { sequential_statement } ⟧
>   **end if** ⟦ *if*_label ⟧ ;

At first sight, this may appear somewhat complicated, so we start with some simple examples and work up to examples showing the general case. The label may be used to identify the if statement. A simple example of an if statement is

```
if en then
  stored_value := data_in;
end if;
```

The condition after the keyword **if** is used to control whether or not the statement after the keyword **then** is executed. If the condition is true, the statement is executed. In this example, if the value of the object **en** is '1', the assignment is made; otherwise it is skipped. We can also specify actions to be performed if the condition is false. For example:

```
if sel = 0 then
   result <= input_0;   -- executed if sel = 0
else
   result <= input_1;   -- executed if sel /= 0
end if;
```

Here, as the comments indicate, the first signal assignment statement is executed if the condition is true, and the second signal assignment statement is executed if the condition is false.

In many models, we may need to check a number of different conditions and execute a different sequence of statements for each case. We can construct a more elaborate form of if statement to do this, for example:

```
if mode = immediate then
   operand := immed_operand;
elsif opcode = load or opcode = add or opcode = subtract then
   operand := memory_operand;
else
   operand := address_operand;
end if;
```

In this example, the first condition is evaluated, and if true, the statement after the first **then** keyword is executed. If the first condition is false, the second condition is evaluated, and if it evaluates to true, the statement after the second **then** keyword is executed. If the second condition is false, the statement after the **else** keyword is executed.

In general, we can construct an if statement with any number of **elsif** clauses (including none), and we may include or omit the **else** clause. Execution of the if statement starts by evaluating the first condition. If it is false, successive conditions are evaluated, in order, until one is found to be true, in which case the corresponding statements are executed. If none of the conditions is true, and we have included an **else** clause, the statements after the **else** keyword are executed.

We are not restricted to just one statement in each part of the if statement. This is illustrated by the following if statement:

```
if opcode = halt_opcode then
   PC := effective_address;
   executing := false;
   halt_indicator <= true;
end if;
```

If the condition is true, all three statements are executed, one after another. On the other hand, if the condition is false, none of the statements are executed. Furthermore, each statement contained in an if statement can be any sequential statement. This means we can nest if statements, for example:

```
if phase = wash then
  if cycle_select = delicate_cycle then
    agitator_speed <= slow;
  else
    agitator_speed <= fast;
  end if;
  agitator_on <= true;
end if;
```

In this example, the condition **phase = wash** is first evaluated, and if true, the nested if statement and the following signal assignment statement are executed. Thus the assignment **agitator_speed <= slow** is executed only if both conditions evaluate to true, and the assignment **agitator_speed <= fast** is executed only if the first condition is true and the second condition is false.

EXAMPLE 3.1   *A heater thermostat*

Let us develop a behavioral model for a simple heater thermostat. The device can be modeled as an entity with two integer inputs, one that specifies the desired temperature and another that is connected to a thermometer, and one Boolean output that turns a heater on and off. The thermostat turns the heater on if the measured temperature falls below two degrees less than the desired temperature, and turns the heater off if the measured temperature rises above two degrees greater than the desired temperature. The entity and architecture body for the thermostat are:

```
entity thermostat is
  port ( desired_temp, actual_temp : in integer;
         heater_on : out boolean );
end entity thermostat;

-------------------------------------------------

architecture example of thermostat is
begin

  controller : process (desired_temp, actual_temp) is
  begin
    if actual_temp < desired_temp - 2 then
      heater_on <= true;
    elsif actual_temp > desired_temp + 2 then
      heater_on <= false;
    end if;
  end process controller;

end architecture example;
```

The entity declaration defines the input and output ports. Since it is a behavioral model, the architecture body contains only a process statement that implements the required behavior. The process statement includes a *sensitivity list* after the keyword **process**. This is a list of signals to which the process is sensitive. When any of these signals changes value, the process resumes and executes the sequential statements. After it has executed the last statement, the process suspends again. In this example, the process is sensitive to changes on either of the input ports. Thus, if we adjust the desired temperature, or if the measured temperature from the thermometer varies, the process is resumed. The body of the process contains an if statement that compares the actual temperature with the desired temperature. If the actual temperature is too low, the process executes the first signal assignment to turn the heater on. If the actual temperature is too high, the process executes the second signal assignment to turn the heater off. If the actual temperature is within the range, the state of the heater is not changed, since there is no **else** clause in the if statement.

VHDL-87, -93, and -2002

These versions of VHDL do not perform implicit conversion of conditions to **boolean**. Conditions in if statements must yield **boolean** results without conversion. Hence, we must write the if statement on page 65 as:

```
if en = '1' then
   ...
end if;
```

VHDL-87

If statements may not be labeled in VHDL-87.

3.2   Case Statements

If we have a model in which the behavior is to depend on the value of a single expression, we can use a *case statement*. The syntax rules are as follows:

```
case_statement ⇐
    〖 case_label : 〗
    case expression is
        ( when choices => 〖 sequential_statement 〗 )
        〖 ₀₀₀ 〗
    end case 〖 case_label 〗 ;
```

choices ⇐ (simple_expression 〗 discrete_range 〗 **others**) 〖 | ₀₀₀ 〗

The label may be used to identify the case statement. We start with some simple examples of case statements and build up from them. First, suppose we are modeling an arithmetic/logic unit, with a control input, **func**, declared to be of the enumeration type:

```
type alu_func is (pass1, pass2, add, subtract);
```

We could describe the behavior using a case statement:

```
case func is
  when pass1 =>
    result := operand1;
  when pass2 =>
    result := operand2;
  when add =>
    result := operand1 + operand2;
  when subtract =>
    result := operand1 - operand2;
end case;
```

At the head of this case statement is the *selector expression*, between the keywords **case** and **is**. In this example it is a simple expression consisting of just a primary value. The value of this expression is used to select which statements to execute. The body of the case statement consists of a series of *alternatives*. Each alternative starts with the keyword **when** and is followed by one or more *choices* and a sequence of statements. The choices are values that are compared with the value of the selector expression. There must be exactly one choice for each possible value. The case statement finds the alternative whose choice value is equal to the value of the selector expression and executes the statements in that alternative. In this example, the choices are all simple expressions of type alu_func. If the value of func is pass1, the statement result := operand1 is executed; if the value is pass2, the statement result := operand2 is executed; and so on.

A case statement bears some similarity to an if statement in that they both select among alternative groups of sequential statements. The difference lies in how the statements to be executed are chosen. We saw in the previous section that an if statement evaluates successive Boolean expressions in turn until one is found to be true. The group of statements corresponding to that condition is then executed. A case statement, on the other hand, evaluates a single selector expression to derive a selector value. This value is then compared with the choice values in the case statement alternatives to determine which statement to execute. An if statement provides a more general mechanism for selecting between alternatives, since the conditions can be arbitrarily complex Boolean expressions. However, case statements are an important and useful modeling mechanism, as the examples in this section show.

The selector expression of a case statement must result in a value of a discrete type, or a one-dimensional array of character elements, such as a character string or bit string (see Chapter 4). Thus, we can have a case statement that selects an alternative based on an integer value. If we assume index_mode and instruction_register are declared as

```
subtype index_mode is integer range 0 to 3;
```

```
variable instruction_register : integer range 0 to 2**16 - 1;
```

then we can write a case statement that uses a value of this type:

```
case index_mode'((instruction_register / 2**12) rem 2**2) is
  when 0 =>
    index_value := 0;
  when 1 =>
    index_value := accumulator_A;
  when 2 =>
    index_value := accumulator_B;
  when 3 =>
    index_value := index_register;
end case;
```

Notice that in this example, we use a qualified expression in the selector expression. If we had omitted this, the result of the expression would have been **integer**, and we would have had to include alternatives to cover all possible integer values. The type qualification avoids this need by limiting the possible values of the expression.

Another rule to remember is that the type of each choice must be the same as the type resulting from the selector expression. Thus in the above example, it is illegal to include an alternative such as

```
when 'a' => ...    -- illegal!
```

since the choice listed cannot be an integer. Such a choice does not make sense, since it can never match a value of type **integer**.

We can include more than one choice in each alternative by writing the choices separated by the "|" symbol. For example, if the type **opcodes** is declared as

```
type opcodes is
  (nop, add, subtract, load, store, jump, jumpsub, branch, halt);
```

we could write an alternative including three of these values as choices:

```
when load | add | subtract =>
  operand := memory_operand;
```

If we have a number of alternatives in a case statement and we want to include an alternative to handle all possible values of the selector expression not mentioned in previous alternatives, we can use the special choice **others**. For example, if the variable opcode is a variable of type **opcodes**, declared above, we can write

```
case opcode is
  when load | add | subtract =>
    operand := memory_operand;
  when store | jump | jumpsub | branch =>
    operand := address_operand;
  when others =>
    operand := 0;
end case;
```

In this example, if the value of **opcode** is anything other than the choices listed in the first and second alternatives, the last alternative is selected. There may only be one alternative that uses the **others** choice, and if it is included, it must be the last alternative in the case statement. An alternative that includes the **others** choice may not include any other choices. Note that, if all of the possible values of the selector expression are covered by previous choices, we may still include the **others** choice, but it can never be matched.

The remaining form of choice that we have not yet mentioned is a *discrete range*, specified by these simplified syntax rules:

discrete_range ⟸
    *discrete*_subtype_indication
      ⟦ simple_expression ⟦ **to** ⟦ **downto** ⟧ simple_expression

subtype_indication ⟸
    type_mark
        ⟦ **range** simple_expression ⟦ **to** ⟦ **downto** ⟧ simple_expression ⟧

These forms allow us to specify a range of values in a case statement alternative. If the value of the selector expression matches any of the values in the range, the statements in the alternative are executed. The simplest way to specify a discrete range is just to write the left and right bounds of the range, separated by a direction keyword. For example, the case statement above could be rewritten as

```
case opcode is
  when add to load =>
    operand := memory_operand;
  when branch downto store =>
    operand := address_operand;
  when others =>
    operand := 0;
end case;
```

Another way of specifying a discrete range is to use the name of a discrete type, and possibly a range constraint to narrow down the values to a subset of the type. For example, if we declare a subtype of **opcodes** as

```
subtype control_transfer_opcodes is opcodes range jump to branch;
```

we can rewrite the second alternative as

```
when control_transfer_opcodes | store =>
  operand := address_operand;
```

Note that we may only use a discrete range as a choice if the selector expression is of a discrete type. We may not use a discrete range if the selector expression is of an array type, such as a bit-vector type. If we specify a range by writing the bounds and a direction, the direction has no significance except to identify the contents of the range.

An important point to note about the choices in a case statement is that they must all be written using *locally static* values. This means that the values of the choices must be determined during the analysis phase of design processing. All of the above examples satisfy this requirement. To give an example of a case statement that fails this requirement, suppose we have an integer variable N, declared as

```
variable N : integer := 1;
```

If we wrote the case statement

```
case expression is              -- example of an illegal case statement
  when N | N+1 => ...
  when N+2 to N+5 => ...
  when others => ...
end case;
```

the values of the choices depend on the value of the variable N. Since this might change during the course of execution, these choices are not locally static. Hence the case statement as written is illegal. On the other hand, if we had declared C to be a constant integer, for example with the declaration

```
constant C : integer := 1;
```

then we could legally write the case statement

```
case expression is
  when C | C+1 => ...
  when C+2 to C+5 => ...
  when others => ...
end case;
```

This is legal, since we can determine, by analyzing the model, that the first alternative includes choices 1 and 2, the second includes numbers between 3 and 6 and the third covers all other possible values of the expression.

The previous examples all show only one statement in each alternative. As with the if statement, we can write an arbitrary number of sequential statements of any kind in each alternative. This includes writing nested case statements, if statements or any other form of sequential statements in the alternatives.

Although the preceding rules governing case statements may seem complex, in practice there are just a few things to remember, namely:

- all possible values of the selector expression must be covered by one and only one choice,

- the values in the choices must be locally static and

- if the **others** choice is used it must be in the last alternative and must be the only choice in that alternative.

EXAMPLE 3.2 *A four-input multiplexer*

We can write a behavioral model of a multiplexer with a select input **sel**; four data inputs **d0**, **d1**, **d2** and **d3**; and a data output **z**. The data inputs and outputs are of the IEEE standard-logic type, and the select input is of type **sel_range**, which we assume to be declared elsewhere as

```
type sel_range is range 0 to 3;
```

We described in Section 2.2 how we define a type in a package for use in an entity declaration. The entity declaration defining the ports and a behavioral architecture body are:

```
library ieee;  use ieee.std_logic_1164.all;

entity mux4 is
  port ( sel : in sel_range;
         d0, d1, d2, d3 : in std_ulogic;
         z : out std_ulogic );
end entity mux4;

--------------------------------------------------

architecture demo of mux4 is
begin

  out_select : process (sel, d0, d1, d2, d3) is
  begin
    case sel is
      when 0 =>
        z <= d0;
      when 1 =>
        z <= d1;
      when 2 =>
        z <= d2;
      when 3 =>
        z <= d3;
    end case;
  end process out_select;

end architecture demo;
```

The architecture body contains just a process declaration. Since the output of the multiplexer must change if any of the data or select inputs change, the process must be sensitive to all of the inputs. It makes use of a case statement to select which of the data inputs is to be assigned to the data output.

VHDL-87
_____

Case statements may not be labeled in VHDL-87.

3.3 Null Statements

Sometimes when writing models we need to state that when some condition arises, no action is to be performed. This need often arises when we use case statements, since we must include an alternative for every possible value of the selector expression. Rather than just leaving the statement part of an alternative blank, we can use a *null statement* to state explicitly that nothing is to be done. The syntax rule for the null statement is simply

null_statement $\Leftarrow$ ⟦ label : ⟧ **null** ;

The optional label serves to identify the statement. A simple, unlabeled null statement is

```
null;
```

An example of its use in a case statement is

```
case opcode is
  when add =>
    Acc := Acc + operand;
  when subtract =>
    Acc := Acc - operand;
  when nop =>
    null;
end case;
```

We can use a null statement in any place where a sequential statement is required, not just in a case statement alternative. A null statement may be used during the development phase of model writing. If we know, for example, that we will need an entity as part of a system, but we are not yet in a position to write a detailed model for it, we can write a behavioral model that does nothing. Such a model just includes a process with a null statement in its body:

```
control_section : process ( sensitivity_list ) is
begin
  null;
end process control_section;
```

Note that the process must include the sensitivity list, for reasons that are explained in Chapter 5.

VHDL-87
_____

Null statements may not be labeled in VHDL-87.

3.4 Loop Statements

Often we need to write a sequence of statements that is to be repeatedly executed. We use a *loop statement* to express this behavior. There are several different forms of loop statements in VHDL; the simplest is a loop that repeats a sequence of statements indefinitely, often called an *infinite loop*. The syntax rule for this kind of loop is

loop_statement ⇐
    〚 *loop*_label : 〛
    loop
       〚 sequential_statement 〛
    end loop 〚 *loop*_label 〛 ;

In most computer programming languages, an infinite loop is not desirable, since it means that the program never terminates. However, when we are modeling digital systems, an infinite loop can be useful, since many hardware devices repeatedly perform the same function until we turn off the power. Typically a model for such a system includes a loop statement in a process body; the loop, in turn, contains a wait statement.

EXAMPLE 3.3 *A modulo-16 counter*

The following is a model for a counter that starts from zero and increments on each clock transition from '0' to '1'. When the counter reaches 15, it wraps back to zero on the next clock transition. The architecture body for the counter contains a process that first initializes the count output to zero, then repeatedly waits for a clock transition before incrementing the count value.

```
entity counter is
  port ( clk : in bit;  count : out natural );
end entity counter;

-------------------------------------------------

architecture behavior of counter is
begin

  incrementer : process is
    variable count_value : natural := 0;
  begin
    count <= count_value;
    loop
      wait until clk;
      count_value := (count_value + 1) mod 16;
      count <= count_value;
    end loop;
  end process incrementer;

end architecture behavior;
```

The wait statement in this example causes the process to suspend in the middle of the loop. When the **clk** signal changes from '0' to '1', the process resumes and updates the count value and the **count** output. The loop is then repeated starting with the wait statement, so the process suspends again.

Another point to note in passing is that the process statement does not include a sensitivity list. This is because it includes a wait statement. A process may contain either a sensitivity list or wait statements, but not both. We will return to this in detail in Chapter 5.

3.4.1 Exit Statements

In the previous example, the loop repeatedly executes the enclosed statements, with no way of stopping. Usually we need to exit the loop when some condition arises. We can use an *exit statement* to exit a loop. The syntax rule is

exit_statement ⇐
    ⟦ label : ⟧ **exit** ⟦ *loop*_label ⟧ ⟦ **when** condition ⟧ ;

The optional label at the start of the exit statement serves to identify the statement. The simplest form of exit statement is just

    exit;

When this statement is executed, any remaining statements in the loop are skipped, and control is transferred to the statement after the **end loop** keywords. So in a loop we can write

```
if condition then
  exit;
end if;
```

Since this is perhaps the most common use of the exit statement, VHDL provides a shorthand way of writing it, using the when clause. We use an exit statement with the when clause in a loop of the form

```
loop
  ...
  exit when condition;
  ...
end loop;
...           -- control transferred to here
              -- when condition becomes true within the loop
```

EXAMPLE 3.4 *A modulo-16 counter with reset*

We now revise the counter model from Example 3.3 to include a **reset** input that, when '1', causes the **count** output to be reset to zero. The output stays at zero as long as the **reset** input is '1' and resumes counting on the next clock transition after **reset** changes to '0'. The revised entity declaration includes the new input port.

```vhdl
entity counter is
  port ( clk, reset : in bit;  count : out natural );
end entity counter;

--------------------------------------------------

architecture behavior of counter is
begin

  incrementer : process is
    variable count_value : natural := 0;
  begin
    count <= count_value;
    loop
      loop
        wait until clk or reset;
        exit when reset;
        count_value := (count_value + 1) mod 16;
        count <= count_value;
      end loop;
      -- at this point, reset = '1'
      count_value := 0;
      count <= count_value;
      wait until not reset;
    end loop;
  end process incrementer;

end architecture behavior;
```

The architecture body is revised by nesting the loop inside another loop statement and adding the **reset** signal to the original wait statement. The inner loop performs the same function as before, except that when **reset** changes to '1', the process is resumed, and the exit statement causes the inner loop to be terminated. Control is transferred to the statement just after the end of the inner loop. As the comment indicates, we know that this point can only be reached when **reset** is '1'. The count value and count outputs are reset, and the process then waits for **reset** to return to '0'. While it is suspended at this point, any changes on the clock input are ignored. When **reset** changes to '0', the process resumes, and the outer loop repeats.

This example also illustrates another important point. When we have nested loop statements, with an exit statement inside the inner loop, the exit statement causes control to be transferred out of the inner loop only, not the outer loop. By default, an exit statement transfers control out of the immediately enclosing loop.

In some cases, we may wish to transfer control out of an inner loop and also a containing loop. We can do this by labeling the outer loop and using the label in the exit statement. We can write

```
loop_name : loop
  ...
  exit loop_name;
  ...
end loop loop_name;
```

This labels the loop with the name **loop_name**, so that we can indicate which loop to exit in the exit statement. The loop label can be any valid identifier. The exit statement referring to this label can be located within nested loop statements.

To illustrate how loops can be nested, labeled and exited, let us consider the following statements:

```
outer : loop
  ...
  inner : loop
    ...
    exit outer when condition_1;    -- exit 1
    ...
    exit when condition_2;          -- exit 2
    ...
  end loop inner;
  ...                               -- target A
  exit outer when condition_3;      -- exit 3
  ...
end loop outer;
...                                 -- target B
```

This example contains two loop statements, one labeled **inner** nested inside another labeled **outer**. The first exit statement, tagged with the comment **exit 1**, transfers control to the statement tagged **target B** if its condition is true. The second exit statement, tagged **exit 2**, transfers control to **target A**. Since it does not refer to a label, it only exits the immediately enclosing loop statement, namely, loop **inner**. Finally, the exit statement tagged **exit 3** transfers control to **target B**.

VHDL-87, -93, and -2002

Since these versions of VHDL do not perform implicit conversion of conditions to **boolean**, conditions in exit statements must yield **boolean** results without conversion. Hence, we must write the exit statement in Example 3.4 as:

```
exit when reset = '1';
```

VHDL-87

Exit statements may not be labeled in VHDL-87.

3.4.2   Next Statements

Another kind of statement that we can use to control the execution of loops is the *next statement*. When this statement is executed, the current iteration of the loop is completed without executing any further statements, and the next iteration is begun. The syntax rule is

next_statement ⇐
  ⟦ label : ⟧ **next** ⟦ *loop*_label ⟧ ⟦ **when** condition ⟧ ;

The optional label at the start of the next statement serves to identify the statement. A next statement is very similar in form to an exit statement, the difference being the keyword **next** instead of **exit**. The simplest form of next statement is

```
next;
```

which starts the next iteration of the immediately enclosing loop. We can also include a condition to test before completing the iteration:

```
next when condition;
```

and we can include a loop label to indicate for which loop to complete the iteration:

```
next loop-label;
```

or

```
next loop-label when condition;
```

A next statement that exits the immediately enclosing loop can be easily rewritten as an equivalent loop with an if statement replacing the next statement. For example, the following two loops are equivalent:

```
loop                              loop
   statement-1;                      statement-1;
   next when condition;              if not condition then
   statement-2;                         statement-2;
end loop;                            end if;
                                  end loop;
```

However, nested labeled loops that contain next statements referring to outer loops cannot be so easily rewritten. As a matter of style, if we find ourselves about to write such a collection of loops and next statements, it's probably time to think more carefully about what we are trying to express. If we check the logic of the model, we may be able to find a simpler formulation of loop statements. Complicated loop/next structures can be confusing, making the model hard to read and understand.

VHDL-87, -93, and -2002

Since these versions of VHDL do not perform implicit conversion of conditions to **boolean**, conditions in next statements must yield **boolean** results without conversion.

VHDL-87

Next statements may not be labeled in VHDL-87.

3.4.3   While Loops

We can augment the basic loop statement introduced previously to form a while loop, which tests a condition before each iteration. If the condition is true, iteration proceeds. If it is false, the loop is terminated. The syntax rule for a while loop is

> loop_statement ⇐
>   ⟦ *loop*_label : ⟧
>   **while** condition **loop**
>   ⦃ sequential_statement ⦄
>   **end loop** ⟦ *loop*_label ⟧ ;

The only difference between this form and the basic loop statement is that we have added the keyword **while** and the condition before the **loop** keyword. All of the things we said about the basic loop statement also apply to a while loop. We can write any sequential statements in the body of the loop, including exit and next statements, and we can label the loop by writing the label before the **while** keyword.

There are three important points to note about while loops. The first point is that the condition is tested before each iteration of the loop, including the first iteration. This means that if the condition is false before we start the loop, it is terminated immediately, with no iterations being executed. For example, given the while loop

```
while index > 0 loop
    ...          -- statement A: do something with index
end loop;
    ...          -- statement B
```

if we can demonstrate that **index** is not greater than zero before the loop is started, then we know that the statements inside the loop will not be executed, and control will be transferred straight to **statement B**.

The second point is that in the absence of exit statements within a while loop, the loop terminates only when the condition becomes false. Thus, we know that the negation of the condition must hold when control reaches the statement after the loop. Similarly, in the absence of next statements within a while loop, the loop performs an iteration only when the condition is true. Thus, we know that the condition holds when we start the statements in the loop body. In the above example, we know that **index** must be greater then zero when we execute the statement tagged **statement A**, and also that index must be less than or equal to zero when we reach **statement B**. This knowledge can help us reason about the correctness of the model we are writing.

The third point is that when we write the statements inside the body of a while loop, we must make sure that the condition will eventually become false, or that an exit statement will eventually exit the loop. Otherwise the while loop will never terminate. Presumably, if we had intended to write an infinite loop, we would have used a simple loop statement.

EXAMPLE 3.5   *A cosine module*

We can develop a model for an entity **cos** that might be used as part of a specialized signal processing system. The entity has one input, **theta**, which is a real number representing an angle in radians, and one output, **result**, representing the cosine function of the value of **theta**. We can use the relation

$$\cos\theta = 1 - \frac{\theta^2}{2!} + \frac{\theta^4}{4!} - \frac{\theta^6}{6!} + \cdots$$

by adding successive terms of the series until the terms become smaller than one millionth of the result. The entity and architecture body declarations are:

```
entity cos is
  port ( theta : in real;  result : out real );
end entity cos;

-----------------------------------------------------

architecture series of cos is
begin

  summation : process (theta) is
    variable sum, term : real;
    variable n : natural;
  begin
    sum := 1.0;
    term := 1.0;
    n := 0;
    while abs term > abs (sum / 1.0E6) loop
      n := n + 2;
      term := (-term) * theta**2 / real(((n-1) * n));
      sum := sum + term;
    end loop;
    result <= sum;
  end process summation;
```

```
end architecture series;
```

   The architecture body consists of a process that is sensitive to changes in the input signal **theta**. Initially, the variables **sum** and **term** are set to 1.0, representing the first term in the series. The variable **n** starts at 0 for the first term. The cosine function is computed using a while loop that increments **n** by two and uses it to calculate the next term based on the previous term. Iteration proceeds as long as the last term computed is larger in magnitude than one millionth of the sum. When the last term falls below this threshold, the while loop is terminated. We can determine that the loop will terminate, since the values of successive terms in the series get progressively smaller. This is because the factorial function grows at a greater rate than the exponential function.

VHDL-87, -93, and -2002

Since these versions of VHDL do not perform implicit conversion of conditions to **boolean**, conditions in while loops must yield **boolean** results without conversion.

3.4.4   For Loops

Another way we can augment the basic loop statement is the for loop. A for loop includes a specification of how many times the body of the loop is to be executed. The syntax rule for a for loop is

loop_statement ⇐
   ⟦ *loop*_label : ⟧
   for identifier **in** discrete_range **loop**
      ⟦ sequential_statement ⟧
   end loop ⟦ *loop*_label ⟧ ;

We saw on page 71 that a discrete range can be of the form

simple_expression ⟨ **to** ⟦ **downto** ⟩ simple_expression

representing all the values between the left and right bounds, inclusive. The identifier is called the *loop parameter*, and for each iteration of the loop, it takes on successive values of the discrete range, starting from the left element. For example, in this for loop:

```
for count_value in 0 to 127 loop
   count_out <= count_value;
   wait for 5 ns;
end loop;
```

the identifier **count_value** takes on the values 0, 1, 2 and so on, and for each value, the assignment and wait statements are executed. Thus the signal **count_out** will be assigned values 0, 1, 2 and so on, up to 127, at 5 ns intervals.

We also saw that a discrete range can be specified using a discrete type or subtype name, possibly further constrained to a subset of values by a range constraint. For example, if we have the enumeration type

```
type controller_state is (initial, idle, active, error);
```

we can write a for loop that iterates over each of the values in the type:

```
for state in controller_state loop
  ...
end loop;
```

Within the sequence of statements in the for loop body, the loop parameter is a constant whose type is the base type of the discrete range. This means we can use its value by including it in an expression, but we cannot make assignments to it. Unlike other constants, we do not need to declare it. Instead, the loop parameter is implicitly declared over the for loop. It only exists when the loop is executing, and not before or after it. For example, the following process statement shows how not to use the loop parameter:

```
erroneous : process is
  variable i, j : integer;
begin
  i := loop_param;                 -- error!
  for loop_param in 1 to 10 loop
    loop_param := 5;               -- error!
  end loop;
  j := loop_param;                 -- error!
end process erroneous;
```

The assignments to i and j are illegal since the loop parameter is defined neither before nor after the loop. The assignment within the loop body is illegal because loop_param is a constant and thus may not be modified.

A consequence of the way the loop parameter is defined is that it *hides* any object of the same name defined outside the loop. For example, in this process:

```
hiding_example : process is
  variable a, b : integer;
begin
  a := 10;
  for a in 0 to 7 loop
    b := a;
  end loop;
  -- a = 10, and b = 7
  ...
end process hiding_example;
```

the variable a is initially assigned the value 10, and then the for loop is executed, creating a loop parameter also called a. Within the loop, the assignment to b uses the loop parameter, so the final value of b after the last iteration is 7. After the loop, the loop parameter no longer exists, so if we use the name **a**, we are referring to the variable object, whose value is still 10.

As we mentioned above, the for loop iterates with the loop parameter assuming successive values from the discrete range starting from the leftmost value. An important point to note is that if we specify a null range, the for loop body does not execute at all. A null range can arise if we specify an ascending range with the left bound greater than the right bound, or a descending range with the left bound less than the right bound. For example, the for loop

```
for i in 10 to 1 loop
  . . .
end loop;
```

completes immediately, without executing the enclosed statements. If we really want the loop to iterate with i taking values 10, 9, 8 and so on, we should write

```
for i in 10 downto 1 loop
  . . .
end loop;
```

One final thing to note about for loops is that, like basic loop statements, they can enclose arbitrary sequential statements, including next and exit statements, and we can label a for loop by writing the label before the **for** keyword.

EXAMPLE 3.6   *A revised cosine module*

We now rewrite the cosine model in Example 3.5 to calculate the result by summing the first 10 terms of the series. The entity declaration is unchanged. The revised architecture body, shown below, consists of a process that uses a for loop instead of a while loop. As before, the variables **sum** and **term** are set to 1.0, representing the first term in the series. The variable n is replaced by the for loop parameter. The loop iterates nine times, calculating the remaining nine terms of the series.

```
architecture fixed_length_series of cos is
begin

  summation : process (theta) is
    variable sum, term : real;
  begin
    sum := 1.0;
    term := 1.0;
    for n in 1 to 9 loop
      term := (-term) * theta**2 / real(((2*n-1) * 2*n));
      sum := sum + term;
    end loop;
    result <= sum;
  end process summation;
```

> **end architecture** fixed_length_series;

3.4.5   Summary of Loop Statements

The preceding sections describe the various forms of loop statements in detail. It is worth summarizing this information in one place, to show the few basic points to remember. First, the syntax rule for all loop statements is

> loop_statement ⇐
>   ⟦ *loop*_label : ⟧
>   ⟦ **while** condition ▯ **for** identifier **in** discrete_range ⟧ **loop**
>   ⦃ sequential_statement ⦄
>   **end loop** ⟦ *loop*_label ⟧ ;

Second, in the absence of exit and next statements, the while loop iterates as long as the condition is true, and the for loop iterates with the loop parameter assuming successive values from the discrete range. If the condition in a while loop is initially false, or if the discrete range in a for loop is a null range, then no iterations occur.

Third, the loop parameter in a for loop cannot be explicitly declared, and it is a constant within the loop body. It also shadows any other object of the same name declared outside the loop.

Finally, an exit statement can be used to terminate any loop, and a next statement can be used to complete the current iteration and commence the next iteration. These statements can refer to loop labels to terminate or complete iteration for an outer level of a nested set of loops.

3.5   Assertion and Report Statements

One of the reasons for writing models of computer systems is to verify that a design functions correctly. We can partially test a model by applying sample inputs and checking that the outputs meet our expectations. If they do not, we are then faced with the task of determining what went wrong inside the design. This task can be made easier using *assertion statements* that check that expected conditions are met within the model. An assertion statement is a sequential statement, so it can be included anywhere in a process body. The full syntax rule for an assertion statement is

> assertion_statement ⇐
>   ⟦ label : ⟧ **assert** condition
>   ⟦ **report** expression ⟧ ⟦ **severity** expression ⟧ ;

The optional label allows us to identify the assertion statement. The simplest form of assertion statement just includes the keyword **assert** followed by a condition that we expect to be true when the assertion statement is executed. If the condition is not met, we say that an *assertion violation* has occurred. If an assertion violation arises during simulation of a model, the simulator reports the fact. During synthesis, the condition in an assertion statement may be interpreted as a condition that the synthesizer may assume to be true. During formal verification, the condition may be interpreted as a condition to be proven by the verifier. For example, if we write

```
assert initial_value <= max_value;
```

and initial_value is larger than **max_value** when the statement is executed during simulation, the simulator will let us know. During synthesis, the synthesizer may assume that initial_value <= max_value and optimize the circuit based on that information. During formal verification, the verifier may attempt to prove initial_value <= max_value for all possible input stimuli and execution paths leading to the assertion statement.

If we have a number of assertion statements throughout a model, it is useful to know which assertion is violated. We can get the simulator to provide extra information by including a **report** clause in an assertion statement, for example:

```
assert initial_value <= max_value
  report "initial value too large";
```

The string that we provide is used to form part of the assertion violation message. We can write any expression in the **report** clause provided it yields a string value, for example:

```
assert current_character >= '0' and current_character <= '9'
  report "Input number " & input_string & " contains a non-digit";
```

Here the message is derived by concatenating three string values together. We can use the **to_string** operation to get a string representation of a value to include in a message, for example:

```
assert initial_value <= max_value
  report "initial value " & to_string(initial_value)
         & " too large";
```

In Section 2.2, we mentioned a predefined enumeration type **severity_level**, defined as

```
type severity_level is (note, warning, error, failure);
```

We can include a value of this type in a **severity** clause of an assertion statement. This value indicates the degree to which the violation of the assertion affects operation of the model. The value **note** can be used to pass informative messages out from a simulation, for example:

```
assert free_memory >= low_water_limit
  report "low on memory, about to start garbage collect"
  severity note;
```

The severity level **warning** can be used if an unusual situation arises in which the model can continue to execute, but may produce unusual results, for example:

```
assert packet_length /= 0
  report "empty network packet received"
  severity warning;
```

We can use the severity level **error** to indicate that something has definitely gone wrong and that corrective action should be taken, for example:

```
assert clock_pulse_width >= min_clock_width
  severity error;
```

Finally, the value **failure** can be used if we detect an inconsistency that should never arise, for example:

```
assert (last_position - first_position + 1) = number_of_entries
  report "inconsistency in buffer model"
  severity failure;
```

We have seen that we can write an assertion statement with either a **report** clause or a **severity** clause, or both. If both are present, the syntax rule shows us that the **report** clause must come first. If we omit the **report** clause, the default string in the error message is "Assertion violation." If we omit the **severity** clause, the default value is error. The severity value is usually used by a simulator to determine whether or not to continue execution after an assertion violation. Most simulators allow the user to specify a severity threshold, beyond which execution is stopped. The VHDL standard recommends that, in the absence of such a specification, simulation continue for assertion violations with severity error or less.

Usually, failure of an assertion means either that the entity is being used incorrectly as part of a larger design or that the model for the entity has been incorrectly written. We illustrate both cases.

EXAMPLE 3.7   *A set/reset flipflop including a check for correct usage*

A set/reset (SR) flipflop has two inputs, S and R, and an output Q. When S is '1', the output is set to '1', and when R is '1', the output is reset to '0'. However, S and R may not both be '1' at the same time. If they are, the output value is not specified. A behavioral model for an SR flipflop that includes a check for this illegal condition is:

```
entity SR_flipflop is
  port ( S, R : in bit;  Q : out bit );
end entity SR_flipflop;

--------------------------------------------------

architecture checking of SR_flipflop is
begin

    set_reset : process (S, R) is
    begin
      assert S nand R;
```

```
      if S then
        Q <= '1';
      end if;
      if R then
        Q <= '0';
      end if;
    end process set_reset;

  end architecture checking;
```

The architecture body contains a process sensitive to the S and R inputs. Within the process body we write an assertion statement that requires that S and R not both be '1'. If both are '1', the assertion is violated, so the simulator writes an "Assertion violation" message with severity error. If execution continues after the violated assertion, the value '1' will first be assigned to Q, followed by the value '0'. The resulting value is '0'. This is allowed, since the state of Q was not specified for this illegal condition, so we are at liberty to choose any value. If the assertion is not violated, then at most one of the following if statements is executed, correctly modeling the behavior of the SR flipflop.

EXAMPLE 3.8   *Sanity check on calculation of the maximum value*

To illustrate the use of an assertion statement as a "sanity check," let us look at a model for an entity that has three integer inputs, a, b and c, and produces an integer output z that is the largest of its inputs.

```
entity max3 is
  port ( a, b, c : in integer;  z : out integer );
end entity max3;

--------------------------------------------------

architecture check_error of max3 is
begin

    maximizer : process (a, b, c)
      variable result : integer;
    begin
      if a > b then
        if a > c then
          result := a;
        else
          result := a;  -- Oops!  Should be: result := c;
        end if;
      elsif  b > c then
        result := b;
      else
        result := c;
```

```
      end if;
      assert result >= a and result >= b and result >= c
        report "inconsistent result for maximum: "
               & to_string(result)
        severity failure;
      z <= result;
    end process maximizer;

end architecture check_error;
```

The architecture body is written using a process containing nested if statements. For this example we have introduced an "accidental" error into the model. If we simulate this model and put the values a = 7, b = 3 and c = 9 on the ports of this entity, we expect that the value of **result**, and hence the output port, is 9. The assertion states that the value of **result** must be greater than or equal to all of the inputs. However, our coding error causes the value 7 to be assigned to **result**, and so the assertion is violated. This violation causes us to examine our model more closely, and correct the error.

Another important use for assertion statements is in checking timing constraints that apply to a model. For example, most clocked devices require that the clock pulse be longer than some minimum duration. We can use the predefined primary **now** in an expression to calculate durations. We return to **now** in a later chapter. Suffice it to say that it yields the current simulation time when it is evaluated.

EXAMPLE 3.9 *An edge-triggered register with timing check*

An edge-triggered register has a data input and a data output of type **real** and a clock input of type **bit**. When the clock changes from '0' to '1', the data input is sampled, stored and transmitted through to the output. Let us suppose that the clock input must remain at '1' for at least 5 ns. The following is a model for this register, including a check for legal clock pulse width.

```
entity edge_triggered_register is
  port ( clock : in bit;
         d_in : in real;  d_out : out real );
end entity edge_triggered_register;

-------------------------------------------------------

architecture check_timing of edge_triggered_register is
begin

  store_and_check : process (clock) is
    variable stored_value : real;
    variable pulse_start : time;
  begin
    if rising_edge(clock) then
```

```
            pulse_start := now;
            stored_value := d_in;
            d_out <= stored_value;
        else
            assert now = 0 ns or (now - pulse_start) >= 5 ns
                report "clock pulse too short: "
                        & to_string(now - pulse_start);
        end if;
    end process store_and_check;

  end architecture check_timing;
```

The architecture body contains a process that is sensitive to changes on the clock input. When the clock changes from '0' to '1', the input is stored, and the current simulation time is recorded in the variable **pulse_start**. Otherwise, when the clock changes from '1' to '0', the difference between **pulse_start** and the current simulation time is checked by the assertion statement.

VHDL-87

Assertion statements may not be labeled in VHDL-87.

VHDL also provides us with a *report statement*, which is similar to an assertion statement. The syntax rule for the report statement shows this similarity:

report_statement ⇐
    ⟦ label : ⟧ **report** expression ⟦ **severity** expression ⟧ ;

The differences are that there is no condition, and if the severity level is not specified, the default is **note**. Indeed, the report statement can be thought of as an assertion statement in which the condition is the value **false** and the severity is **note**, hence it always produces the message. One way in which the report statement is useful is as a means of including "trace writes" in a model as an aid to debugging.

EXAMPLE 3.10   *Trace messages using a report statement*

Suppose we are writing a complex model and we are not sure that we have got the logic quite right. We can use report statements to get the processes in the model to write out messages, so that we can see when they are activated and what they are doing. An example process is

```
transmit_element : process (transmit_data) is
    ...         -- variable declarations
begin
  report "transmit_element: data = "
        & to_string(transmit_data);
```

```
      ...
   end process transmit_element;
```

Both assertion statements and report statements allow inclusion of a message string to provide useful information. In some cases, the information we wish to provide may be extensive and not fit entirely on a single line when displayed. We can include the line-feed character in the message string to break the message over multiple lines. A line-feed is represented by the identifier LF of type **character**. For example:

```
assert data = expected_data
   report "%%%ERROR data value miscompare." & LF &
          " Actual value = " & to_string(data) & LF &
          " Expected value = " & to_string(expdata) & LF &
          " at time: " & to_string(now) );
```

The message produced when this assertion is violated consists of four lines of text. A VHDL tool interprets the line feed characters using the appropriate convention for the host operating system. For example, if a Unix-based system were to write the message to a file, it would just include the line-feed characters. A Windows-based system, on the other hand, would write a carriage-return/line-feed pair for every line-feed in the message.

VHDL-87, -93, and -2002

These versions of VHDL do not make any recommendation about continuing simulation based on the severity of an assertion violation from an assertion statement or report statement. Different simulators take different approaches, which can make it difficult to write portable models with consistent simulation behavior on different tools.

These versions also do not necessarily interpret line-feed characters in message strings as denoting line breaks. Interpretation of line feeds is implementation defined.

VHDL-87

Report statements are not provided in VHDL-87. We achieve the same effect by writing an assertion statement with the condition **false** and a severity level of **note**. For example, the VHDL-93 or VHDL-2002 report statement

```
report "Initialization complete";
```

can be written in VHDL-87 as

```
assert false
   report "Initialization complete" severity note;
```

Exercises

1. [❶ 3.1] Write an if statement that sets a variable **odd** to '1' if an integer **n** is odd, or to '0' if it is even.

2. [❶ 3.1] Write an if statement that, given the year of today's date in the variable **year**, sets the variable **days_in_February** to the number of days in February. A year is a leap year if it is divisible by four, except for years that are divisible by 100. However, years that are divisible by 400 are leap years. February has 29 days in a leap year and 28 days otherwise.

3. [❶ 3.2] Write a case statement that strips the strength information from a standard-logic variable **x**. If **x** is '0' or 'L', set it to '0'. If **x** is '1' or 'H', set it to '1'. If **x** is 'X', 'W', 'Z', 'U' or '–', set it to 'X'. (This is the conversion performed by the standard-logic function to_X01.)

4. [❶ 3.2] Write a case statement that sets an integer variable **character_class** to 1 if the character variable **ch** contains a letter, to 2 if it contains a digit, to 3 if it contains some other printable character or to 4 if it contains a non-printable character. Note that the VHDL character set contains accented letters, as shown in Section 2.2.5 on page 44.

5. [❶ 3.4] Write a loop statement that samples a bit input **d** when a clock input **clk** changes to '1'. So long as **d** is '0', the loop continues executing. When **d** is '1', the loop exits.

6. [❶ 3.4] Write a while loop that calculates the exponential function of **x** to an accuracy of one part in 104 by summing terms of the following series:

$$e^x = 1 + \frac{x}{1} + \frac{x^2}{2!} + \frac{x^3}{3!} + \frac{x^4}{4!} + \cdots$$

7. [❶ 3.4] Write a for loop that calculates the exponential function of **x** by summing the first eight terms of the series in Exercise 6.

8. [❶ 3.5] Write an assertion statement that expresses the requirement that a flipflop's two outputs, **q** and **q_n**, of type **std_ulogic**, are complementary.

9. [❶ 3.5] We can use report statements in VHDL to achieve the same effect as using "trace writes" in software programming languages, to report a message when part of the model is executed. Insert a report statement in the model of Example 3.4 to cause a trace message when the counter is reset.

10. [❷ 3.1] Develop a behavioral model for a limiter with three integer inputs, **data_in**, **lower** and **upper**; an integer output, **data_out**; and a bit output, **out_of_limits**. The **data_out** output follows **data_in** so long as it is between **lower** and **upper**. If **data_in** is less than **lower**, **data_out** is limited to **lower**. If **data_in** is greater than **upper**, **data_out** is limited to **upper**. The **out_of_limit** output indicates when **data_out** is limited.

11. [❷ 3.2] Develop a model for a floating-point arithmetic unit with data inputs **x** and **y**, data output **z** and function code inputs **f1** and **f0** of type **bit**. Function codes **f1** = '0'

and f0 = '0' produce addition; f1 = '0' and f0 = '1' produce subtraction of y from x; f1 = '1' and f0 = '0' produce multiplication; and f1 = '1' and f0 = '1' produce division of x by y.

12. [❷ 3.4] Write a model for a counter with an output port of type **natural**, initially set to 15. When the clk input changes to '1', the counter decrements by one. After counting down to zero, the counter wraps back to 15 on the next clock edge.

13. [❷ 3.4] Modify the counter of Exercise 12 to include an asynchronous load input and a data input. When the load input is '1', the counter is preset to the data input value. When the load input changes back to '0', the counter continues counting down from the preset value.

14. [❷ 3.4] Develop a model of an averaging module that calculates the average of batches of 16 real numbers. The module has clock and data inputs and a data output. The module accepts the next input number when the clock changes to '1'. After 16 numbers have been accepted, the module places their average on the output port, then repeats the process for the next batch.

15. [❷ 3.5] Write a model that causes assertion violations with different severity levels. Experiment with your simulator to determine its behavior when an assertion violation occurs. See if you can specify a severity threshold above which it stops execution.

Chapter 4

Composite Data Types and Operations

Now that we have seen the basic data types and sequential operations from which the behavioral part of a VHDL model is formed, it is time to look at composite data types. We first mentioned them in the classification of data types in Chapter 2. Composite data objects consist of related collections of data elements in the form of either an *array* or a *record*. We can treat an object of a composite type as a single object or manipulate its constituent elements individually. In this chapter, we see how to define composite types and how to manipulate them using operators and sequential statements.

4.1 Arrays

An *array* consists of a collection of values, all of which are of the same type as each other. The position of each element in an array is given by a scalar value called its *index*. To create an array object in a model, we first define an array type in a type declaration. The syntax rule for an array type definition is

> array_type_definition ⇐
>   **array** (discrete_range ⟦ , ₒₒₒ ⟧) **of** *element*_subtype_indication

This defines an array type by specifying one or more index ranges (the list of discrete ranges) and the element type or subtype.

Recall from previous chapters that a discrete range is a subset of values from a discrete type (an integer or enumeration type), and that it can be specified as shown by the simplified syntax rule

> discrete_range ⇐
>   *discrete*_subtype_indication
>   ⟦ simple_expression ⟦ **to** ⟦ **downto** ⟧ simple_expression

Recall also that a subtype indication can be just the name of a previously declared type (a type mark) and can include a range constraint to limit the set of values from that type, as shown by the simplified rule

subtype_indication ⇐
    type_mark 〚 **range** simple_expression (**to** 〛 **downto**) simple_expression 〛

We illustrate these rules for defining arrays with a series of examples. We start with single-dimensional arrays, in which there is just one index range. Here is a simple example to start off with, showing the declaration of an array type to represent words of data:

    type word **is array** (0 **to** 31) **of** bit;

Each element is a bit, and the elements are indexed from 0 up to 31. An alternative declaration of a word type, more appropriate for "little-endian" systems, is

    type word **is array** (31 **downto** 0) **of** bit;

The difference here is that index values start at 31 for the leftmost element in values of this type and continue down to 0 for the rightmost.

The index values of an array do not have to be numeric. For example, given this declaration of an enumeration type:

    type controller_state **is** (initial, idle, active, error);

we could then declare an array as follows:

    type state_counts **is array** (idle **to** error) **of** natural;

This kind of array type declaration relies on the type of the index range being clear from the context. If there were more than one enumeration type with values **idle** and **error**, it would not be clear which one to use for the index type. To make it clear, we can use the alternative form for specifying the index range, in which we name the index type and include a range constraint. The previous example could be rewritten as

    type state_counts **is**
      array (controller_state **range** idle **to** error) **of** natural;

If we need an array element for every value in an index type, we need only name the index type in the array declaration without specifying the range. For example:

    subtype coeff_ram_address **is** integer **range** 0 **to** 63;
    type coeff_array **is array** (coeff_ram_address) **of** real;

Once we have declared an array type, we can define objects of that type, including constants, variables and signals. For example, using the types declared above, we can declare variables as follows:

    variable buffer_register, data_register : word;
    variable counters : state_counts;
    variable coeff : coeff_array;

Each of these objects consists of the collection of elements described by the corresponding type declaration. An individual element can be used in an expression or as the target of an assignment by referring to the array object and supplying an index value, for example:

```
coeff(0) := 0.0;
```

If **active** is a variable of type **controller_state**, we can write

```
counters(active) := counters(active) + 1;
```

An array object can also be used as a single composite object. For example, the assignment

```
data_register := buffer_register;
```

copies all of the elements of the array **buffer_register** into the corresponding elements of the array **data_register**.

EXAMPLE 4.1 *A memory module for real-number coefficients*

The following is a model for a memory that stores 64 real-number coefficients, initialized to 0.0. We assume the type **coeff_ram_address** is previously declared as above. The architecture body contains a process with an array variable representing the coefficient storage. When the process starts, it initializes the array using a for loop. It then repetitively waits for any of the input ports to change. When **rd** is '1', the array is indexed using the address value to read a coefficient. When **wr** is '1', the address value is used to select which coefficient to change.

```
entity coeff_ram is
  port ( rd, wr : in bit;  addr : in coeff_ram_address;
         d_in : in real;  d_out : out real );
end entity coeff_ram;

--------------------------------------------------

architecture abstract of coeff_ram is
begin

  memory : process is
    type coeff_array is array (coeff_ram_address) of real;
    variable coeff : coeff_array;
  begin
    for index in coeff_ram_address loop
      coeff(index) := 0.0;
    end loop;
    loop
      wait on rd, wr, addr, d_in;
      if rd then
        d_out <= coeff(addr);
      end if;
      if wr then
```

```
            coeff(addr) := d_in;
        end if;
      end loop;
    end process memory;

  end architecture abstract;
```

4.1.1   Multidimensional Arrays

VHDL also allows us to create multidimensional arrays, for example, to represent matrices or tables indexed by more than one value. A multidimensional array type is declared by specifying a list of index ranges, as shown by the syntax rule on page 95. For example, we might include the following type declarations in a model for a finite-state machine:

```
type symbol is ('a', 't', 'd', 'h', digit, cr, error);
type state is range 0 to 6;

type transition_matrix is array (state, symbol) of state;
```

Each index range can be specified as shown above for single-dimensional arrays. The index ranges for each dimension need not all be from the same type, nor have the same direction. An object of a multidimensional array type is indexed by writing a list of index values to select an element. For example, if we have a variable declared as

```
variable transition_table : transition_matrix;
```

we can index it as follows:

```
transition_table(5, 'd');
```

EXAMPLE 4.2   *Transformation matrices*

In three-dimensional graphics, a point in space may be represented using a three-element vector [x, y, z] of coordinates. Transformations, such as scaling, rotation and reflection, may be done by multiplying a vector by a 3×3 transformation matrix to get a new vector representing the transformed point. We can write VHDL type declarations for points and transformation matrices:

```
type point is array (1 to 3) of real;
type matrix is array (1 to 3, 1 to 3) of real;
```

We can use these types to declare point variables **p** and **q** and a matrix variable transform:

```
variable p, q : point;
variable transform : matrix;
```

The transformation can be applied to the point **p** to produce a result in **q** with the following statements:

```
      for i in 1 to 3 loop
        q(i) := 0.0;
        for j in 1 to 3 loop
          q(i) := q(i) + transform(i, j) * p(j);
        end loop;
      end loop;
```

4.1.2   Array Aggregates

We have seen how we can write literal values of scalar types. Often we also need to write literal array values, for example, to initialize a variable or constant of an array type. We can do this using a VHDL construct called an array aggregate, according to the syntax rule

$$\text{aggregate} \Leftarrow (\llbracket\; \llbracket\; \text{choices} => \rrbracket\; \text{expression}\; \rrbracket\; \{\; ,\; \ldots \}\;)$$

Let us look first at the form of aggregate without the choices part. It simply consists of a list of the elements enclosed in parentheses, for example:

```
type point is array (1 to 3) of real;
constant origin : point := (0.0, 0.0, 0.0);
variable view_point : point := (10.0, 20.0, 0.0);
```

This form of array aggregate uses *positional association* to determine which value in the list corresponds to which element of the array. The first value is the element with the leftmost index, the second is the next index to the right, and so on, up to the last value, which is the element with the rightmost index. There must be a one-to-one correspondence between values in the aggregate and elements in the array.

An alternative form of aggregate uses *named association*, in which the index value for each element is written explicitly using the choices part shown in the syntax rule. The choices may be specified in exactly the same way as those in alternatives of a case statement, discussed in Chapter 3. As a reminder, here is the syntax rule for choices:

$$\text{choices} \Leftarrow \llparenthesis\; \text{simple\_expression} \;\rVert\; \text{discrete\_range} \;\rVert\; \textbf{others}\; \rrparenthesis\; \{\;\rvert\; \ldots \}$$

For example, the variable declaration and initialization could be rewritten as

```
variable view_point : point := (1 => 10.0, 2 => 20.0, 3 => 0.0);
```

The main advantage of named association is that it gives us more flexibility in writing aggregates for larger arrays. To illustrate this, let us return to the coefficient memory described above. The type declaration was

```
type coeff_array is array (coeff_ram_address) of real;
```

Suppose we want to declare the coefficient variable, initialize the first few locations to some non-zero value and initialize the remainder to zero. Following are a number of ways of writing aggregates that all have the same effect:

```
variable coeff : coeff_array
        := (0 => 1.6, 1 => 2.3, 2 => 1.6, 3 to 63 => 0.0);
```

Here we are using a range specification to initialize the bulk of the array value to zero.

```
variable coeff : coeff_array
        := (0 => 1.6, 1 => 2.3, 2 => 1.6, others => 0.0);
```

The keyword **others** stands for any index value that has not been previously mentioned in the aggregate. If the keyword **others** is used, it must be the last choice in the aggregate.

```
variable coeff : coeff_array
        := (0 | 2 => 1.6, 1 => 2.3, others => 0.0);
```

The "|" symbol can be used to separate a list of index values, for which all elements have the same value.

Note that we may not mix positional and named association in an array aggregate, except for the use of an **others** choice in the final postion. Thus, the following aggregate is illegal:

```
variable coeff : coeff_array
        := (1.6, 2.3, 2 => 1.6, others => 0.0);   -- illegal
```

We can also use aggregates to write multidimensional array values. In this case, we treat the array as though it were an array of arrays, writing an array aggregate for each of the leftmost index values first.

EXAMPLE 4.3   *Transition matrix for a modem finite-state machine*

We can use a two-dimensional array to represent the transition matrix of a finite-state machine (FSM) that interprets simple modem commands. A command must consist of the string "atd" followed by a string of digits and a **cr** character, or the string "ath" followed by **cr**. The state transition diagram is shown in Figure 4.1. The symbol "other" represents a character other than 'a', 't', 'd', 'h', a digit or **cr**.

An outline of a process that implements the FSM is:

```
modem_controller : process is

    type symbol is ('a', 't', 'd', 'h', digit, cr, other);
    type symbol_string is array (1 to 20) of symbol;
    type state is range 0 to 6;
    type transition_matrix is array (state, symbol) of state;

    constant next_state : transition_matrix :=
      ( 0 => ('a' => 1, others => 6),
        1 => ('t' => 2, others => 6),
        2 => ('d' => 3, 'h' => 5, others => 6),
        3 => (digit => 4, others => 6),
        4 => (digit => 4, cr => 0, others => 6),
```

FIGURE 4.1

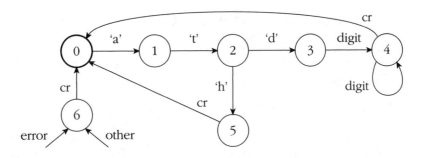

The state transition diagram for a modem command finite-state machine. State 0 is the initial state. The machine returns to this state after recognizing a correct command. State 6 is the error state, to which the machine goes if it detects an illegal or unexpected character.

```
        5 => (cr => 0, others => 6),
        6 => (cr => 0, others => 6) );
    variable command : symbol_string;
    variable current_state : state := 0;
  begin
    . . .
    for index in 1 to 20 loop
      current_state := next_state( current_state, command(index) );
      case current_state is
        . . .
      end case;
    end loop;
    . . .
  end process modem_controller;
```

The type declarations for **symbol** and **state** represent the command symbols and the states for the FSM. The transition matrix, **next_state**, is a two-dimensional array constant indexed by the state and symbol type. An element at position (i, j) in this matrix indicates the next state the FSM should move to when it is in state i and the next input symbol is j. The matrix is initialized according to the transition diagram. The process uses the **current_state** variable and successive input symbols as indices into the transition matrix to determine the next state. For each transition, it performs some action based on the new state. The actions are implemented within the case statement.

In the array aggregates we have seen so far, each value in the aggregate corresponds to a single array element. VHDL also allows an alternate form of aggregate in which we write a combination of individual element values and sub-array values. The element values and sub-array values are joined together to form a complete array value. For example, given the declarations

```
type byte is array (7 downto 0) of bit;
variable d_reg : byte;
variable a, b : bit;
```

we could assign an aggregate value as follows:

```
d_reg := (a, "1001", b, "00");
```

The aggregate represents a value consisting of an element taken from the bit variable **a**, followed by a sub-array of the four bits, an element taken from the bit variable **b**, and a further sub-array of two bits. We could also write this using named association:

```
d_reg := (7 => a, 6 downto 3 => "1001",
          2 => b, 1 downto 0 => "00");
```

Note that when we write an aggregate containing a sub-array using named association, the choice for the sub-array must take the form of a discrete range, the number of choice values in the range must be the same as the number of elements in the sub-array, and the direction of the range must match the context in which the aggregate appears. Thus, in the preceding example, we used descending ranges for the choices, since the aggregate is assigned to a variable with a descending range.

Another place in which we may use an aggregate is the target of a variable assignment or a signal assignment. The full syntax rule for a variable assignment statement is

variable_assignment_statement ⇐
    〚 label : 〛 〖 name 〗 aggregate 〗 := expression ;

If the target is an aggregate, it must contain a variable name at each position. Furthermore, the expression on the right-hand side of the assignment must produce a composite value of the same type as the target aggregate. Each element of the right-hand side is assigned to the corresponding variable in the target aggregate. The variable names in the target aggregate can represent a combination of array elements and sub-arrays. For a sub-array variable, the corresponding elements of the right-hand side are assigned to the variable elements.

The full syntax rule for a signal assignment also allows the target to be in the form of an aggregate, with a signal name at each position in the aggregate. We can use assignments of this form to split a composite value among a number of scalar signals. For example, if we have a variable **flag_reg**, which is a four-element bit vector, we can perform the following signal assignment to four signals of type **bit**:

```
( z_flag, n_flag, v_flag, c_flag ) <= flag_reg;
```

Since the right-hand side is a bit vector, the target is taken as a bit-vector aggregate. The leftmost element of **flag_reg** is assigned to **z_flag**, the second element of **flag_reg** is assigned to **n_flag**, and so on. This form of multiple assignment is much more compact to write than four separate assignment statements.

As another example, suppose we have signals declared as follows:

```
signal status_reg : bit_vector(7 downto 0);
signal int_priority, cpu_priority : bit_vector(2 downto 0);
signal int_enable, cpu_mode : bit;
```

where the type **bit_vector** is declared to be an array of bit elements (see Section 4.2). We can then write the assignment:

```
(2 downto 0 => int_priority,
 6 downto 4 => cpu_priority,
 3 => int_en, 7 => cpu_mode) <= status_reg;
```

This specifies that the bits of the **status_reg** value are assigned in left-to-right order to **cpu_mode**, **cpu_priority**, **int_en**, and **int_priority**, respectively.

VHDL-87, -93, and -2002

These earlier versions to not allow aggregates with sub-arrays. Instead, each value in an aggregate must be an individual element value. Similarly, where an aggregate of names is used as the target of an assignment, each name must be an object of the same type as the elements of the right-hand side expression.

4.1.3 Array Attributes

In Chapter 2 we saw that attributes could be used to refer to information about scalar types. There are also attributes applicable to array types; they refer to information about the index ranges. Array attributes can also be applied to array objects, such as constants, variables and signals, to refer to information about the types of the objects. Given some array type or object A, and an integer N between 1 and the number of dimensions of A, VHDL defines the following attributes:

A'left(N)	Left bound of index range of dimension N of A
A'right(N)	Right bound of index range of dimension N of A
A'low(N)	Lower bound of index range of dimension N of A
A'high(N)	Upper bound of index range of dimension N of A
A'range(N)	Index range of dimension N of A
A'reverse_range(N)	Reverse of index range of dimension N of A
A'length(N)	Length of index range of dimension N of A
A'ascending(N)	**true** if index range of dimension N of A is an ascending range, **false** otherwise
A'element	The element subtype of A

For example, given the array declaration

type A **is array** (1 **to** 4, 31 **downto** 0) **of** boolean;

some attribute values are

A'left(1) = 1	A'low(1) = 1
A'right(2) = 0	A'high(2) = 31
A'range(1) *is* 1 **to** 4	A'reverse_range(2) *is* 0 **to** 31
A'length(1) = 4	A'length(2) = 32
A'ascending(1) = true	A'ascending(2) = false
A'element *is* boolean	

For all of these attributes (except **'element**), to refer to the first dimension (or if there is only one dimension), we can omit the dimension number in parentheses, for example:

A'low = 1   A'length = 4

In the next section, we see how these array attributes may be used to deal with array ports. We will also see, in Chapter 6, how they may be used with subprogram parameters that are arrays. Another major use is in writing for loops to iterate over elements of an array. For example, given an array variable **free_map** that is an array of bits, we can write a for loop to count the number of '1' bits without knowing the actual size of the array:

```
count := 0;
for index in free_map'range loop
  if free_map(index) then
    count := count + 1;
  end if;
end loop;
```

The **'range** and **'reverse_range** attributes can be used in any place in a VHDL model where a range specification is required, as an alternative to specifying the left and right bounds and the range direction. Thus, we may use the attributes in type and subtype definitions, in subtype constraints, in for loop parameter specifications, in case statement choices and so on. The advantage of taking this approach is that we can specify the size of the array in one place in the model and in all other places use array attributes. If we need to change the array size later for some reason, we need only change the model in one place.

The **'element** attribute allows us to declare objects of the same type as the elements of an array. We will see examples where that is useful in the next section.

VHDL-87, -93, and -2002

The array attribute **'element** is not provided in these earlier versions of VHDL.

VHDL-87

The array attribute 'ascending is not provided in VHDL-87.

4.2 Unconstrained Array Types

The array types we have seen so far in this chapter are called *constrained* arrays, since the type definition constrains index values to be within a specific range. VHDL also allows us to define *unconstrained* array types, in which we just indicate the type of the index values, without specifying bounds. An unconstrained array type definition is described by the alternate syntax rule

array_type_definition ⇐
    array (⟦ type_mark **range** <> ⟧ ⟨ , ... ⟩) **of** *element*_subtype_indication

The symbol "<>", often called "box," can be thought of as a placeholder for the index range, to be filled in later when the type is used. An example of an unconstrained array type declaration is

type sample **is array** (natural **range** <>) **of** integer;

An important point to understand about unconstrained array types is that when we declare an object of such a type, we need to provide a constraint that specifies the index bounds. We can do this in several ways. One way is to provide the constraint when an object is created, for example:

variable short_sample_buf : sample(0 **to** 63);

This indicates that index values for the variable **short_sample_buf** are natural numbers in the ascending range 0 to 63. Another way to specify the constraint is to declare a subtype of the unconstrained array type. Objects can then be created using this subtype, for example:

subtype long_sample **is** sample(0 **to** 255);
variable new_sample_buf, old_sample_buf : long_sample;

These are both examples of a new form of subtype indication that we have not yet seen. The syntax rule is

subtype_indication ⇐ type_mark ⟦ (discrete_range ⟨ , ... ⟩) ⟧

The type mark is the name of the unconstrained array type, and the discrete range specifications constrain the index type to a subset of values used to index array elements. Each discrete range must be of the same type as the corresponding index type.

When we declare a constant of an unconstrained array type, there is a third way in which we can provide a constraint. We can infer it from the expression used to initialize the constant. If the initialization expression is an array aggregate written using named association, the index values in the aggregate imply the index range of the constant. For example, in the constant declaration

```
constant lookup_table : sample
         := ( 1 => 23, 3 => -16, 2 => 100, 4 => 11);
```

the index range is 1 to 4.

If the expression is an aggregate using positional association, the index value of the first element is assumed to be the leftmost value in the array subtype. For example, in the constant declaration

```
constant beep_sample : sample
         := ( 127, 63, 0, -63, -127, -63, 0, 63 );
```

the index range is 0 to 7, since the index subtype is **natural**. The index direction is ascending, since **natural** is defined to be an ascending range.

4.2.1 Predefined Array Types

VHDL predefines a number of unconstrained array types. In many models, these types are sufficient to represent our data. We list the predefined array types in this section.

Strings

VHDL provides a predefined unconstrained array type called **string**, declared as

```
type string is array (positive range <>) of character;
```

In principle the index range for a constrained string may be either an ascending or descending range, with any positive integers for the index bounds. However, most applications simply use an ascending range starting from 1. For example:

```
constant LCD_display_len : positive := 20;
subtype LCD_display_string is string(1 to LCD_display_len);
variable LCD_display : LCD_display_string := (others => ' ');
```

Boolean Vectors, Integer Vectors, Real Vectors, and Time Vectors

VHDL also provides predefined unconstrained types for arrays of **boolean**, **integer**, **real**, and **time** elements, respectively. They are declared as:

```
type boolean_vector is array (natural range <>) of boolean;
type integer_vector is array (natural range <>) of integer;
type real_vector is array (natural range <>) of real;
type time_vector is array (natural range <>) of time;
```

These types can be used to represent collections of data of the respective element types. For example, a subtype representing a collection of comparator thresholds can be declared as:

subtype thresholds **is** integer_vector(15 **downto** 0);

Alternatively, we can supply the constraint for a vector when an object is declared, for example:

variable max_temperatures : real_vector(1 **to** 10);

The **time_vector** type, in particular, is useful for specifying collection of timing parameters. For example, we can declare a constant representing individual propagation delays for each of eight output bits as follows:

constant Tpd_result : time_vector
  := (0 **to** 3 => 100 ps, 4 **to** 7 => 150 ps);

VHDL-87, -93, and -2002

The types **boolean_vector**, **integer_vector**, **real_vector**, and **time_vector** are not predefined in these earlier versions of VHDL. Instead, they (or similar types) must be explicitly defined.

Bit Vectors

VHDL provides a further predefined unconstrained array type called **bit_vector**, declared as

type bit_vector **is array** (natural **range** <>) **of** bit;

This type can be used to represent words of data at the architectural level of modeling. For example, subtypes for representing bytes of data in a little-endian processor might be declared as

subtype byte **is** bit_vector(7 **downto** 0);

Alternatively, we can supply the constraint when an object is declared, for example:

variable channel_busy_register : bit_vector(1 **to** 4);

Standard-Logic Arrays

The standard-logic package **std_logic_1164** provides an unconstrained array type for vectors of standard-logic values. It is declared as

type std_ulogic_vector **is array** (natural **range** <>) **of** std_ulogic;

This type can be used in a way similar to bit vectors, but provides more detail in representing the electrical levels used in a design. We can define subtypes of the standard-logic vector type, for example:

```
subtype std_ulogic_word is std_ulogic_vector(0 to 31);
```

Or we can directly create an object of the standard-logic vector type:

```
signal csr_offset : std_ulogic_vector(2 downto 1);
```

String and Bit-String Literals

In Chapter 1, we saw that a string literal may be used to write a value representing a sequence of characters. We can use a string literal in place of an array aggregate for a value of type string. For example, we can initialize a string constant as follows:

```
constant ready_message  : string := "Ready      ";
```

We can also use string literals for any other one-dimensional array type whose elements are of an enumeration type that includes characters. The IEEE standard-logic array type **std_ulogic_vector** is an example. Thus we could declare and initialize a variable as follows:

```
variable current_test : std_ulogic_vector(0 to 13)
          := "ZZZZZZZZZZ----";
```

In Chapter 1 we also saw bit-string literals as a way of writing a sequence of bit values. Bit strings can be used in place of array aggregates to write values of bit-vector types. For example, the variable **channel_busy_register** defined above may be initialized with an assignment:

```
channel_busy_register := b"0000";
```

We can also use bit-string literals for other one-dimensional array types whose elements are of an enumeration type that includes the characters '0' and '1'. Each character in the bit-string literal represents one, three or four successive elements of the array value, depending on whether the base specified in the literal is binary, octal or hexadecimal. Again, using **std_ulogic_vector** as an example type, we can write a constant declaration using a bit-string literal:

```
constant all_ones : std_ulogic_vector(15 downto 0) := X"FFFF";
```

VHDL-87

In VHDL-87, bit-string literals may only be used as literals for array types in which the elements are of type **bit**. The predefined type **bit_vector** is such a type. However, the standard-logic type **std_ulogic_vector** is not. We may use string literals for array types such as **std_ulogic_vector**.

4.2.2 Unconstrained Array Element Types

In the preceding examples of unconstrained array types, the elements were all of scalar subtypes. In general, arrays can have elements of almost any type, including other array types. The array element types can themselves be constrained or unconstrained. Strictly, we just use the term unconstrained to refer to an array type in which the top-level type has its index range unspecified and the element type, if an array type, is also unconstrained. For example, the type **sample** that we declared as

type sample **is array** (natural **range** <>) **of** integer;

is unconstrained, since its index range is unspecified and the element type is scalar rather than an array type. If we declare a type for a collection of samples:

type sample_set **is array** (positive **range** <>) **of** sample;

this type also is unconstrained. The top-level array type, **sample_set**, has an unspecified index range, and the element type is unconstrained. There is no constraint information specified at any level of the type's hierarchy.

We use the term *fully constrained* for a type in which all index ranges are constrained at all levels of the type's hierarchy. For example, the type that we declared for points,

type point **is array** (1 **to** 3) **of** real;

is fully constrained, since there is only one index range, and it is constrained to be 1 to 3. Similarly, if we declare a type for a line segment determined by two points:

type line_segment **is array** (1 **to** 2) **of** point;

that type is also fully constrained. It constrains the top-level index range to 1 to 2 and the element index range to 1 to 3.

In between unconstrained and fully constrained types, we have what are called *partially constrained* types. Such types have one or more index ranges unspecified and others that are constrained. For example, we can declare a type for fixed-sized collections of samples:

type dozen_samples **is array** (1 **to** 12) **of** sample;

The top-level index range is constrained to 1 to 12, but the element index range is unspecified. Similarly, we can declare a type for a path consisting of an unspecified number of points:

type path **is array** (positive **range** <>) **of** point;

The top-level index range is unspecified, but the element index range is 1 to 3.

We mentioned that when we declare an object of an array type, we must provide constraints for index ranges. If the type used in the declaration is fully constrained, the constraints from the type provide sufficient information. On the other hand, if the type is unconstrained or partially constrained, we need to provide the missing constraints. We saw how to do that for the simple case of an unconstrained array of scalar elements. We do something similar for an unconstrained array with array elements. For example, to declare a variable of type **sample_set** to store 100 samples each of 20 values, we can write

    variable main_sample_set : sample_set(1 **to** 100)(1 **to** 20);

The first index range, 1 to 100, is used for the top level of the type's hierarchy, and the second index range, 1 to 20, is used for the second level. We can use the same type for a second object with a different size:

    variable alt_sample_set : sample_set(1 **to** 50)(1 **to** 10);

This represents a collection of 50 samples, each with 10 values. Both variables are of the same type, **sample_set**, but they are of different sizes and have different element array sizes.

    If we are to use a partially constrained type to declare an object, we specify constraints only for the index ranges not specified by the type. We can use the preceding notation for the case of the top-level index range being the one we have to specify. For example, we can declare a variable for a path connecting five points:

    variable short_path : path(5 **downto** 1);

The index range 5 down to 1 is used for the top level of the type's hierarchy, and the constraint 1 to 3 for the second level comes from the type itelf.

    For the case in which we need to specify only a second-level index range, we need to use the reserved word **open** in place of the top-level index range. An example is

    variable bakers_samples : dozen_samples(**open**)(0 **to** 9);

In this example, we write **open** for the top-level index range, since the type itself specifies 1 to 12 for that index range. Using the word **open** allows us to advance to the second-level index range, where we specify 0 to 9 as the constraint.

    We can use this notation in subtype declarations as well as in declarations of objects. For example, if we want to declare several objects with the same constraints, we could write the subtype declaration

    subtype dozen_short_samples **is** dozen_samples(**open**)(0 **to** 9);

Since this subtype is fully constrained, we can use it to declare objects without adding any further constraint information.

    When we declare a subtype, we do not need to constrain all of the index ranges to make a fully constrained subtype. We can add index constraints for some of the index ranges to declare partially constrained subtypes. For example:

    subtype short_sample_set **is** sample_set(**open**)(0 **to** 9);

In this case, we use the word **open** to skip over the unspecified index range at the top level and add a constraint at the second level. The top-level index range remains unspecified, and so the subtype is partially constrained. When using this subtype to declare an object, we would have to specify the top-level index range for the object, for example:

```
variable unprocessed_samples : short_sample_set(1 to 20);
```

We mentioned earlier that, when declaring a constant of an unconstrained array type, we can infer the index range of the constant from the value of the expression used to initialize the constant. That applies not only to unconstrained arrays of scalar elements, but also to unconstrained arrays of array elements and to partially constrained arrays. For example, if we write:

```
constant default_sample_pair : sample_set
        := ( 1 => (39, 25, 6, -4, 5),
             2 => (9, 52, 100, 0, -1),
             3 => (0, 0, 0, 0, 0) );
```

the top-level index range is inferred to be 1 to 3 (from the choices in the outer level of the aggregate), and the second-level index range is inferred to be 0 to 4 (from the fact that the index subtype of **sample** is natural). Similarly, if we write:

```
constant default_samples : short_sample_set
        := ( 1 to 20 => (0, 0, 0, 0, 0, 0, 0, 0, 0, 0) );
```

the top-level index range is inferred to be 1 to 20 (from the choice in the outer level of the aggregate), but the second-level index range is 0 to 9, specified in the subtype.

4.2.3 Unconstrained Array Ports

An important use of an unconstrained array type is to specify the type of an array port. This use allows us to write an entity interface in a general way, so that it can connect to array signals of any size or with any range of index values. When we instantiate the entity, the index bounds of the array signal connected to the port are used as the bounds of the port. If the port type is an unconstrained array of unconstrained array elements, the index ranges at all levels of the type's hierarchy come from the connected signal.

EXAMPLE 4.4   *Multiple-input and gates*

Suppose we wish to model a family of and gates, each with a different number of inputs. We declare the entity interface as shown below. The input port is of the unconstrained type **bit_vector**. The architecture body includes a process that is sensitive to changes on the input port. When any element changes, the process performs a logical and operation across the input array. It uses the 'range attribute to determine the index range of the array, since the index range is not known until the entity is instantiated.

```
entity and_multiple is
  port ( i : in bit_vector;  y : out bit );
end entity and_multiple;
```

```vhdl
architecture behavioral of and_multiple is
begin

  and_reducer : process ( i ) is
    variable result : bit;
  begin
    result := '1';
    for index in i'range loop
      result := result and i(index);
    end loop;
    y <= result;
  end process and_reducer;

end architecture behavioral;
```

To illustrate the use of the multiple-input gate entity, suppose we have the following signals:

```vhdl
signal count_value : bit_vector(7 downto 0);
signal terminal_count : bit;
```

We instantiate the entity, connecting its input port to the bit-vector signal:

```vhdl
tc_gate : entity work.and_multiple(behavioral)
  port map ( i => count_value, y => terminal_count);
```

For this instance, the input port is constrained by the index range of the signal. The instance acts as an eight-input and gate.

EXAMPLE 4.5   *Multiple-input and-or-invert gates*

We can model a family of and-or-invert gates with varying numbers of groups of input bits. Each group of input bits is and-ed, the results are or-ed, and the final result negated to derive the output. The inputs are represented using an array of arrays:

```vhdl
type bv_array is array (natural range <>) of bit_vector;
```

Each array element of type **bit_vector** is a group of bits that are to be and-ed together. The entity and architecture are:

```vhdl
entity and_or_invert is
  port ( a : in bv_array; z : out bit );
end entity and_or_invert;

architecture behavioral of and_or_invert is

  reducer : process ( a ) is
    variable and_result, result : bit;
  begin
    result := '0';
```

```
    for i in a'range loop
      and_result := '1';
      for j in a'element'range loop
        and_result := and_result and a(i)(j);
      end loop;
      result := result or and_result;
    end loop;
    z <= not result;
  end process reducer;

end architecture behavioral;
```

The **reducer** process contains an outer loop that iterates over the array of groups. It uses the input array's top-level index range to govern the loop parameter. The inner loop iterates over the bits in a group represented by a particular element of **a**. This loop uses the index range of the elements of **a**, given by the **'range** attribute of the **'element** attribute of **a**. Note that we could have used the reducing **and** operator, described in Section 4.3.1, in place of the inner loop, as follows:

```
and_result := and a(i);
```

For this example, however, we have included the loop to illustrate use of the **'element** attribute in cases where the index ranges of array elements are determined by the signal connected to the port of an instance.

We can also use partially constrained types for ports of entities. In such cases, the index ranges of the signal connected to the port are used to determine the those bounds of the port that are not specified in the port's subtype. For example, if we declare an entity using the subtype **short_sample_set** subtype from Section 4.2.2:

```
entity sample_processor is
  port ( samples : in short_sample_set; ... );
end entity sample_processor;
```

and instantiate it as follows:

```
signal sensor_samples : short_sample_set(1 to 3);
...

preprocessor : entity sample_processor
  port map ( samples => sensor_samples, ... );
```

then, for the **preprocessor** instance, the top-level index range of the samples port would be 1 to 3, obtained from the **samples** signal. The second-level index range for the **samples** port would be 0 to 9, obtained from the subtype **short_sample_set**, the declared subtype of the port.

4.3 Array Operations and Referencing

Although an array is a collection of values, much of the time we operate on arrays one element at a time, using the operators described in Chapter 2. However, if we are working with one-dimensional arrays of scalar values, we can use some of the operators to operate on whole arrays. In this section, we describe the operators that can be applied to arrays and introduce a number of other ways in which arrays can be referenced.

4.3.1 Logical Operators

The logical operators (**and**, **or**, **nand**, **nor**, **xor** and **xnor**) can be applied to two one-dimensional arrays of bit or Boolean elements. That includes the predefined types bit_vector and boolean vector, as well as any array types with bit or boolean elements that we might declare. The operators can also be applied to two arrays of type std_ulogic_vector defined by the **std_logic_1164** package. In each case, the operands must be of the same length and type, and the result is computed by applying the operator to matching elements from each array to produce an array of the same length. Elements are matched starting from the leftmost position in each array. An element at a given position from the left in one array is matched with the element at the same position from the left in the other array. The operator **not** can also be applied to a single array of any of these types, with the result being an array of the same length and type as the operand. The following declarations and statements illustrate this use of logical operators when applied to bit vectors:

```
subtype pixel_row is bit_vector (0 to 15);
variable current_row, mask : pixel_row;

current_row := current_row and not mask;
current_row := current_row xor X"FFFF";
```

The logical operators **and**, **or**, **nand**, **nor**, **xor** and **xnor** can also be applied to a pair of operands, one of which is a one-dimensional arrays of the types mentioned above, and the other of which is a scalar of the same type as the array elements. The result is an array of the same length and type as the array operand. Each element of the result is computed by applying the operator to the scalar operand and the corresponding element of the array operand. Some examples are

```
B"0011" and '1' = B"0011"      B"0011" and '0' = B"0000"

B"0011" xor '1' = B"1100"      B"0011" xor '0' = B"0011"
```

EXAMPLE 4.6 *Select signal for a data bus*

Suppose the outputs of three registers are provided on **std_ulogic_vector** signals a, b, and c. We can use three select signals, a_sel, b_sel and c_sel, to select among the register outputs for assignment to a data bus signal. The declarations and statements are

```
signal a, b, c, data_bus : std_ulogic_vector(31 downto 0);
signal a_sel, b_sel, c_sel : std_ulogic;
...

data_bus <= (a and a_sel) or (b and b_sel) or (c and c_sel);
```

Further, these operators can be applied in unary form to a single one-dimensional array of the types mentioned above, reducing the array to a single scalar result of the same type as the array elements. The reduction **and**, **or**, and **xor** operators form the logical and, or, and exclusive or, respectively of the array elements. Thus:

and "0110" = '0' **and** '1' **and** '1' **and** '0' = '0'

 or "0110" = '0' **or** '1' **or** '1' **or** '0' = '1'

xor "0110" = '0' **xor** '1' **xor** '1' **xor** '0' = '0'

In each case, if the array has only one element, the result is the value of that element. If the array is a null array (that is, it has no elements), the result of the **and** operator is '1', and the result of the **or** and xor operators is '0'.

The reduction **nand**, **nor**, and **xnor** operators are the negation of the reduction **and**, **or**, and **xor** operators, respectively. Thus:

nand "0110" = **not** ('0' **and** '1' **and** '1' **and** '0') = **not** '0' = '1'

 nor "0110" = **not** ('0' **or** '1' **or** '1' **or** '0') = **not** '1' = '0'

xnor "0110" = **not** ('0' **xor** '1' **xor** '1' **xor** '0') = **not** '0' = '1'

In each case, application to a single-element array produces the negation of the element value. Application of **nand** to a null array produces '0' and application of **nor** or **xnor** to a null array produces '1'.

The logical reduction operators have the same precedence as the unary **not** and **abs** operators. In the absence of parentheses, they are evaluated before binary operators. So the expression:

and A **or** B

involves applying the reduction **and** operator to A, then applying the binary **or** operator to the result and B. In some cases, we need to include parentheses to make an expression legal. For example, the expression:

and **not** X

is not legal without parentheses, since we cannot chain unary operators. Instead, we must write the expression as:

and (**not** X)

EXAMPLE 4.7   *Parity reduction*

Given a signal **data** of type bit_vector, we can calculate parity using the reduction **xor** operator:

```
parity <= xor data;
```

Since reduction operators have higher precedence than binary logical operators, the following two statements produce the same value:

```
parity_error1 <= (xor data) and received_parity;

parity_error2 <= xor data and received_parity;
```

However, the parentheses make the first form more readable.

VHDL-87

The logical operator **xnor** is not provided in VHDL-87.

4.3.2   Shift Operators

The shift operators introduced in Chapter 2 (**sll**, **srl**, **sla**, **sra**, **rol** and **ror**) can be used with a one-dimensional array of bit or Boolean values as the left operand and an integer value as the right operand. The **sll**, **srl**, **rol** and **ror** operators can be used with a left operand of type std_ulogic_vector, defined in the std_logic_1164 package. A shift-left logical operation shifts the elements in the array n places to the left (n being the right operand), filling in the vacated positions with '0' or **false** and discarding the leftmost n elements. If n is negative, the elements are instead shifted to the right. Some examples are

```
B"10001010" sll 3 = B"01010000"      B"10001010" sll -2 = B"00100010"
```

The shift-right logical operation similarly shifts elements n positions to the right for positive n, or to the left for negative n, for example:

```
B"10010111" srl 2 = B"00100101"      B"10010111" srl -6 = B"11000000"
```

The next two shift operations, shift-left arithmetic and shift-right arithmetic, operate similarly, but instead of filling vacated positions with '0' or **false**, they fill them with a copy of the element at the end being vacated, for example:

```
B"01001011" sra 3 = B"00001001"      B"10010111" sra 3 = B"11110010"
B"00001100" sla 2 = B"00110000"      B"00010001" sla 2 = B"01000111"
```

As with the logical shifts, if n is negative, the shifts work in the opposite direction, for example:

```
B"00010001" sra -2 = B"01000111"      B"00110000" sla -2 = B"00001100"
```

A rotate-left operation moves the elements of the array *n* places to the left, transferring the *n* elements from the left end of the array around to the vacated positions at the right end. A rotate-right operation does the same, but in the opposite direction. As with the shift operations, a negative right argument reverses the direction of rotation. Some examples are

B"10010011" **rol** 1 = B"00100111"   B"10010011" **ror** 1 = B"11001001"

VHDL-87

The shift operators **sll**, **srl**, **sla**, **sra**, **rol** and **ror** are not provided in VHDL-87.

4.3.3 Relational Operators

Relational operators can also be applied to one-dimensional arrays. For the ordinary relation operators ("=", "/=", "<", "<=", ">" and "=>"), the array elements can be of any discrete type. The two operands need not be of the same length, so long as they have the same element type. The "=" and "/=" operators are quite straightforward. If two arrays have the same length and the corresponding elements are pairwise equal, then the arrays are equal. The "/=" operator is simply the negation of the "=" operator. The way the remaining operators work can be most easily seen when they are applied to strings of characters, in which case they are compared according to case-sensitive dictionary ordering.

To see how dictionary comparison can be generalized to one-dimensional arrays of other element types, let us consider the "<" operator applied to two arrays a and b. If both a and b have length 0, a < b is false. If a has length 0, and b has non-zero length, then a < b. Alternatively, if both a and b have non-zero length, then a < b if a(1) < b(1), or if a(1) = b(1) and the rest of a < the rest of b. In the remaining case, where a has non-zero length and b has length 0, a < b is false. Comparison using the other relational operators is performed analogously.

An important point that follows from this definition of "<" ordering is that, if we apply it to bit vectors representing binary-coded numbers, it does not correspond to numeric ordering. For example, consider the comparison B"001000" < B"10". Since the first element of the left operand is '0' and the first element of the right operand is '1', and since '0' < '1', the result of the comparison is true. However, if we interpret the vectors as unsigned binary numbers, the left operand represents 8 and the right operand represents 2. We would then expect the comparison to yield false. Clearly, the predefined relational operators are inappropriate for this interpretation of bit vectors. We will see in Chapter 9 how we can perform the right kind of comparisons on binary-coded numbers.

In Section 2.2.5, we introduced the matching equality ("?=") and inequality ("?/=") operators for comparing **bit** or **std_ulogic** operands. These operators can also be applied to operands that are one-dimensional arrays of **bit** or **std_ulogic** elements to yield a **std_ulogic** result. The operands must be of the same type and length. For the "?=" operator, corresponding elements are compared using the scalar version of the operator, and the results reduced using the logical **and** reduction operator. The "?/=" operator is computed similarly, with the **not** operator applied to the reduced **and** result.

EXAMPLE 4.8   *Chip-select and address decoding*

We can write a Boolean equation for a **std_ulogic** select signal that includes chip-select control signals and an address signal. We can use the "?=" operator, which returns a **std_ulogic** result. We can combine that result with the **std_ulogic** control signals to produce a **std_ulogic** form of the Boolean equation:

```
dev_sel1 <= cs1 and not ncs2 and addr ?= X"A5";
```

We can also use this form of expression in a condition, since the value is implictly converted to **boolean** (see Section 2.2.5):

```
if cs1 and not ncs2 and addr ?= X"A5" then
   . . .
```

or similarly:

```
if cs1 and ncs2 ?= '0' and addr ?= X"A5" then
   . . .
```

VHDL-87, -93, and -2002

The matching relational operators are not provided in these versions of VHDL. The assignment in the above example would have to be written as:

```
dev_sel1 <= '1' when cs1 = '1' and
                     ncs2 = '0' and addr = X"A5" else '0';
```

Similarly, since condition values are not implicitly converted to **boolean**, the conditions in the if statements would be written as:

```
if cs1 = '1' and ncs2 = '0' and addr = X"A5" then
   . . .
```

or

```
if (cs1 and not ncs2) = '1' and addr = X"A5" then
   . . .
```

Maximum and Minimum Operations

In Chapter 2, we introduced the **maximum** and **minimum** operations for scalar types. These operations can also be applied to arrays of discrete-type elements. The "<" operator is defined for such arrays, and the **maximum** and **minimum** operations are defined in terms of the "<" operator. Thus, for example:

```
minimum(B"0001", B"0110") = B"0001"
maximum(B"001000", B"10") = B"10"
```

Note that the same argument that we made above about comparing binary-coded numbers using the "<" operator applies to use of the maximum and minimum operations. Again, we will see in Chapter 9 how to perform the operation correctly for binary-coded numbers.

The **maximum** and **minimum** operations are further defined as reduction operations on one-dimensional arrays of any scalar type. The **maximum** function of this form returns the largest element in the array, and the **minimum** function returns the smallest element in the array. Again, the comparisons are performed using the predefined "<" operator for the element type. Thus,

```
maximum(string'("WXYZ")) = 'Z'

minimum(string'("WXYZ")) = 'W'

maximum(time_vector'(10 ns, 50 ns, 20 ns)) = 50 ns

minimum(time_vector'(10 ns, 50 ns, 20 ns)) = 10 ns
```

For a null array (one with no elements), the **maximum** function returns the smallest value of the element type, and the **minimum** function returns the largest value of the element type.

VHDL-87, -93, and -2002

The **maximum** and **minimum** operations are not provided in earlier versions of VHDL.

4.3.4 The Concatenation Operator

The one remaining operator that can be applied to one-dimensional arrays is the concatenation operator ("&"), which joins two array values end to end. For example, when applied to bit vectors, it produces a new bit vector with length equal to the sum of the lengths of the two operands. Thus, b"0000" & b"1111" produces b"0000_1111".

The concatenation operator can be applied to two operands, one of which is an array and the other of which is a single scalar element. It can also be applied to two scalar values to produce an array of length 2. Some examples are

```
"abc" & 'd'   =   "abcd"
'w'   & "xyz" =   "wxyz"
'a'   & 'b'   =   "ab"
```

4.3.5 To_String Operations

In Section 2.5, we described the predefined **to_string** operation on scalar types. **To_string** can also be applied to values of one-dimensional array types that contain only character-literal elements. Examples of such types include the predefined types **bit_vector** and **string** and the type **std_ulogic_vector** defined in **std_logic_1164**. Applying **to_string** to a **string** value is not of much use, since it just yields the operand unchanged. For other array types, the operation yields a **string** value with the same characters as the operand. This can be useful for including such array values in message strings. For example:

```
signal x : bit_vector(7 downto 0);

...

report "Trace: x = " & to_string(x);
```

The value of **x** is an array of **bit** elements, whereas the report statement expects a **string** value, which is an array of **character** elements. The to_string operation deals with the conversion. Thus, if **x** has the **bit_vector** value "00110101", the result of the **to_string** operation would be the character string "00110101".

VHDL also provides operations, to_ostring and to_hstring, for converting **bit_vector** operands to strings in octal and hexadecimal form, respectively. **To_ostring** takes each group of three bits from the operand, starting from the right, and includes the corresponding octal-digit character in the result. If the operand is not a multiple of three in length, additional '0' bits are assumed on the left of the operand. Some examples are:

```
to_ostring(B"101_011_000") = "530"
to_ostring( B"11_000_111") = "307"
```

The **to_hstring** operation similarly takes each group of four bits and includes the corresponding hexadecimal-digit character in the result. The digits A to F appear in uppercase. Some examples are:

```
to_hstring(B"0110_1100") = "6C"
to_hstring(  B"11_0101") = "35"
```

Note that we don't necessarily need a separate **to_bstring** operation, since the **to_string** operation would serve that purpose. However, in the interest of completeness and consistency, VHDL does provide a **to_bstring** operation with exactly the same behavior. (In fact, **to_bstring** is an alias for **to_string**. We discuss aliases in detail in Chapter 10.) In addition, VHDL provides alternate names for all of these operations: **to_binary_string**, **to_octal_string** and **to_hex_string**. Some designers may consider these to be more readable than the shorter names. Their use is a matter of taste or organizational coding style.

4.3.6 Array Slices

Often we want to refer to a contiguous subset of elements of an array, but not the whole array. We can do this using *slice* notation, in which we specify the left and right index values of part of an array object. For example, given arrays **a1** and **a2** declared as follows:

```
type array1 is array (1 to 100) of integer;
type array2 is array (100 downto 1) of integer;

variable a1 : array1;
variable a2 : array2;
```

we can refer to the array slice a1(11 **to** 20), which is an array of 10 elements having the indices 11 to 20. Similarly, the slice a2(50 **downto** 41) is an array of 10 elements but with a descending index range. Note that the slices a1(10 **to** 1) and a2(1 **downto** 10) are null slices, since the index ranges specified are null. Furthermore, the ranges specified in the slice must have the same direction as the original array. Thus we may not legally write a1(10 **downto** 1) or a2(1 **to** 10).

EXAMPLE 4.9   *A byte-swapper module*

We can write a behavioral model for a byte-swapper that has one input port and one output port, each of which is a bit vector of subtype **halfword**, declared as follows:

```
subtype halfword is bit_vector(0 to 15);
```

The entity and architecture are:

```
entity byte_swap is
  port (input : in halfword;  output : out halfword);
end entity byte_swap;

-------------------------------------------------

architecture behavior of byte_swap is

begin

  swap : process (input)
  begin
    output(8 to 15) <= input(0 to 7);
    output(0 to 7) <= input(8 to 15);
  end process swap;

end architecture behavior;
```

The process in the architecture body swaps the two bytes of input with each other. It shows how the slice notation can be used for signal array objects in signal assignment statements.

VHDL-87

In VHDL-87, the range specified in a slice may have the opposite direction to that of the index range of the array. In this case, the slice is a null slice.

4.3.7   Array Type Conversions

In Chapter 2 we introduced the idea of type conversion of a numeric value of one type to a value of a so-called *closely related* type. A value of an array type can also be converted to a value of another array type, provided the array types are closely related. Two array types are closely related if they have the same number of dimensions and their element types can be converted (that is, the element types are closely related). The type conversion simply produces a new array value of the specified type containing the converted elements of the original array in the same order.

To illustrate the idea of type-converting array values, suppose we have the following declarations in a model:

```
subtype name is string(1 to 20);
type display_string is array (integer range 0 to 19) of character;

variable item_name : name;
variable display : display_string;
```

We cannot directly assign the value of **item_name** to **display**, since the types are different. However, we can write the assignment using a type conversion:

```
display := display_string(item_name);
```

This produces a new array, with the left element having index 0 and the right element having index 19, which is compatible with the assignment target.

The rule that the element types of the converted expression and the target type must be convertible allows us to perform the following conversions:

```
subtype integer_vector_10 is integer_vector(1 to 10);
subtype real_vector_10 is real_vector(1 to 10);

variable i_vec : integer_vector_10;
variable r_vec : real_vector_10;
...

i_vec := integer_vector_10(r_vec);
r_vec := real_vector_10(i_vec);
```

Since we can convert between values of type **integer** and **real**, we can also convert between arrays with **integer** and **real** elements, respectively. Each element of the converted expression is converted to the element subtype of the target type.

The index ranges need not all be numeric for a type conversion to be performed. For example, suppose we have array types and signals declared as follows:

```
type exception_type is (int, ovf, div0, undef, trap);
type exception_vector is array (exception_type) of bit;
signal d_in, d_out: bit_vector(31 downto 0);
signal exception_reg : exception_vector;
```

Then the type conversion:

```
exception_vector( d_in(4 downto 0) )
```

yields a vector of bits indexed from **int** to **trap**, with each element being the matching element of the slice of **d_in**, from left to right. Since the element types for the expression and the target type are both **bit**, conversion of the elements is trivial.

The above examples illustrate the case of a type conversion in which the target type is fully constrained, specifying the index range for the result. In general, we can convert to a target type that is fully constrained, partially constrained, or unconstrained. (We described array index constraints in Section 4.2.2.) If the target type of the conversion specifies an index range at any level of the type's hierarchy, that index range is used, as in the examples. On the other hand, if the target type leaves some index range or ranges unspecified (that is, the target type is unconstrained or partially constrained), the correponding index range or ranges for the result depend on the index subtypes. If the index subtypes of the original array and the target type are both numeric, the index range of the result has the same numeric bounds and direction as the index range of the original array. For example, in the type conversion

```
integer_vector(r_vec)
```

the index range of the result is 1 to 10, taken from the index range of **r_vec**. If, however, one or both index ranges are enumeration types, the index range of the result is determined from the index subtype of the target type. The direction is the same as that of the index subtype, the left bound is the leftmost value in the index subtype, and the right bound depends on the number of elements. For example, in the type conversion

```
bit_vector( exception_reg )
```

the index range of the result comes from the index subtype defined for **bit_vector**, namely, **natural**. The subtype **natural** is declared to be an ascending range with a left bound of 0. This direction and left bound are used as the direction and left bound of the type-conversion result. The right bound comes from the number of elements. Thus, the result is a **bit_vector** value indexed from 0 to 4.

A common case in which we do not need a type conversion is the assignment of an array value of one subtype to an array signal or variable of a different subtype of the same base type. This occurs where the index ranges of the target and the operand have different bounds or directions. VHDL automatically includes an implicit subtype conversion in the assignment. For example, given the subtypes and variables declared thus:

```
subtype big_endian_upper_halfword is bit_vector(0 to 15);
subtype little_endian_upper_halfword is bit_vector(31 downto 16);

variable big : big_endian_upper_halfword;
variable little : little_endian_upper_halfword;
```

we could make the following assignments without including explicit type conversions:

```
big := little;
little := big;
```

A final point to make about conversions relates to type qualification, introduced in Section 2.3.2. There, we mentioned that the operand of a type qualification has to be of the specified type, but not necessarily of the specific subtype. In the case of type qualification for arrays, we can qualify an array operand as being of some different subtype to that of the operand. The operand is then converted to that subtype, as described above.

VHDL-87, -93, and -2002

The rules for array type conversions in these earlier versions of VHDL were more strict. Array types were only closely related if they had the same element type, the same number of dimensions and index types that could be type converted. The restriction on index subtypes effectively meant that both had to be numeric or both had to be the same enumeration type. In addition, for type qualification, no subtype conversion was performed. If the qualified type was a constrained array subtype, the operand had to have exactly the index range or ranges specified in the subtype.

4.3.8   Arrays in Case Statements

In Section 3.2, we introduced case statements, and described a number of requirements on the selector expression and choices. In our examples, we just used scalar types for the selector expression. However, VHDL also allows us to write a selector expression of a one-dimensional character array type, that is, an array type whose element type includes character literals. Examples of such types are **bit_vector**, **std_ulogic_vector**, and similar types. The choices are typically string literals, bit-string literals, or, less commonly, aggregates, and all must have the same length. When the case statement is executed, the value of the selector expression is checked to ensure it has the same length as the choices, and then compared with the choices to determine which alternative to execute. When the case statement is executed, the value of the expression must have the same length as the choices. For example, in the following:

```
variable s : bit_vector(3 downto 0);
variable c : bit;
...

case c & s is
   when "00000" => ...
   when "10000" => ...
   when others  => ...
end case;
```

all of the choices (except the **others** choice) are of length five, so that determines the required length for the result of the concatenation.

We saw in Section 4.1.2 that we can include the word others in an array aggregate to refer to all elements not identified in the preceding part of the aggregate. If we write an aggregate containing **others** as a choice in a case statement, the index range of the case expression must be locally static, that is, determined during the analysis phase of design processing. For example, we can write a case statement as follows:

```
variable s : bit_vector(3 downto 0);
...

case s is
   ('0', others => '1') => ...
   ('1', others => '0') => ...
```

```
  . . .
end case;
```

In this example, the index range of the expression s can be determined at analysis time as being 3 **downto** 0. That means the analyzer can use the index range for the choice values. If the analyzer cannot work out the index range for the case expression, it cannot determine the index values represented by **others** in the aggregates.

VHDL-87, -93, and -2002

In these versions of VHDL, if the selector expression in a case statement was of an array type, the index range had to be locally static, regardless of whether the choices used the word **others** or not. Thus, the expression c & s in the example above would be illegal. Instead, we would have to write the example as:

```
variable s : bit_vector(3 downto 0);
variable c : bit;
subtype bv5 is bit_vector(0 to 4);
  . . .
case bv5'(c & s) is
  . . .
end case;
```

4.3.9 Matching Case Statements

In the previous subsection, we saw how we can write a case statement with a selector expression of an array type. The choices are compared for exact equality with the expression value to select an alternative to execute. If the type of the case expression and choices is a vector of **std_ulogic** values, exact comparison is not always what we want. In particular, we would like to be able to include don't care elements ('–') in the choices to indicate that we don't care about some elements of the selector expression when selecting an alternative. We can do this with a new form of case statement, called a *matching case statement*, that uses the predefined "?=" operator described in Section 4.3.3 to compare choice values with the expression value. We include a question mark symbol after the keyword **case**, as follows:

```
case? expression is
  . . .
end case?;
```

The most common use of a matching case statement is with an expression of a vector type whose elements are **std_ulogic** values, such as the standard type **std_ulogic_vector** defined in the **std_logic_1164** package. It also includes vector types that we might define. With a case expression of such a type, we can write choice values that include '–' elements to specify don't care matching.

EXAMPLE 4.10   *A priority arbiter*

Suppose we have vectors of request and grant values, declared as follows:

```
variable request, grant : std_ulogic_vector(0 to 3);
```

We can use a matching case statement in a priority arbiter, with request 0 having highest priority:

```
case? request is
  when "1---" => grant := "1000";
  when "01--" => grant := "0100";
  when "001-" => grant := "0010";
  when "0001" => grant := "0001";
  when others => grant := "0000";
end case?;
```

Each choice is compared with the case expression using the predefined "?=" operator. Thus, the first choice matches values "1000", "1001", "100X", "H000", and so on, and similarly for the remaining choices. This is a much more succinct way of describing the arbiter than using an ordinary case statement. Moreover, unlike a sequence of tests in an if statement, it does not imply chained decision logic.

When we use a matching case statement with a vector-type expression, the value of the expression must not include any '–' elements. (This is different from the choice values, which can include '–' elements.) The reason is that an expression value with a '–' element would match multiple choice values, making selection of an alternative ambiguous. Normally, this rule is not a problem, since we don't usually assign '–' values to signals or variables. They usually just occur in literal values for comparison and in test bench assertions.

In an ordinary case statement, we need to include choices for all possible values of the case expression. A related rule applies in a matching case statement. Each possible value of the case expression, except those that include any '–' elements, must be represented by exactly one choice. By "represented," we mean that comparison of the choice and the expression value using the "?=" operator yields '1'. Hence, our choice values would generally just include '0', '1', and '–' elements, matching with '0', 'L', '1', 'H' elements in the case expression value. We could also include 'L' and 'H' elements in a choice. However, we would not include 'U', 'X', 'W', or 'Z' choice elements, since they only ever produce 'U' or 'X' results, and so never match. As with an ordinary case statement, we can include an **others** choice to represent expression values not otherwise represented. Unlike an ordinary case statement, a choice can represent multiple expression values if it contains a '–' element.

We mentioned that a vector type including **std_ulogic** values is the most common type for a matching case statement. Less commonly, we can write a selector expression of type **std_ulogic**, **bit**, or a vector of **bit** elements (such as **bit_vector**). These are the other types for which the "?=" operator is predefined. For **std_ulogic** expressions, the choice values would typically be either '0' (matching an expression value of '0' or 'L') or '1' (matching an expression value of '1' or 'H'). We would not write a choice of '–', since that would match all expression values, preventing us from selecting distinct alternatives. For case expressions of type **bit** or a vector of **bit** elements, a matching case statement has exactly the same behavior as an ordinary case statement. VHDL allows matching case statements of this form to allow synthesizable models to be written uniformly regardless of whether **bit** or **std_ulogic** data types are used.

VHDL-87, -93, and -2002

These versions of VHDL do not provide matching case statements.

4.4 Records

In this section, we discuss the second class of composite types, *records*. We start with record types, and return to record natures subsequently, since there are some significant differences between them. A record is a composite value comprising elements that may be of different types from one another. Each element is identified by a name, which is unique within the record. This name is used to select the element from the record value. The syntax rule for a record type definition is

record_type_definition ⇐
    record
        (identifier { , ₀₀₀ } : subtype_indication ;)
        { ₀₀₀ }
    end record ⟦ identifier ⟧

Each of the names in the identifier lists declares an element of the indicated type or subtype. Recall that the curly brackets in the syntax rule indicate that the enclosed part may be repeated indefinitely. Thus, we can include several elements of different types within the record. The identifier at the end of the record type definition, if included, must repeat the name of the record type.

VHDL-87

The record type name may not be included at the end of a record type definition in VHDL-87.

The following is an example record type declaration and variable declarations using the record type:

```
type time_stamp is record
    seconds : integer range 0 to 59;
    minutes : integer range 0 to 59;
    hours : integer range 0 to 23;
  end record time_stamp;
```

```
variable sample_time, current_time : time_stamp;
```

Whole record values can be assigned using assignment statements, for example:

```
sample_time := current_time;
```

We can also refer to an element in a record using a *selected name,* for example:

```
sample_hour := sample_time.hours;
```

In the expression on the right of the assignment symbol, the prefix before the dot names the record value, and the suffix after the dot selects the element from the record. A selected name can also be used on the left side of an assignment to identify a record element to be modified, for example:

```
current_time.seconds := clock mod 60;
```

EXAMPLE 4.11   *Representing CPU instructions and data using records*

In the early stages of designing a new instruction set for a CPU, we don't want to commit to an encoding of opcodes and operands within an instruction word. Instead we use a record type to represent the components of an instruction. We illustrate this in an outline of a system-level behavioral model of a CPU and memory that uses record types to represent instructions and data:

```
architecture system_level of computer is

  type opcodes is
        (add, sub, addu, subu, jmp, breq, brne, ld, st, ...);
  type reg_number is range 0 to 31;
  constant r0 : reg_number := 0;  constant r1 : reg_number := 1;
  ...

  type instruction is record
     opcode : opcodes;
     source_reg1, source_reg2, dest_reg : reg_number;
     displacement : integer;
   end record instruction;

  type word is record
     instr : instruction;
     data : bit_vector(31 downto 0);
   end record word;

  signal address : natural;
  signal read_word, write_word : word;
  signal mem_read, mem_write : bit := '0';
  signal mem_ready : bit := '0';

begin
```

```
cpu : process is
  variable instr_reg : instruction;
  variable PC : natural;
  ...      -- other declarations for register file, etc.
begin
  address <= PC;
  mem_read <= '1';
  wait until mem_ready;
  instr_reg := read_word.instr;
  mem_read <= '0';
  PC := PC + 4;
  case instr_reg.opcode is   -- execute the instruction
    ...
  end case;
end process cpu;

memory : process is
  subtype address_range is natural range 0 to 2**14 - 1;
  type memory_array is array (address_range) of word;
  variable store : memory_array :=
    ( 0   =>      ( ( ld, r0, r0, r2, 40 ), X"00000000" ),
      1   =>      ( ( breq, r2, r0, r0, 5 ), X"00000000" ),
      ...
      40  =>      ( ( nop, r0, r0, r0, 0 ), X"FFFFFFFE"),
      others => ( ( nop, r0, r0, r0, 0 ), X"00000000") );
begin
  ...
end process memory;

end architecture system_level;
```

The record type **instruction** represents the information to be included in each instruction of a program and includes the opcode, source and destination register numbers and a displacement. The record type **word** represents a word stored in memory. Since a word might represent an instruction or data, elements are included in the record for both possibilities. Unlike many conventional programming languages, VHDL does not provide variant parts in record values. The record type **word** illustrates how composite data values can include elements that are themselves composite values. The signals in the model are used for the address, data and control connections between the CPU and the memory.

Within the CPU process the variable **instr_reg** represents the instruction register containing the current instruction to be executed. The process fetches a word from memory and copies the instruction element from the record into the instruction register. It then uses the opcode field of the value to determine how to execute the instruction.

The memory process contains a variable that is an array of word records representing the memory storage. The array is initialized with a program and data. Words representing instructions are initialized with a record aggregate containing an instruction record aggregate and a bit vector, which is ignored. Similarly, words representing data are initialized with an aggregate containing an instruction aggregate, which is ignored, and the bit vector of data.

4.4.1 Record Aggregates

We can use a record aggregate to write a literal value of a record type, for example, to initialize a record variable or constant. Using a record aggregate is analogous to using an array aggregate for writing a literal value of an array type (see Section 4.1.2). A record aggregate is formed by writing a list of the elements enclosed in parentheses. An aggregate using positional association lists the elements in the same order as they appear in the record type declaration. For example, given the record type **time_stamp** shown above, we can initialize a constant as follows:

```
constant midday : time_stamp := (0, 0, 12);
```

We can also use named association, in which we identify each element in the aggregate by its name. The order of elements identified using named association does not affect the aggregate value. The example above could be rewritten as

```
constant midday : time_stamp
            := (hours => 12, minutes => 0, seconds => 0);
```

Unlike array aggregates, we can mix positional and named association in record aggregates, provided all of the named elements follow any positional elements. We can also use the symbols "|" and **others** when writing choices. Here are some more examples, using the types **instruction** and **time_stamp** declared above:

```
constant nop_instr : instruction :=
    ( opcode => addu,
      source_reg1 | source_reg2 | dest_reg => 0,
      displacement => 0 );

variable latest_event : time_stamp
            := (others => 0); -- initially midnight
```

Note that unlike array aggregates, we can't use a range of values to identify elements in a record aggregate, since the elements are identified by names, not indexed by a discrete range.

4.4.2 Unconstrained Record Element Types

In Section 4.2.2, we showed how the element type of an array type can be unconstrained, leading to unconstrained and partially constrained array types. In a similar way, an element of a record type can be of an unconstrained or partially constrained composite type. We use the terms unconstrained, partially constrained, and fully constrained to describe a record type in an analogous way to the use of the terms for array types. Specifically, an unconstrained record type is one that has one or more elements of composite types, all of which are unconstrained. For example, the following type

```
type test_vector is record
    id : natural;
    stimulus : bit_vector;
    response : bit_vector;
  end record test_vector;
```

is unconstrained, since the elements stimulus and response are both of an unconstrained array type.

A fully constrained record type is one in which all composite elements (if any) are fully constrained. For example, the types **instruction** and **word** in Example 4.11 are both fully constrained. The type **instruction** has no composite elements, so there is no place in the type's hierarchy where a constraint is needed. The type **word** has one element, **data**, of a composite subtype, which is fully constrained.

As with array types, a partially constrained record type is one that is neither unconstrained nor fully constrained. It may have a mix of unconstrained, partially constrained, and fully constrained elements, or it may just have one or more partially constrained elements. For example, if we declare a fully constrained record type

```
type test_times is record
    stimulus_time : time;
    response_delay : delay_length;
  end record test_times;
```

we can use this and the **test_vector** type as element types for a larger record type:

```
type test_application is record
    test_to_apply : test_vector;
    application_times : test_times;
  end record;
```

Since the **test_to_apply** element is unconstrained and the **application_times** element is fully constrained, the **test_application** type is partially constrained.

As another example, recall the types **sample** and **dozen_samples** defined in Section 4.2.2 as

```
type sample is array (natural range <>) of integer;
type dozen_samples is array (1 to 12) of sample;
```

If we declare a type as follows:

```
type analyzed_samples is record
    samples : dozen_samples;
    result : real;
  end record analyzed_samples;
```

this type is partially constrained, since it has just one composite element, **samples**, that is itself partially constrained.

We have mentioned that, when we declare an object of an array type, we must provide constraints for any index ranges that remain unspecified by the type. This rule applies to composite types in general, including record types. If any of the record elements are arrays, their index ranges must be specified. For a fully constrained record type, the type itself specifies the index ranges, if any. Thus, in Example 4.11, we were able to declare signals and variables of the fully constrained types **instruction** and **word** without supplying any further information beyond the type names.

For an unconstrained or partially constrained record type, we need to fill in any unspecified index ranges, and we need to specify which element of the type each index range constrains. The way in which we do so is illustrated by the following declaration using the unconstrained type **test_vector**:

```
variable next_test_vector : test_vector(stimulus(0 to 7),
                                        response(0 to 9));
```

For those elements of the type that we need to constrain, we write the element name followed by the index constraint. If the index range to be constrained is nested more deeply within the type's hierarchy, we can nest the constraint notation. For example, to declare a variable of type **test_application**, we could write:

```
variable scheduled_test :
        test_application(test_to_apply(stimulus(0 to 7),
                                       response(0 to 9)));
```

Since the **application_times** element of the **test_application** type is fully constrained, we do not mention it in the record constraint. As a second example, the declaration

```
variable analysis : analyzed_samples(samples(open)(1 to 100));
```

constrains the samples element of the record type. The constraint uses the word **open** to skip over the top-level index range of the element, since that index range is specified by the element type **dozen_samples**. The nested index range is constrained to be 1 to 100.

Just as we did for array types, we can use this notation to declare subtypes of record types. Some examples are:

```
subtype byte_test_vector is test_vector(stimulus(7 downto 0),
                                        response(7 downto 0));
```

```
subtype analyzed_short_samples is
        analyzed_samples(samples(open)(1 to 100));
```

We do not need to constrain every element. For example, if we write:

```
subtype test_application_word is
        test_application(test_to_apply(stimulus(0 to 31)));
```

only the **stimulus** element of the nested record element is constrained, and so the subtype **test_application_word** remains partially constrained. This is equivalent to writing

```
    subtype test_application_word is
            test_application(test_to_apply(stimulus(0 to 31),
                                            response(open)));
```

We could then further constrain it as follows:

```
    subtype test_application_word_byte is
            test_application_word(test_to_apply(response(0 to 7)));
```

or equivalently:

```
    subtype test_application_word_byte is
            test_application_word(test_to_apply(stimulus(open),
                                                response(0 to 7)));
```

Finally, the rule that index ranges for a constant can be inferred from the initial value also applies to a constant of an unconstrained or partially constrained record type. For example, if we declare a constant as follows:

```
    constant first_test_vector : test_vector
            := (id => 0,
                stimulus => B"100010",
                response => B"00000001");
```

the index ranges for the **stimulus** and **response** elements are inferred to be 0 to 5 and 0 to 7, respectively, since they are both of type **bit_vector**, which has natural as its index subtype.

Exercises

1. **[❶ 4.1]** Write an array type declaration for an array of 30 integers, and a variable declaration for a variable of the type. Write a for loop to calculate the average of the array elements.

2. **[❶ 4.1]** Write an array type declaration for an array of bit values, indexed by standard-logic values. Then write a declaration for a constant, **std_ulogic_to_bit**, of this type that maps standard-logic values to the corresponding bit value. (Assume unknown values map to '0'.) Given a standard-logic vector **v1** and a bit-vector variable **v2**, both indexed from 0 to 15, write a for loop that uses the constant **std_ulogic_to_bit** to map the standard-logic vector to the bit vector.

3. **[❶ 4.1]** The data on a diskette is arranged in 18 sectors per track, 80 tracks per side and two sides per diskette. A computer system maintains a map of free sectors. Write a three-dimensional array type declaration to represent such a map, with a '1' element representing a free sector and a '0' element representing an occupied sector. Write a set of nested for loops to scan a variable of this type to find the location of the first free sector.

4. **[❶ 4.2]** Write a declaration for a subtype of **std_ulogic_vector**, representing a byte. Declare a constant of this subtype, with each element having the value 'Z'.

5. [❶ 4.2] Write a type declaration for an unconstrained array of **time_vector** elements, indexed by **positive** values. Then write a subtype declaration representing an array with 4 unconstrained elements. Last, write a variable declaration using the subtype with each element having 10 subelements.

6. [❶ 4.2] Write a for loop to count the number of '1' elements in a bit-vector variable **v**.

7. [❶ 4.3] An 8-bit vector **v1** representing a two's-complement binary integer can be sign-extended into a 32-bit vector **v2** by copying it to the leftmost eight positions of **v2**, then performing an arithmetic right shift to move the eight bits to the rightmost eight positions. Write variable assignment statements that use slicing and shift operations to express this procedure.

8. [❶ 4.4] Write a record type declaration for a test stimulus record containing a stimulus bit vector of three bits, a delay value and an expected response bit vector of eight bits.

9. [❷ 4.1] Develop a model for a register file that stores 16 words of 32 bits each. The register file has data input and output ports, each of which is a 32-bit word; read-address and write-address ports, each of which is an integer in the range 0 to 15; and a write-enable port of type **bit**. The data output port reflects the content of the location whose address is given by the read-address port. When the write-enable port is '1', the input data is written to the register file at the location whose address is given by the write-address port.

10. [❷ 4.1] Develop a model for a priority encoder with a 16-element bit-vector input port, an output port of type **natural** that encodes the index of the leftmost '1' value in the input and an output of type **bit** that indicates whether any input elements are '1'.

11. [❷ 4.2] Write a package that declares an unconstrained array type whose elements are integers. Use the type in an entity declaration for a module that finds the maximum of a set of numbers. The entity has an input port of the unconstrained array type and an integer output. Develop a behavioral architecture body for the entity. How should the module behave if the actual array associated with the input port is empty (i.e., of zero length)?

12. [❷ 4.2/4.3] Develop a model for a general and-or-invert gate, with two standard-logic vector input ports **a** and **b** and a standard-logic output port **y**. The output of the gate is

$$\overline{a_0 \cdot b_0 + a_1 \cdot b_1 + \cdots + a_{n-1} \cdot b_{n-1}}$$

13. [❷ 4.4] Develop a model of a 3-to-8 decoder and a test bench to exercise the decoder. In the test bench, declare the record type that you wrote for Exercise 8 and a constant array of test record values. Initialize the array to a set of test vectors for the decoder, and use the vectors to perform the test.

Chapter 5

Basic Modeling Constructs

The description of a module in a digital system can be divided into two facets: the external view and the internal view. The external view describes the interface to the module, including the number and types of inputs and outputs. The internal view describes how the module implements its function. In VHDL, we can separate the description of a module into an *entity declaration*, which describes the external interface, and one or more *architecture bodies*, which describe alternative internal implementations. These were introduced in Chapter 1 and are discussed in detail in this chapter. We also look at how a design is processed in preparation for simulation or synthesis.

5.1 Entity Declarations and Architecture Bodies

Let us first examine the syntax rules for an entity declaration and then show some examples. We start with a simplified description of entity declarations and move on to a full description later in this chapter. The syntax rules for this simplified form of entity declaration are

entity_declaration ⇐
    entity identifier **is**
        ⟦ **port** (*port*_interface_list) ; ⟧
        { entity_declarative_item }
    end ⟦ **entity** ⟧ ⟦ identifier ⟧ ;

interface_list ⇐
    (identifier {, … } : ⟦ mode ⟧ subtype_indication ⟦ := expression ⟧) { ; … }

mode ⇐ **in** ⎮ **out** ⎮ **buffer** ⎮ **inout**

The identifier in an entity declaration names the module so that it can be referred to later. If the identifier is included at the end of the declaration, it must repeat the name of the entity. The port clause names each of the *ports*, which together form the interface to the entity. We can think of ports as being analogous to the pins of a circuit; they are the means by which information is fed into and out of the circuit. In VHDL, each port of an entity has a *type*, which specifies the kind of information that can be communicated, and a *mode*, which specifies how information flows into or out from the entity through the port. These aspects of type and direction are in keeping with the strong typing philosophy of VHDL, which helps us avoid erroneous circuit descriptions. A simple example of an entity declaration is

```
entity adder is
  port ( a : in word;
         b : in word;
         sum : out word );
end entity adder;
```

This example describes an entity named **adder**, with two input ports and one output port, all of type **word**, which we assume is defined elsewhere. We can list the ports in any order; we do not have to put inputs before outputs. Also, we can include a list of ports of the same mode and type instead of writing them out individually. Thus the above declaration could equally well be written as follows:

```
entity adder is
  port ( a, b : in word;
         sum : out word );
end entity adder;
```

In this example we have seen input and output ports. An input port allows us to model a device that senses data provided externally on a pin. An output port allows us to model a device that drives a pin to provide data to external connections. VHDL also allows us to specify the mode **buffer** for a port that not only provides data to external connections, but also provides that same data for use internally. We could achieve the same effect with an **out**-mode port, since VHDL does allow us to read the driven value of an **out**-mode port internally. However, we prefer to use an **out**-mode port when the value is read internally just for verification purposes, for example, using assertion statements. The real device we are modeling in this case does not have an internal connection to implement its functionality. For a device that does have such an internal connection, we use a **buffer** port to make our design intent clear.

As an example, suppose we want to model an SR-latch and allow for an implementation using cross-coupled gates. Since each output is also fed back internally to an input of a gate, we use buffer-mode ports for the outputs. The entity declaration is:

```
entity SR_latch is
  port ( S, R : in bit; Q, Q_n : buffer bit );
end entity SR_latch;
```

The syntax rules for entities show that we can also have bidirectional ports, with mode **inout**. These can be used to model devices that alternately sense and drive data through a pin. Such models must deal with the possibility of more than one connected device driving a given signal at the same time. VHDL provides a mechanism for this, *signal resolution*, which we will return to in Chapter 8.

The similarity between the description of a port in an entity declaration and the declaration of a variable may be apparent. This similarity is not coincidental, and we can extend the analogy by specifying a default value on a port description; for example:

```
entity and_or_inv is
  port ( a1, a2, b1, b2 : in bit := '1';
         y : out bit );
end entity and_or_inv;
```

The default value, in this case the '1' on the input ports, indicates the value each port should assume if it is left unconnected in an enclosing model. We can think of it as describing the value that the port "floats to." On the other hand, if the port is used, the default value is ignored. We say more about use of default values when we look at the execution of a model.

Another point to note about entity declarations is that the port clause is optional. So we can write an entity declaration such as

```
entity top_level is
end entity top_level;
```

which describes a completely self-contained module. As the name in this example implies, this kind of module usually represents the top level of a design hierarchy.

Finally, if we return to the first syntax rule on page 135, we see that we can include declarations of items within an entity declaration. These include declarations of constants, types, signals and other kinds of items that we will see later in this chapter. The items can be used in all architecture bodies corresponding to the entity. Thus, it makes sense to include declarations that are relevant to the entity and all possible implementations. Anything that is part of only one particular implementation should instead be declared within the corresponding architecture body.

EXAMPLE 5.1 *A ROM entity including the ROM contents*

Suppose we are designing an embedded controller using a microprocessor with a program stored in a read-only memory (ROM). The program to be stored in the ROM is fixed, but we still need to model the ROM at different levels of detail. We can include declarations that describe the program in the entity declaration for the ROM:

```
entity program_ROM is
  port ( address : in std_ulogic_vector(14 downto 0);
         data : out std_ulogic_vector(7 downto 0);
         enable : in std_ulogic );

  subtype instruction_byte is bit_vector(7 downto 0);
  type program_array is
         array (0 to 2**14 - 1) of instruction_byte;
  constant program : program_array
     := ( X"32", X"3F", X"03",   -- LDA  $3F03
          X"71", X"23",          -- BLT     $23
```

```
        . . .
    );
end entity program_ROM;
```

The declarations within the ROM entity are not directly accessible to a user of the entity, but serve to document the contents of the ROM. Each architecture body corresponding to the entity can use the constant program to initialize whatever structure it uses internally to implement the ROM.

The internal operation of a module is described by an architecture body. An architecture body generally applies some operations to values on input ports, generating values to be assigned to output ports. The operations can be described either by processes, which contain sequential statements operating on values, or by a collection of components representing sub-circuits. Where the operation requires generation of intermediate values, these can be described using *signals*, analogous to the internal wires of a module. The syntax rule for architecture bodies shows the general outline:

architecture_body ⇐
    architecture identifier **of** *entity*_name **is**
        { block_declarative_item }
    begin
        { concurrent_statement }
    end [**architecture**] [identifier] ;

The identifier names this particular architecture body, and the entity name specifies which module has its operation described by this architecture body. If the identifier is included at the end of the architecture body, it must repeat the name of the architecture body. There may be several different architecture bodies corresponding to a single entity, each describing an alternative way of implementing the module's operation. The block declarative items in an architecture body are declarations needed to implement the operations. The items may include type and constant declarations, signal declarations and other kinds of declarations that we will look at in later chapters.

VHDL-87, -93, and -2002

These versions of VHDL do not allow reading of an **out**-mode port within an entity or a corresponding architecture body. Instead, the model must declare an internal signal for the driven value and read that internally. The model can then assign the value of the signal to the **out**-mode port using a concurrent signal assignment statement (see Section 5.2.7).

    In VHDL-2002, another alternative would be to use a **buffer**-mode port instead of an **out**-mode port. However, if the port is only read for verification purposes, using a **buffer**-mode port would be counter to the design intent.

VHDL-87

In VHDL-87, the keyword **entity** may not be included at the end of an entity declaration, and the keyword **architecture** may not be included at the end of an architecture body.

5.1.1 Concurrent Statements

The *concurrent statements* in an architecture body describe the module's operation. One form of concurrent statement, which we have already seen, is a process statement. Putting this together with the rule for writing architecture bodies, we can look at a simple example of an architecture body corresponding to the **adder** entity on page 136:

```
architecture abstract of adder is
begin

  add_a_b : process (a, b) is
  begin
    sum <= a + b;
  end process add_a_b;

end architecture abstract;
```

The architecture body is named **abstract**, and it contains a process **add_a_b**, which describes the operation of the entity. The process assumes that the operator "+" is defined for the type **word**, the type of **a** and **b**. We will see in Chapter 6 how such a definition may be written. We could also envisage additional architecture bodies describing the adder in different ways, provided they all conform to the external interface laid down by the entity declaration.

We have looked at processes first because they are the most fundamental form of concurrent statement. All other forms can ultimately be reduced to one or more processes. Concurrent statements are so called because conceptually they can be activated and perform their actions together, that is, concurrently. Contrast this with the sequential statements inside a process, which are executed one after another. Concurrency is useful for modeling the way real circuits behave. If we have two gates whose inputs change, each evaluates its new output independently of the other. There is no inherent sequencing governing the order in which they are evaluated. We look at process statements in more detail in Section 5.2. Then, in Section 5.3, we look at another form of concurrent statement, the component instantiation statement, used to describe how a module is composed of interconnected sub-modules.

5.1.2 Signal Declarations

When we need to provide internal signals in an architecture body, we must define them using *signal declarations*. The syntax for a signal declaration is very similar to that for a variable declaration:

signal_declaration ⇐
    signal identifier ⟦ , ₀₀₀ ⟧ : subtype_indication ⟦ := expression ⟧ ;

This declaration simply names each signal, specifies its type and optionally includes an initial value for all signals declared by the declaration.

EXAMPLE 5.2   *An and-or-invert architecture with internal signals*

The following is an example of an architecture body for the entity **and_or_inv**, defined on page 137. The architecture body includes declarations of some signals that are internal to the architecture body. They can be used by processes within the architecture body but are not accessible outside, since a user of the module need not be concerned with the internal details of its implementation. Values are assigned to signals using signal assignment statements within processes. Signals can be sensed by processes to read their values.

```
architecture primitive of and_or_inv is

  signal and_a, and_b : bit;
  signal or_a_b : bit;

begin

  and_gate_a : process (a1, a2) is
  begin
    and_a <= a1 and a2;
  end process and_gate_a;

  and_gate_b : process (b1, b2) is
  begin
    and_b <= b1 and b2;
  end process and_gate_b;

  or_gate : process (and_a, and_b) is
  begin
    or_a_b <= and_a or and_b;
  end process or_gate;

  inv : process (or_a_b) is
  begin
    y <= not or_a_b;
  end process inv;

end architecture primitive;
```

An important point illustrated by this example is that the ports of the entity are also visible to processes inside the architecture body and are used in the same way as signals. This corresponds to our view of ports as external pins of a circuit: from the internal point of view, a pin is just a wire with an external connection. So it makes sense for VHDL to treat ports like signals inside an architecture of the entity.

5.2 Behavioral Descriptions

At the most fundamental level, the behavior of a module is described by signal assignment statements within processes. We can think of a process as the basic unit of behavioral description. A process is executed in response to changes of values of signals and uses the present values of signals it reads to determine new values for other signals. A signal assignment is a sequential statement and thus can only appear within a process. In this section, we look in detail at the interaction between signals and processes.

5.2.1 Signal Assignment

In all of the examples we have looked at so far, we have used a simple form of signal assignment statement. Each assignment just provides a new value for a signal. The value is determined by evaluating an expression, the result of which must match the type of the signal. What we have not yet addressed is the issue of timing: when does the signal take on the new value? This is fundamental to modeling hardware, in which events occur over time. First, let us look at the syntax for a basic signal assignment statement in a process:

> signal_assignment_statement ⇐
>   ⟦ label : ⟧ name <= ⟦ delay_mechanism ⟧ waveform ;
>
> waveform ⇐ ⟮ *value*_expression ⟦ **after** *time*_expression ⟧ ⟯ ⟨ , ... ⟩
>   ⟦ **unaffected**

The optional label allows us to identify the statement. The syntax rules tell us that we can specify a delay mechanism, which we come to soon, and one or more waveform elements, each consisting of a new value and an optional delay time. We will return to the use of the reserved word **unaffected** as a waveform shortly. It is these delay times in a signal assignment that allow us to specify when the new value should be applied. For example, consider the following assignment:

> y <= **not** or_a_b **after** 5 ns;

This specifies that the signal y is to take on the new value at a time 5 ns later than that at which the statement executes. The delay can be read in one of two ways, depending on whether the model is being used purely for its descriptive value or for simulation. In the first case, the delay can be considered in an abstract sense as a specification of the module's propagation delay: whenever the input changes, the output is updated 5 ns later. In the second case, it can be considered in an operational sense, with reference to a host machine simulating operation of the module by executing the model. Thus if the above assignment is executed at time 250 ns, and or_a_b has the value '1' at that time, then the signal y will take on the value '0' at time 255 ns. Note that the statement itself executes in zero modeled time.

The time dimension referred to when the model is executed is *simulation time*, that is, the time in which the circuit being modeled is deemed to operate. This is distinct from real execution time on the host machine running a simulation. We measure simulation time starting from zero at the start of execution and increasing in discrete steps as events occur in the model. Not surprisingly, this technique is called *discrete event simulation*. A discrete event simulator must have a simulation time clock, and when a signal assignment statement is executed, the delay specified is added to the current simulation time to determine when the new value is to be applied to the signal. We say that the signal assignment schedules a *transaction* for the signal, where the transaction consists of the new value and the simulation time at which it is to be applied. When simulation time advances to the time at which a transaction is scheduled, the signal is updated with the new value. We say that the signal is *active* during that simulation cycle. If the new value is not equal to the old value it replaces on a signal, we say an *event* occurs on the signal. The importance of this distinction is that processes respond to events on signals, not to transactions.

The syntax rules for signal assignments show that we can schedule a number of transactions for a signal, to be applied after different delays. For example, a clock driver process might execute the following assignment to generate the next two edges of a clock signal (assuming T_pw is a constant that represents the clock pulse width):

```
clk <= '1' after T_pw, '0' after 2*T_pw;
```

If this statement is executed at simulation time 50 ns and T_pw has the value 10 ns, one transaction is scheduled for time 60 ns to set clk to '1', and a second transaction is scheduled for time 70 ns to set clk to '0'. If we assume that clk has the value '0' when the assignment is executed, both transactions produce events on clk.

This signal assignment statement shows that when more than one transaction is included, the delays are all measured from the current time, not the time in the previous element. Furthermore, the transactions in the list must have strictly increasing delays, so that the list reads in the order that the values will be applied to the signal.

EXAMPLE 5.3   *A clock generator process*

We can write a process declaration for a clock generator using the above signal assignment statement to generate a symmetrical clock signal with pulse width T_pw. The difficulty is to get the process to execute regularly every clock cycle. One way to do this is by making it resume whenever the clock changes and scheduling the next two transitions when it changes to '0'. A process using this approach is

```
clock_gen : process (clk) is
begin
  if not clk then
    clk <= '1' after T_pw, '0' after 2*T_pw;
  end if;
end process clock_gen;
```

Since a process is the basic unit of a behavioral description, it makes intuitive sense to be allowed to include more than one signal assignment statement for a given signal within a single process. We can think of this as describing the different ways in which a signal's value can be generated by the process at different times.

EXAMPLE 5.4   *A process for a two-input multiplexer*

We can write a process that models a two-input multiplexer as shown below. The value of the **sel** port is used to select which signal assignment to execute to determine the output value.

```
mux : process (a, b, sel) is
begin
  case sel is
    when '0' =>
      z <= a after prop_delay;
    when '1' =>
      z <= b after prop_delay;
  end case;
end process mux;
```

We say that a process defines a *driver* for a signal if and only if it contains at least one signal assignment statement for the signal. So this example defines a driver for the signal **z**. If a process contains signal assignment statements for several signals, it defines drivers for each of those signals. A driver is a *source* for a signal in that it provides values to be applied to the signal. An important rule to remember is that for normal signals, there may only be one source. This means that we cannot write two different processes, each containing signal assignment statements for the one signal. If we want to model such things as buses or wired-or signals, we must use a special kind of signal called a *resolved signal*, which we will discuss in Chapter 8.

We now return to the use of the reserved word **unaffected** as a waveform in a signal assignment statement, as shown in the syntax rule on page 141. This simply represents no change to the value of the assigned signal. The assignment is equivalent to a null statement, except that it allows us to explicitly document the intention of not changing the target signal. For example, in the following:

```
if device_busy then
  collision_count := collision_count + 1;
  device_req <= unaffected;
else
  accepted_count := accepted_count + 1;
  device_req <= '1';
end if;
```

the assignment with **unaffected** explicitly document that we are not changing device_req in the alternative where device_busy is true. Had we omitted the assignment, on later examination of the model, the omission might appear inadvertent.

VHDL-87, -93, and -2002

These versions of VHDL do not allow the reserved word **unaffected** to appear as a waveform in a sequential signal assignment. It can only be used in concurrent signal assignments (see Section 5.2.7). If a target signal is to remain unchanged as a result of executing sequential statements, a model in the earlier versions of VHDL must either omit an assignment or use a null statement.

VHDL-87

Signal assignment statements may not be labeled in VHDL-87.

Conditional Signal Assignments

VHDL provides conditional signal assignments as a shorthand for signal assignment statements within if statements. The syntax rule is:

```
conditional_signal_assignment ⇐
    ⟦ label : ⟧
    name <= ⟦ delay_mechanism ⟧
            waveform when condition
            ⟨ else waveform when condition ⟩
            ⟦ else waveform ⟧ ;
```

We will return to the delay mechanism part in Section 5.2.5. As an example, we can model a register with synchronous reset using a conditional assignment within a process as follows:

```
reg : process (clk) is
begin
  if rising_edge(clk) then
    q <= (others => '0') when reset else d;
  end if;
end process reg;
```

The conditional assignment in the process is equivalent to the if statement:

```
if reset then
  q <= (others => '0')
else
  q <= d;
end if;
```

The waveforms in a conditional signal assignment are the same as those described earlier, consisting of one or more values to be assigned after successive delays, or the reserved word **unaffected** if we want to leave the signal unchanged. For example, in a stimulus-generator process, we could write the assignment:

```
req <= '1', '0' after T_fixed when fixed_delay_mode else
       '1', '0' after next_random_delay(ran_seed);
```

VHDL-87, -93, and -2002

These versions of VHDL do not provide the conditional signal assignment shorthand notation. We must write an if statement with a separate signal assignment for each condition.

Selected Signal Assignments

VHDL also provides a selected signal assignment statement that is short for a case statement containing simple assignments to the target signal. The syntax rule is:

selected_signal_assignment ⇐
    ⟦ label : ⟧
    with expression **select**
        name <= ⟦ delay_mechanism ⟧
                ⟨ waveform **when** choices , ⟩
             waveform **when** choices ;

We will return to the delay mechanism part in Section 5.2.5. As an example, we can write a process containing a selected signal assignment for a multiplexer as follows:

```
with d_sel select
  q <= source0 when "00",
       source1 when "01",
       source2 when "10",
       source3 when "11";
```

The assignment is equivalent to the following case statement and nested assignments:

```
case d_sel is
  when "00" =>
    q <= source0;
  when "01"
    q <= source1;
  when "10"
    q <= source2;
  when "11"
    q <= source3;
end case;
```

This form of signal assignment is particularly useful for describing the next-state logic of a finite-state machine, as is shown by the following process outline:

```
next_state_logic : process (all) is
begin
  with current_state select
    idle =>
      next_state <= pending1 when request and busy     else
                    active1  when request and not busy else
                    idle;
    pending1 =>
      ...
    ...
  end case;
end process next_state_logic;
```

We can also include the reserved word **unaffected** as a waveform in an alternative of a selected signal assignment, for example:

```
with dut_state select
  dut_req <= '1' when ready,
             '0' when ack,
             unaffected when others;
```

As a further variant of the selected signal assignment, we can write the "?" symbol after the reserved word **select** to specify a matching case statement in the equivalent form. For example, if we write

```
with request select?
  grant <= "1000" when "1---",
           "0100" when "01--",
           "0010" when "001-",
           "0001" when "0001",
           "0000" when others;
```

the equivalent statement is

```
case? request is
  when "1---" =>
    grant <= "1000";
  when "01--" =>
    grant <=  "0100";
  when "001-" =>
    grant <=  "0010";
  when "0001" =>
    grant =>  "0001";
  when others =>
    grant =>  "0000";
end case?;
```

The rules for case statements covering the type of the selector expression and the way in which choices are matched apply to the selected signal assignment.

VHDL-87, -93, and -2002

These versions of VHDL do not provide the selected signal assignment shorthand notation. We must write a case statement with a separate signal assignment for each alternative.

5.2.2 Signal Attributes

In Chapter 2 we introduced the idea of attributes of types, which give information about allowed values for the types. Then, in Chapter 4, we saw how we could use attributes of array objects to get information about their index ranges. We can also refer to attributes of signals to find information about their history of transactions and events. Given a signal S, and a value T of type **time**, VHDL defines the following attributes:

S'delayed(T)	A signal that takes on the same values as S but is delayed by time T.
S'stable(T)	A Boolean signal that is true if there has been no event on S in the time interval T up to the current time, otherwise false.
S'quiet(T)	A Boolean signal that is true if there has been no transaction on S in the time interval T up to the current time, otherwise false.
S'transaction	A signal of type bit that changes value from '0' to '1' or vice versa each time there is a transaction on S.
S'event	True if there is an event on S in the current simulation cycle, false otherwise.
S'active	True if there is a transaction on S in the current simulation cycle, false otherwise.
S'last_event	The time interval since the last event on S.
S'last_active	The time interval since the last transaction on S.
S'last_value	The value of S just before the last event on S.

The first three attributes take an optional time parameter. If we omit the parameter, the value 0 fs is assumed. These attributes are often used in checking the timing behavior within a model. For example, we can verify that a signal d meets a minimum setup time requirement of Tsu before a rising edge on a clock clk of type **std_ulogic** as follows:

```
if clk'event and (clk = '1' or clk = 'H')
            and (clk'last_value = '0'
                    or clk'last_value = 'L') then
    assert d'last_event >= Tsu
```

```
      report "Timing error: d changed within setup time of clk";
  end if;
```

The condition in the if statement performs the same test as the **rising_edge** operation on **std_ulogic** signals. Similarly, we might check that the pulse width of a clock signal input to a module doesn't exceed a maximum frequency by testing its pulse width:

```
assert (not clk'event) or clk'delayed'last_event >= Tpw_clk
  report "Clock frequency too high";
```

Note that we test the time since the last event on a delayed version of the clock signal. When there is currently an event on a signal, the **'last_event** attribute returns the value 0 fs. In this case, we determine the time since the previous event by applying the **'last_event** attribute to the signal delayed by 0 fs. We can think of this as being an infinitesimal delay. We will return to this idea later in this chapter, in our discussion of delta delays.

EXAMPLE 5.5   *An edge-triggered flipflop using the* 'event *attribute*

We can use a similar test for the rising edge of a clock signal to model an edge-triggered module, such as a flipflop. The flipflop should load the value of its **D** input on a rising edge of **clk**, but asynchronously clear the outputs whenever **clr** is '1'. The entity declaration and a behavioral architecture body are:

```
entity edge_triggered_Dff is
  port ( D : in bit;  clk : in bit;  clr : in bit;
         Q : out bit );
end entity edge_triggered_Dff;

--------------------------------------------------

architecture behavioral of edge_triggered_Dff is
begin
  state_change : process (clk, clr) is
  begin
    if clr then
      Q <= '0' after 2 ns;
    elsif clk'event and clk = '1' then
      Q <= D after 2 ns;
    end if;
  end process state_change;

end architecture behavioral;
```

The condition in this if statement performs the same test as the predefined **rising_edge** operation on **bit** signals. If the flipflop did not have the asynchronous clear input, the model could have used a simple wait statement such as

```
wait until clk;
```

to trigger on a rising edge. However, with the clear input present, the process must be sensitive to changes on both **clk** and **clr** at any time. Hence it uses the **'event** attribute to distinguish between **clk** changing to '1' and **clr** going back to '0' while **clk** is stable at '1'. Note that we cannot write the condition as

> clk'event **and** clk

since **clk'event** yields a **boolean** value, and **clk** is of type **bit**. The **and** operator is not defined for this mixture of operand types. Instead, we compare the **clk** value with '1' using the "=" operator, as shown in the if statement.

VHDL-87

In VHDL-87, the **'last_value** attribute for a composite signal returns the aggregate of last values for each of the scalar elements of the signal. For example, suppose a bit-vector signal **s** initially has the value B"00" and changes to B"01" and then B"11" in successive events. After the last event, the result of **s'last_value** is B"00" in VHDL-87. In VHDL-93 and VHDL-2002 it is B"01", since that is the last value of the entire composite signal.

5.2.3 Wait Statements

Now that we have seen how to change the values of signals over time, the next step in behavioral modeling is to specify when processes respond to changes in signal values. This is done using *wait statements*. A wait statement is a sequential statement with the following syntax rule:

wait_statement ⇐
    〖 label : 〗 **wait** 〖 **on** *signal*_name 〖 , � � ⁀ 〗 〗
               〖 **until** condition 〗
               〖 **for** *time*_expression 〗 ;

The optional label allows us to identify the statement. The purpose of the wait statement is to cause the process that executes the statement to suspend execution. The *sensitivity* clause, *condition* clause and *timeout* clause specify when the process is subsequently to resume execution. We can include any combination of these clauses, or we may omit all three. Let us go through each clause and describe what it specifies.

The sensitivity clause, starting with the word **on**, allows us to specify a list of signals to which the process responds. If we just include a sensitivity clause in a wait statement, the process will resume whenever any one of the listed signals changes value, that is, whenever an event occurs on any of the signals. This style of wait statement is useful in a process that models a block of combinatorial logic, since any change on the inputs may result in new output values; for example:

```
half_add : process is
begin
```

```
  sum <= a xor b after T_pd;
  carry <= a and b after T_pd;
  wait on a, b;
end process half_add;
```

The process starts execution by generating values for **sum** and **carry** based on the initial values of **a** and **b**, then suspends on the wait statement until either **a** or **b** (or both) change values. When that happens, the process resumes and starts execution from the top.

This form of process is so common in modeling digital systems that VHDL provides the shorthand notation that we have seen in many examples in preceding chapters. A process with a sensitivity list in its heading is exactly equivalent to a process with a wait statement at the end, containing a sensitivity clause naming the signals in the sensitivity list. So the **half_add** process above could be rewritten as

```
half_add : process (a, b) is
begin
  sum <= a xor b after T_pd;
  carry <= a and b after T_pd;
end process half_add;
```

EXAMPLE 5.6 *A revised model of a two-input multiplexer*

Let us return to the model of a two-input multiplexer in Example 5.4. The process in that model is sensitive to all three input signals. This means that it will resume on changes on either data input, even though only one of them is selected at any time. If we are concerned about this slight lack of efficiency in simulation, we can write the process differently, using wait statements to be more selective about the signals to which the process is sensitive each time it suspends. The revised model is shown below. In this model, when input **a** is selected, the process only waits for changes on the select input and on **a**. Any changes on **b** are ignored. Similarly, if **b** is selected, the process waits for changes on **sel** and on **b**, ignoring changes on **a**.

```
entity mux2 is
  port ( a, b, sel : in bit;
          z : out bit );
end entity mux2;

--------------------------------------------------

architecture behavioral of mux2 is

  constant prop_delay : time := 2 ns;

begin

  slick_mux : process is
  begin
    case sel is
      when '0' =>
        z <= a after prop_delay;
```

```
          wait on sel, a;
        when '1' =>
          z <= b after prop_delay;
          wait on sel, b;
      end case;
    end process slick_mux;

  end architecture behavioral;
```

The condition clause in a wait statement, starting with the word **until**, allows us to specify a condition that must be true for the process to resume. For example, the wait statement

wait until clk;

causes the executing process to suspend until the value of the signal **clk** changes to '1'. The condition expression is tested while the process is suspended to determine whether to resume the process. A consequence of this is that even if the condition is true when the wait statement is executed, the process will still suspend until the appropriate signals change and cause the condition to be true again. If the wait statement doesn't include a sensitivity clause, the condition is tested whenever an event occurs on any of the signals mentioned in the condition.

EXAMPLE 5.7   *A revised clock generator process*

The clock generator process in Example 5.3 can be rewritten using a wait statement with a condition clause, as shown below. Each time the process executes the wait statement, **clk** has the value '0'. However, the process still suspends, and the condition is tested each time there is an event on **clk**. When **clk** changes to '1', nothing happens, but when it changes to '0' again, the process resumes and schedules transactions for the next cycle.

```
clock_gen : process is
begin
  clk <= '1' after T_pw, '0' after 2*T_pw;
  wait until not clk;
end process clock_gen;
```

If a wait statement includes a sensitivity clause as well as a condition clause, the condition is only tested when an event occurs on any of the signals in the sensitivity clause. For example, if a process suspends on the following wait statement:

wait on clk **until not** reset;

the condition is tested on each change in the value of **clk**, regardless of any changes on reset.

The timeout clause in a wait statement, starting with the word **for**, allows us to specify a maximum interval of simulation time for which the process should be suspended. If we also include a sensitivity or condition clause, these may cause the process to be resumed earlier. For example, the wait statement

wait until trigger **for** 1 ms;

causes the executing process to suspend until **trigger** changes to '1', or until 1 ms of simulation time has elapsed, whichever comes first. If we just include a timeout clause by itself in a wait statement, the process will suspend for the time given.

EXAMPLE 5.8   *The clock generator process further revised*

We can rewrite the clock generator process in Example 5.3 yet again, this time using a wait statement with a timeout clause, as shown in below. In this case we specify the clock period as the timeout, after which the process is to be resumed.

```
clock_gen : process is
begin
  clk <= '1' after T_pw, '0' after 2*T_pw;
  wait for 2*T_pw;
end process clock_gen;
```

If we refer back to the syntax rule for a wait statement shown on page 149, we note that it is legal to write

wait;

This form causes the executing process to suspend for the remainder of the simulation. Although this may at first seem a strange thing to want to do, in practice it is quite useful. One place it is used is in a process whose purpose is to generate stimuli for a simulation. Such a process should generate a sequence of transactions on signals connected to other parts of a model and then stop. For example, the process

```
test_gen : process is
begin
  test0 <= '0' after 10 ns, '1' after 20 ns,
           '0' after 30 ns, '1' after 40 ns;
  test1 <= '0' after 10 ns, '1' after 30 ns;
  wait;
end process test_gen;
```

generates all four possible combinations of values on the signals **test0** and **test1**. If the final wait statement were omitted, the process would cycle forever, repeating the signal assignment statements without suspending, and the simulation would make no progress.

VHDL-87, -93, and -2002

These versions of VHDL do not perform implicit conversion of conditions to **boolean**. Conditions in the **until** clauses of wait statements must yield **boolean** results without conversion.

VHDL-87

Wait statements may not be labeled in VHDL-87.

5.2.4 Delta Delays

Let us now return to the topic of delays in signal assignments. In many of the example signal assignments in previous chapters, we omitted the delay part of waveform elements. This is equivalent to specifying a delay of 0 fs. The value is to be applied to the signal at the current simulation time. However, it is important to note that the signal value does not change as soon as the signal assignment statement is executed. Rather, the assignment schedules a transaction for the signal, which is applied after the process suspends. Thus the process does not see the effect of the assignment until the next time it resumes, even if this is at the same simulation time. For this reason, a delay of 0 fs in a signal assignment is called a *delta delay*.

To understand why delta delays work in this way, it is necessary to review the simulation cycle, introduced in Chapter 1 on page 15. Recall that the simulation cycle consists of two phases: a signal update phase followed by a process execution phase. In the signal update phase, simulation time is advanced to the time of the earliest scheduled transaction, and the values in all transactions scheduled for this time are applied to their corresponding signals. This may cause events to occur on some signals. In the process execution phase, all processes that respond to these events are resumed and execute until they suspend again on wait statements. The simulator then repeats the simulation cycle.

Let us now consider what happens when a process executes a signal assignment statement with delta delay, for example:

```
data <= X"00";
```

Suppose this is executed at simulation time *t* during the process execution phase of the current simulation cycle. The effect of the assignment is to schedule a transaction to put the value X"00" on **data** at time *t*. The transaction is not applied immediately, since the simulator is in the process execution phase. Hence the process continues executing, with **data** unchanged. When all processes have suspended, the simulator starts the next simulation cycle and updates the simulation time. Since the earliest transaction is now at time *t*, simulation time remains unchanged. The simulator now applies the value X"00" in the scheduled transaction to **data**, then resumes any processes that respond to the new value.

Writing a model with delta delays is useful when we are working at a high level of abstraction and are not yet concerned with detailed timing. If all we are interested in is describing the order in which operations take place, delta delays provide a means of ignoring the complications of timing. We have seen this in many of the examples in previous chapters. However, we should note a common pitfall encountered by most beginner VHDL designers when using delta delays: they forget that the process does not see the effect of the assignment immediately. For example, we might write a process that includes the following statements:

```
s <= '1';
...
if s then ...
```

and expect the process to execute the if statement assuming s has the value '1'. We would then spend fruitless hours debugging our model until we remembered that s still has its old value until the next simulation cycle, after the process has suspended.

EXAMPLE 5.9   *Using delta delays to synchronize communication*

The following is an outline of an abstract model of a computer system. The CPU and memory are connected with address and data signals. They synchronize their operation with the **mem_read** and **mem_write** control signals and the **mem_ready** status signal. No delays are specified in the signal assignment statements, so synchronization occurs over a number of delta delay cycles, as shown in Figure 5.1.

```
architecture abstract of computer_system is

    subtype word is bit_vector(31 downto 0);

    signal address : natural;
    signal read_data, write_data : word;
    signal mem_read, mem_write : bit := '0';
    signal mem_ready : bit := '0';

begin

    cpu : process is
      variable instr_reg : word;
      variable PC : natural;
      ...       -- other declarations
    begin
      loop
        address <= PC;
        mem_read <= '1';
        wait until mem_ready;
        instr_reg := read_data;
        mem_read <= '0';
        wait until not mem_ready;
        PC := PC + 4;
        ...       -- execute the instruction
      end loop;
    end process cpu;
```

FIGURE 5.1

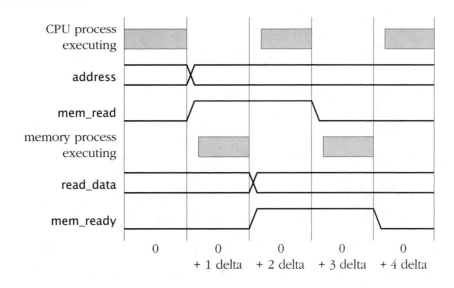

Synchronization over successive delta cycles in a simulation of a read operation between the CPU and memory.

```
memory : process is
  type memory_array is array (0 to 2**14 - 1) of word;
  variable store : memory_array := ( ... );
begin
  wait until mem_read or mem_write;
  if mem_read then
    read_data <= store( address / 4 );
    mem_ready <= '1';
    wait until not mem_read;
    mem_ready <= '0';
  else
    ...        -- perform write access
  end if;
end process memory;

end architecture abstract;
```

When the simulation starts, the CPU process begins executing its statements and the memory suspends. The CPU schedules transactions to assign the next instruction address to the **address** signal and the value '1' to the **mem_read** signal, then suspends. In the next simulation cycle, these signals are updated and the memory process resumes, since it is waiting for an event on **mem_read**. The memory process schedules the data on the **read_data** signal and the value '1' on **mem_ready**, then suspends. In the third cycle, these signals are updated and the CPU process resumes. It schedules the value '0' on **mem_read** and suspends. Then, in the fourth cycle, **mem_read** is updated and the memory process is resumed, scheduling the value '0' on **mem_ready** to complete the handshake. Finally, on the fifth cycle, **mem_ready** is updated and the CPU process resumes and executes the fetched instruction.

5.2.5   Transport and Inertial Delay Mechanisms

So far in our discussion of signal assignments, we have implicitly assumed that there were no pending transactions scheduled for a signal when a signal assignment statement was executed. In many models, particularly at higher levels of abstraction, this will be the case. If, on the other hand, there are pending transactions, the new transactions are merged with them in a way that depends on the *delay mechanism* used in the signal assignment statement. This is an optional part of the signal assignment syntax shown on page 141. The syntax rule for the delay mechanism is

delay_mechanism ⇐ **transport** ⎸ ⟦ **reject** *time*_expression ⟧ **inertial**

A signal assignment with the delay mechanism part omitted is equivalent to specifying **inertial**. We look at the *transport* delay mechanism first, since it is simpler, and then return to the *inertial* delay mechanism.

We use the transport delay mechanism when we are modeling an ideal device with infinite frequency response, in which any input pulse, no matter how short, produces an output pulse. An example of such a device is an ideal transmission line, which transmits all input changes delayed by some amount. A process to model a transmission line with delay 500 ps is

```
transmission_line : process (line_in) is
begin
  line_out <= transport line_in after 500 ps;
end process transmission_line;
```

In this model the output follows any changes in the input, but delayed by 500 ps. If the input changes twice or more within a period shorter than 500 ps, the scheduled transactions are simply queued by the driver until the simulation time at which they are to be applied, as shown in Figure 5.2.

In this example, each new transaction that is generated by a signal assignment statement is scheduled for a simulation time that is later than the pending transactions queued by the driver. The situation gets a little more complex when variable delays are used, since we can schedule a transaction for an earlier time than a pending transaction. The semantics of the transport delay mechanism specify that if there are pending transactions on a driver that are scheduled for a time later than or equal to a new transaction, those later transactions are deleted.

FIGURE 5.2

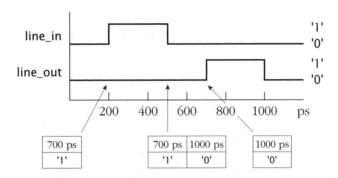

Transactions queued by a driver using transport delay. At time 200 ps the input changes, and a transaction is scheduled for 700 ps. At time 500 ps, the input changes again, and another transaction is scheduled for 1000 ps. This is queued by the driver behind the earlier transaction. When simulation time reaches 700 ps, the first transaction is applied, and the second transaction remains queued. Finally, simulation time reaches 1000 ps, and the final transaction is applied, leaving the driver queue empty.

EXAMPLE 5.10   *An asymmetric delay element using transport delay*

The following is a process that describes the behavior of an asymmetric delay element, with different delay times for rising and falling transitions. The delay for rising transitions is 800 ps and for falling transitions, 500 ps.

```
asym_delay : process (a) is
  constant Tpd_01 : time := 800 ps;
  constant Tpd_10 : time := 500 ps;
begin
  if a then
    z <= transport a after Tpd_01;
  else  -- not a
    z <= transport a after Tpd_10;
  end if;
end process asym_delay;
```

If we apply an input pulse of only 200 ps duration, we would expect the output not to change, since the delayed falling transition should "overtake" the delayed rising transition. If we were simply to add each transition to the driver queue when a signal assignment statement is executed, we would not get this behavior. However, the semantics of the transport delay mechanism produce the desired behavior, as Figure 5.3 shows.

FIGURE 5.3

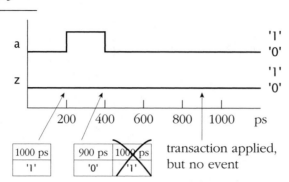

Transactions in a driver using asymmetric transport delay. At time 200 ps the input changes, and a transaction is scheduled for 1000 ps. At time 400 ps, the input changes again, and another transaction is scheduled for 900 ps. Since this is earlier than the pending transaction at 1000 ps, the pending transaction is deleted. When simulation time reaches 900 ps, the remaining transaction is applied, but since the value is '0', no event occurs on the signal.

Most real electronic circuits don't have infinite frequency response, so it is not appropriate to model them using transport delay. In real devices, changing the values of internal nodes and outputs involves moving electronic charge around in the presence of capacitance, inductance and resistance. This gives the device some inertia; it tends to stay in the same state unless we force it by applying inputs for a sufficiently long duration. This is why VHDL includes the inertial delay mechanism, to allow us to model devices that reject input pulses too short to overcome their inertia. Inertial delay is the mechanism used by default in a signal assignment, or we can specify it explicitly by including the word **inertial**.

To explain how inertial delay works, let us first consider a model in which all the signal assignments for a given signal use the same delay value, say, 3 ns, as in the following inverter model:

```
inv : process (a) is
begin
  y <= inertial not a after 3 ns;
end process inv;
```

So long as input events occur more than 3 ns apart, this model does not present any problems. Each time a signal assignment is executed, there are no pending transactions, so a new transaction is scheduled, and the output changes value 3 ns later. However, if an input changes less than 3 ns after the previous change, this represents a pulse less than the propagation delay of the device, so it should be rejected. This behavior is shown at the top of Figure 5.4. In a simple model such as this, we can interpret inertial delay by saying if a signal assignment produces an output pulse shorter than the propagation delay, then the output pulse does not happen.

FIGURE 5.4

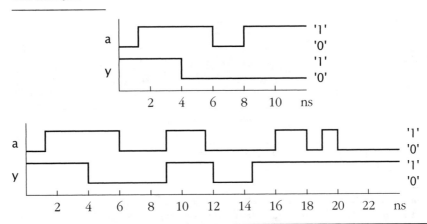

Results of signal assignments using the inertial delay mechanism. In the top waveform, an inertial delay of 3 ns is specified. The input change at time 1 ns is reflected in the output at time 4 ns. The pulse from 6 to 8 ns is less than the propagation delay, so it doesn't affect the output. In the bottom waveform, an inertial delay of 3 ns and a pulse rejection limit of 2 ns are specified. The input changes at 1, 6, 9 and 11.5 ns are all reflected in the output, since they occur greater than 2 ns apart. However, the subsequent input pulses are less than or equal to the pulse rejection limit in length, and so do not affect the output.

Next, let us extend this model by specifying a pulse rejection limit, after the word **reject** in the signal assignment:

```
inv : process (a) is
begin
   y <= reject 2 ns inertial not a after 3 ns;
end process inv;
```

We can interpret this by saying if a signal assignment produces an output pulse shorter than (or equal to) the pulse rejection limit, the output pulse does not happen. In this simple model, so long as input changes occur more than 2 ns apart, they produce output changes 3 ns later, as shown at the bottom of Figure 5.4. Note that the pulse rejection limit specified must be between 0 fs and the delay specified in the signal assignment. Omitting a pulse rejection limit is the same as specifying a limit equal to the delay, and specifying a limit of 0 fs is the same as specifying transport delay.

Now let us look at the full story of inertial delay, allowing for varying the delay time and pulse rejection limit in different signal assignments applied to the same signal. As with transport delay, the situation becomes more complex, and it is best to describe it in terms of deleting transactions from the driver. Those who are unlikely to be writing models that deal with timing at this level of detail may wish to move on to the next section.

An inertially delayed signal assignment involves examining the pending transactions on a driver when adding a new transaction. Suppose a signal assignment schedules a new transaction for time t_{new}, with a pulse rejection limit of t_r. First, any pending transactions scheduled for a time later than or equal to t_{new} are deleted, just as they are when trans-

FIGURE 5.5

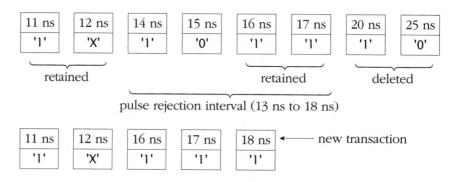

Transactions before (top) and after (bottom) an inertial delay signal assignment. The transactions at 20 and 25 ns are deleted because they are scheduled for later than the new transaction. Those at 11 and 12 ns are retained because they fall before the pulse rejection interval. The transactions at 16 and 17 ns fall within the rejection interval, but they form a run leading up to the new transaction, with the same value as the new transaction; hence they are also retained. The other transactions in the rejection interval are deleted.

port delay is used. Then the new transaction is added to the driver. Second, any pending transactions scheduled in the interval $t_{new} - t_r$ to t_{new} are examined. If there is a run of consecutive transactions immediately preceding the new transaction with the same value as the new transaction, they are kept in the driver. All other transactions in the interval are deleted.

An example will make this clearer. Suppose a driver for signal s contains pending transactions as shown at the top of Figure 5.5, and the process containing the driver executes the following signal assignment statement at time 10 ns:

```
s <= reject 5 ns inertial '1' after 8 ns;
```

The pending transactions after this assignment are shown at the bottom of Figure 5.5.

A further point to note about specifying the delay mechanism in a signal assignment statement is that if a number of waveform elements are included, the specified mechanism only applies to the first element. All the subsequent elements schedule transactions using transport delay. Since the delays for multiple waveform elements must be in ascending order, this means that all of the transactions after the first are just added to the driver transaction queue in the order written.

EXAMPLE 5.11   *An and gate with detailed timing*

A detailed model of a two-input and gate is shown below. The process **gate** implements the logical function of the entity, and the process **delay** implements its detailed timing characteristics using inertially delayed signal assignments. A delay of 1.5 ns is used for rising transitions, and 1.2 ns for falling transitions. When a change on either of the input signals results in a change scheduled for the output, the **delay** process determines the propagation delay to be used. On a rising output transition, spikes of less than 400 ps are rejected, and on a falling or unknown transition, spikes of less than 300 ps are rejected.

```vhdl
library ieee;  use ieee.std_logic_1164.all;

entity and2 is
  port ( a, b : in std_ulogic;  y : out std_ulogic );
end entity and2;

-- ------------------------------------------------

architecture detailed_delay of and2 is

  signal result : std_ulogic;

begin

  gate : process (a, b) is
  begin
    result <= a and b;
  end process gate;

  delay : process (result) is
  begin
    if result then
      y <= reject 400 ps inertial '1' after 1.5 ns;
    elsif not result then
      y <= reject 300 ps inertial '0' after 1.2 ns;
    else
      y <= reject 300 ps inertial 'X' after 500 ps;
    end if;
  end process delay;

end architecture detailed_delay;
```

The final point to make about delay mechanisms is that they can be specified in the conditional and selected forms of signal assignment, as shown by the syntax rules on pages 144 and 145. For example, we can write a sequential conditional assignment using transport delay as:

```vhdl
wire_out <= transport
  wire_in after T_wire_delay when delay_mode = fixed else
  wire_in after delay_lookup("wire_out");
```

Likewise, we can write a sequential conditional assignment using inertial delay as:

```vhdl
with speed_grade select
  z <= reject Tpr inertial
    result after Tpd_std when std_grade,
```

```
        result after Tpd_fast when fast_grade,
        result after Tpd_redhot when redhot_grade;
```

If we include a delay mechanism in a conditional or selected assignment containing multiple waveform elements in the alternatives, the delay mechanism applies to the first waveform element in each alternative, with any subsequent waveform elements using transport delay.

VHDL-87

VHDL-87 does not allow specification of the pulse rejection limit in a delay mechanism. The syntax rule in VHDL-87 is

delay_mechanism ⇐ **transport**

If the delay mechanism is omitted, inertial delay is used, with a pulse rejection limit equal to the delay specified in the waveform element.

5.2.6 Process Statements

We have been using processes quite extensively in examples in this and previous chapters, so we have seen most of the details of how they are written and used. To summarize, let us now look at the formal syntax for a process statement and review the operation of processes. The syntax rule is

process_statement ⇐
    〚 *process*_label : 〛
    process 〚 (*signal*_name 〚 , ₒₒₒ 〛 | **all**) 〛 〚 **is** 〛
        〚 process_declarative_item 〛
    begin
        〚 sequential_statement 〛
    end process 〚 *process*_label 〛 ;

Recall that a process statement is a concurrent statement that can be included in an architecture body to implement all or part of the behavior of a module. The process label identifies the process. While it is optional, it is a good idea to include a label on each process. A label makes it easier to debug a simulation of a system, since most simulators provide a way of identifying a process by its label. Most simulators also generate a default name for a process if we omit the label in the process statement. Having identified a process, we can examine the contents of its variables or set breakpoints at statements within the process.

The declarative items in a process statement may include constant, type and variable declarations, as well as other declarations that we will come to later. Note that ordinary variables may only be declared within process statements, not outside of them. The variables are used to represent the state of the process, as we have seen in the examples. The sequential statements that form the process body may include any of those that we introduced in Chapter 3, plus signal assignment and wait statements. When a process is activated during simulation, it starts executing from the first sequential statement and continues until it reaches the last. It then starts again from the first. This would be an infinite loop, with no progress being made in the simulation, if it were not for the inclusion of wait statements, which suspend process execution until some relevant event occurs. Wait statements are the only statements that take more than zero simulation time to execute. It is only through the execution of wait statements that simulation time advances.

A process may include a sensitivity list in parentheses after the keyword **process**. The sensitivity list identifies a set of signals that the process monitors for events. If the sensitivity list is omitted, the process should include one or more wait statements. On the other hand, if the sensitivity list is included, then the process body cannot include any wait statements. Instead, there is an implicit wait statement, just before the **end process** keywords, that includes the signals listed in the sensitivity list as signals in an **on** clause.

The sensitivity list can be just the reserved word **all** instead of a list of signals, in which case the process is sensitive to all of the signals that it reads as inputs. This form of sensitivity list allows us to write models for combinational logic much more simply. If we change the model to include more inputs, we don't need to remember to revise the sensitivity list of the process.

EXAMPLE 5.12   *A combinational process for a finite-state machine*

One place where assembling the sensitivity list for a combinational process often causes problems is the next-state and output logic for a finite-state machine. The logic has, as inputs, the current state signal and signals whose values determine the next state and the output values. An example is:

```
next_state_logic : process (all) is
begin
  out1 <= '0'; out2 <= '0'; ...
  case current_state is
    when idle =>
      out1 <= '1';
      if in1 and not in2 then
        out2 <= '1';
        next_state <= busy1;
      elsif in1 and in2 then
        next_state <= busy2;
      else
        next_state <= idle;
      end if;
      ...
  end case;
end process next_state;
```

As we revise the finite-state machine, we might include more signals as inputs. Using the reserved word **all** instead of explicitly listing the input signals makes the process easier to write and maintain.

VHDL-87, -93, and -2002

These versions of VHDL do not allow the reserved word **all** in a sensitivity list. Instead, the list of signals to which a process is sensitive must be written out explicitly.

VHDL-87

The keyword **is** may not be included in the header of a process statement in VHDL-87.

5.2.7 Concurrent Signal Assignment Statements

The form of process statement that we have been using is the basis for all behavioral modeling in VHDL, but for simple cases, it can be a little cumbersome and verbose. For this reason, VHDL provides us with some useful shorthand notations for *functional modeling*, that is, behavioral modeling in which the operation to be described is a simple combinatorial transformation of inputs to an output. *Concurrent signal assignment statements* are equivalent to sequential signal assignments contained in process statements. Unlike ordinary signal assignments, concurrent signal assignment statements can be included in the statement part of an architecture body. There are simple, conditional, and selected forms of concurrent signal assignments. The syntax rules are essentially the same as those for the corresponding sequential signal assignments.

Concurrent Simple Signal Assignments

A very common case in function modeling is to write a simple unconditional signal assignment, as in the following example:

```
PC_incr : next_PC <= PC + 4 after 5 ns;
```

At first sight this appears to be an ordinary sequential signal assignment statement, which by rights ought to be inside a process body. However, if it appears as a concurrent statement in an architecture body, it is equivalent to the following process statement:

```
PC_incr : process is
begin
  next_PC <= PC + 4 after 5 ns;
  wait on PC;
end process PC_incr;
```

Looking at the equivalent process shows us something important about the concurrent signal assignment statement, namely, that it is sensitive to the **PC** signal. In fact, a concurrent signal assignment is sensitive to all of the signals mentioned in the waveform. So whenever any of those signals change value, the assignment is reevaluated and a new transaction is scheduled on the driver for the target signal.

EXAMPLE 5.13 *A flipflop with complementary outputs*

We can model a flipflop with a process that assigns to a data output port. If the flipflop also has a complementary data output port, we can use a conditional signal assignment with no condition to drive that output. The entity and architecture body are

```
entity Dff is
  port ( clk, d : in bit; q, q_n : out bit );
end entity Dff;

-----------------------------------------------------

architecture rtl of Dff is
begin
  ff : process (clk) is
  begin
    if clk then
      q <= d;
    end if;
  end process ff;
  q_n <= not q;
end architecture rtl;
```

Concurrent Conditional Signal Assignment

The concurrent conditional signal assignment statement is a shorthand for a collection of simple signal assignments contained in an if statement, which is in turn contained in a process statement. Let us look at some examples and show how each conditional signal assignment can be transformed into an equivalent process statement.

EXAMPLE 5.14 *A multiplexer using a concurrent conditional assignment*

First, here is a functional description of a multiplexer, with four data inputs (d0, d1, d2 and d3), two select inputs (sel0 and sel1) and a data output (z). All of these signals are of type bit.

```
zmux : z <= d0 when not sel1 and not sel0 else
            d1 when not sel1 and     sel0 else
            d2 when     sel1 and not sel0 else
            d3 when     sel1 and     sel0;
```

This statement has exactly the same meaning as the following process statement:

```
zmux : process is
begin
  if not sel1 and not sel0 then
    z <= d0;
```

```
      elsif not sel1 and sel0 then
        z <= d1;
      elsif sel1 and not sel0 then
        z <= d2;
      elsif sel1 and sel0 then
        z <= d3;
      end if;
      wait on d0, d1, d2, d3, sel0, sel1;
    end process zmux;
```

If we look at the equivalent process, we see that the concurrent conditional signal assignment statement is sensitive to all of the signals mentioned in the waveforms and in the conditions. So whenever any of these change value, the assignment is reevaluated and a new transaction is scheduled on the driver for the target signal.

On closer inspection, we note that the last condition is redundant, since the signals **sel0** and **sel1** are of type **bit**. If none of the previous conditions are true, the signal should always be assigned the last waveform. So we can rewrite the example as follows:

```
zmux : z <= d0 when not sel1 and not sel0 else
            d1 when not sel1 and     sel0 else
            d2 when     sel1 and not sel0 else
            d3;
```

The equivalent process is

```
zmux : process is
begin
  if not sel1 and not sel0 then
    z <= d0;
  elsif not sel1 and sel0 then
    z <= d1;
  elsif sel1 and not sel0 then
    z <= d2;
  else
    z <= d3;
  end if;
  wait on d0, d1, d2, d3, sel0, sel1;
end process zmux;
```

Another case that sometimes arises when writing functional models is the need for a process that schedules an initial set of transactions and then does nothing more for the remainder of the simulation.

EXAMPLE 5.15 *Reset signal generation*

An example of "one-shot" activity is the generation of a reset signal. One way of doing this is as follows:

```
reset_gen : reset <= '1', '0' after 200 ns when extended_reset else
                     '1', '0' after 50 ns;
```

The thing to note here is that there are no signals named in any of the waveforms or the conditions (assuming that **extended_reset** is a constant). This means that the statement is executed once when simulation starts, schedules two transactions on re-set and remains quiescent thereafter. The equivalent process is

```
reset_gen : process is
begin
  if extended_reset then
    reset <= '1', '0' after 200 ns;
  else
    reset <= '1', '0' after 50 ns;
  end if;
  wait;
end process reset_gen;
```

Since there are no signals involved, the wait statement has no sensitivity clause. Thus, after the if statement has executed, the process suspends forever.

If we include a delay mechanism specification in a conditional signal assignment state-ment, it is used whichever waveform is chosen. So we might rewrite the model for the asymmetric delay element shown in Example 5.10 as

```
asym_delay : z <= transport a after Tpd_01 when a else
                  a after Tpd_10;
```

In Section 5.2.1 we saw the use of the reserved word **unaffected** as a waveform to specify that the target signal not be changed by an assignment. We can use **unaffected** in a concurrent assignement also.

EXAMPLE 5.16 *A scheduler for a server*

A scheduler selects among requests for a server, but when the server is busy, no re-quest is scheduled. We can use **unaffected** to indicate that there should be no change on the signal representing the selected request, as follows:

```
scheduler :
  request <=
    first_priority_request after scheduling_delay
      when priority_waiting and server_status = ready else
```

```
      first_normal_request after scheduling_delay
        when not priority_waiting and server_status = ready else
      unaffected
        when server_status = busy else
      reset_request after scheduling_delay;
```

The equivalent process is

```
    scheduler : process is
    begin
      if priority_waiting and server_status = ready then
        request <= first_priority_request after scheduling_delay;
      elsif not priority_waiting and server_status = ready then
        request <= first_normal_request after scheduling_delay;
      elsif server_status = busy then
        null;
      else
        request <= reset_request after scheduling_delay;
      end if;
      wait on first_priority_request, priority_waiting,
              server_status, first_normal_request, reset_request;
    end process scheduler;
```

The effect of the **unaffected** waveform is to include a null statement in the equivalent process, causing it to bypass scheduling a transaction when the corresponding condition is true. (Recall that the effect of the null sequential statement is to do nothing.)

VHDL-87

In VHDL-87 the syntax rule for a conditional signal assignment statement is

conditional_signal_assignment ⇐
    name <= ⟦ **transport** ⟧
            ⦃ waveform **when** condition **else** ⦄
            waveform ;

The delay mechanism is restricted to the keyword **transport**, as discussed on page 162. The final waveform may not be conditional. Furthermore, we may not use the keyword **unaffected**. If the required behavior cannot be expressed with these restrictions, we must write a full process statement instead of a conditional signal assignment statement.

Concurrent Selected Signal Assignments

The concurrent selected signal assignment statement is shorthand for a number of simple signal assignments embedded in a case statement, which is in turn contained in a process. Let us look at some examples.

EXAMPLE 5.17 *An ALU using a concurrent selected assignment*

The following concurrent selected signal assignment models an ALU that performs addition, subtraction, logical and, logical or, and pass operations:

```
alu : with alu_function select
        result <= a + b after Tpd    when alu_add |
                                          alu_add_unsigned,
                  a - b after Tpd    when alu_sub |
                                          alu_sub_unsigned,
                  a and b after Tpd when alu_and,
                  a or b after Tpd  when alu_or,
                  a after Tpd        when alu_pass_a;
```

This has the same meaning as the following process statement containing a case statement:

```
alu : process is
begin
  case alu_function is
    when alu_add |
         alu_add_unsigned =>  result <= a + b after Tpd;
    when alu_sub |
         alu_sub_unsigned =>  result <= a - b after Tpd;
    when alu_and            =>  result <= a and b after Tpd;
    when alu_or             =>  result <= a or b after Tpd;
    when alu_pass_a         =>  result <= a after Tpd;
  end case;
  wait on alu_function, a, b;
end process alu;
```

A concurrent selected signal assignment statement is sensitive to all of the signals in the selector expression and in the waveforms. This means that the selected signal assignment for the ALU is always sensitive to **b** and will resume if **b** changes value, even if the value of **alu_function** is **alu_pass_a** and the value of **b** is not used.

Apart from the difference in the equivalent process, the concurrent selected signal assignment is similar to the concurrent conditional assignment. Thus the special waveform **unaffected** can be used to specify that no assignment take place for some values of the selector expression. Also, if a delay mechanism is specified in the statement, that mechanism is used on each sequential signal assignment within the equivalent process.

EXAMPLE 5.18   *A full adder in truth-table form*

We can use a selected signal assignment to express a combinatorial logic function in truth-table form. In the following entity declaration and an architecture body for a full adder, the selected signal assignment statement has, as its selector expression, a bit vector formed by aggregating the input signals. The choices list all possible values of inputs, and for each, the values for the **c_out** and **s** outputs are given.

```
entity full_adder is
  port ( a, b, c_in : bit;  s, c_out : out bit );
end entity full_adder;

----------------------------------------------------

architecture truth_table of full_adder is
begin

  with bit_vector'(a, b, c_in) select
    (c_out, s) <= bit_vector'("00") when "000",
                  bit_vector'("01") when "001",
                  bit_vector'("01") when "010",
                  bit_vector'("10") when "011",
                  bit_vector'("01") when "100",
                  bit_vector'("10") when "101",
                  bit_vector'("10") when "110",
                  bit_vector'("11") when "111";

end architecture truth_table;
```

This example illustrates the most common use of aggregate targets in signal assignments. Note that the type qualification is required in the selector expression to specify the type of the aggregate. The type qualification is needed in the output values to distinguish the bit-vector string literals from character string literals.

We can include the symbol "?" after the reserved word select in a concurrent selected signal assignment to specify matching case statement in the equivalent form, just as we did in the sequential form of the statement. Thus, we could write the assignment

```
with request select?
  grant <= "1000" when "1---",
           "0100" when "01--",
           "0010" when "001-",
           "0001" when "0001",
           "0000" when others;
```

as a concurrent statement in an architecture body.

VHDL-87, -93, and -2002

These versions of VHDL do not provide the matching concurrent selected signal assignment notation.

VHDL-87

In VHDL-87, the delay mechanism is restricted to the keyword **transport**, as discussed on page 162. Furthermore, the keyword **unaffected** may not be used. If the required behavior cannot be expressed without using the keyword **unaffected**, we must write a full process statement instead of a selected signal assignment statement.

5.2.8 Concurrent Assertion Statements

VHDL provides another shorthand process notation, the *concurrent assertion statement*, which can be used in behavioral modeling. As its name implies, a concurrent assertion statement represents a process whose body contains an ordinary sequential assertion statement. The syntax rule is

concurrent_assertion_statement ⇐
    〚 label : 〛
    assert condition
        〚 **report** expression 〛 〚 **severity** expression 〛 ;

This syntax appears to be exactly the same as that for a sequential assertion statement, but the difference is that it may appear as a concurrent statement. The optional label on the statement serves the same purpose as that on a process statement: to provide a way of referring to the statement during simulation or synthesis. The process equivalent to a concurrent assertion contains a sequential assertion with the same condition, report clause and severity clause. The sequential assertion is then followed by a wait statement whose sensitivity list includes the signals mentioned in the condition expression. Thus the effect of the concurrent assertion statement is to check that the condition holds true each time any of the signals mentioned in the condition change value. Concurrent assertions provide a very compact and useful way of including timing and correctness checks in a model.

EXAMPLE 5.19   *A set/reset flipflop with usage check*

We can use concurrent assertion statements to check for correct use of a set/reset flipflop, with two inputs s and r and two outputs q and q_n, all of type **bit**. The requirement for use is that s and r are not both '1' at the same time. The entity and architecture body are

```
entity S_R_flipflop is
  port ( s, r : in bit;  q, q_n : out bit );
end entity S_R_flipflop;
```

```
-----------------------------------------------------------
architecture functional of S_R_flipflop is

begin

  q <= '1' when s else
       '0' when r;

  q_n <= '0' when s else
         '1' when r;

  check : assert not (s and r)
            report "Incorrect use of S_R_flip_flop: " &
                   "s and r both '1'";

end architecture functional;
```

The first and second concurrent statements implement the functionality of the model. The third checks for correct use and is resumed when either **s** or **r** changes value, since these are the signals mentioned in the Boolean condition. If both of the signals are '1', an assertion violation is reported. The equivalent process for the concurrent assertion is

```
check : process is
begin
  assert not (s  and r)
    report "Incorrect use of S_R_flip_flop: " &
           "s and r both '1'";
  wait on s, r;
end process check;
```

5.2.9   Entities and Passive Processes

We complete this section on behavioral modeling by returning to declarations of entities. We can include certain kinds of concurrent statements in an entity declaration, to monitor use and operation of the entity. The extended syntax rule for an entity declaration that shows this is

entity_declaration ⇐
    entity identifier **is**
        ⟦ **port** (*port*_interface_list) ; ⟧
        { entity_declarative_item }
    ⟦ **begin**
        { concurrent_assertion_statement
        ⏐ *passive*_concurrent_procedure_call_statement
        ⏐ *passive*_process_statement } ⟧
    end ⟦ **entity** ⟧ ⟦ identifier ⟧ ;

The concurrent statements included in an entity declaration must be *passive*; that is, they may not affect the operation of the entity in any way. A concurrent assertion statement meets this requirement, since it simply tests a condition whenever events occur on signals to which it is sensitive. A process statement is passive if it contains no signal assignment statements or calls to procedures containing signal assignment statements. Such a process can be used to trace events that occur on the entity's inputs. We will describe the remaining alternative, concurrent procedure call statements, when we discuss procedures in Chapter 6. A concurrent procedure call is passive if the procedure called contains no signal assignment statements or calls to procedures containing signal assignment statements.

EXAMPLE 5.20   *A revised set/reset flipflop with usage check*

We can rewrite the entity declaration for the set/reset flipflop of Example 5.19 as shown below, using a concurrent assertion statement for the usage check. If we do this, the check is included for every possible implementation of the flipflop and does not need to be included in the corresponding architecture bodies.

```
entity S_R_flipflop is
  port ( s, r : in bit;  q, q_n : out bit );

begin

  check : assert not (s and r)
            report "Incorrect use of S_R_flip_flop: "
                   "s and r both '1'";

end entity S_R_flipflop;
```

EXAMPLE 5.21   *A ROM that traces read operations*

The following entity declaration for a read-only memory (ROM) includes a passive process, **trace_reads**, that is sensitive to changes on the **enable** port. When the value of the port changes to '1', the process reports a message tracing the time and address of the read operation. The process does not affect the course of the simulation in any way, since it does not include any signal assignments.

```
entity ROM is
  port ( address : in natural;
         data : out bit_vector(0 to 7);
         enable : in bit );

begin

  trace_reads : process (enable) is
  begin
    if enable then
      report "ROM read at time " & to_string(now)
```

```
                      & " from address " & to_string(address);
               end if;
          end process trace_reads;

     end entity ROM;
```

5.3   Structural Descriptions

A structural description of a system is expressed in terms of subsystems interconnected by
signals. Each subsystem may in turn be composed of an interconnection of sub-
subsystems, and so on, until we finally reach a level consisting of primitive components,
described purely in terms of their behavior. Thus the top-level system can be thought of
as having a hierarchical structure. In this section, we look at how to write structural architecture bodies to express this hierarchical organization.

   We have seen earlier in this chapter that the concurrent statements in an architecture
body describe an implementation of an entity interface. In order to write a structural implementation, we must use a concurrent statement called a *component instantiation statement*, the simplest form of which is governed by the syntax rule

> component_instantiation_statement ⇐
>   *instantiation*_label :
>   **entity** *entity*_name 〚 (*architecture*_identifier) 〛
>   〚 **port map** (port_association_list) 〛 ;

This form of component instantiation statement performs *direct instantiation* of an
entity. We can think of component instantiation as creating a copy of the named entity,
with the corresponding architecture body substituted for the component instance. The
port map specifies which ports of the entity are connected to which signals in the enclosing architecture body. The simplified syntax rule for a port association list is

> port_association_list ⇐
>   (〚 *port*_name => 〛 (*signal*_name ▯ expression ▯ **open**)) { , … }

Each element in the association list associates one port of the entity either with one
signal of the enclosing architecture body or with the value of an expression, or leaves the
port unassociated, as indicated by the keyword **open**.

   Let us look at some examples to illustrate component instantiation statements and the
association of ports with signals. Suppose we have an entity declared as

```
entity DRAM_controller is
  port ( rd, wr, mem : in bit;
         ras, cas, we, ready : out bit  );
end entity DRAM_controller;
```

and a corresponding architecture called **fpld**. We might create an instance of this entity as
follows:

```
main_mem_controller : entity work.DRAM_controller(fpld)
  port map ( cpu_rd, cpu_wr, cpu_mem,
                mem_ras, mem_cas, mem_we, cpu_rdy );
```

In this example, the name **work** refers to the current working library in which entities and architecture bodies are stored. We return to the topic of libraries in the next section. The port map of this example lists the signals in the enclosing architecture body to which the ports of the copy of the entity are connected. *Positional association* is used: each signal listed in the port map is connected to the port at the same position in the entity declaration. So the signal **cpu_rd** is connected to the port **rd**, the signal **cpu_wr** is connected to the port **wr** and so on.

One of the problems with positional association is that it is not immediately clear which signals are being connected to which ports. Someone reading the description must refer to the entity declaration to check the order of the ports in the entity interface. A better way of writing a component instantiation statement is to use *named association*, as shown in the following example:

```
main_mem_controller : entity work.DRAM_controller(fpld)
  port map ( rd => cpu_rd, wr => cpu_wr,
                mem => cpu_mem, ready => cpu_rdy,
                ras => mem_ras, cas => mem_cas, we => mem_we );
```

Here, each port is explicitly named along with the signal to which it is connected. The order in which the connections are listed is immaterial. The advantage of this approach is that it is immediately obvious to the reader how the entity is connected into the structure of the enclosing architecture body.

In the preceding example we have explicitly named the architecture body to be used corresponding to the entity instantiated. However, the syntax rule for component instantiation statements shows this to be optional. If we wish, we can omit the specification of the architecture body, in which case the one to be used may be chosen when the overall model is processed for simulation, synthesis or some other purpose. At that time, if no other choice is specified, the most recently analyzed architecture body is selected. We return to the topic of analyzing models in the next section.

EXAMPLE 5.22   *A structural model for a two-digit counter*

In Example 5.5 we looked at a behavioral model of an edge-triggered flipflop. We can use the flipflop as the basis of a 4-bit edge-triggered register, described by the following entity declaration and structural architecture body.

```
entity reg4 is
  port ( clk, clr, d0, d1, d2, d3 : in bit;
          q0, q1, q2, q3 : out bit );
end entity reg4;
```

```
architecture struct of reg4 is
begin

  bit0 : entity work.edge_triggered_Dff(behavioral)
    port map (d0, clk, clr, q0);
  bit1 : entity work.edge_triggered_Dff(behavioral)
    port map (d1, clk, clr, q1);
  bit2 : entity work.edge_triggered_Dff(behavioral)
    port map (d2, clk, clr, q2);
  bit3 : entity work.edge_triggered_Dff(behavioral)
    port map (d3, clk, clr, q3);

end architecture struct;
```

We can use the register entity, along with other entities, as part of a structural architecture for the two-digit decimal counter represented by the schematic of Figure 5.6.

FIGURE 5.6

A schematic for a two-digit counter using the reg4 *entity.*

Suppose a digit is represented as a bit vector of length four, described by the subtype declaration

```
subtype digit is bit_vector(3 downto 0);
```

An entity declaration for the counter, along with an outline of the structural architecture body, are:

```
entity counter is
  port ( clk, clr : in bit;
          q0, q1 : out digit );
end entity counter;

-------------------------------------------------

architecture registered of counter is

  signal current_val0, current_val1, next_val0, next_val1 : digit;

begin

  val0_reg : entity work.reg4(struct)
    port map ( d0 => next_val0(0), d1 => next_val0(1),
                d2 => next_val0(2), d3 => next_val0(3),
                q0 => current_val0(0), q1 => current_val0(1),
                q2 => current_val0(2), q3 => current_val0(3),
                clk => clk, clr => clr );

  val1_reg : entity work.reg4(struct)
    port map ( d0 => next_val1(0), d1 => next_val1(1),
                d2 => next_val1(2), d3 => next_val1(3),
                q0 => current_val1(0), q1 => current_val1(1),
                q2 => current_val1(2), q3 => current_val1(3),
                clk => clk, clr => clr );

  incr0 : entity work.add_1(boolean_eqn) ...;

  incr1 : entity work.add_1(boolean_eqn) ...;

  buf0 : entity work.buf4(basic) ...;

  buf1 : entity work.buf4(basic) ...;

end architecture registered;
```

This example illustrates a number of important points about component instances and port maps. First, the two component instances val0_reg and val1_reg are both instances of the same entity/architecture pair. This means that two distinct copies of the architecture **struct** of **reg4** are created, one for each of the component instances. We return to this point when we discuss the topic of elaboration in the next section. Second, in each of the port maps, ports of the entity being instantiated are associated with separate elements of array signals. This is allowed, since a signal that is of a composite type, such as an array, can be treated as a collection of signals, one per element.

Third, some of the signals connected to the component instances are signals declared within the enclosing architecture body, **registered**, whereas the **clk** signal is a port of the entity **counter**. This again illustrates the point that within an architecture body, the ports of the corresponding entity are treated as signals.

We saw in the above example that we can associate separate ports of an instance with individual elements of an actual signal of a composite type, such as an array or record type. If an instance has a composite port, we can write associations the other way around; that is, we can associate separate actual signals with individual elements of the port. This is sometimes called *subelement association*. For example, if the instance **DMA_buffer** has a port **status** of type **FIFO_status**, declared as

```
type FIFO_status is record
    nearly_full, nearly_empty, full, empty : bit;
  end record FIFO_status;
```

we could associate a signal with each element of the port as follows:

```
DMA_buffer : entity work.FIFO
  port map ( ...,
              status.nearly_full => start_flush,
              status.nearly_empty => end_flush,
              status.full => DMA_buffer_full,
              status.empty => DMA_buffer_empty, ... );
```

This illustrates two important points about subelement association. First, all elements of the composite port must be associated with an actual signal. We cannot associate some elements and leave the rest unassociated. Second, all of the associations for a particular port must be grouped together in the association list, without any associations for other ports among them.

We can use subelement association for ports of an array type by writing an indexed element name on the left side of an association. Furthermore, we can associate a slice of the port with an actual signal that is a one-dimensional array, as the following example shows.

EXAMPLE 5.23   *Using subelement association for bus connections*

Suppose we have a register entity, declared as follows. The ports **d** and **q** are arrays of bits.

```
entity reg is
  port ( d : in bit_vector(7 downto 0);
         q : out bit_vector(7 downto 0);
         clk : in bit );
end entity reg;
```

The architecture body for a microprocessor, outlined below, instantiates this entity as the program status register (PSR). Individual bits within the register represent condition and interrupt flags, and the field from bit 6 down to bit 4 represents the current interrupt priority level.

```
architecture RTL of microprocessor is

  signal interrupt_req : bit;
  signal interrupt_level : bit_vector(2 downto 0);
  signal carry_flag, negative_flag,
         overflow_flag, zero_flag : bit;
  signal program_status : bit_vector(7 downto 0);
  signal clk_PSR : bit;
  ...

begin

  PSR : entity work.reg
    port map ( d(7) => interrupt_req,
               d(6 downto 4) => interrupt_level,
               d(3) => carry_flag,     d(2) => negative_flag,
               d(1) => overflow_flag,  d(0) => zero_flag,
               q => program_status,
               clk => clk_PSR );

  ...

end architecture RTL;
```

In the port map of the instance, subelement association is used for the input port d to connect individual elements of the port with separate actual signals of the architecture. A slice of the port is connected to the **interrupt_level** signal. The output port q, on the other hand, is associated wholly with the bit-vector signal **program_status**.

We may also use subelement association for a port that is of an unconstrained or partially constrained array type whose top-level index bounds are not defined. The index bounds of the port are determined by the least and greatest index values used in the association list, and the index range direction is determined by the port type. For example, suppose we declare an and gate entity:

```
entity and_gate is
  port ( i : in bit_vector;  y : out bit );
end entity and_gate;
```

and a number of signals:

```
signal serial_select, write_en, bus_clk, serial_wr : bit;
```

We can instantiate the entity as a three-input and gate:

```
serial_write_gate : entity work.and_gate
  port map ( i(1) => serial_select,
             i(2) => write_en,
             i(3) => bus_clk,
             y => serial_wr );
```

Since the input port i is unconstrained, the index values in the subelement associations determine the index bounds for this instance. The least value is one and the greatest value is three. The port type is **bit_vector**, which has an ascending index range. Thus, the index range for the port in the instance is an ascending range from one to three.

This method of determining index ranges also applies to subelements with undefined index bounds. For example, given a type

```
type bv_pair is array (1 to 2) of bit_vector;
```

and a port declared in an entity as

```
entity ent3 is
  port ( p : in bv_pair );
end entity ent3;
```

we can write an instance of the entity:

```
signal s1, s2 : bit;
signal sv1, sv2 : bit_vector(4 to 7);
...

inst3 : entity work.ent3
  port map ( p(1)(0) => s1, p(1)(1 to 4) => sv1,
             p(2)(0) => s2, p(2)(1 to 4) => sv2 );
```

Here, the index range for the top level of **p** is 1 to 2, determined from the subtype **bv_pair**. However, for the elements, the subtype index range is not defined, so the index range for **p** comes from the formal element and slice names. Combining these effects, the index ranges for **p** are 1 to 2 for the top level, and 0 to 4 for the elements. Note that the index range determined for the two elements **p(1)** and **p(2)** must be the same. It would be illegal to write the instance as:

```
signal s1, s2 : bit;
signal sv1, sv2 : bit_vector(4 to 7);
...

inst3 : entity work.ent3
  port map ( p(1)(0) => s1, p(1)(1 to 4) => sv1,
             p(2)(15) => s2, p(2)(11 to 14) => sv2 ); -- illegal
```

since that would imply two different index ranges: 0 to 4 for **p(1)** and 11 to 15 for **p(2)**. An array must have the same index ranges for all elements.

The syntax rule for a port association list shows that a port of a component instance may be associated with an expression instead of a signal. There are two possibilities for this case. First, if the expression is *globally static*, the value of the expression is used as a constant value for the port throughout the simulation. For an expression to be globally static, we must be able to determine the value from constants defined when the model is elaborated. So, for example, the expression must not include references to any signals. If real hardware is synthesized from the model, the port of the component instance would be tied to a fixed value determined by the expression. Association with an expression of this form is useful when we have an entity provided as part of a library, but we do not need to use all of the functionality provided by the entity.

EXAMPLE 5.24   *Using a four-input multiplexer as a two-input multiplexer*

Given a four-input multiplexer described by the entity declaration

```
entity mux4 is
  port ( i0, i1, i2, i3, sel0, sel1 : in bit;
         z : out bit );
end entity mux4;
```

we can use it as a two-input multiplexer by instantiating it as follows:

```
a_mux : entity work.mux4
  port map ( sel0 => select_line, i0 => line0, i1 => line1,
             z => result_line,
             sel1 => '0', i2 => '1', i3 => '1' );
```

For this component instance, the high-order select bit is fixed at '0', ensuring that only one of **line0** or **line1** is passed to the output. We have also followed the practice, recommended for many logic families, of tying unused inputs to a fixed value, in this case '1'.

In the second case of association with an expression, the expression is not static, but instead involves the values of signals. This allows us to include a small amount of functional logic in a port map, and avoids the need to express the logic with a separate assignment statement and an intermediate signal. If the expression is not static, the port association is defined to be equivalent to association with an anonymous signal that is the target of a signal assignment with the expression on the right-hand side.

EXAMPLE 5.25   *Including select logic in a port map*

Suppose an I/O controller connected to a CPU bus is to be enabled when bus control signals indicate a read from I/O address space and the bus address matches the controller's address. We can include the select logic in the port map for the controller instance:

```
io_ctrl_1 : entity work.io_controller(rtl)
  port map ( en => rd_en and io_sel and addr ?= io_base,
             ... );
```

This is a much more succinct way of expressing the model than the equivalent:

```
signal en_tmp : std_ulogic;
...

en_tmp <= rd_en and io_sel and addr ?= io_base;

io_ctrl_1 : entity work.io_controller(rtl)
  port map ( en => en_tmp,
             ... );
```

Some entities may be designed to allow inputs to be left open by specifying a default value for a port. When the entity is instantiated, we can specify that a port is to be left open by using the keyword **open** in the port association list, as shown in the syntax rule on page 174.

EXAMPLE 5.26 *And-or-invert with an unconnected input*

The and_or_inv entity declaration on page 137 includes a default value of '1' for each of its input ports, as again shown here:

```
entity and_or_inv is
  port ( a1, a2, b1, b2 : in bit := '1';
         y : out bit );
end entity and_or_inv;
```

We can write a component instantiation to perform the function **not** ((A **and** B) **or** C) using this entity as follows:

```
f_cell : entity work.and_or_inv
  port map ( a1 => A, a2 => B, b1 => C, b2 => open, y => F );
```

The port b2 is left open, so it assumes the default value '1' specified in the entity declaration.

There is some similarity between specifying a default value for an input port and associating an input port with a globally static expression. In both cases we must be able to determine the expression's value when the model is elaborated. The difference is that a default value is only used if the port is left open when the entity is instantiated, whereas association with a globally static expression specifies that the expression value is to be used to drive the port for the entire simulation or life of the component instance. If a port is declared with a default value and then associated with an expression, the expression value is used, overriding the default value.

Output and bidirectional ports may also be left unassociated using the **open** keyword, provided they are not of an unconstrained or partially constrained composite type. If a port of mode **out** or **buffer** is left open, any value driven by the entity is ignored. If a port of mode **inout** is left open, the value used internally by the entity (the *effective value*) is the value that it drives on to the port.

A final point to make about unassociated ports is that we can simply omit a port from a port association list to specify that it remain open. So, given an entity declared as follows:

```
entity and3 is
  port ( a, b, c : in bit := '1';
         z, not_z : out bit);
end entity and3;
```

the component instantiation

```
g1 : entity work.and3 port map ( a => s1, b => s2, not_z => ctrl1 );
```

has the same meaning as

```
g1 : entity work.and3 port map ( a => s1, b => s2, not_z => ctrl1,
                                 c => open, z => open );
```

The difference is that the second version makes it clear that the unused ports are deliberately left open, rather than being accidentally overlooked in the design process. This is useful information for someone reading the model.

VHDL-87, -93, and -2002

These earlier versions of VHDL do not allow a non-static expression in a port map. Instead, we must write the equivalent intermediate signal declaration and assignment explicitly.

VHDL-87 and VHDL-93

VHDL-87 and VHDL-93 impose a number of restrictions on how **buffer**-mode ports may be interconnected with other ports in structural designs. First, if the actual object associated with a buffer port of a component instance is a port of the enclosing entity, it must also be a **buffer** port. Second, if we associate a **buffer** as an actual object with some formal port of a component instance, the formal port must be of mode **in** or **buffer**. It may not be a port of mode **out**. There are also restrictions on the number of sources contributing to a **buffer** port or to a signal that is associated with a **buffer** port. These restrictions severely limit the uses of **buffer** ports, so they are not commonly used in VHDL-87 or VHDL-93.

VHDL-87

VHDL-87 does not allow direct instantiation. Instead, we must declare a *component* with a similar interface to the entity, instantiate the component and *bind* each component instance to the entity and an associated architecture body. Component declarations and binding are described in Chapter 12.

VHDL-87 does not allow association of an expression with a port in a port map. However, we can achieve a similar effect by declaring a signal, initializing it to the value of the expression and associating the signal with the port. For example, if we declare two signals

```
signal tied_0 : bit := '0';
signal tied_1 : bit := '1';
```

we can rewrite the port map shown in Example 5.24 as

```
port map ( sel0 => select_line, i0 => line0, i1 => line1,
           z => result_line,
           sel1 => tied_0, i2 => tied_1, i3 => tied_1 );
```

5.4   Design Processing

Now that we have seen how a design may be described in terms of entities, architectures, component instantiations, signals and processes, it is time to take a practical view. A VHDL description of a design is usually used to simulate the design and perhaps to synthesize the hardware. This involves processing the description using computer-based tools to create a simulation program to run or a hardware net-list to build. Both simulation and synthesis require two preparatory steps: analysis and elaboration. Simulation then involves executing the elaborated model, whereas synthesis involves creating a net-list of primitive circuit elements that perform the same function as the elaborated model. In this section, we look at the analysis, elaboration and execution operations introduced in Chapter 1. We will leave a discussion of synthesis to Chapter 14.

5.4.1   Analysis

The first step in processing a design is to analyze the VHDL descriptions. A correct description must conform to the rules of syntax and semantics that we have discussed at length. An *analyzer* is a tool that verifies this. If a description fails to meet a rule, the analyzer provides a message indicating the location of the problem and which rule was broken. We can then correct the error and retry the analysis. Another task performed by the analyzer in most VHDL systems is to translate the description into an internal form more easily processed by the remaining tools. Whether such a translation is done or not, the analyzer places each successfully analyzed description into a *design library*.

A complete VHDL description usually consists of a number of entity declarations and their corresponding architecture bodies. Each of these is called a *design unit*. Organizing a design as a hierarchy of modules, rather than as one large flat design, is good engineering practice. It makes the description much easier to understand and manage.

The analyzer analyzes each design unit separately and places the internal form into the library as a *library unit*. If a unit being analyzed uses another unit, the analyzer extracts information about the other unit from the library to check that the unit is used correctly. For example, if an architecture body instantiates an entity, the analyzer needs to check the number, type and mode of ports of the entity to make sure it is instantiated correctly. To do this, it requires that the entity be previously analyzed and stored in the library. Thus, we see that there are dependency relations between library units in a complete description that enforce an order of analysis of the original design units.

To clarify this point, we divide design units into *primary units*, which include entity declarations, and *secondary units*, which include architecture bodies. There are other kinds of design units in each class, which we come to in later chapters. A primary unit defines the external view or interface to a module, whereas a secondary unit describes an implementation of the module. Thus the secondary unit depends on the corresponding primary unit and must be analyzed after the primary unit has been analyzed. In addition, a library unit may draw upon the facilities defined in some other primary unit, as in the case of an architecture body instantiating some other entity. In this case, there is a further dependency between the secondary unit and the referenced primary unit. Thus we may build up a network of dependencies of units upon primary units. Analysis must be done in such an order that a unit is analyzed before any of its dependents. Furthermore, whenever we change and reanalyze a primary unit, all of the dependent units must also be reanalyzed. Note, however, that there is no way in which any unit can be dependent upon a secondary unit; that is what makes a secondary unit "secondary." This may seem rather complicated, and indeed, in a large design, the dependency relations can form a complex network. For this reason, most VHDL systems include tools to manage the dependencies, automatically reanalyzing units where necessary to ensure that an outdated unit is never used.

EXAMPLE 5.27   *Dependencies in the counter model*

The structural architecture of the **counter** module, described in Example 5.22, leads to the network of dependencies shown in Figure 5.7. One possible order of compilation for this set of design units is

> entity **edge_triggered_Dff**
> architecture **behav** of **edge_triggered_Dff**
>
> entity **reg4**
> architecture **struct** of reg4
>
> entity **add_1**
> architecture **boolean_eqn** of **add_1**
>
> entity **buf4**
> architecture **basic** of **buf4**

FIGURE 5.7

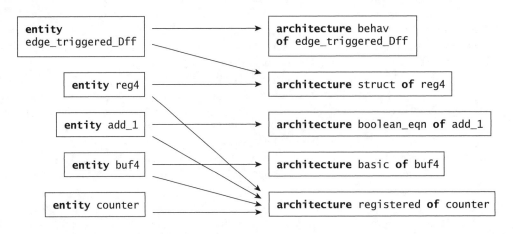

The dependency network for the counter module. The arrows point from a primary unit to a dependent secondary unit.

entity **counter**
architecture **registered** of **counter**

In this order, each primary unit is analyzed immediately before its corresponding secondary unit, and each primary unit is analyzed before any secondary unit that instantiates it. This is not the only possible order. Another alternative is to analyze all of the entity declarations first, then analyze the architecture bodies in arbitrary order.

5.4.2 Design Libraries and Contexts

So far, we have not actually said what a design library is, other than that it is where library units are stored. Indeed, this is all that is defined by the VHDL language specification, since to go further is to enter into the domain of the host operating system under which the VHDL tools are run. Some systems may use a database to store analyzed units, whereas others may simply use a directory in the host file system as the design library. The documentation for each VHDL tool suite indicates what we need to know about how the suite deals with design libraries.

A VHDL tool suite must also provide some means of using a number of separate design libraries. When a design is analyzed, we nominate one of the libraries as the *working library*, and the analyzed design is stored in this library. We use the special library name **work** in our VHDL models to refer to the current working library. We have seen examples of this in this chapter's component instantiation statements, in which a previously analyzed entity is instantiated in an architecture body.

If we need to access library units stored in other libraries, we refer to the libraries as *resource libraries*. We do this by including a *library clause* immediately preceding a design unit that accesses the resource libraries. The syntax rule for a library clause is library_clause ⇐ **library** identifier ⟨ , ... ⟩ ;

The identifiers are used by the analyzer and the host operating system to locate the design libraries, so that the units contained in them can be used in the description being analyzed. The exact way that the identifiers are used varies between different tool suites and is not defined by the VHDL language specification. Note that we do not need to include the library name **work** in a library clause; the current working library is automatically available.

EXAMPLE 5.28   *Using library cells*

Suppose we are working on part of a large design project code-named Wasp, and we are using standard cell parts supplied by Widget Designs, Inc. Our system administrator has loaded the design library for the Widget cells in a directory called /local/widget/cells in our workstation file system, and our project leader has set up another design library in /projects/wasp/lib for some in-house cells we need to use. We consult the manual for our VHDL analyzer and use operating system commands to set up the appropriate mapping from the identifiers **widget_cells** and **wasp_lib** to these library directories. We can then instantiate entities from these libraries, along with entities we have previously analyzed, into our own working library, as follows:

```
library widget_cells, wasp_lib;

architecture cell_based of filter is

  -- declaration of signals, etc
  ...

begin

  clk_pad : entity wasp_lib.in_pad
    port map ( i => clk, z => filter_clk );

  accum : entity widget_cells.reg32
    port map ( en => accum_en, clk => filter_clk, d => sum,
               q => result );

  alu : entity work.adder
    port map ( a => alu_op1, b => alu_op2, y => sum, c => carry );

  -- other component instantiations
  ...

end architecture cell_based;
```

If we need to make frequent reference to library units from a design library, we can include a use clause in our model to avoid having to write the library name each time. The simplified syntax rules are

use_clause ⇐ **use** selected_name ⟨ , ... ⟩ ;

selected_name ⇐ name . ((identifier ▯ **all**))

If we include a use clause with a library name as the prefix of the selected name (preceding the dot), and a library unit name from the library as the suffix (after the dot), the library unit is made *directly visible*. This means that subsequent references in the model to the library unit need not prefix the library unit name with the library name. For example, we might precede the architecture body in the previous example with the following library and use clauses:

```
library widget_cells, wasp_lib;

use widget_cells.reg32;
```

This makes `reg32` directly visible within the architecture body, so we can omit the library name when referring to it in component instantiations; for example:

```
accum : entity reg32
  port map ( en => accum_en, clk => filter_clk, d => sum,
             q => result );
```

If we include the keyword **all** in a use clause, all of the library units within the named library are made directly visible. For example, if we wanted to make all of the Wasp project library units directly visible, we might precede a library unit with the use clause

```
use wasp_lib.all;
```

Care should be taken when using this form of use clause with several libraries at once. If two libraries contain library units with the same name, VHDL avoids ambiguity by making neither of them directly visible. The solution is either to use the full selected name to refer to the particular library unit required, or to include in use clauses only those library units really needed in a model.

Use clauses can also be included to make names from packages directly visible. We will return to this idea when we discuss packages in detail in Chapter 7.

5.4.3   Elaboration

Once all of the units in a design hierarchy have been analyzed, the design hierarchy can be *elaborated*. The effect of elaboration is to "flesh out" the hierarchy, producing a collection of processes interconnected by *nets*. This is done by substituting the contents of an architecture body for every instantiation of its corresponding entity. Each net in the elaborated design consists of a signal and the ports of the substituted architecture bodies to which the signal is connected. (Recall that a port of an entity is treated as a signal within a corresponding architecture body.) Let us outline how elaboration proceeds, illustrating it step by step with an example.

Elaboration is a recursive operation, started at the topmost entity in a design hierarchy. We use the **counter** design from Example 5.22 as our topmost entity. The first step is to create the ports of the entity. Next, an architecture body corresponding to the entity is chosen. If we do not explicitly specify which architecture body to choose, the most recently analyzed architecture body is used. For this illustration, we use the architecture registered. This architecture body is then elaborated, first by creating any signals that it declares, then by elaborating each of the concurrent statements in its body. Figure 5.8 shows the **counter** design with the signals created.

The concurrent statements in this architecture are all component instantiation statements. Each of them is elaborated by creating new instances of the ports specified by the instantiated entity and joining them into the nets represented by the signals with which they are associated. Then the internal structure of the specified architecture body of the instantiated entity is copied in place of the component instance, as shown in Figure 5.9. The architectures substituted for the instances of the **add_1** and **buf4** entities are both behavioral, consisting of processes that read the input ports and make assignments to the output ports. Hence elaboration is complete for these architectures. However, the architecture **struct**, substituted for each of the instances of **reg4**, contains further signals and component instances. Hence they are elaborated in turn, producing the structure shown

FIGURE 5.8

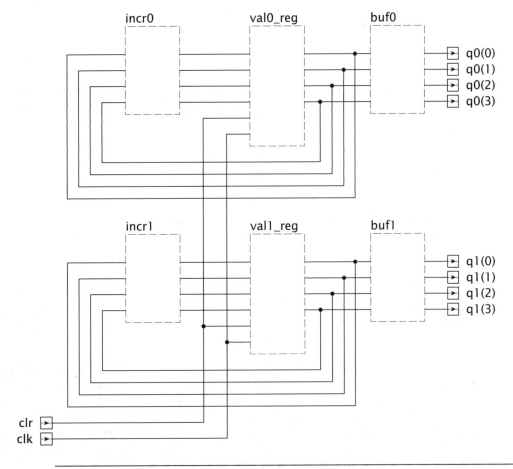

The first stage of elaboration of the **counter** *entity. The ports have been created, the architecture* **registered** *selected and the signals of the architecture created.*

FIGURE 5.9

The counter design further elaborated. Behavioral architectures, consisting of just processes, have been substituted for instances of the **add_1** *and* **buf4** *entities. A structural architecture has been substituted for each instance of the* **reg4** *entity.*

in Figure 5.10 for each instance. We have now reached a stage where we have a collection of nets comprising signals and ports, and processes that sense and drive the nets.

Each process statement in the design is elaborated by creating new instances of the variables it declares and by creating a driver for each of the signals for which it has signal assignment statements. The drivers are joined to the nets containing the signals they drive. For example, the **storage** process within **bit0** of **val0_reg** has a driver for the port **q**, which is part of the net based on the signal **current_val0(0)**.

FIGURE 5.10

A register within the counter structure elaborated down to architectures that consist only of processes and signals.

Once all of the component instances and all of the resulting processes have been elaborated, elaboration of the design hierarchy is complete. We now have a fully fleshed-out version of the design, consisting of a number of process instances and a number of nets connecting them. Note that there are several distinct instances of some of the processes, one for each use of an entity containing the process, and each process instance has its own distinct version of the process variables. Each net in the elaborated design consists of a signal, a collection of ports associated with it and a driver within a process instance.

5.4.4   Execution

Now that we have an elaborated design hierarchy, we can execute it to simulate operation of the system it describes. Much of our previous discussion of VHDL statements was in terms of what happens when they are executed, so we do not go over statement execution again here. Instead, we concentrate on the simulation algorithm introduced in Chapter 1.

Recall that the simulation algorithm consists of an initialization phase followed by a repeated simulation cycle. The simulator keeps a clock to measure out the passage of simulation time. In the initialization phase, the simulation time is set to zero. Each driver is initialized to drive its signal with the initial value declared for the signal or the default value for the signal if no initial value was declared. Next, each of the process instances in the design is started and executes the sequential statements in its body. We usually write a

model so that at least some of these initial statements schedule some transactions to get
the simulation under way, then suspend by executing a wait statement. When all of the
process instances have suspended, initialization is complete and the simulator can start
the first simulation cycle.

At the beginning of a simulation cycle, there may be a number of drivers with transactions scheduled on them and a number of process instances that have scheduled
timeouts. The first step in the simulation cycle is to advance the simulation time clock to
the earliest time at which a transaction or process timeout has been scheduled. Second,
all of the transactions scheduled for this time are performed, updating the corresponding
signals and possibly causing events on those signals. Third, all process instances that are
sensitive to any of these events are resumed. In addition, process instances whose timeout
expires at the current simulation time are resumed during this step. All of these processes
execute their sequential statements, possibly scheduling more transactions or timeouts,
and eventually suspend again by executing wait statements. When they have all suspended, the simulation cycle is done and the next cycle can start. If there are no more transactions or timeouts scheduled, or if simulation time reaches **time'high** (the largest
representable time value), the simulation is complete.

Describing the operation of a simulator in this way is a little like setting a play in a
theater without any seats—nobody is there to watch it, so what's the point! In reality, a
simulator is part of a suite of VHDL tools and provides us with various means to control
and monitor the progress of the simulation. Typical simulators allow us to step through
the model one line at a time or to set breakpoints, causing the simulation to stop when a
line of the model is executed or a signal is assigned a particular value. They usually provide commands to display the value of signals or variables. Many simulators also provide
a graphical waveform display of the history of signal values similar to a logic analyzer display, and allow storage and subsequent redisplay of the history for later analysis. It is these
facilities that make the simulation useful. Unfortunately, since there is a great deal of variation between the facilities provided by different simulators, it is not practical to go into
any detail in this book. Simulator vendors usually provide training documentation and lab
courses that explain how to use the facilities provided by their products.

Exercises

1. [❶ 5.1] Write an entity declaration for a lookup table ROM modeled at an abstract level.
    The ROM has an address input of type **lookup_index**, which is an integer range from
    0 to 31, and a data output of type **real**. Include declarations within the declarative part
    of the entity to define the ROM contents, initialized to numbers of your choice.

2. [❶ 5.2] Write an architecture body for the ROM described in Exercise 1. Include a sig-
    nal assignment that uses the address input to index the ROM content and assigns the
    resulting value to the data output with a delay of 200 ps.

3. [❶ 5.2] Trace the transactions applied to the signal **s** in the following process. At what
    times is the signal active, and at what times does an event occur on it?

```
process is
begin
  s <= 'Z', '0' after 10 ns, '1' after 30 ns;
```

```
      wait for 50 ns;
      s <= '1' after 5 ns; 'H' after 15 ns;
      wait for 50 ns;
      s <= 'Z';
      wait;
   end process;
```

4. [❶ 5.2] Given the assignments to the signal s made by the process in Exercise 3, trace the values of the signals s'delayed(5 ns), s'stable(5 ns), s'quiet(5 ns) and s'transaction. What are the values of s'last_event, s'last_active and s'last_value at time 60 ns?

5. [❶ 5.2] Write a wait statement that suspends a process until a signal s changes from '1' to '0' while an enable signal en is '1'.

6. [❶ 5.2] Write a wait statement that suspends a process until a signal ready changes to '1' or until a maximum of 5 ms has elapsed.

7. [❶ 5.2] Suppose the signal s currently has the value '0'. What is the value of the Boolean variables v1 and v2 after execution of the following statements within a process?

```
      s <= '1';
      v1 := s = '1';
      wait on s;
      v2 := s = '1';
```

8. [❶ 5.2] Trace the transactions scheduled on the driver for z by the following statements, and show the values taken on by z during simulation.

```
      z <= transport '1' after 6 ns;
      wait for 3 ns;
      z <= transport '0' after 4 ns;
      wait for 5 ns;
      z <= transport '1' after 6 ns;
      wait for 1 ns;
      z <= transport '0' after 4 ns;
```

9. [❶ 5.2] Trace the transactions scheduled on the driver for x by the following statements, and show the values taken on by x during simulation. Assume x initially has the value zero.

```
      x <= reject 5 ns inertial  1 after  7 ns,
                                23 after  9 ns,
                                 5 after 10 ns,
                                23 after 12 ns,
                                -5 after 15 ns;
      wait for 6 ns;
      x <= reject 5 ns inertial 23 after 7 ns;
```

10. [❶ 5.2] Identify the signals to which the following process is sensitive:

```
logic_block : process (all) is
begin
  out1 <= '0'; out2 <= '0';
  case current_state is
    when s0 => if in1 then
                 next_state <= s1;
                 out1 <= '1';
               else
                 next_state <= idle;
               end if;
    when s1 => next_state <= s2;
               out2 <= '1';
    when s2 => next_state <= idle;
  end case;
end process logic_block;
```

11. [❶ 5.2] Write the equivalent process for the conditional signal assignment statement

```
mux_logic :
  z <= a and not b after 5 ns
         when enable and not sel else
       x or y after 6 ns
         when enable and sel else
       '0' after 4 ns;
```

12. [❶ 5.2] Write the equivalent process for the selected signal assignment statement

```
with bit_vector'(s, r) select
  q <= unaffected when "00",
       '0' when "01",
       '1' when "10" | "11";
```

13. [❶ 5.2] Write a concurrent assertion statement that verifies that the time between changes of a clock signal, clk, is at least T_pw_clk.

14. [❶ 5.3] Write component instantiation statements to model the structure shown by the schematic diagram in Figure 5.11. Assume that the entity ttl_74x74 and the corresponding architecture basic have been analyzed into the library work.

FIGURE 5.11

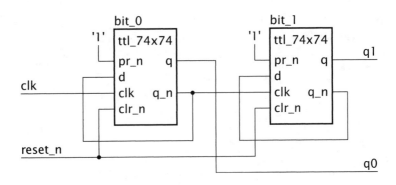

A schematic diagram of a 2-bit counter.

15. [❶ 5.3] Sketch a schematic diagram of the structure modeled by the following component instantiation statements.

```
decode_1 : entity work.ttl_74x138(basic)
  port map ( c => a(2), b => a(1), a => a(0),
             g1 => a(3), g2a_n => sel_n, g2b_n => '0',
             y7_n => en_n(15), y6_n => en_n(14),
             y5_n => en_n(13), y4_n => en_n(12),
             y3_n => en_n(11), y2_n => en_n(10),
             y1_n => en_n(9), y0_n => en_n(8) );

decode_0 : entity work.ttl_74x138(basic)
  port map ( c => a(2), b => a(1), a => a(0),
             g1 => '1', g2a_n => sel_n, g2b_n => a(3),
             y7_n => en_n(7), y6_n => en_n(6),
             y5_n => en_n(5), y4_n => en_n(4),
             y3_n => en_n(3), y2_n => en_n(2),
             y1_n => en_n(1), y0_n => en_n(0) );
```

16. [❶ 5.4] Example 5.27 shows one possible order of analysis of the design units in the counter of Figure 5.7. Show two other possible orders of analysis.

17. [❶ 5.4] Write a context clause that makes the resource libraries company_lib and project_lib accessible and that makes directly visible the entities in_pad and out_pad from company_lib and all entities from project_lib.

18. [❶ 5.4] Write a context declaration that includes a library clause for libraries ieee, IP_worx, and phantom_lib, and use clauses for the package std_logic_1164 from ieee and for all library units from the other two libraries.

19. [❷ 5.2] Develop a behavioral model for a four-input multiplexer, with ports of type bit and a propagation delay from data or select input to data output of 4.5 ns. You should

declare a constant for the propagation delay, rather than writing it as a literal in signal assignments in the model.

20. [❷ 5.2] Develop a behavioral model for a negative-edge-triggered 4-bit counter with asynchronous parallel load inputs. The entity declaration is

```
entity counter is
  port ( clk_n, load_en : in std_ulogic;
         d : in std_ulogic_vector(3 downto 0);
         q : out std_ulogic_vector(3 downto 0) );
end entity counter;
```

21. [❷ 5.2] Develop a behavioral model for a D-latch with a clock-to-output propagation delay of 3 ns and a data-to-output propagation delay of 4 ns.

22. [❷ 5.2] Develop a behavioral model for an edge-triggered flipflop that includes tests to verify the following timing constraints: data setup time of 3 ns, data hold time of 2 ns and minimum clock pulse width of 5 ns.

23. [❷ 5.2] Develop a model of an adder whose interface is specified by the following entity declaration:

```
entity adder is
  port ( a, b : in integer;  s : out integer );
end entity adder;
```

For each pair of integers that arrive on the inputs, the adder produces their sum on the output. Note that successive integers on each input may have the same value, so the adder must respond to transactions rather than to events. While integers in a pair may arrive in the inputs at different times, you may assume that neither value of the following pair will arrive until both values of the first pair have arrived. The adder should produce the sum only when both input values of a pair have arrived.

24. [❷ 5.2] Develop a behavioral model for a two-input Muller-C element, with two input ports and one output, all of type **bit**. The inputs and outputs are initially '0'. When both inputs are '1', the output changes to '1'. It stays '1' until both inputs are '0', at which time it changes back to '0'. Your model should have a propagation delay for rising output transitions of 3.5 ns, and for falling output transitions of 2.5 ns.

25. [❷ 5.2] The following process statement models a producer of data:

```
producer : process is
  variable next_data : natural := 0;
begin
  data <= next_data;  next_data := next_data + 1;
  data_ready <= '1';
  wait until data_ack;
  data_ready <= '0';
  wait until not data_ack;
end process producer;
```

The process uses a four-phase handshaking protocol to synchronize data transfer with a consumer process. Develop a process statement to model the consumer. It, too, should use delta delays in the handshaking protocol. Include the process statements in a test-bench architecture body, and experiment with your simulator to see how it deals with models that use delta delays.

26. [❷ 5.2] Develop a behavioral model for a multitap delay line, with the following interface:

```
entity delay_line is
  port ( input : in std_ulogic;
         output : out std_ulogic_vector );
end entity delay_line;
```

Each element of the output port is a delayed version of the input. The delay to the leftmost output element is 5 ns, to the next element is 10 ns and so on. The delay to the rightmost element is 5 ns times the length of the output port. Assume the delay line acts as an ideal transmission line.

27. [❷ 5.2] Develop a functional model using conditional signal assignment statements of an address decoder for a microcomputer system. The decoder has an address input port of type natural and a number of active-low select outputs, each activated when the address is within a given range. The outputs and their corresponding ranges are

ROM_sel_n	16#0000# to 16#3FFF#
RAM_sel_n	16#4000# to 16#5FFF#
PIO_sel_n	16#8000# to 16#8FFF#
SIO_sel_n	16#9000# to 16#9FFF#
INT_sel_n	16#F000# to 16#FFFF#

28. [❷ 5.2] Develop a functional model of a BCD-to-seven-segment decoder for a light-emitting diode (LED) display. The decoder has a 4-bit input that encodes a numeric digit between 0 and 9. There are seven outputs indexed from 'a' to 'g', corresponding to the seven segments of the LED display as shown in the margin. An output bit being '1' causes the corresponding segment to illuminate. For each input digit, the decoder activates the appropriate combination of segment outputs to form the displayed representation of the digit. For example, for the input "0010", which encodes the digit 2, the output is "1101101". Your model should use a selected signal assignment statement to describe the decoder function in truth-table form.

29. [❷ 5.2] Write an entity declaration for a 4-bit counter with an asynchronous reset input. Include a process in the entity declaration that measures the duration of each reset pulse and reports the duration at the end of each pulse.

30. [❷ 5.3] Develop a structural model of an 8-bit odd-parity checker using instances of an exclusive-or gate entity. The parity checker has eight inputs, i0 to i7, and an output, p, all of type **std_ulogic**. The logic equation describing the parity checker is

$$P = ((I_0 \oplus I_1) \oplus (I_2 \oplus I_3)) \oplus ((I_4 \oplus I_5) \oplus (I_6 \oplus I_7))$$

31. [❸ 5.3] Develop a structural model of a 14-bit counter with parallel load inputs, using instances of the 4-bit counter described in Exercise 20. Ensure that any unused inputs are properly connected to a constant driving value.

32. [❸ 5.2] Develop a behavioral model for a D-latch with tristate output. The entity declaration is

```
entity d_latch is
  port ( latch_en, out_en, d : in std_ulogic;
         q : out std_ulogic );
end entity d_latch;
```

When latch_en is asserted, data from the d input enters the latch. When latch_en is negated, the latch maintains the stored value. When out_en is asserted, data passes through to the output. When out_en is negated, the output has the value 'Z' (high-impedance). The propagation delay from latch_en to q is 3 ns and from d to q is 4 ns. The delay from out_en asserted to q active is 2 ns and from out_en negated to q high-impedance is 5 ns.

33. [❸ 5.2] Develop a functional model of a 4-bit carry-look-ahead adder. The adder has two 4-bit data inputs, a(3 **downto** 0) and b(3 **downto** 0); a 4-bit data output, s(3 **downto** 0); a carry input, c_in; a carry output, c_out; a carry generate output, g; and a carry propagate output, p. The adder is described by the logic equations and associated propagation delays:

$$S_i = A_i \oplus B_i \oplus C_{i-1} \quad \text{(delay is 5 ns)}$$

$$G_i = A_i B_i \quad \text{(delay is 2 ns)}$$

$$P_i = A_i + B_i \quad \text{(delay is 3 ns)}$$

$$C_i = G_i + P_i C_{i-1}$$

$$\quad = G_i + P_i G_{i-1} + P_i P_{i-1} G_{i-2} + \cdots + P_i P_{i-1} ... P_0 C_{-1} \quad \text{(delay is 5 ns)}$$

$$G = G_3 + P_3 G_2 + P_3 P_2 G_1 + P_3 P_2 P_1 G_0 \quad \text{(delay is 5 ns)}$$

$$P = P_3 P_2 P_1 P_0 \quad \text{(delay is 3 ns)}$$

where the G_i are the intermediate carry generate signals, the P_i are the intermediate carry propagate signals and the C_i are the intermediate carry signals. C_{-1} is c_in and C_3 is c_out. Your model should use the expanded equation to calculate the intermediate carries, which are then used to calculate the sums.

34. [❸ 5.2] Develop a behavioral model for a four-input arbiter with the following entity interface:

```
entity arbiter is
  port ( request : in bit_vector(0 to 3);
```

```
            acknowledge : out bit_vector(0 to 3) );
    end entity arbiter;
```

The arbiter should use a round-robin discipline for responding to requests. Include a concurrent assertion statement that verifies that no more than one acknowledgment is issued at once and that an acknowledgment is only issued to a requesting client.

35. [❸ 5.2] Write an entity declaration for a 7474 positive edge-triggered JK-flipflop with asynchronous active-low preset and clear inputs, and Q and $\overline{Q}$ outputs. Include concurrent assertion statements and passive processes as necessary in the entity declaration to verify that

- the preset and clear inputs are not activated simultaneously,

- the setup time of 6 ns from the J and K inputs to the rising clock edge is observed,

- the hold time of 2 ns for the J and K inputs after the rising clock edge is observed and

- the minimum pulse width of 5 ns on each of the clock, preset and clear inputs is observed.

Write a behavioral architecture body for the flipflop and a test bench that exercises the statements in the entity declaration.

36. [❸ 5.3] Define entity interfaces for a microprocessor, a ROM, a RAM, a parallel I/O controller, a serial I/O controller, an interrupt controller and a clock generator. Use instances of these entities and an instance of the address decoder described in Exercise 27 to develop a structural model of a microcomputer system.

37. [❸ 5.3] Develop a structural model of a 16-bit carry-look-ahead adder, using instances of the 4-bit adder described in Exercise 33. You will need to develop a carry-look-ahead generator with the following interface:

```
entity carry_look_ahead_generator is
  port ( p0, p1, p2, p3, g0, g1, g2, g3 : in bit;
         c_in : in bit;  c1, c2, c3 : out bit );
end entity carry_look_ahead_generator;
```

The carry-look-ahead generator is connected to the 4-bit adders as shown in Figure 5.12 on page 200. It calculates the carry output signals using the generate, propagate and carry inputs in the same way that the 4-bit counters calculate their internal carry signals.

FIGURE 5.12

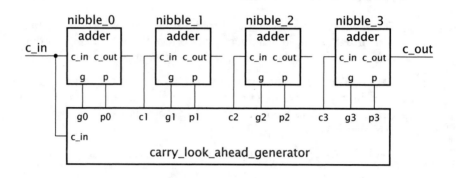

Connections between a carry-look-ahead generator and adders.

Chapter 6

Subprograms

When we write complex behavioral models it is useful to divide the code into sections, each dealing with a relatively self-contained part of the behavior. VHDL provides a *subprogram* facility to let us do this. In this chapter, we look at the two kinds of subprograms: *procedures* and *functions*. The difference between the two is that a procedure encapsulates a collection of sequential statements that are executed for their effect, whereas a function encapsulates a collection of statements that compute a result. Thus a procedure is a generalization of a statement, whereas a function is a generalization of an expression.

6.1 Procedures

We start our discussion of subprograms with procedures. There are two aspects to using procedures in a model: first the procedure is declared, then elsewhere the procedure is *called*. The syntax rule for a procedure declaration is

> subprogram_body ⟸
>   **procedure** identifier ⟦ (*parameter*_interface_list) ⟧ **is**
>   { subprogram_declarative_part }
>   **begin**
>   { sequential_statement }
>   **end** [**procedure**] [identifier] ;

For now we will just look at procedures without the parameter list part; we will come back to parameters in the next section.

The *identifier* in a procedure declaration names the procedure. The name may be repeated at the end of the procedure declaration. The sequential statements in the body of a procedure implement the algorithm that the procedure is to perform and can include any of the sequential statements that we have seen in previous chapters. A procedure can declare items in its declarative part for use in the statements in the procedure body. The declarations can include types, subtypes, constants, variables and nested subprogram declarations. The items declared are not accessible outside of the procedure; we say they are *local* to the procedure.

EXAMPLE 6.1   *Averaging an array of data samples*

The following procedure calculates the average of a collection of data values stored in an array called **samples** and assigns the result to a variable called **average**. This procedure has a local variable **total** for accumulating the sum of array elements. Unlike variables in processes, procedure local variables are created anew and initialized each time the procedure is called.

```
procedure average_samples is
  variable total : real := 0.0;
begin
  assert samples'length > 0 severity failure;
  for index in samples'range loop
    total := total + samples(index);
  end loop;
  average := total / real(samples'length);
end procedure average_samples;
```

The actions of a procedure are invoked by a *procedure call* statement, which is yet another VHDL sequential statement. A procedure with no parameters is called simply by writing its name, as shown by the syntax rule

procedure_call_statement ⇐ ⟦ label : ⟧ *procedure*_name ;

The optional label allows us to identify the procedure call statement. As an example, we might include the following statement in a process:

```
average_samples;
```

The effect of this statement is to invoke the procedure **average_samples**. This involves creating and initializing a new instance of the local variable **total**, then executing the statements in the body of the procedure. When the last statement in the procedure is completed, we say the procedure *returns*; that is, the thread of control of statement execution returns to the process from which the procedure was called, and the next statement in the process after the call is executed.

We can write a procedure declaration in the declarative part of an architecture body or a process. We can also declare procedures within other procedures, but we will leave that until a later section. If a procedure is included in an architecture body's declarative part, it can be called from within any of the processes in the architecture body. On the other hand, declaring a procedure within a process hides it away from use by other processes.

EXAMPLE 6.2   *A procedure to implement behavior within a process*

The outline below illustrates a procedure defined within a process. The procedure **do_arith_op** encapsulates an algorithm for arithmetic operations on two values, producing a result and a flag indicating whether the result is zero. It has a variable **result**, which it uses within the sequential statements that implement the algorithm. The statements also use the signals and other objects declared in the architecture body. The process **alu** invokes **do_arith_op** with a procedure call statement. The advantage of separating the statements for arithmetic operations into a procedure in this example is that it simplifies the body of the **alu** process.

```
architecture rtl of control_processor is

  type func_code is (add, subtract);

  signal op1, op2, dest : integer;
  signal Z_flag : boolean;
  signal func : func_code;
  ...

begin

  alu : process is

    procedure do_arith_op is
      variable result : integer;
    begin
      case func is
        when add =>
          result := op1 + op2;
        when subtract =>
          result := op1 - op2;
      end case;
      dest  <=  result after Tpd;
      Z_flag  <=  result = 0 after Tpd;
    end procedure do_arith_op;

  begin
    ...
    do_arith_op;
    ...
  end process alu;

  ...

end architecture rtl;
```

Another important use of procedures arises when some action needs to be performed several times at different places in a model. Instead of writing several copies of the statements to perform the action, the statements can be encapsulated in a procedure, which is then called from each place.

EXAMPLE 6.3   *A memory read procedure invoked from several places in a model*

The process outlined below is taken from a behavioral model of a CPU. The process fetches instructions from memory and interprets them. Since the actions required to fetch an instruction and to fetch a data word are identical, the process encapsulates them in a procedure, **read_memory**. The procedure copies the address from the memory address register to the address bus, sets the read signal to '1', then activates the request signal. When the memory responds, the procedure copies the data from the data bus signal to the memory data register and acknowledges to the memory by setting the request signal back to '0'. When the memory has completed its operation, the procedure returns.

```
instruction_interpreter : process is

    variable mem_address_reg, mem_data_reg,
             prog_counter, instr_reg, accumulator, index_reg : word;
    ...

    procedure read_memory is
    begin
      address_bus <= mem_address_reg;
      mem_read <= '1';
      mem_request <= '1';
      wait until mem_ready;
      mem_data_reg := data_bus_in;
      mem_request <= '0';
      wait until not mem_ready;
    end procedure read_memory;

begin
    ...   -- initialization
    loop
      -- fetch next instruction
      mem_address_reg := prog_counter;
      read_memory;        -- call procedure
      instr_reg := mem_data_reg;
      ...
      case opcode is
        ...
        when load_mem =>
          mem_address_reg := index_reg + displacement;
          read_memory;  -- call procedure
          accumulator := mem_data_reg;
        ...
      end case;
    end loop;
end process instruction_interpreter;
```

The procedure is called in two places within the process. First, it is called to fetch an instruction. The process copies the program counter into the memory address register and calls the procedure. When the procedure returns, the process copies the data from the memory data register, placed there by the procedure, to the instruction register. The second call to the procedure takes place when a "load memory" instruction is executed. The process sets the memory address register using the values of the index register and some displacement, then calls the memory read procedure to perform the read operation. When it returns, the process copies the data to the accumulator.

Since a procedure call is a form of sequential statement and a procedure body implements an algorithm using sequential statements, there is no reason why one procedure cannot call another procedure. In this case, control is passed from the calling procedure to the called procedure to execute its statements. When the called procedure returns, the calling procedure carries on executing statements until it returns to its caller.

EXAMPLE 6.4 *Nested procedure calls in a control sequencer*

The process outlined below is a control sequencer for a register-transfer-level model of a CPU. It sequences the activation of control signals with a two-phase clock on signals **phase1** and **phase2**. The process contains two procedures, **control_write_back** and **control_arith_op**, that encapsulate parts of the control algorithm. The process calls **control_arith_op** when an arithmetic operation must be performed. This procedure sequences the control signals for the source and destination operand registers in the data path. It then calls **control_write_back**, which sequences the control signals for the register file in the data path, to write the value from the destination register. When this procedure is completed, it returns to the first procedure, which then returns to the process.

```
control_sequencer : process is

  procedure control_write_back is
  begin
    wait until phase1;
    reg_file_write_en <= '1';
    wait until not phase2;
    reg_file_write_en <= '0';
  end procedure control_write_back;

  procedure control_arith_op is
  begin
    wait until phase1;
    A_reg_out_en <= '1';
    B_reg_out_en <= '1';
    wait until not phase1;
    A_reg_out_en <= '0';
    B_reg_out_en <= '0';
```

```
        wait until phase2;
        C_reg_load_en <= '1';
        wait until not phase2;
        C_reg_load_en <= '0';
        control_write_back;  -- call procedure
      end procedure control_arith_op;

      ...

  begin
      ...
      control_arith_op;   -- call procedure
      ...
  end process control_sequencer;
```

VHDL-87

The keyword **procedure** may not be included at the end of a procedure declaration in VHDL-87. Procedure call statements may not be labeled in VHDL-87.

6.1.1   Return Statement in a Procedure

In all of the examples above, the procedures completed execution of the statements in their bodies before returning. Sometimes it is useful to be able to return from the middle of a procedure, for example, as a way of handling an exceptional condition. We can do this using a *return* statement, described by the simplified syntax rule

return_statement ⇐ ⟦ label : ⟧ return ;

The optional label allows us to identify the return statement. The effect of the return statement, when executed in a procedure, is that the procedure is immediately terminated and control is transferred back to the caller.

EXAMPLE 6.5   *A revised memory read procedure*

The following is a revised version of the instruction interpreter process from Example 6.3. The procedure to read from memory is revised to check for the reset signal becoming active during a read operation. If it does, the procedure returns immediately, aborting the operation in progress. The process then exits the fetch/execute loop and starts the process body again, reinitializing its state and output signals.

```
  instruction_interpreter : process is

      ...

      procedure read_memory is
      begin
```

```
                address_bus <= mem_address_reg;
                mem_read <= '1';
                mem_request <= '1';
                wait until mem_ready or reset;
                if reset then
                  return;
                end if;
                mem_data_reg := data_bus_in;
                mem_request <= '0';
                wait until not mem_ready;
              end procedure read_memory;
          begin
            ...      -- initialization
            loop
              ...
              read_memory;
              exit when reset;
                ...
            end loop;
          end process instruction_interpreter;
```

VHDL-87

Return statements may not be labeled in VHDL-87.

6.2 Procedure Parameters

Now that we have looked at the basics of procedures, we will discuss procedures that include parameters. A *parameterized procedure* is much more general in that it can perform its algorithm using different data objects or values each time it is called. The idea is that the caller passes parameters to the procedure as part of the procedure call, and the procedure then executes its statements using the parameters.

When we write a parameterized procedure, we include information in the *parameter interface list* (or *parameter list*, for short) about the parameters to be passed to the procedure. The syntax rule for a procedure declaration on page 201 shows where the parameter list fits in. Following is the syntax rule for a parameter list:

interface_list ⇐
    (⟦ **constant** ⟦ **variable** ⟦ **signal** ⟧
        identifier { , ₒₒₒ } : ⟦ mode ⟧ subtype_indication
                            ⟦ := *static*_expression ⟧) { ; ₒₒₒ }

mode ⇐ **in** ⟦ **out** ⟦ **inout**

As we can see, it is similar to the port interface list used in declaring entities. This similarity is not coincidental, since they both specify information about objects upon which the user and the implementation must agree. In the case of a procedure, the user is the caller of the procedure, and the implementation is the body of statements within the procedure. The objects defined in the parameter list are called the *formal parameters* of the procedure. We can think of them as placeholders that stand for the *actual parameters*, which are to be supplied by the caller when it calls the procedure. Since the syntax rule for a parameter list is quite complex, let us start with some simple examples and work up from them.

EXAMPLE 6.6   *Using a parameter to select an arithmetic operation to perform*

Let's rewrite the procedure **do_arith_op** from Example 6.2 so that the function code is passed as a parameter. The new version is

```
procedure do_arith_op ( op : in func_code ) is
  variable result : integer;
begin
  case op is
    when add =>
      result := op1 + op2;
    when subtract =>
      result := op1 - op2;
  end case;
  dest  <=  result after Tpd;
  Z_flag  <=  result = 0 after Tpd;
end procedure do_arith_op;
```

In the parameter interface list we have identified one formal parameter named **op**. This name is used in the statements in the procedure to refer to the value that will be passed as an actual parameter when the procedure is called. The mode of the formal parameter is **in**, indicating that it is used to pass information into the procedure from the caller. This means that the statements in the procedure can use the value but cannot modify it. In the parameter list we have specified the type of the parameter as func_code. This indicates that the operations performed on the value in the statements must be appropriate for a value of this type, and that the caller may only pass a value of this type as an actual parameter.

Now that we have parameterized the procedure, we can call it from different places passing different function codes each time. For example, a call at one place might be

```
do_arith_op ( add );
```

The procedure call simply includes the actual parameter value in parentheses. In this case we pass the literal value **add** as the actual parameter. At another place in the model we might pass the value of the signal **func** shown in the model in Example 6.2:

```
do_arith_op ( func );
```

In this example, we have specified the mode of the formal parameter as **in**. Note that the syntax rule for a parameter list indicates that the mode is an optional part. If we leave it out, mode **in** is assumed, so we could have written the procedure as

procedure do_arith_op (op : func_code) **is** ...

While this is equally correct, it's not a bad idea to include the mode specification for **in** parameters, to make our intention explicitly clear.

The syntax rule for a parameter list also shows us that we can specify the *class* of a formal parameter, namely, whether it is a constant, a variable or a signal within the procedure. If the mode of the parameter is **in**, the class is assumed to be *constant*, since a constant is an object that cannot be updated by assignment. It is just a quirk of VHDL that we can specify both **constant** and **in**, even though to do so is redundant. Usually we simply leave out the keyword **constant**, relying on the mode to make our intentions clear. For an **in**-mode constant-class parameter, we write an expression as the actual parameter. The value of this expression must be of the type specified in the parameter list. The value is passed to the procedure for use in the statements in its body.

Let us now turn to formal parameters of mode **out**. Such a parameter lets us transfer information out from the procedure back to the caller. Here is an example, before we delve into the details.

EXAMPLE 6.7   *A procedure for addition with overflow output*

The procedure below performs addition of two unsigned numbers represented as bit vectors of type **word32**, which we assume is defined elsewhere. The procedure has two **in**-mode parameters a and b, allowing the caller to pass two bit-vector values. The procedure uses these values to calculate the sum and overflow flag. Within the procedure, the two **out**-mode parameters, **sum** and **overflow**, appear as variables. The procedure performs variable assignments to update their values, thus transferring information back to the caller.

```
procedure addu ( a, b : in word32;
                 sum : out word32;
                 overflow : out bit ) is
  variable carry : bit := '0';
begin
  for index in sum'reverse_range loop
    sum(index) := a(index) xor b(index) xor carry;
    carry := ( a(index) and b(index) )
             or ( carry and ( a(index) xor b(index) ) );
  end loop;
  overflow := carry;
end procedure addu;
```

A call to this procedure may appear as follows:

```
variable PC, next_PC : word32;
variable overflow_flag : bit;
...

addu ( PC, X"0000_0004", next_PC, overflow_flag);
```

In this procedure call statement, the first two actual parameters are expressions whose values are passed in through the formal parameters a and b. The third and fourth actual parameters are the names of variables. When the procedure returns, the values assigned by the procedure to the formal parameters sum and overflow are used to update the variables next_PC and overflow_flag.

In the above example, the **out**-mode parameters are of the class *variable*. Since this class is assumed for **out** parameters, we usually leave out the class specification **variable**, although it may be included if we wish to state the class explicitly. We will come back to signal-class parameters in a moment. The mode **out** indicates that the procedure may update the formal parameters by variable assignment to transfer information back to the caller. The procedure may also read the values of the parameters, just as it can with **in**-mode parameters. The difference is that an **out**-mode parameter is not initialized with the value of the actual parameter. Instead, it is initalized in the same way as a locally declared variable, with the default initial value for the type of the parameter. When the procedure reads the parameter, it reads the parameter's current value, yielding the value most recently assigned within the procedure, or the initial value if no assignments have been made. For an **out** mode, variable-class parameter, the caller must supply a variable as an actual parameter. Both the actual parameter and the value returned must be of the type specified in the parameter list. When the procedure returns, the value of the formal parameter is copied back to the actual parameter variable.

The third mode we can specify for formal parameters is **inout**, which is a combination of **in** and **out** modes. It is used for objects that are to be both read and updated by a procedure. As with **out** parameters, they are assumed to be of class variable if the class is not explicitly stated. For **inout**-mode variable parameters, the caller supplies a variable as an actual parameter. The value of this variable is used to initialize the formal parameter, which may then be used in the statements of the procedure. The procedure may also perform variable assignments to update the formal parameter. When the procedure returns, the value of the formal parameter is copied back to the actual parameter variable, transferring information back to the caller.

EXAMPLE 6.8   *A procedure to negate a binary-coded number*

The following procedure negates a number represented as a bit vector, using the "complement and add one" method:

```
procedure negate ( a : inout word32 ) is
  variable carry_in : bit := '1';
  variable carry_out : bit;
begin
  a := not a;
```

```
      for index in a'reverse_range loop
        carry_out :=  a(index) and carry_in;
        a(index) := a(index) xor carry_in;
        carry_in := carry_out;
      end loop;
    end procedure negate;
```

Since **a** is an **inout**-mode parameter, we can refer to its value in expressions in the procedure body. (This differs from the parameter **result** in the **addu** procedure of the previous example.) We might include the following call to this procedure in a model:

```
variable op1 : word32;
...
negate ( op1 );
```

This uses the value of **op1** to initialize the formal parameter **a**. The procedure body is then executed, updating **a**, and when it returns, the final value of **a** is copied back into **op1**.

VHDL-87, -93, and -2002

These versions of VHDL do not allow an **out**-mode parameter to be read. Instead, if the value must be read within the procedure, the procedure must declare and read a local variable. The final value of the local variable can then be assigned to the **out**-mode parameter immediately before the procedure returns.

6.2.1 Signal Parameters

The third class of object that we can specify for formal parameters is *signal*, which indicates that the algorithm performed by the procedure involves a signal passed by the caller. A signal parameter can be of any of the modes **in**, **out** or **inout**. The way that signal parameters work is somewhat different from constant and variable parameters, so it is worth spending a bit of time understanding them.

When a caller passes a signal as a parameter of mode **in**, instead of passing the value of the signal, it passes the signal object itself. Any reference to the formal parameter within the procedure is exactly like a reference to the actual signal itself. The statements within the procedure can read the signal value, include it in sensitivity lists in wait statements, and query its attributes. A consequence of passing a reference to the signal is that if the procedure executes a wait statement, the signal value may be different after the wait statement completes and the procedure resumes. This behavior differs from that of constant parameters of mode **in**, which have the same value for the whole of the procedure.

EXAMPLE 6.9   *A procedure to receive network packets*

Suppose we wish to model the receiver part of a network interface. It receives fixed-length packets of data on the signal **rx_data**. The data is synchronized with changes, from '0' to '1', of the clock signal **rx_clock**. An outline of part of the model is

```
architecture behavioral of receiver is

    ...     -- type declarations, etc

    signal recovered_data : bit;
    signal recovered_clock : bit;
    ...

    procedure receive_packet ( signal rx_data : in bit;
                               signal rx_clock : in bit;
                               data_buffer : out packet_array ) is
    begin
      for index in packet_index_range loop
        wait until rx_clock;
        data_buffer(index) := rx_data;
      end loop;
    end procedure receive_packet;

begin

    packet_assembler : process is
      variable packet : packet_array;
    begin
      ...
      receive_packet ( recovered_data, recovered_clock, packet );
      ...
    end process packet_assembler;

    ...

end architecture behavioral;
```

The receive_packet procedure has signal parameters of mode **in** for the network-data and clock signals. During execution of the model, the process **packet_assembler** calls the procedure **receive_packet**, passing the signals **recovered_data** and **recovered_clock** as actual parameters. We can think of the procedure as executing "on behalf of" the process. When it reaches the wait statement, it is really the calling process that suspends. The wait statement mentions **rx_clock**, and since this stands for **recovered_clock**, the process is sensitive to changes on **recovered_clock** while it is suspended. Each time it resumes, it reads the current value of **rx_data** (which represents the actual signal **recovered_data**) and stores it in an element of the array parameter data_buffer.

Now let's look at signal parameters of mode **out**. In this case, the caller must name a signal as the actual parameter, and the procedure is passed a reference to the driver for the signal. The procedure is not allowed to read the formal parameter. When the procedure performs a signal assignment statement on the formal parameter, the transactions are scheduled on the driver for the actual signal parameter. In Chapter 5, we said that a process that contains a signal assignment statement contains a driver for the target signal, and that an ordinary signal may only have one driver. When such a signal is passed as an actual **out**-mode parameter, there is still only the one driver. We can think of the signal assignments within the procedure as being performed on behalf of the process that calls the procedure.

EXAMPLE 6.10   *A procedure to generate pulses on a signal*

The following is an outline of an architecture body for a signal generator. The procedure **generate_pulse_train** has **in**-mode constant parameters that specify the characteristics of a pulse train and an **out**-mode signal parameter on which it generates the required pulse train. The process **raw_signal_generator** calls the procedure, supplying **raw_signal** as the actual signal parameter for s. A reference to the driver for **raw_signal** is passed to the procedure, and transactions are generated on it.

```
library ieee;  use ieee.std_logic_1164.all;

architecture top_level of signal_generator is

  signal raw_signal : std_ulogic;
  ...

  procedure generate_pulse_train
    ( width, separation : in delay_length;
      number : in natural;
      signal s : out std_ulogic ) is
  begin
    for count in 1 to number loop
      s <= '1', '0' after width;
      wait for width + separation;
    end loop;
  end procedure generate_pulse_train;

begin

  raw_signal_generator : process is
  begin
    ...
    generate_pulse_train ( width => period / 2,
                           separation => period - period / 2,
                           number => pulse_count,
                           s => raw_signal );
    ...
  end process raw_signal_generator;
```

> ...
> **end architecture** top_level;

An incidental point to note is the way we have specified the actual value for the **separation** parameter in the procedure call. This ensures that the sum of the **width** and **separation** values is exactly equal to **period**, even if **period** is not an even multiple of the time resolution limit. This illustrates an approach sometimes called "defensive programming," in which we try to ensure that the model works correctly in all possible circumstances.

As with variable-class parameters, we can also have a signal-class parameter of mode **inout**. When the procedure is called, both the signal and a reference to its driver are passed to the procedure. The statements within it can read the signal value, include it in sensitivity lists in wait statements, query its attributes, and schedule transactions using signal assignment statements.

An important point to note about procedures with signal parameters relates to procedure calls within processes with the reserved word **all** in their sensitivity lists. Such a process is sensitive to all signals read within the process. That includes signals used as actual **in**-mode and **inout**-mode parameters in procedure calls within the process. It also includes other signals that aren't parameters but that are read within the procedure body. (We will see in Section 6.6 how a procedure can reference such signals.) Since it could become difficult to determine which signals are read by such a process when procedure calls are involved, VHDL simplifies things somewhat by requiring that a procedure called by the process only read signals that are formal parameters or that are declared in the same design unit as the process. In most models this is not a problem.

A final point to note about signal parameters relates to procedures declared immediately within an architecture body. The target of any signal assignment statements within such a procedure must be a signal parameter, rather than a direct reference to a signal declared in the enclosing architecture body. The reason for this restriction is that the procedure may be called by more than one process within the architecture body. Each process that performs assignments on a signal has a driver for the signal. Without the restriction, we would not be able to tell easily by looking at the model where the drivers for the signal were located. The restriction makes the model more comprehensible and, hence, easier to maintain.

6.2.2 Default Values

The one remaining part of a procedure parameter list that we have yet to discuss is the optional default value expression, shown in the syntax rule on page 207. Note that we can only specify a default value for a formal parameter of mode **in**, and the parameter must be of the class constant or variable. If we include a default value in a parameter specification, we have the option of omitting an actual value when the procedure is called. We can either use the keyword **open** in place of an actual parameter value or, if the actual value would be at the end of the parameter list, simply leave it out. If we omit an actual value, the default value is used instead.

EXAMPLE 6.11 *A procedure to increment an integer*

The procedure below increments an unsigned integer represented as a bit vector. The amount to increment by is specified by the second parameter, which has a default value of the bit-vector representation of 1.

```
procedure increment ( a : inout word32;
                      by : in word32 := X"0000_0001" ) is
  variable sum : word32;
  variable carry : bit := '0';
begin
  for index in a'reverse_range loop
    sum(index) := a(index) xor by(index) xor carry;
    carry := ( a(index) and by(index) )
             or ( carry and ( a(index) xor by(index) ) );
  end loop;
  a := sum;
end procedure increment;
```

If we have a variable **count** declared to be of type **word32**, we can call the procedure to increment it by 4, as follows:

```
increment(count, X"0000_0004");
```

If we want to increment the variable by 1, we can make use of the default value for the second parameter and call the procedure without specifying an actual value to increment by, as follows:

```
increment(count);
```

This call is equivalent to

```
increment(count, by => open);
```

6.2.3 Unconstrained Array Parameters

In Chapter 4 we described unconstrained and partially constrained types, in which index ranges of arrays or array elements were left unspecified. For such types, we constrain the index bounds when we create an object, such as a variable or a signal, or when we associate an actual signal with a port. Another use of an unconstrained or partially constrained type is as the type of a formal parameter to a procedure. This use allows us to write a procedure in a general way, so that it can operate on composite values of any size or with any ranges of index values. When we call the procedure and provide a constrained array or record as the actual parameter, the index bounds of the actual parameter are used as the bounds of the formal parameter. The same rules apply as those we described in Section 4.2.3 for ports. Let us look at an example to show how unconstrained parameters work.

EXAMPLE 6.12   *A procedure to find the first set bit*

Following is a procedure that finds the index of the first bit set to '1' in a bit vector. The formal parameter v is of type **bit_vector**, which is an unconstrained array type. Note that in writing this procedure, we do not explicitly refer to the index bounds of the formal parameter v, since they are not known. Instead, we use the **'range** attribute.

```
procedure find_first_set ( v : in bit_vector;
                           found : out boolean;
                           first_set_index : out natural ) is
begin
  for index in v'range loop
    if v(index) then
      found := true;
      first_set_index := index;
      return;
    end if;
  end loop;
  found := false;
end procedure find_first_set;
```

When the procedure is executed, the formal parameters stand for the actual parameters provided by the caller. So if we call this procedure as follows:

```
variable int_req : bit_vector (7 downto 0);
variable top_priority : natural;
variable int_pending : boolean;
...

find_first_set ( int_req, int_pending, top_priority );
```

v'range returns the range 7 **downto** 0, which is used to ensure that the loop parameter **index** iterates over the correct index values for v. If we make a different call:

```
variable free_block_map : bit_vector(0 to block_count-1);
variable first_free_block : natural;
variable free_block_found : boolean;
...

find_first_set ( free_block_map,
                 free_block_found, first_free_block );
```

v'range returns the index range of the array **free_block_map**, since that is the actual parameter corresponding to v.

When we have formal parameters that are of array types, whether fully constrained, partially constrained, or unconstrained, we can use any of the array attributes mentioned in Chapter 4 to refer to the index bounds and range of the actual parameters. We can use the attribute values to define new local constants or variables whose index bounds and ranges depend on those of the parameters. The local objects are created anew each time the procedure is called.

EXAMPLE 6.13   *A procedure to compare binary-coded signed integers*

The following procedure has two bit-vector parameters, which it assumes represent signed integer values in two's-complement form. It performs an arithmetic comparison of the numbers.

```
procedure bv_lt ( bv1, bv2 : in bit_vector;
                      result : out boolean ) is
  variable tmp1 : bit_vector(bv1'range) := bv1;
  variable tmp2 : bit_vector(bv2'range) := bv2;
begin
  tmp1(tmp1'left) := not tmp1(tmp1'left);
  tmp2(tmp2'left) := not tmp2(tmp2'left);
  result :=   tmp1 < tmp2;
end procedure bv_lt;
```

The procedure operates by taking temporary copies of each of the bit-vector parameters, inverting the sign bits and performing a lexical comparison using the built-in "<" operator. This is equivalent to an arithmetic comparison of the original numbers. Note that the temporary variables are declared to be of the same size as the parameters by using the 'range attribute, and the sign bits (the leftmost bits) are indexed using the 'left attribute.

EXAMPLE 6.14   *A procedure to swap array values*

Given an unconstrained type representing arrays of bit vectors declared as follows:

```
type bv_vector is array (natural range <>) of bit_vector;
```

we can declare a procedure to swap the values of two variables of the type:

```
procedure swap_bv_arrays ( a1, a2 : inout bv_array ) is
  variable temp : a1'subtype;
begin
  assert a1'length = a2'length and
         a1'element'length = a2'element'length;
  temp := a1; a1 := a2; a2 := temp;
end procedure swap;
```

Since the type **bv_array** is not fully constrained, we cannot use it as the type of the variable **temp**. Instead, we use the 'subtype attribute to get a fully constrained subtype with the same shape as **a1**. Once we've verified that **a1** and **a2** are the same shape, we can then swap their values in the usual way using **temp** as the intermediate variable. We use the 'length attribute to refer to the lengths of the top-level arrays, and the 'length attribute applied to the 'subtype attribute to refer to the lengths of the element arrays.

6.2.4   Summary of Procedure Parameters

Let us now summarize all that we have seen in specifying and using parameters for procedures. The syntax rule on page 207 shows that we can specify five aspects of each formal parameter. First, we may specify the class of object, which determines how the formal parameter appears within the procedure, namely, as a constant, a variable or a signal. Second, we give a name to the formal parameter so that it can be referred to in the procedure body. Third, we may specify the mode, **in**, **out** or **inout**, which determines the direction in which information is passed between the caller and the procedure and whether the procedure can assign to the formal parameter. Fourth, we must specify the type or subtype of the formal parameter, which restricts the type of actual parameters that can be provided by the caller. This is important as a means of preventing inadvertent misuse of the procedure. Fifth, we may include a default value, giving a value to be used if the caller does not provide an actual parameter. These five aspects clearly define the interface between the procedure and its callers, allowing us to partition a complex behavioral model into sections and concentrate on each section without being distracted by other details.

Once we have encapsulated some operations in a procedure, we can then call that procedure from different parts of a model, providing actual parameters to specialize the operation at each call. The syntax rule for a procedure call is

> procedure_call_statement ⇐
>   〚 label : 〛 *procedure*_name 〚 (*parameter*_association_list) 〛 ;

This is a sequential statement, so it may be used in a process or inside another subprogram body. If the procedure has formal parameters, the call can specify actual parameters to associate with the formal parameters. The actual associated with a constant-class formal is the value of an expression. The actual associated with a variable-class formal must be a variable, and the actual associated with a signal-class formal must be a signal. The simplified syntax rule for the parameter association list is

> parameter_association_list ⇐
>   (〚 *parameter*_name => 〛
>   expression ❘ *signal*_name ❘ *variable*_name ❘ **open**) { , … }

This is in fact the same syntax rule that applies to port maps in component instantiations, seen in Chapter 5. Most of what we said there also applies to procedure parameter association lists. For example, we can use positional association in the procedure call by providing one actual parameter for each formal parameter in the order listed in the procedure declaration. Alternatively, we can use named association by identifying explicitly which formal corresponds to which actual parameter in the call. In this case, the parameters can be in any order. Also, we can use a mix of positional and named association, provided all of the positional parameters come first in the call.

EXAMPLE 6.15 *Positional and named association for parameters*

Suppose we have a procedure declared as

```
procedure p ( f1 : in t1;  f2 : in t2;
              f3 : out t3; f4 : in t4 := v4 ) is
begin
  ...
end procedure p;
```

We could call this procedure, providing actual parameters in a number of ways, including

```
p ( val1, val2, var3, val4 );
p ( f1 => val1, f2 => val2, f4 => val4, f3 => var3 );
p ( val1, val2, f4 => open, f3 => var3 );
p ( val1, val2, var3 );
```

6.3 Concurrent Procedure Call Statements

In Chapter 5 we saw that VHDL provides concurrent signal assignment statements and concurrent assertions as shorthand notations for commonly used kinds of processes. Now that we have looked at procedures and procedure call statements, we can introduce another shorthand notation, the *concurrent procedure call statement*. As its name implies, it is short for a process whose body contains a sequential procedure call statement. The syntax rule is

concurrent_procedure_call_statement ⇐
   〚 label : 〛 *procedure*_name 〚 (*parameter*_association_list) 〛 ;

This looks identical to an ordinary sequential procedure call, but the difference is that it appears as a concurrent statement, rather than as a sequential statement. A concurrent procedure call is exactly equivalent to a process that contains a sequential procedure call to the same procedure with the same actual parameters. For example, a concurrent procedure call of the form

```
call_proc : p ( s1, s2, val1 );
```

where s1 and s2 are signals and val1 is a constant, is equivalent to the process

```
call_proc : process is
begin
  p ( s1, s2, val1 );
  wait on s1, s2;
end process call_proc;
```

This also shows that the equivalent process contains a wait statement, whose sensitivity clause includes the signals mentioned in the actual parameter list. This is useful, since it results in the procedure being called again whenever the signal values change. Note that only signals associated with **in**-mode or **inout**-mode parameters are included in the sensitivity list.

EXAMPLE 6.16   *A procedure to check setup time*

We can write a procedure that checks setup timing of a data signal with respect to a clock signal, as shown follows:

```
procedure check_setup ( signal data, clock : in bit;
                        constant Tsu : in time ) is
begin
  if rising_edge(clock) then
    assert data'last_event >= Tsu
      report "setup time violation" severity error;
  end if;
end procedure check_setup;
```

When the procedure is called, it tests to see if there is a rising edge on the clock signal, and if so, checks that the data signal has not changed within the setup time interval. We can invoke this procedure using a concurrent procedure call; for example:

```
check_ready_setup : check_setup ( data => ready,
                                  clock => phi2,
                                  Tsu => Tsu_rdy_clk );
```

The procedure is called whenever either of the signals in the actual parameter list, **ready** or phi2, changes value. When the procedure returns, the concurrent procedure call statement suspends until the next event on either signal. The advantage of using a concurrent procedure call like this is twofold. First, we can write a suite of commonly used checking procedures and reuse them whenever we need to include a check in a model. This is potentially a great improvement in productivity. Second, the statement that invokes the check is more compact and readily understandable than the equivalent process written in-line.

Another point to note about concurrent procedure calls is that if there are no signals associated with **in**-mode or **inout**-mode parameters, the wait statement in the equivalent process does not have a sensitivity clause. If the procedure ever returns, the process suspends indefinitely. This may be useful if we want the procedure to be called only once at startup time. On the other hand, we may write the procedure so that it never returns. If we include wait statements within a loop in the procedure, it behaves somewhat like a process itself. The advantage of this is that we can declare a procedure that performs some commonly needed behavior and then invoke one or more instances of it using concurrent procedure call statements.

EXAMPLE 6.17 *A procedure to generate a clock waveform*

The following procedure generates a periodic clock waveform on a signal passed as
a parameter. The **in**-mode constant parameters specify the shape of a clock waveform.
The procedure waits for the initial phase delay, then loops indefinitely, scheduling a
new rising and falling transition on the clock signal parameter on each iteration. It
never returns to its caller.

```
procedure generate_clock ( signal clk : out std_ulogic;
                           constant Tperiod,
                                    Tpulse,
                                    Tphase : in time ) is
begin
  wait for Tphase;
  loop
    clk <= '1', '0' after Tpulse;
    wait for Tperiod;
  end loop;
end procedure generate_clock;
```

We can use this procedure to generate a two-phase non-overlapping pair of clock
signals, as follows:

```
signal phi1, phi2 : std_ulogic := '0';
...

gen_phi1 : generate_clock ( phi1, Tperiod => 50 ns,
                                  Tpulse => 20 ns,
                                  Tphase => 0 ns );

gen_phi2 : generate_clock ( phi2, Tperiod => 50 ns,
                                  Tpulse => 20 ns,
                                  Tphase => 25 ns );
```

Each of these calls represents a process that calls the procedure, which then executes the clock generation loop on behalf of its parent process. The advantage of this
approach is that we only had to write the loop once in a general-purpose procedure.
Also, we have made the model more compact and understandable.

6.4 Functions

Let us now turn our attention to the second kind of subprogram in VHDL: *functions*. We
can think of a function as a generalization of expressions. The expressions that we described in Chapter 2 combined values with operators to produce new values. A function
is a way of defining a new operation that can be used in expressions. We define how the
new operation works by writing a collection of sequential statements that calculate the
result. The syntax rule for a function declaration is very similar to that for a procedure
declaration:

```
subprogram_body ⟸
    ⟦ pure ▯ impure ⟧
    function identifier ⟦ ( parameter_interface_list ) ⟧ return type_mark is
        ⟅ subprogram_declarative_item ⟆
    begin
        ⟅ sequential_statement ⟆
    end ⟦ function ⟧ ⟦ identifier ⟧ ;
```

The identifier in the declaration names the function. It may be repeated at the end of the declaration. Unlike a procedure subprogram, a function calculates and returns a result that can be used in an expression. The function declaration specifies the type of the result after the keyword **return**. The parameter list of a function takes the same form as that for a procedure, with two restrictions. First, the parameters of a function may not be of the class variable. If the class is not explicitly mentioned, it is assumed to be constant. Second, the mode of each parameter must be **in**. If the mode is not explicitly specified, it is assumed to be **in**. We come to the reasons for these restrictions in a moment. Like a procedure, a function can declare local items in its declarative part for use in the statements in the function body.

A function passes the result of its computation back to its caller using a return statement, given by the syntax rule

```
return_statement ⟸ ⟦ label : ⟧ return expression ;
```

The optional label allows us to identify the return statement. The form described by this syntax rule differs from the return statement in a procedure subprogram in that it includes an expression to provide the function result. Furthermore, a function must include at least one return statement of this form, and possibly more. The first to be executed causes the function to complete and return its result to the caller. A function cannot simply run into the end of the function body, since to do so would not provide a way of specifying a result to pass back to the caller.

A function call looks exactly like a procedure call. The syntax rule is

```
function_call ⟸ function_name ⟦ ( parameter_association_list ) ⟧
```

The difference is that a function call is part of an expression, rather than being a sequential statement on its own, like a procedure call. Since a function is called as part of evaluation of an expression, a function is not allowed to include a wait statement (nor call a procedure that includes a wait statement). Expressions must always be evaluated within a single simulation cycle.

EXAMPLE 6.18   *A function to limit a value to be within bounds*

The following function calculates whether a value is within given bounds and returns a result limited to those bounds.

```
function limit ( value, min, max : integer ) return integer is
begin
  if value > max then
```

```
      return max;
    elsif value < min then
      return min;
    else
      return value;
    end if;
  end function limit;
```

A call to this function might be included in a variable assignment statement, as follows:

```
new_temperature := limit ( current_temperature
                            + increment, 10, 100 );
```

In this statement, the expression on the right-hand side of the assignment consists of just the function call, and the result returned is assigned to the variable **new_temperature**. However, we might also use the result of a function call in further computation, for example:

```
new_motor_speed := old_motor_speed
                     + scale_factor * limit ( error, -10, +10 );
```

EXAMPLE 6.19   *A bit-vector to numeric conversion function*

The function below determines the number represented in binary by a bit-vector value. The algorithm scans the bit vector from the most-significant end. For each bit, it multiplies the previously accumulated value by two and then adds in the integer value of the bit. The accumulated value is then used as the result of the function, passed back to the caller by the return statement.

```
function bv_to_natural ( bv : in bit_vector ) return natural is
  variable result : natural := 0;
begin
  for index in bv'range loop
    result := result * 2 + bit'pos(bv(index));
  end loop;
  return result;
end function bv_to_natural;
```

As an example of using this function, consider a model for a read-only memory, which represents the stored data as an array of bit vectors, as follows:

```
type rom_array is array (natural range 0 to rom_size-1)
                  of bit_vector(0 to word_size-1);
variable rom_data : rom_array;
```

If the model has an address port that is a bit vector, we can use the function to convert the address to a natural value to index the ROM data array, as follows:

```
    data <= rom_data ( bv_to_natural(address) ) after Taccess;
```

VHDL-87

The keyword **function** may not be included at the end of a function declaration in VHDL-87. Return statements may not be labeled in VHDL-87.

6.4.1 Functional Modeling

In Chapter 5 we looked at concurrent signal assignment statements for functional modeling of designs. We can use functions in VHDL to help us write functional models more expressively by defining a function that encapsulates the data transformation to be performed and then calling the function in a concurrent signal assignment statement. For example, given a declaration of a function to add two bit vectors:

```
function bv_add ( bv1, bv2 : in bit_vector ) return bit_vector is
begin
    . . .
end function bv_add;
```

and signals declared in an architecture body:

```
signal source1, source2, sum : bit_vector(0 to 31);
```

we can write a concurrent signal assignment statement as follows:

```
adder : sum <= bv_add(source1, source2) after T_delay_adder;
```

6.4.2 Pure and Impure Functions

Let us now return to the reason for the restrictions on the class and mode of function formal parameters stated above. These restrictions are in keeping with our idea that a function is a generalized form of operator. If we pass the same values to an operator, such as the addition operator, in different expressions, we expect the operator to return the same result each time. By restricting the formal parameters of a function in the way described above, we go part of the way to ensuring the same property for function calls. One additional restriction we need to make is that the function may not refer to any variables or signals declared by its parents, that is, by any process, subprogram or architecture body in which the function declaration is nested. Otherwise the variables or signals might change values between calls to the function, thus influencing the result of the function. We call a function that makes no such reference a *pure* function. We can explicitly declare a function to be pure by including the keyword **pure** in its definition, as shown by the syntax rule on page 222. If we leave it out, the function is assumed to be pure. Both of the above examples of function declarations are pure functions.

On the other hand, we may deliberately relax the restriction about a function referencing its parents' variables or signals by including the keyword **impure** in the function declaration. This is a warning to any caller of the function that it might produce different results on different calls, even when passed the same actual parameter values.

EXAMPLE 6.20   *A function returning unique sequence numbers*

Many network protocols require a sequence number in the packet header so that they can handle packets getting out of order during transmission. We can use an impure function to generate sequence numbers when creating packets in a behavioral model of a network interface. The following is an outline of a process that represents the output side of the network interface.

```
network_driver : process is

  constant seq_modulo : natural := 2**5;
  subtype seq_number is natural range 0 to seq_modulo-1;
  variable next_seq_number : seq_number := 0;
  . . .

  impure function generate_seq_number return seq_number is
    variable number : seq_number;
  begin
    number := next_seq_number;
    next_seq_number := (next_seq_number + 1) mod seq_modulo;
    return number;
  end function generate_seq_number;

begin   -- network_driver
  . . .
  new_header := pkt_header'( dest => target_host_id,
                            src => my_host_id,
                            pkt_type => control_pkt,
                            seq => generate_seq_number );

  . . .
end process network_driver;
```

In this model, the process has a variable **next_seq_number**, used by the function **generate_seq_number** to determine the return value each time it is called. The function has the side effect of incrementing this variable, thus changing the value to be returned on the next call. Because of the reference to the variable in the function's parent, the function must be declared to be impure. The advantage of writing the function this way lies in the expressive power of its call. The function call is simply part of an expression, in this case yielding an element in a record aggregate of type **pkt_header**. Writing it this way makes the process body more compact and easily understandable.

6.4.3 The Function **now**

VHDL provides a predefined function, **now**, that returns the current simulation time when it is called. It is defined as

> **impure function** now **return** delay_length;

Recall that the type **delay_length** is a predefined subtype of the physical type **time**, constrained to non-negative time values. The function **now** is often used to check that the inputs to a model obey the required timing constraints.

EXAMPLE 6.21   *A process to check hold time*

The process below checks the clock and data inputs of an edge-triggered flipflop for adherence to the minimum hold time constraint, **Thold_d_clk**. When the clock signal changes to '1', the process saves the current simulation time in the variable **last_clk_edge_time**. When the data input changes, the process tests whether the current simulation time has advanced beyond the time of the last clock edge by at least the minimum hold time, and reports an error if it has not.

```
hold_time_checker : process ( clk, d ) is
  variable last_clk_edge_time : time := 0 fs;
begin
  if rising_edge(clk) then
    last_clk_edge_time := now;
  end if;
  if d'event then
    assert now - last_clk_edge_time >= Thold_d_clk
      report "hold time violation";
  end if;
end process hold_time_checker;
```

VHDL-93 and -2002

The function **now** was originally defined to be impure in VHDL-93. As a consequence, it could not be used in an expression that must be globally static. While the need to do this is rare, it did lead to **now** being pure in VHDL-2002. However, that caused more problems than it solved, so the change was reversed in VHDL-2002.

VHDL-87

The function **now** returns a value of type **time** in VHDL-87, since the subtype **delay_length** is not predefined in VHDL-87.

6.5 Overloading

When we are writing subprograms, it is a good idea to choose names for our subprograms that indicate what operations they perform to make it easier for a reader to understand our models. This raises the question of how to name two subprograms that perform the same kind of operation but on parameters of different types. For example, we might wish to write two procedures to increment variables holding numeric values, but in some cases the values are represented as type integer, and in other cases they are represented using type bit_vector. Ideally, since both procedures perform the same operation, we would like to give them the same name, such as increment. But if we did that, would we be able to tell them apart when we wanted to call them? Recall that VHDL strictly enforces the type rules, so we have to refer to the right procedure depending on the type of the variable we wish to increment.

Fortunately, VHDL allows us to define subprograms in this way, using a technique called *overloading* of subprogram names. We can define two distinct subprograms with the same name but with different numbers or types of formal parameters. When we call one of them, the number and types of the actual parameters we supply in the call are used to determine which subprogram to invoke. It is the context of the call that determines how to resolve the apparent ambiguity. We have already seen overloading applied to identifiers used as literals in enumeration types (see Chapter 2). We saw that if two enumeration types included the same identifier, the context of use in a model is used to determine which type is meant.

The precise rules used to disambiguate a subprogram call when the subprogram name is overloaded are quite complex, so we will not enumerate them all here. Fortunately, they are sufficiently complete to sort out most situations that arise in practice. Instead, we look at some examples to show how overloading of procedures and functions works in straightforward cases. First, here are some procedure outlines for the increment operation described above:

```
procedure increment ( a : inout integer;
                      n : in integer := 1 ) is ...

procedure increment ( a : inout bit_vector;
                      n : in bit_vector := B"1" ) is ...

procedure increment ( a : inout bit_vector;
                      n : in integer := 1 ) is ...
```

Suppose we also have some variables declared as follows:

```
variable count_int : integer := 2;
variable count_bv : bit_vector (15 downto 0) := X"0002";
```

If we write a procedure call using count_int as the first actual parameter, it is clear that we are referring to the first procedure, since it is the only one whose first formal parameter is an integer. Both of the following calls can be disambiguated in this way:

```
increment ( count_int, 2 );
increment ( count_int );
```

Similarly, both of the next two calls can be sorted out:

```
increment ( count_bv, X"0002");
increment ( count_bv, 1 );
```

The first call refers to the second procedure, since the actual parameters are both bit vectors. Similarly, the second call refers to the third procedure, since the actual parameters are a bit vector and an integer. Problems arise, however, if we try to make a call as follows:

```
increment ( count_bv );
```

This could equally well be a call to either the second or the third procedure, both of which have default values for the second formal parameter. Since it is not possible to determine which procedure is meant, a VHDL analyzer rejects such a call as an error.

6.5.1   Overloading Operator Symbols

When we introduced function subprograms in Section 6.4, we described them as a generalization of operators used in expressions, such as "+", "–", **and**, **or** and so on. Looking at this the other way around, we could say that the predefined operators are specialized functions, with a convenient notation for calling them. In fact, this is exactly what they are. Furthermore, since each of the operators can be applied to values of various types, we see that the functions they represent are overloaded, so the operand types determine the particular version of each operator used in an expression.

Given that we can define our own types in VHDL, it would be convenient if we could extend the predefined operators to work with these types. For example, if we are using bit vectors to model integers using two's-complement notation, we would like to use the addition operator to add two bit vectors in this form. Fortunately, VHDL provides a way for us to define new functions using the operator symbols as names. The extended syntax rules for subprogram declarations are shown in Appendix B. Our bit-vector addition function can be declared as

```
function "+" ( left, right : in bit_vector ) return bit_vector is
begin
  ...
end function "+";
```

We can then call this function using the infix "+" operator with bit-vector operands; for example:

```
variable addr_reg : bit_vector(31 downto 0);
...
addr_reg := addr_reg + X"0000_0004";
```

Operators denoted by reserved words can be overloaded in the same way. For example, we can declare a bit-vector absolute-value function as

```
function "abs" ( right : in bit_vector ) return bit_vector is
begin
  ...
end function "abs";
```

We can use this operator with a bit-vector operand, for example:

```
variable accumulator : bit_vector(31 downto 0);
...
accumulator := abs accumulator;
```

We can overload any of the operator symbols shown in Table 2.2. One important point to note, however, is that overloaded versions of the logical operators **and**, **nand**, **or** and **nor** are not evaluated in the short-circuit manner described in Chapter 2. For any type of operands other than **bit** and **boolean**, both operands are evaluated first, then passed to the function.

EXAMPLE 6.22 *Use of overloaded logical operations in control logic*

The **std_logic_1164** package defines functions for logical operators applied to values of type **std_ulogic** and **std_ulogic_vector**. We can use them in functional models to write Boolean equations that represent the behavior of a design. For example, the following model describes a block of logic that controls an input/output register in a microcontroller system. The architecture body describes the behavior in terms of Boolean equations. Its concurrent signal assignment statements use the logical operators **and** and **not**, referring to the overloaded functions defined in the std_logic_1164 package.

```
library ieee;  use ieee.std_logic_1164.all;

entity reg_ctrl is
  port ( reg_addr_decoded,
         rd, wr, io_en, cpu_clk : in std_ulogic;
         reg_rd, reg_wr : out std_ulogic );
end entity reg_ctrl;

-------------------------------------------------

architecture bool_eqn of reg_ctrl is
begin
  rd_ctrl : reg_rd <= reg_addr_decoded and rd and io_en;
  rw_ctrl : reg_wr <= reg_addr_decoded and wr and io_en
                        and not cpu_clk;
end architecture bool_eqn;
```

VHDL-87

Since VHDL-87 does not provide the shift operators **sll**, **srl**, **sla**, **sra**, **rol**, and **ror** and the logical operator **xnor**, they cannot be used as operator symbols.

6.6 Visibility of Declarations

The last topic we need to discuss in relation to subprograms is the use of names declared within a model. We have seen that names of types, constants, variables and other items defined in a subprogram can be used in that subprogram. Also, in the case of procedures and impure functions, names declared in an enclosing process, subprogram or architecture body can also be used. The question we must answer is: What are the limits of use of each name?

To answer this question, we introduce the idea of the *visibility* of a declaration, which is the region of the text of a model in which it is possible to refer to the declared name. We have seen that architecture bodies, processes and subprograms are each divided into two parts: a declarative part and a body of statements. A name declared in a declarative part is visible from the end of the declaration itself down to the end of the corresponding statement part. Within this area we can refer to the declared name. Before the declaration, within it and beyond the end of the statement part, we cannot refer to the name because it is not visible.

EXAMPLE 6.23   *Visibility of declarations within an architecture body*

Figure 6.1 shows an outline of an architecture body of a model. It contains a number of declarations, including some procedure declarations. The visibility of each of the declarations is indicated. The first item to be declared is the type t; its visibility extends to the end of the architecture body. Thus it can be referred in other declarations, such as the variable declarations. The second declaration is the signal s; its visibility likewise extends to the end of the architecture body. So the assignment within procedure p1 is valid. The third and final declaration in the declarative part of the architecture body is that of the procedure p1, whose visibility extends to the end of the architecture body, allowing it to be called in either of the processes. It includes a local variable, v1, whose visibility extends only to the end of p1. This means it can be referred to in p1, as shown in the signal assignment statement, but neither process can refer to it.

In the statement part of the architecture body, we have two process statements, **proc1** and **proc2**. The first includes a local variable declaration, **v2**, whose visibility extends to the end of the process body. Hence we can refer to **v2** in the process body and in the procedure **p2** declared within the process. The visibility of **p2** likewise extends to the end of the body of **proc1**, allowing us to call **p2** within **proc1**. The procedure **p2** includes a local variable declaration, **v3**, whose visibility extends to the end of the statement part of **p2**. Hence we can refer to **v3** in the statement part of **p2**. However, we cannot refer to **v3** in the statement part of **proc1**, since it is not visible in that part of the model.

FIGURE 6.1

```
architecture arch of ent is                                              t
    type t is ...;                                                     s
    signal s : t;                                                   p1
    procedure p1 ( ... ) is
        variable v1 : t;                            v1
    begin
        v1 := s;
    end procedure p1;
begin   -- arch
    proc1 : process is
        variable v2 : t;                                    v2
        procedure p2 ( ... ) is                        p2
            variable v3 : t;                   v3
        begin
            p1 ( v2, v3, ... );
        end procedure p2;
    begin   -- proc1
        p2 ( v2, ... );
    end process proc1;
    proc2 : process is
        ...
    begin   -- proc2
        p1 ( ... );
    end process proc2;
end architecture arch;
```

An outline of an architecture body, showing the visibility of declared names within it.

Finally, we come to the second process, **proc2**. The only items we can refer to here are those declared in the architecture body declarative part, namely, **t**, **s** and **p1**. We cannot call the procedure **p2** within **proc2**, since it is local to **proc1**.

One point we mentioned earlier about subprograms but did not go into in detail was that we can include nested subprogram declarations within the declarative part of a subprogram. This means we can have local procedures and functions within a procedure or a function. In such cases, the simple rule for the visibility of a declaration still applies, so any items declared within an outer procedure before the declaration of a nested procedure can be referred to inside the nested procedure.

EXAMPLE 6.24 *Nested subprograms for memory read operations*

The following is an outline of an architecture of a cache memory for a computer system.

```
architecture behavioral of cache is
begin

  behavior : process is

    ...

    procedure read_block( start_address : natural;
                          entry : out cache_block ) is

      variable memory_address_reg : natural;
      variable memory_data_reg : word;

      procedure read_memory_word is
      begin
        mem_addr <= memory_address_reg;
        mem_read <= '1';
        wait until mem_ack;
        memory_data_reg := mem_data_in;
        mem_read <= '0';
        wait until not mem_ack;
      end procedure read_memory_word;

    begin   -- read_block
      for offset in 0 to block_size - 1 loop
        memory_address_reg := start_address + offset;
        read_memory_word;
        entry(offset) := memory_data_reg;
      end loop;
    end procedure read_block;

  begin   -- behavior
    ...
    read_block( miss_base_address, data_store(entry_index) );
    ...
  end process behavior;

end architecture behavioral;
```

The entity interface (not shown) includes ports named **mem_addr**, **mem_ready**, **mem_ack** and **mem_data_in**. The process behavior contains a procedure, **read_block**, which reads a block of data from main memory on a cache miss. It has the local variables **memory_address_reg** and **memory_data_reg**. Nested inside of this procedure is another procedure, **read_memory_word**, which reads a single word of data from memory. It uses the value placed in **memory_address_reg** by the outer procedure and leaves the data read from memory in **memory_data_reg**.

Now let us consider a model in which we have one subprogram nested inside another, and each declares an item with the same name as the other, as shown in Figure 6.2. Here, the first variable **v** is visible within all of the procedure **p2** and the statement body of **p1**. However, because **p2** declares its own local variable called **v**, the variable belonging to **p1** is not *directly visible* where **p2**'s **v** is visible. We say the inner variable declaration *hides* the outer declaration, since it declares the same name. Hence the addition within **p2** applies to the local variable **v** of **p2** and does not affect the variable **v** of **p1**. If we need to refer to an item that is visible but hidden, we can use a selected name. For example, within **p2** in Figure 6.2, we can use the name **p1.v** to refer to the variable **v** declared in **p1**. Although the outer declaration is not directly visible, it is *visible by selection*. An important point to note about using a selected name in this way is that it can only be used within the construct containing the declaration. Thus, in Figure 6.2, we can only refer to **p1.v** within **p1**. We cannot use the name **p1.v** to "peek inside" of **p1** from places outside **p1**.

The idea of hiding is not restricted to variable declarations within nested procedures. Indeed, it applies in any case where we have one declarative part nested within another, and an item is declared with the same name in each declarative part in such a way that the rules for resolving overloaded names are unable to distinguish between them. The advantage of having inner declarations hide outer declarations, as opposed to the alternative of simply disallowing an inner declaration with the same name, is that it allows us to write local procedures and processes without having to know the names of all items declared at outer levels. This is certainly beneficial when writing large models. In practice, if we are

FIGURE 6.2

```
procedure p1 is                                    v
   variable v : integer;         ────────────┐
   procedure p2 is                       v
      variable v : integer;     ─────────┐
   begin    -- p2                        │    │
      ...                                │    │
      v := v + 1;                        │    │
      ...                                │    │
   end procedure p2;            ─────────┘    │
begin    -- p1                                │
   ...                                        │
   v := 2 * v;                                │
   ...                                        │
end procedure p1;               ──────────────┘
```

Nested procedures showing hiding of names. The declaration of v *in* **p2** *hides the variable* v *declared in* **p1**.

reading a model and need to check the use of a name in a statement against its declaration, we only need to look at successively enclosing declarative parts until we find a declaration of the name, and that is the declaration that applies.

Exercises

1.   [❶ 6.2] Write parameter specifications for the following constant-class parameters:

     *   an integer, operand1,

     *   a bit vector, tag, indexed from 31 down to 16, and

     *   a Boolean, trace, with default value false.

2.   [❶ 6.2] Write parameter specifications for the following variable-class parameters:

     *   a real number, average, used to pass data back from a procedure, and

     *   a string, identifier, modified by a procedure.

3.   [❶ 6.2] Write parameter specifications for the following signal-class parameters:

     *   a bit signal, clk, to be assigned to by a procedure, and

     *   an unconstrained standard-logic vector signal, data_in, whose value is to be read by a procedure.

4.   [❶ 6.2] Given the following procedure declaration:

```
procedure stimulate ( signal target : out bit_vector;
                      delay : in delay_length := 1 ns;
                      cycles : in natural := 1 ) is ...
```

     write procedure calls using a signal s as the actual parameter for target and using the following values for the other parameters:

     *   delay = 5 ns, cycles = 3,

     *   delay = 10 ns, cycles = 1 and

     *   delay = 1 ns, cycles = 15.

5.   [❶ 6.3] Suppose we have a procedure declared as

```
procedure shuffle_bytes
  ( signal d_in : in std_ulogic_vector(0 to 15);
    signal d_out : out std_ulogic_vector(0 to 15);
    signal shuffle_control : in std_ulogic;
    prop_delay : delay_length ) is ...
```

     Write the equivalent process for the following concurrent procedure call:

```
swapper : shuffle_bytes ( ext_data, int_data, swap_control,
                          Tpd_swap );
```

6. [❶ 6.4] Suppose we have a function declared as

```
function approx_log_2 ( a : in bit_vector ) return positive is ...
```

that calculates the minimum number of bits needed to represent a binary-encoded number. Write a variable assignment statement that calculates the minimum number of bits needed to represent the product of two numbers in the variables **multiplicand** and **multiplier** and assigns the result to the variable **product_size**.

7. [❶ 6.4] Write an assertion statement that verifies that the current simulation time has not exceeded 20 ms.

8. [❶ 6.5] Given the declarations of the three procedures named **increment** and the variables **count_int** and **count_bv** shown on page 227, which of the three procedures, if any, is referred to by each of the following procedure calls?

```
increment ( count_bv, -1 );
increment ( count_int );
increment ( count_int, B"1" );
increment ( count_bv, 16#10# );
```

9. [❶ 6.6] Show the parts of the following model in which each of the declared items is visible:

```
architecture behavioral of computer_system is

  signal internal_data : bit_vector(31 downto 0);

  interpreter : process is

    variable opcode : bit_vector(5 downto 0);

    procedure do_write is
      variable aligned_address : natural;
    begin
      ...
    end procedure do_write;

  begin
    ...
  end process interpreter;

end architecture behavioral;
```

10. [❷ 6.1] Write a procedure that calculates the sum of squares of elements of an array variable **deviations**. The elements are real numbers. Your procedure should store the result in a real variable **sum_of_squares**.

11. [❷ 6.1] Write a procedure that generates a 1 µs pulse every 20 µs on a signal **syn_clk**. When the signal **reset** changes to '1', the procedure should immediately set **syn_clk** to '0' and return.

12. [❷ 6.2] Write a procedure called **align_address** that aligns a binary encoded address in a bit-vector variable parameter. The procedure has a second parameter that indicates the alignment size. If the size is 1, the address is unchanged. If the size is 2, the address is rounded to a multiple of 2 by clearing the least-significant bit. If the size is 4, two bits are cleared, and if the size is 8, three bits are cleared. The default alignment size is 4.

13. [❷ 6.2/6.3] Write a procedure that checks the hold time of a data signal with respect to rising edges of a clock signal. Both signals are of the IEEE standard-logic type. The signals and the hold time are parameters of the procedure. The procedure is invoked by a concurrent procedure call.

14. [❷ 6.2/6.3] Write a procedure, to be invoked by a concurrent procedure call, that assigns successive natural numbers to a signal at regular intervals. The signal and the interval between numbers are parameters of the procedure.

15. [❷ 6.4] Write a function, **weaken**, that maps a standard-logic value to the same value, but with weak drive strength. Thus, '0' and 'L' are mapped to 'L', '1' and 'H' are mapped to 'H', 'X' and 'W' are mapped to 'W' and all other values are unchanged.

16. [❷ 6.4] Write a function, returning a Boolean result, that tests whether a standard-logic signal currently has a valid edge. A valid edge is defined to be a transition from '0' or 'L' to '1' or 'H' or vice versa. Other transitions, such as 'X' to '1', are not valid.

17. [❷ 6.4] Write two functions, one to find the maximum value in an array of integers and the other to find the minimum value.

18. [❷ 6.5] Write overloaded versions of the logical operators to operate on integer operands. The operators should treat the value 0 as logical falsehood and any non-zero value as logical truth.

19. [❸ 6.2] Write a procedure called **scan_results** with an **in**-mode bit-vector signal parameter **results**, and **out**-mode variable parameters **majority_value** of type **bit**, **majority_count** of type **natural** and **tie** of type **boolean**. The procedure counts the occurrences of '0' and '1' values in **results**. It sets **majority_value** to the most frequently occurring value, **majority_count** to the number of occurrences and **tie** to true if there are an equal number of occurrences of '0' and '1'.

20. [❸ 6.2/6.3] Write a procedure that stimulates a bit-vector signal passed as a parameter. The procedure assigns to the signal a sequence of all possible bit-vector values. The first value is assigned to the signal immediately, then subsequent values are assigned at intervals specified by a second parameter. After the last value is assigned, the procedure returns.

21. [❸ 6.2/6.3] Write a passive procedure that checks that setup and hold times for a data signal with respect to rising edges of a clock signal are observed. The signals and the setup and hold times are parameters of the procedure. Include a concurrent procedure call to the procedure in the statement part of a D-flipflop entity.

22. [❸ 6.4] Write a function that calculates the cosine of a real number, using the series

$$\cos\theta = 1 - \frac{\theta^2}{2!} + \frac{\theta^4}{4!} - \frac{\theta^6}{6!} + \cdots$$

Next, write a second function that returns a cosine table of the following type:

type table **is array** (0 **to** 1023) **of** real;

Element *i* of the table has the value $\cos(i\pi/2048)$. Finally, develop a behavioral model of a cosine lookup ROM. The architecture body should include a constant of type **table**, initialized using a call to the second function.

Chapter 7

Packages and Use Clauses

Packages in VHDL provide an important way of organizing the data and subprograms declared in a model. In this chapter, we describe the basics of packages and show how they may be used. We will return to packages in Chapter 11, where we will see how they can be extended to make them more reusable than the basic form we discuss here.

7.1 Package Declarations

A VHDL package is simply a way of grouping a collection of related declarations that serve a common purpose. They might be a set of subprograms that provide operations on a particular type of data, or they might just be the set of declarations needed to model a particular design. The important thing is that they can be collected together into a separate design unit that can be worked on independently and reused in different parts of a model.

Another important aspect of packages is that they separate the external view of the items they declare from the implementation of those items. The external view is specified in a *package declaration*, whereas the implementation is defined in a separate *package body*. We will look at package declaration first and return to the package body shortly.

The syntax rule for writing a package declaration is

package_declaration ⇐
    package identifier is
        ⟦ package_declarative_item ⟧
    end ⟦ **package** ⟧ ⟦ identifier ⟧ ;

The identifier provides a name for the package, which we can use elsewhere in a model to refer to the package. Inside the package declaration we write a collection of declarations, including type, subtype, constant, signal and subprogram declarations, as well as several other kinds of declarations that we see in later chapters. These are the declarations that are provided to the users of the package. The advantage of placing them in a package is that they do not clutter up other parts of a model, and they can be shared within and between models without having to rewrite them.

EXAMPLE 7.1   *A package as part of a CPU model*

The following package declares constants and types that we can use in a model of a
CPU:

```
package cpu_types is

    constant word_size : positive := 16;
    constant address_size : positive := 24;

    subtype word is bit_vector(word_size - 1 downto 0);
    subtype address is bit_vector(address_size - 1 downto 0);

    type status_value is ( halted, idle, fetch,
                           mem_read, mem_write,
                           io_read, io_write, int_ack );

end package cpu_types;
```

VHDL-87

The keyword **package** may not be included at the end of a package declaration in
VHDL-87.

Most of the time, we write a package as another form of design unit, along with entity
declarations and architecture bodies. It is separately analyzed and is placed into the working library as a library unit by the analyzer. From there, other library units can refer to an
item declared in the package using the *selected name* of the item. The selected name is
formed by writing the library name, then the package name and then the name of the item,
all separated by dots; for example:

```
work.cpu_types.status_value
```

EXAMPLE 7.2   *An address decoder using the* cpu_types *package*

Suppose the **cpu_types** package, shown in Example 7.1, has been analyzed and
placed into the **work** library. We might make use of the declared items when modeling
an address decoder to go with a CPU. The entity declaration and architecture body of
the decoder are:

```
entity address_decoder is
  port ( addr : in work.cpu_types.address;
         status : in work.cpu_types.status_value;
         mem_sel, int_sel, io_sel : out bit );
end entity address_decoder;
```

```
architecture functional of address_decoder is

  constant mem_low : work.cpu_types.address := X"000000";
  constant mem_high : work.cpu_types.address := X"EFFFFF";
  constant io_low : work.cpu_types.address := X"F00000";
  constant io_high : work.cpu_types.address := X"FFFFFF";

begin

  mem_decoder :
    mem_sel <=
      '1' when ( work.cpu_types."="
                    (status, work.cpu_types.fetch)
                  or work.cpu_types."="(
                      status, work.cpu_types.mem_read)
                  or work.cpu_types."="
                      (status, work.cpu_types.mem_write) )
                and addr >= mem_low
                and addr <= mem_high else
      '0';

  int_decoder :
    int_sel <=
      '1' when work.cpu_types."="
                  (status, work.cpu_types.int_ack) else
      '0';

  io_decoder :
    io_sel <=
      '1' when ( work.cpu_types."="
                    (status, work.cpu_types.io_read)
                  or work.cpu_types."="
                      (status, work.cpu_types.io_write) )
                and addr >= io_low
                and addr <= io_high else
      '0';

end architecture functional;
```

Note that we have to use selected names to refer to the subtype **address**, the type **status_value**, the enumeration literals of **status_value** and the implicitly declared "=" operator, defined in the package **cpu_types**. This is because they are not directly visible within the entity declaration and architecture body. We will see later in this chapter how a use clause can help us avoid long selected names. If we needed to type-qualify the enumeration literals, we would use selected names for both the type name and the literal name; for example:

```
work.cpu_types.status_value'(work.cpu_types.fetch)
```

We have seen that a package, when analyzed, is placed into the working library. Items in the package can be accessed by other library units using selected names starting with **work**. However, if we are writing a package of generally useful declarations, we may wish to place them into a different library, such as a project library, where they can be accessed by other designers. Different VHDL tool suites provide different ways of specifying the library into which a library unit is placed. We must consult the documentation for a particular product to find out what to do. However, once the package has been included in a resource library, we can refer to items declared in it using selected names, starting with the resource library name. As an example, we might consider the IEEE standard-logic package, which must be placed in a resource library called ieee. We can refer to the types declared in that package, for example:

```
variable stored_state : ieee.std_logic_1164.std_ulogic;
```

One kind of declaration we can include in a package declaration is a signal declaration. This gives us a way of defining a signal, such as a master clock or reset signal, that is global to a whole design, instead of being restricted to a single architecture body. Any module that needs to refer to the global signal simply names it using the selected name as described above. This avoids the clutter of having to specify the signal as a port in each entity that uses it, making the model a little less complex. However, it does mean that a module can affect the overall behavior of a system by means other than through its ports, namely, by assigning to global signals. This effectively means that part of the module's interface is implicit, rather than being specified in the port map of the entity. As a matter of style, global signals declared in packages should be used sparingly, and their use should be clearly documented with comments in the model.

EXAMPLE 7.3   *A package containing clock signal declarations*

The following package declares two clock signals for use within an integrated circuit design for an input/output interface controller.

```
library ieee;  use ieee.std_logic_1164.all;

package clock_pkg is
   constant Tpw : delay_length := 4 ns;
   signal clock_phase1, clock_phase2 : std_ulogic;
end package clock_pkg;
```

The top-level architecture of the controller circuit is outlined below. The instance of the **phase_locked_clock_gen** entity uses the **ref_clock** port of the circuit to generate the two-phase clock waveforms on the global clock signals. The architecture also includes an instance of an entity that sequences bus operations using the bus control signals and generates internal register control signals.

```
library ieee;  use ieee.std_logic_1164.all;
```

```
entity io_controller is
  port ( ref_clock : in std_ulogic;  ... );
end entity io_controller;

-------------------------------------------------

architecture top_level of io_controller is

  ...

begin

  internal_clock_gen :
    entity work.phase_locked_clock_gen(std_cell)
      port map ( reference => ref_clock,
                 phi1 => work.clock_pkg.clock_phase1,
                 phi2 => work.clock_pkg.clock_phase2 );

  the_bus_sequencer :
    entity work.bus_sequencer(fsm)
      port map ( rd, wr, sel, width, burst,
                 addr(1 downto 0), ready,
                 control_reg_wr, status_reg_rd,
                 data_fifo_wr, data_fifo_rd,
                 ... );

  ...

end architecture top_level;
```

The architecture body for the sequencer is outlined next. It creates an instance of a register entity and connects the global clock signals to its clock input ports.

```
architecture fsm of bus_sequencer is

  -- This architecture implements the sequencer as
  -- a finite-state machine. NOTE: it uses the clock signals
  -- from clock_pkg to synchronize the fsm.

  signal next_state_vector : ...;

begin

  bus_sequencer_state_register :
    entity work.state_register(std_cell)
      port map ( phi1 => work.clock_pkg.clock_phase1,
                 phi2 => work.clock_pkg.clock_phase2,
                 next_state => next_state_vector,
                 ... );

  ...

end architecture fsm;
```

7.1.1 Subprograms in Package Declarations

Another kind of declaration that may be included in a package declaration is a subprogram declaration—either a procedure or a function declaration. This ability allows us to write subprograms that implement useful operations and to call them from a number of different modules. An important use of this feature is to declare subprograms that operate on values of a type declared by the package. This gives us a way of conceptually extending VHDL with new types and operations, so-called *abstract data types*.

An important aspect of declaring a subprogram in a package declaration is that we only write the header of the subprogram, that is, the part that includes the name and the interface list defining the parameters (and result type for functions). We leave out the body of the subprogram. The reason for this is that the package declaration, as we mentioned earlier, provides only the external view of the items it declares, leaving the implementation of the items to the package body. For items such as types and signals, the complete definition is needed in the external view. However, for subprograms, we need only know the information contained in the header to be able to call the subprogram. As users of a subprogram, we need not be concerned with how it achieves its effect or calculates its result. This is an example of a general principle called *information hiding*: making an interface visible but hiding the details of implementation. To illustrate this idea, suppose we have a package declaration that defines a bit-vector subtype:

```
subtype word32 is bit_vector(31 downto 0);
```

We can include in the package a procedure to do addition on **word32** values that represent signed integers. The procedure declaration in the package declaration is

```
procedure add ( a, b : in word32;
                result : out word32;  overflow : out boolean );
```

Note that we do not include the keyword **is** or any of the local declarations or statements needed to perform the addition. These are deferred to the package body. All we include is the description of the formal parameters of the procedure. Similarly, we might include a function to perform an arithmetic comparison of two **word32** values:

```
function "<" ( a, b : in word32 ) return boolean;
```

Again, we omit the local declarations and statements, simply specifying the formal parameters and the result type of the function.

7.1.2 Constants in Package Declarations

Just as we can apply the principle of information hiding to subprograms declared in a package, we can also apply it to constants declared in a package. The external view of a constant is just its name and type. We need to know these in order to use it, but we do not actually need to know its value. This may seem strange at first, but if we recall that the idea of introducing constant declarations in the first place was to avoid scattering literal values throughout a model, it makes more sense. We defer specifying the value of a constant declared in a package by omitting the initialization expression; for example:

```
constant max_buffer_size : positive;
```

This defines the constant to be a positive integer value. However, since we cannot see the actual value, we are not tempted to write the value as an integer literal in a model that uses the package. The specification of the actual value is deferred to the package body, where it is not visible to a model that uses the package. Given the above deferred constant in a package declaration, the corresponding package body must include the full constant declaration, for example:

```
constant max_buffer_size : positive := 4096;
```

Note that we do not have to defer the value in a constant declaration—it is optional.

EXAMPLE 7.4   *The CPU package extended with operations*

We can extend the package specification from Example 7.1, declaring useful types for a CPU model, by including declarations related to opcode processing. The revised package is shown below. It includes a subtype that represents an opcode value, a function to extract an opcode from an instruction word and a number of constants representing the opcodes for different instructions.

```
package cpu_types is

    constant word_size : positive := 16;
    constant address_size : positive := 24;

    subtype word is bit_vector(word_size - 1 downto 0);
    subtype address is bit_vector(address_size - 1 downto 0);

    type status_value is ( halted, idle, fetch,
                           mem_read, mem_write,
                           io_read, io_write, int_ack );

    subtype opcode is bit_vector(5 downto 0);

    function extract_opcode ( instr_word : word ) return opcode;

    constant op_nop : opcode := "000000";
    constant op_breq : opcode := "000001";
    constant op_brne : opcode := "000010";
    constant op_add : opcode := "000011";
    ...

end package cpu_types;
```

A behavioral model of a CPU that uses these declarations is

```
architecture behavioral of cpu is
begin

    interpreter : process is
```

```
      variable instr_reg : work.cpu_types.word;
      variable instr_opcode : work.cpu_types.opcode;
  begin
    ...  -- initialize
    loop
      ...  -- fetch instruction
      instr_opcode := work.cpu_types.extract_opcode(instr_reg);
      case instr_opcode is
        when work.cpu_types.op_nop => null;
        when work.cpu_types.op_breq => ...
        ...
      end case;
    end loop;
  end process interpreter;

end architecture behavioral;
```

The instruction set interpreter process declares a variable of the **opcode** type and uses the **extract_opcode** function to extract the bits representing the opcode from the fetched instruction word. It then uses the constants from the package as choices in a case statement to decode and execute the instruction specified by the opcode. Note that since the constants are used as choices in the case statement, they must be locally static. If we had deferred the values of the constants to the package body, their value would not be known when the case statement was analyzed. This is why we included the constant values in the package declaration. In general, the value of a deferred constant is not locally static.

7.2 Package Bodies

Now that we have seen how to define the interface to a package, we can turn to the package body. Each package declaration that includes subprogram declarations or deferred constant declarations must have a corresponding package body to fill in the missing details. However, if a package declaration only includes other kinds of declarations, such as types, signals or fully specified constants, no package body is necessary. The syntax rule for a package body is similar to that for the interface, but with the inclusion of the keyword **body**:

> package_body ⇐
>   **package body** identifier **is**
>   ⦃ package_body_declarative_item ⦄
>   **end** ⟦ **package body** ⟧ ⟦ identifier ⟧ ;

The items declared in a package body must include the full declarations of all subprograms defined in the corresponding package declaration. These full declarations must include the subprogram headers exactly as they are written in the package declaration, to ensure that the implementation *conforms* with the interface. This means that the names, types, modes and default values of each of the formal parameters must be repeated ex-

actly. There are only two variations allowed. First, a numeric literal may be written differently, for example, in a different base, provided it has the same value. Second, a simple
name consisting just of an identifier may be replaced by a selected name, provided it refers
to the same item. While this conformance requirement might seem an imposition at first,
in practice it is not. Any reasonable text editor used to create a VHDL model allows the
header to be copied from the package declaration with little difficulty. Similarly, a deferred
constant defined in a package declaration must have its value specified by repeating the
declaration in the package body, this time filling in the initialization expression as in a full
constant declaration.

In addition to the full declarations of items deferred from the package declaration, a
package body may include declarations of additional types, subtypes, constants and subprograms. These items are used to implement the subprograms defined in the package
declaration. Note that the items declared in the package declaration cannot be declared
again in the body (apart from subprograms and deferred constants, as described above),
since they are automatically visible in the body. Furthermore, the package body cannot
include declarations of additional signals. Signal declarations may only be included in the
interface declaration of a package.

EXAMPLE 7.5   *A package of overloaded arithmetic operators*

The package declaration outlined below declares overloaded versions of arithmetic
operators for bit-vector values. The functions treat bit vectors as representing signed
integers in binary form. Only the function headers are included in the package declaration.

```
package bit_vector_signed_arithmetic is

  function "+" ( bv1, bv2 : bit_vector )
    return bit_vector;

  function "-" ( bv : bit_vector )
    return bit_vector;

  function "*" ( bv1, bv2 : bit_vector )
    return bit_vector;

  ...

end package bit_vector_signed_arithmetic;
```

The package body contains the full function bodies. It also includes a function,
mult_unsigned, not defined in the package declaration. It is used internally in the
package body to implement the signed multiplication operator.

```
package body bit_vector_signed_arithmetic is

  function "+" ( bv1, bv2 : bit_vector )
    return bit_vector is ...

  function "-" ( bv : bit_vector )
    return bit_vector is ...
```

```
    function mult_unsigned ( bv1, bv2 : bit_vector )
      return bit_vector is
      ...
    begin
      ...
    end function mult_unsigned;

    function "*" ( bv1, bv2 : bit_vector )
      return bit_vector is
    begin
      if not bv1(bv1'left) and not bv2(bv2'left) then
        return mult_unsigned(bv1, bv2);
      elsif not bv1(bv1'left) and bv2(bv2'left) then
        return -mult_unsigned(bv1, -bv2);
      elsif bv1(bv1'left) and not bv2(bv2'left) then
        return -mult_unsigned(-bv1, bv2);
      else
        return mult_unsigned(-bv1, -bv2);
      end if;
    end function "*";

    ...

  end package body bit_vector_signed_arithmetic;
```

One further point to mention on the topic of packages relates to the order of analysis. We mentioned before that a package is usually a separate design unit that is analyzed separately from other design units, such as entity declarations and architecture bodies. (We will return to the case of a package not being a design unit shortly.) In most cases, a package declaration and its corresponding package body are each separate design units; hence they may be analyzed separately. A package declaration is a primary design unit, and a package body is a secondary design unit. The package body depends on information defined in the package declaration, so the declaration must be analyzed first. Furthermore, the declaration must be analyzed before any other design unit that refers to an item defined by the package. Once the declaration has been analyzed, it does not matter when the body is analyzed in relation to units that use the package, provided it is analyzed before the model is elaborated. In a large suite of models, the dependency relationships can get quite complex, and a correct order of analysis can be difficult to find. A good VHDL tool suite will provide some degree of automating this process by working out the dependency relationships and analyzing those units needed to build a particular target unit to simulate or synthesize.

VHDL-87

The keywords **package body** may not be included at the end of a package body in VHDL-87.

7.2.1 Local Packages

We have mentioned that package declarations and package bodies are usually separate design units, but that there are cases where that is not so. VHDL allows us to declare a package locally within the declarative part of an entity, architecture body, process, or subprogram. This allows the visibility of the package to be contained to just the enclosing declarative part and the corresponding statement part. If the package declaration requires a package body, we must write the package body in the same declarative part after the package declaration. Since declarations written in a package body are not visible outside the package, we can use a local package to provide controlled access to locally declared items.

EXAMPLE 7.6 *A package to manage unique identification numbers*

Suppose we need to generate test cases in a design, with each test case having a unique identification number. We can declare a package locally within a stimulus-generator process. The package encapsulates a variable that tracks the next identification number to be assigned, and provides an operation to yield the next number. The process outline is:

```
stim_gen : process is

  package ID_manager is
    impure function get_ID return natural;
  end package ID_manager;

  package body ID_manager is
    variable next_ID : natural := 0;
    impure function get_ID return natural is
      variable result : natural;
    begin
      result := next_ID;
      next_ID := next_ID + 1;
      return result;
    end function get_ID;
  end package body ID_manager;
  ...

  type test_case is record
    ...
    ID : natural;
  end record test_case;
  variable next_test_case : test_case;
begin
  ...
  next_test_case.ID := ID_manager.get_ID;
  ID_manager.next_ID := 0;  -- Illegal
```

```
   . . .
   end process stim_gen;
```

The variable **next_ID** is declared in the package body, and so is not visible outside the package. The only way to access it is using the **get_ID** function provided by the package declaration. This is shown in the first assignment statement within the process body. The package name is used as a prefix in the selected name for the function. The second assignment statement is illegal, since the variable is not visible at that point. The package provides a measure of safety against inadvertent corruption of the data state.

By writing the package locally within the process, it is only available in the process. Thus, we have achieved greater separation of concerns than if we had written the package as a design unit, making it globally visible. Moreover, since the package is local to a process, there can be no concurrent access by multiple processes. Thus, the encapsulated variable can be an ordinary non-shared variable. If the package were declared as a global design unit, there could be concurrent calls to the **get_ID** function. As a consequence, the variable would have to be declared as a shared variable, which would significantly complicate the design.

We can also declare a local package within an enclosing package declaration, whether that enclosing package be a design unit or itself a local package. If the nested package is to be accessible outside the enclosing package, the nested package declaration must occur within the enclosing package declaration. The nested package body, if required, must then occur within the body of the enclosing package. As an example, the following outline shows an enclosing package **outer** with a nested package **inner** that declares a function **f**:

```
package outer is
   . . .
   package inner is
      impure function f ( ... ) return natural;
   end package inner;
   . . .
end package outer;

package body outer is
   . . .
   package body inner is
      . . .
      impure function f ( ... ) return natural is
         . . .
      end function f;
   end package body inner;
   . . .
end package body outer;
```

Outside the packages, we can refer to the function **f** with the name **outer.inner.f**.

If the enclosing package only requires a local package for private use, we can write both the nested package declaration and nested package body in the body of the enclosing package. The outline is:

```
package outer is
  ...
end package outer;

package body outer is
  ...
  package inner is
    ...
  end package inner;

  package body inner is
    ...
  end package body inner;
  ...
end package body outer;
```

In this case, items in the nested package are only accessible within the enclosing package body. While this scheme would not commonly arise in practice, it does serve to illustrate the consistency and general applicability of the visibility rules we introduced in Section 6.6.

VHDL-87, -93, and -2002

These versions of VHDL do not allow declaration of local packages. A package can only be declared as a design unit.

7.3   Use Clauses

We have seen how we can refer to an item provided by a package by writing its selected name, for example, work.cpu_types.status_value. This name refers to the item status_value in the package cpu_types stored in the library work. If we need to refer to this object in many places in a model, having to write the library name and package name becomes tedious and can obscure the intent of the model. We saw in Chapter 5 that we can write a *use clause* to make a library unit directly visible in a model, allowing us to omit the library name when referring to the library unit. Since an analyzed design-unit package is a library unit, use clauses also apply to making such packages directly visible. So we could precede a model with a use clause referring to the package defined in the example in Example 7.1:

```
use work.cpu_types;
```

This use clause allows us to write declarations in our model more simply; for example:

```
variable data_word : cpu_types.word;
variable next_address : cpu_types.address;
```

In fact, the use clause is more general than this usage indicates and allows us to make any name from a library or package directly visible. Let us look at the full syntax rule for a use clause, then discuss some of the possibilities.

use_clause ⇐ **use** selected_name ⟦ , ... ⟧ ;

selected_name ⇐ name . ⟦ identifier ⟦ character_literal ⟦ operator_symbol ⟦ **all** ⟧

The syntax rule for names, shown in Appendix B, includes the possibility of a name itself being either a selected name or a simple identifier. If we make these substitutions in the above syntax rule, we see that a selected name can be of the form

identifier . identifier . ⟦ identifier ⟦ character_literal ⟦ operator_symbol ⟦ **all** ⟧

One possibility is that the first identifier is a library name, and the second is the name of a package within the library. This form allows us to refer directly to items within a package without having to use the full selected name. For example, we can simplify the above declarations even further by rewriting the use clause as

```
use work.cpu_types.word, work.cpu_types.address;
```

The declarations can then be written as

```
variable data_word : word;
variable next_address : address;
```

We can place a use clause in any declarative part in a model. One way to think of a use clause is that it "imports" the names of the listed items into the part of the model containing the use clause, so that they can be used without writing the library or package name. The names become directly visible after the use clause, according to visibility rules similar to those we discussed in Chapter 6.

The syntax rule for a use clause shows that we can write the keyword **all** instead of the name of a particular item to import from a package. This form is very useful, as it is a shorthand way of importing all of the names defined in the interface of a package. For example, if we are using the IEEE standard-logic package as the basis for the data types in a design, it is often convenient to import everything from the standard-logic package, including all of the overloaded operator definitions. We can do this with a use clause as follows:

```
use ieee.std_logic_1164.all;
```

This use clause means that the model imports all of the names defined in the package **std_logic_1164** residing in the library **ieee**. This explains the "magic" that we have used in previous chapters when we needed to model data using the standard-logic types. The keyword **all** can be included for any package where we want to import all of the declarations from the package into a model.

We can also write use clauses for locally declared packages. Thus, in Example 7.6, we could follow the package declaration with the use clause

use ID_manager.**all**;

and then rewrite the assignment in the process as

next_test_case.ID := get_ID;

EXAMPLE 7.7 *A use clause for the CPU types package*

Following is a revised version of the CPU architecture body outlined in Example 7.4. It includes a use clause referring to items declared in the **cpu_types** package. This makes the rest of the model considerably less cluttered and easier to read. The use clause is included within the declarative part of the instruction set interpreter process. Thus the names "imported" from the package are directly visible in the rest of the declarative part and in the body of the process.

```
architecture behavioral of cpu is
begin

  interpreter : process is

    use work.cpu_types.all;

    variable instr_reg : word;
    variable instr_opcode : opcode;

  begin
    ...  -- initialize
    loop
      ...  -- fetch instruction
      instr_opcode := extract_opcode ( instr_reg );
      case instr_opcode is
        when op_nop => null;
        when op_breq => ...
        ...
      end case;
    end loop;
  end process interpreter;

end architecture behavioral;
```

While using **all** to import all declaration from a package is a common case, there are occasions when we would prefer to use just a type declared in a package. This might occur if we need to draw upon several packages, each of which declares numerous other items that could conflict with our own declarations and with items from other packages. However, just importing a type is not particularly useful, since we typically need to operate on values of the type. Fortunately, VHDL helps us by importing more than just the type name when we refer to a type in a use clause. In addition, the following are imported:

- All of the predefined operations on the type, provided they are not hidden by over-loaded versions also declared in the package.

- Overloaded versions of predefined operations on the type declared in the package.

- For an enumeration type or subtype, all of the enumeration literals. This includes any character literals of the type.

- For a physical type or subtype, all of the unit names for the type.

For example, suppose we declare the following package:

```
package stuff_pkg is

    type color_type is (red, orange, yellow, green, blue, violet);
    subtype warm_color is color_type range red to yellow;

    function "<" ( c1, c2 : color_type ) return boolean;
    function pretty ( c : color_type ) return boolean;

    type resistance is range 0 to 1E9 units
        Ohm;
        kOhm = 1000 Ohm;
        MOhm = 1000 kOhm;
    end units;

    subtype weak_logic is
        IEEE.std_logic_1164.std_ulogic range 'W' to 'H';

end package stuff_pkg;
```

Then the use clause

```
use stuff_pkg.color_type;
```

makes not only the type **color_type** visible, but also the enumeration literals **red** through **violet**, the predefined operations on **color_type** other than "<", and the overloaded "<" operator declared in the package. It does not make the function **pretty** visible, since it is not an overloaded version of a predefined operation. If we write the use clause

```
use stuff_pkg.warm_color;
```

it makes the subtype **warm_color** visible, along with all of the enumeration literals for **color_type** (not just those in the subtype) and the operations for **color_type**.

If we write the use clause

```
use stuff_pkg.resistance;
```

it makes the type **resistance** visible, along with the unit names **Ohm**, **kOhm**, and **MOhm**, and the predefined operations on **resistance**.

Finally, if we write the use clause

use stuff_pkg.weak_logic;

all we get is the subtype name **weak_logic** made visible, since none of the enumeration literals or operations are declared in the package **stuff_pkg**.

VHDL-87, -93, and -2002

According to a strict reading of the VHDL *Language Reference Manual*, these earlier versions do not import additional operations and other items if a use clause refers to a type name. Only the type name itself is imported. However, since that is not useful in practice, many implementations import at least the predefined operations, enumeration literals, and unit names. Implementations differ on whether they do this and whether they import any additional overloaded operations.

7.3.1   Visibility of Used Declarations

In general, a use clause makes a name directly visible in the enclosing declarative part and in the corresponding statement part. One of the most common places in which we write a use clause is at the beginning of a design unit. We saw in Section 5.4 how we may include library clauses, use clauses, and context references at the head of a design unit, such as an entity interface or architecture body. This area of a design unit is called its *context clause*. The names imported here are made directly visible throughout the design unit. For example, if we want to use the IEEE standard-logic type **std_ulogic** in the declaration of an entity, we might write the design unit as follows:

```
library ieee;  use ieee.std_logic_1164.std_ulogic;

entity logic_block is
  port ( a, b : in std_ulogic;
         y, z : out std_ulogic );
end entity logic_block;
```

The library clause and the use clause together form the context clause for the entity declaration in this example. The library clause makes the contents of the library accessible to the model, and the use clause imports the type name **std_ulogic** declared in the package **std_logic_1164** in the library **ieee**. By including the use clause in the context clause of the entity declaration, the **std_ulogic** type name is available when declaring the ports of the entity.

The names imported by a use clause in this way are made directly visible in the entire design unit after the use clause. In addition, if the design unit is a primary unit (such as an entity declaration or a package declaration), the visibility is extended to any corresponding secondary unit. Thus, if we include a use clause in the primary unit, we do not need to repeat it in the secondary unit, as the names are automatically visible there.

When we write use clauses in a model, there is potential to introduce conflicting names. The rules for dealing with such conflicts are related to those for dealing with overloading of subprograms and enumeration literals.

One form of conflict arises when we use an item declared in a package, and the declarative part containing the use clause declares another item with the same name. For example, our **cpu_types** package in earlier examples declares the subtype **address**. We might use this package in an architecture body as follows:

```
use work.cpu_types.all;
architecture behavior of cpu is
  signal address : bit_vector(15 downto 0);
  ...
end architecture behavior;
```

The subtype name **address** identified by the use clause conflicts with the signal name **address** declared within the architecture body. VHDL resolves this conflict by not making the subtype name directly visible. Any reference to the simple name **address** in the architecture body refers to the signal. Of course, we can still use the selected name **work.cpu_types.address** within the architecture body to refer to the subtype if necessary. In general, this form of conflict arises when an item identified by a use clause has the same name as a locally declared item and either or both are not overloadable (that is, not a subprogram or an enumeration literal). The conflict is resolved by not making the item identified by the use clause directly visible. If both of the items are overloadable, then there is no conflict, since the normal rules for disambiguating subprogram calls apply.

Another form of conflict arises when we use two items of the same name declared in different packages. The rules for dealing with this form of conflict are more involved, and depend on whether the items are overloadable and whether either is a predefined operation. We'll consider the cases in turn.

First, if one item is a predefined operation and the other is explicitly declared, only the explicitly declared item is made directly visible. Explicitly declared items in this case include overloaded versions of predefined operations, as well as other non-overloadable items. For example, suppose we declare two packages as follows:

```
package short_int_types is
  type short_int is range 0 to 255;
end package short_int_types

use work.short_int_types.all;
package short_int_ops is
  function "+" ( L, R : short_int ) return short_int;
  constant maximum : short_int := 255;
  ...
end package short_int_ops;
```

The package **short_int_types** declares the integer type **short_int**. The predefined operations "+" and **maximum** are implicitly declared within this package also. The package **short_int_ops** explicitly declares an overloaded version of the "+" operation to perform modulo addition. It also declares the constant **maximum**, which is a non-overloadable item. Now suppose we include a use clause for both of these packages in an architecture body:

```
use work.short_int_types.all, work.short_int_ops.all;
architecture behavior of alu is
  ...
end architecture behavior;
```

Within the architecture body, the explicitly declared "+" operation and **maximum** constant from the **short_int_ops** package are made directly visible. If we wanted to refer to the original predefined operations, we would have to write **work.short_int_types."+"** and **work.short_int.maximum**.

The second case of conflict from two items of the same name used from different packages arises if both items are explicitly declared and either or both are not overloadable. In this case, neither item is made directly visible. For example, if we declare the following package:

```
package controller_types is
  subtype address is bit_vector(2 downto 0);
  constant int_ack : address := "100";
end package controller_types;
```

and use it together with the **cpu_types** package from earlier examples:

```
use work.cpu_types.all, work.controller_types.all;
architecture rtl of system is
  ...
end architecture rtl;
```

the names address and **int_ack** are not made directly visible in the architecture. Both packages explicitly declare **address** as a subtype, which is a non-overloadable item. The package **cpu_types** declares **int_ack** as an enumeration type, which is overloadable, but **controller_types** declares **int_ack** as a constant which is not overloadable.

There is one case where what we might consider a conflict arises, but in fact a different rule comes into play. Suppose we write two packages, each of which explicitly declares overloaded subprograms, as follows:

```
package int_ops is
  function increment ( a : inout integer; n : in integer := 1 );
end package int_ops;

package counter_ops is
  function increment ( c : inout integer; n : in integer := 1 );
end package counter_ops;
```

If we use these two packages in a given design unit, as follows:

```
use work.int_ops.all, work.counter_ops.all;
```

we might be tempted to say that, since the names and the types of the parameters are the same, the declarations conflict, and so neither version of **increment** would be made directly visible. However, the rules for disambiguating calls to overloaded procedures allow parameter names used in named association to be taken into account. Thus, the following two calls are unambiguous:

```
increment ( a => count_value, n => -1 );
increment ( c => count_value, n => -1 );
```

The first call refers to the **increment** procedure from package **int_ops**, whereas the second call refers to the **increment** procedure from package **counter_ops**. In order for this rule to come into play, the two subprogram names must be directly visible. Rather than there being a conflict, there may be an ambiguity in the call if positional association is used.

VHDL-87, -93, and -2002

According to a strict reading of the VHDL *Language Reference Manual*, these earlier versions did not resolve a conflict between an implicitly declared predefined operation in one package and an explicitly declared overloaded version in another package in the same way as VHDL-2008. Instead, both are made directly visible, and the rules for overload resolution are required to disambiguate calls.

Complicating this is the widely held, but incorrect, view that versions of a subprogram with the same names and parameter types used from different packages do conflict and are not made directly visible. Some tools implement this view, rather than making both subprograms directly visible, as described for the **increment** procedures above.

Exercises

1. [❶ 7.1] Write a package declaration for use in a model of an engine management system. The package contains declarations of a physical type, **engine_speed**, expressed in units of revolutions per minute (RPM); a constant, **peak_rpm**, with a value of 6000 RPM; and an enumeration type, **gear**, with values representing first, second, third, fourth and reverse gears. Assuming the package is analyzed and stored in the current working library, write selected names for each of the items declared in the package.

2. [❶ 7.1] Write a declaration for a procedure that increments an integer, as the procedure declaration would appear in a package declaration.

3. [❶ 7.1] Write a declaration for a function that tests whether an integer is odd, as the function declaration would appear in a package declaration.

4. [❶ 7.1] Write a deferred constant declaration for the real constant $e = 2.71828$.

5. [❶ 7.2] Is a package body required for the package declaration described in Exercise 1?

6. [❶ 7.3] Write a use clause that makes the **engine_speed** type from the package described in Exercise 1 directly visible.

7. [❶ 7.3] Write a context clause that makes a library **DSP_lib** accessible and that makes an entity **systolic_FFT** and all items declared in a package **DSP_types** in the library directly visible.

8. [❸ 7.1/7.2] Develop a package declaration and body that provide operations for dealing with time-of-day values. The package defines a time-of-day value as a record containing hours, minutes and seconds since midnight and provides deferred constants representing midnight and midday. The operations provided by the package are

   • comparison ("<", ">", "<=" and ">="),

   • addition of a time-of-day value and a number of seconds to yield a time-of-day result and

   • subtraction of two time-of-day values to yield a number-of-seconds result.

9. [❸ 7.1/7.2] Develop a package declaration and body to provide operations on character strings representing identifiers. An outline of the package declaration is

```
package identifier_pkg is

  subtype identifier is string(1 to 15);

  constant max_table_size : integer := 50;
  subtype table_index is integer range 1 to max_table_size;
  type table is array (table_index) of identifier;

  . . .

end package identifier_pkg;
```

The package also declares a procedure to convert alphabetic characters in a string to lowercase and a procedure to search for an occurrence of a given identifier in a table. The search procedure has two **out**-mode parameters: a Boolean value indicating whether the sought string is in the table and a **table_index** value indicating its position, if present.

Chapter 8

Resolved Signals

Throughout the previous chapters we have studiously avoided considering the case of multiple output ports connecting one signal. The problem that arises in such a case is determining the final value of the signal when multiple sources drive it. In this chapter we discuss *resolved signals*, the mechanism provided by VHDL for modeling such cases.

8.1 Basic Resolved Signals

If we consider a real digital system with two outputs driving one signal, we can fairly readily determine the resulting value based on some analog circuit theory. The signal is driven to some intermediate state, depending on the drive capacities of the conflicting drivers. This intermediate state may or may not represent a valid logic state. Usually we only connect outputs in a design if at most one is active at a time, and the rest are in some high-impedance state. In this case, the resulting value should be the driving value of the single active output. In addition, we include some form of "pull-up" that determines the value of the signal when all outputs are inactive.

While this simple approach is satisfactory for some models, there are other cases where we need to go further. One of the reasons for simulating a model of a design is to detect errors such as multiple simultaneously active connected outputs. In this case, we need to extend the simple approach to detect such errors. Another problem arises when we are modeling at a higher level of abstraction and are using more complex types. We need to specify what, if anything, it means to connect multiple outputs of an enumeration type together.

The approach taken by VHDL is a very general one: the language requires the designer to specify precisely what value results from connecting multiple outputs. It does this through *resolved signals*, which are an extension of the basic signals we have used in previous chapters. A resolved signal includes in its definition a function, called the *resolution function*, that is used to calculate the final signal value from the values of all of its sources.

Let us see how this works by developing an example. We can model the values driven by a tristate output using a simple extension to the predefined type **bit**, for example:

```
type tri_state_logic is ('0', '1', 'Z');
```

The extra value, 'Z', is used by an output to indicate that it is in the high-impedance state. Next, we need to write a function that takes a collection of values of this type, representing the values driven by a number of outputs, and return the resulting value to be applied to the connected signal. For this example, we assume that at most one driver is active ('0' or '1') at a time and that the rest are all driving 'Z'. The difficulty with writing the function is that we should not restrict it to a fixed number of input values. We can avoid this by giving it a single parameter that is an unconstrained array of **tri_state_logic** values, defined by the type declaration

```
type tri_state_logic_array is
  array (integer range <>) of tri_state_logic;
```

The declaration of the resolution function is

```
function resolve_tri_state_logic
  ( values : in tri_state_logic_array )
  return tri_state_logic is
  variable result : tri_state_logic := 'Z';
begin
  for index in values'range loop
    if values(index) /= 'Z' then
      result := values(index);
    end if;
  end loop;
  return result;
end function resolve_tri_state_logic;
```

The final step to making a resolved signal is to declare the signal, as follows:

```
signal s1 : resolve_tri_state_logic tri_state_logic;
```

This declaration is almost identical to a normal signal declaration, but with the addition of the resolution function name before the signal type. The signal still takes on values from the type **tri_state_logic**, but inclusion of a function name indicates that the signal is a re-solved signal, with the named function acting as the resolution function. The fact that s1 is resolved means that we are allowed to have more than one source for it in the design. (Sources include drivers within processes and output ports of components associated with the signal.) When a transaction is scheduled for the signal, the value is not applied to the signal directly. Instead, the values of all sources connected to the signal, including the new value from the transaction, are formed into an array and passed to the resolution function. The result returned by the function is then applied to the signal as its new value.

Let us look at the syntax rule that describes the VHDL mechanism we have used in the above example. It is an extension of the rules for the subtype indication, which we first introduced in Chapters 2 and 4. The combined rule is

subtype_indication ⇐
    ⟦ *resolution_function*_name ⟧
    type_mark ⟦ **range**⦅ *range*_attribute_name

〚 simple_expression 〘 **to** 〛 **downto** 〙 simple_expression 〛
〚 (discrete_range { , ... }) 〛

This rule shows that a subtype indication can optionally include the name of a function to be used as a resolution function. Given this new rule, we can include a resolution function name anywhere that we specify a type to be used for a signal. For example, we could write a separate subtype declaration that includes a resolution function name, defining a *resolved subtype*, then use this subtype to declare a number of resolved signals, as follows:

```
subtype resolved_logic is
  resolve_tri_state_logic tri_state_logic;

signal s2, s3 : resolved_logic;
```

The subtype **resolved_logic** is a resolved subtype of **tri_state_logic**, with **resolve_tri_state_logic** acting as the resolution function. The signals **s2** and **s3** are resolved signals of this subtype. Where a design makes extensive use of resolved signals, it is good practice to define resolved subtypes and use them to declare the signals and ports in the design.

The resolution function for a resolved signal is also invoked to initialize the signal. At the start of a simulation, the drivers for the signal are initialized to the expression included in the signal declaration, or to the default initial value for the signal type if no initialization expression is given. The resolution function is then invoked using these driver values to determine the initial value for the signal. In this way, the signal always has a properly resolved value, right from the start of the simulation.

Let us now return to the tristate logic type we introduced earlier. In the previous example, we assumed that at most one driver is '0' or '1' at a time. In a more realistic model, we need to deal with the possibility of driver conflicts, in which one source drives a resolved signal with the value '0' and another drives it with the value '1'. In some logic families, such driver conflicts cause an indeterminate signal value. We can represent this indeterminate state with a fourth value of the logic type, 'X', often called an *unknown* value. This gives us a complete and consistent *multivalued logic* type, which we can use to describe signal values in a design in more detail than we can using just bit values.

EXAMPLE 8.1   *A four-state multivalued logic type and its use*

The following package declaration and body define a four-state multivalued logic type.

```
package MVL4 is

  -- unresolved logic type
  type MVL4_ulogic is ('X', '0', '1', 'Z');

  type MVL4_ulogic_vector is
    array (natural range <>) of MVL4_ulogic;

  function resolve_MVL4
    ( contribution : MVL4_ulogic_vector ) return MVL4_ulogic;
```

```vhdl
    subtype MVL4_logic is resolve_MVL4 MVL4_ulogic;

    function "not" ( r : MVL4_ulogic ) return MVL4_ulogic;
    function "and" ( l, r : MVL4_ulogic ) return MVL4_ulogic;
    function "or"  ( l, r : MVL4_ulogic ) return MVL4_ulogic;
    ...

    function to_X01 ( a : MVL4_ulogic ) return MVL4_ulogic;

end package MVL4;

--------------------------------------------------

package body MVL4 is

  type table is
    array (MVL4_ulogic, MVL4_ulogic) of MVL4_ulogic;

  constant resolution_table : table :=
    --  'X'  '0'  '1'  'Z'
    --  ------------------
    ( ( 'X', 'X', 'X', 'X' ),     -- 'X'
      ( 'X', '0', 'X', '0' ),     -- '0'
      ( 'X', 'X', '1', '1' ),     -- '1'
      ( 'X', '0', '1', 'Z' ) );   -- 'Z'

  function resolve_MVL4 ( contribution : MVL4_ulogic_vector )
                       return MVL4_ulogic is
    variable result : MVL4_ulogic := 'Z';
  begin
    for index in contribution'range loop
      result := resolution_table(result, contribution(index));
    end loop;
    return result;
  end function resolve_MVL4;

  function "not" ( r : MVL4_ulogic ) return MVL4_ulogic is
  begin
    case r is
      when '1' => return '0';
      when '0' => return '1';
      when others => return 'X';
    end case;
  end function "not";

  function "and" ( l, r : MVL4_ulogic ) return MVL4_ulogic is ...

  function "or"  ( l, r : MVL4_ulogic ) return MVL4_ulogic is ...

  ...

  function to_X01 ( a : MVL4_ulogic ) return MVL4_ulogic is
  begin
```

```
      case a is
        when '0' | '1' => return a;
        when 'X' | 'Z' => return 'X';
      end case;
    end function to_X01;

  end package body MVL4;
```

The constant **resolution_table** is a lookup table used to determine the value resulting from two source contributions to a signal of the resolved logic type. The resolution function uses this table, indexing it with each element of the array passed to the function. If any source contributes 'X', or if there are two sources with conflicting '0' and '1' contributions, the result is 'X'. If one or more sources are '0' and the remainder 'Z', the result is '0'. Similarly, if one or more sources are '1' and the remainder 'Z', the result is '1'. If all sources are 'Z', the result is 'Z'. The lookup table is a compact way of representing this set of rules. The package also declares overloaded versions of the logical operators and other functions. The **to_X01** function ensures that a value is either a proper logic value ('0' or '1') or an unknown value.

We can use this package in a design for a tristate buffer. The entity declaration and a behavioral architecture body are

```
use work.MVL4.all;

entity tri_state_buffer is
  port ( a, enable : in MVL4_ulogic;  y : out MVL4_ulogic );
end entity tri_state_buffer;

--------------------------------------------------

architecture behavioral of tri_state_buffer is
begin

  y <= to_X01(a) when enable = '1' else
       'Z'        when enable = '0' else
       'X';

end architecture behavioral;
```

When the buffer is enabled, the buffer copies the input to the output, but with a 'Z' input value changed to 'X' by the **to_X01** function. When the buffer is not enabled, it drives the value 'Z' on its output. If the **enable** port is not a proper logic level, both conditions are false, so the buffer drives the unknown value on its output.

An architecture body for a logic block that uses the tristate buffer is:

```
use work.MVL4.all;

architecture gate_level of misc_logic is

  signal src1, src1_enable : MVL4_ulogic;
  signal src2, src2_enable : MVL4_ulogic;
  signal selected_val : MVL4_logic;
  ...
```

```
begin
    src1_buffer : entity work.tri_state_buffer(behavioral)
        port map ( a => src1, enable => src1_enable,
                   y => selected_val );
    src2_buffer : entity work.tri_state_buffer(behavioral)
        port map ( a => src2, enable => src2_enable,
                   y => selected_val );
    ...
end architecture gate_level;
```

The signal **selected_val** is a resolved signal of the multivalued logic type. It is driven by the two buffer output ports. The resolution function for the signal is used to determine the final value of the signal whenever a new transaction is applied to either of the buffer outputs.

8.1.1 Composite Resolved Subtypes

The above examples have all shown resolved subtypes of scalar enumeration types. In fact, VHDL's resolution mechanism is more general. We can use it to define a resolved subtype of any type that we can legally use as the type of a signal. Thus, we can define resolved integer subtypes, resolved composite subtypes and others. In the latter case, the resolution function is passed an array of composite values and must determine the final composite value to be applied to the signal.

EXAMPLE 8.2   *A package for a resolved array subtype*

The package declaration and body below define a resolved array subtype. Each element of an array value of this subtype can be 'X', '0', '1' or 'Z'. The unresolved type **uword** is an unconstrained array of these values. The resolution function has an unconstrained array parameter consisting of elements of type **uword**. The function uses the lookup table to resolve corresponding elements from each of the contributing sources and produces an array result. The subtype **word** is the final resolved array subtype.

```
package words is
    type X01Z is ('X', '0', '1', 'Z');
    type uword is array (natural range <>) of X01Z;

    type uword_vector is array (natural range <>) of uword;

    function resolve_word
        ( contribution : uword_vector ) return uword;

    subtype word is resolve_word uword;

end package words;
```

```
-------------------------------------------------

package body words is

  type table is array (X01Z, X01Z) of X01Z;

  constant resolution_table : table :=
    --  'X'  '0'  '1'  'Z'
    --  -----------------
    ( ( 'X', 'X', 'X', 'X' ),     -- 'X'
      ( 'X', '0', 'X', '0' ),     -- '0'
      ( 'X', 'X', '1', '1' ),     -- '1'
      ( 'X', '0', '1', 'Z' ) );   -- 'Z'

  function resolve_word
    ( contribution : uword_vector ) return uword is
    variable result : uword(contribution'element'range)
              := (others => 'Z');
  begin
    for index in contribution'range loop
      for element in result'range loop
        result(element) :=
          resolution_table( result(element),
                            contribution(index)(element) );
      end loop;
    end loop;
    return result;
  end function resolve_word;

end package body words;
```

We can use these types to declare array ports in entity declarations and resolved array signals with multiple sources. For example, the following CPU entity and memory entity have bidirectional data ports of the unresolved array type.

```
use work.words.all;

entity cpu is
  port ( address : out uword(23 downto 0);
         data : inout uword(31 downto 0);  ... );
end entity cpu;
```

```
-------------------------------------------------

use work.words.all;

entity memory is
  port ( address : in uword(23 downto 0);
         data : inout uword(31 downto 0); ... );
end entity memory;
```

The architecture body for a computer system declares a signal of the resolved subtype and connects it to the data ports of the instances of the CPU and memory:

```
architecture top_level of computer_system is

  use work.words.all;

  signal address : uword(23 downto 0);
  signal data : word(31 downto 0);
  ...

begin

  the_cpu : entity work.cpu(behavioral)
    port map ( address, data, ... );

  the_memory : entity work.memory(behavioral)
    port map ( address, data, ... );

  ...

end architecture top_level;
```

A resolved composite subtype works well provided every source for a resolved signal of the subtype is connected to every element of the signal. For the **data** signal shown in the example, every source must be a 32-element array and must connect to all 32 elements of the data signal. However, in a realistic computer system, sources are not always connected in this way. For example, we may wish to connect an 8-bit-wide device to the low-order eight bits of a 32-bit-wide data bus. We might attempt to express such a connection in a component instantiation statement, as follows:

```
boot_rom : entity work.ROM(behavioral)
  port map ( a => address, d => data(24 to 31), ... );  -- illegal
```

If we add this statement to the architecture body in Example 8.2, we have two sources for elements 0 to 23 of the data signal and three for elements 24 to 31. A problem arises when resolving the signal, since we are unable to construct an array containing the contributions from the sources. For this reason, VHDL does not allow us to write such a description; it is illegal.

The solution to this problem is to describe the data signal as an array of resolved elements, rather than as a resolved array of elements. One way of doing this is to declare an array type whose elements are values of the **MVL4_logic** type, shown in Example 8.2. The array type declaration is

```
type MVL4_logic_vector is array (natural range <>) of MVL4_logic;
```

This approach has the advantage that the array type is unconstrained, so we can use it to create signals of different widths, each element of which is resolved. The problem, however, is that the type **MVL4_logic_vector** is distinct from the type **MVL4_ulogic_vector**, since they are defined by separate type declarations. Neither is a subtype of the other. Hence we cannot legally associate a signal of type **MVL4_logic_vector** with a port of type

MVL4_ulogic_vector, or a signal of type MVL4_ulogic_vector with a port of type
MVL4_logic_vector.

A better way to describe arrays of resolved elements is to declare an array subtype in
which we associate the resolution function with the elements. In our example, the array
base type is MVL4_ulogic_vector, which has unresolved elements. We declare the subtype
as:

```
subtype MVL4_logic_vector is (resolve_MVL4) std_ulogic_vector;
```

The parentheses around the resolution function name, resolve_MVL4, indicates that
the resolution function is associated with each element of the array type, rather than with
the array type as a whole. Since MVL4_logic_vector is now a subtype of
MVL4_ulogic_vector, not a distinct type, we can freely assign and associate signals and
ports of the two types.

This example illustrates a more general form of *resolution indication* to be included
in a subtype indication or signal declaration, rather than just naming a resolution function
by itself. The syntax rule is:

resolution_indication ⇐
    *resolution_function*_name
      ⟦ (resolution_indication
           ⟦ ⟨ *record_element*_identifier resolution_indication ⟩ ⟨ , ... ⟩)

If we want to associate a resolution function with an entire subtype, the resolution
indication just consists of the resolution function name, as in the declaration of
MVL4_logic:

```
subtype MVL4_logic is resolve_MVL4 MVL4_ulogic;
```

The resolution indication here is just the resolution function name, resolve_MVL4. In
the case of an array whose elements are to be resolved, we write the resolution function
name in parentheses, as in the declaration of MVL4_logic_vector. We can also resolve the
elements of an array type that is itself an array element type. For example, given the following declaration:

```
type unresolved_RAM_content_type is
  array (natural range <>) of MVL4_ulogic_vector;
```

we can declare a subtype with resolved nested elements:

```
subtype RAM_content_type is
  ((resolve_MVL4)) unresolved_RAM_content_type;
```

The degree of nesting of parentheses indicates how deeply nested in the type structure the resolution function is associated. Two levels indicate that the resolution function
is associated with the elements of the elements of the type.

If we have a record type, one of whose elements is to be resolved, we include the
element name in the resolution indication. For example, given the following record type
with no associated resolution information:

```
type unresolved_status_type is record
  valid : MVL4_ulogic;
  dirty : MVL4_ulogic;
  tag : MVL4_ulogic_vector;
end record unresolved_status_type;
```

we can declare a subtype with the **valid** element resolved by the function **wired_and** as follows:

```
subtype status_resolved_valid is
  (valid wired_and) unresolved_status_type;
```

We can include resolution functions with multiple elements of the record type by listing the element names and the resolution function associated with each, for example:

```
subtype status_resolved_flags is
  (valid wired_and, dirty wired_or) unresolved_status_type;
```

For a record element that is itself of a composite type, we can associate a resolution function with subelements of the record element by writing a parenthesized resolution indication for the element. Thus, to resolve the elements of the **tag** element of the above record type, we would declare a subtype as follows:

```
subtype status_resolved_tag is
  (tag(resolve_MVL4)) unresolved_status_type;
```

We could combine all of these examples together, resolving all of the scalar subelements, as follows:

```
subtype resolved_status_type is
  ( tag(resolve_MVL4),
    valid wired_and,
    dirty wired_or ) unresolved_status_type;
```

This declaration illustrates that we do not have to write the resolution indications for the record elements in the same order as the declaration of elements in the record types. The record element names in the resolution indication determine the element with which the resolution function is associated.

EXAMPLE 8.3   *Connection to parts of a bus signal*

Let us assume that the type **MVL4_logic_vector** described above has been added to the package **MVL4**. Below are entity declarations for a ROM entity and a single in-line memory module (SIMM), using the **MVL4_ulogic_vector** type for their data ports. The data port of the SIMM is 32 bits wide, whereas the data port of the ROM is only 8 bits wide.

```
use work.MVL4.all;
```

```
entity ROM is
  port ( a : in MVL4_ulogic_vector(15 downto 0);
         d : out MVL4_ulogic_vector(7 downto 0);
         rd : in MVL4_ulogic );
end entity ROM;
```

```
use work.MVL4.all;

entity SIMM is
  port ( a : in MVL4_ulogic_vector(9 downto 0);
         d : inout MVL4_ulogic_vector(31 downto 0);
         ras, cas, we, cs : in MVL4_ulogic );
end entity SIMM;
```

The following architecture body uses these two entities. It declares a signal, **internal_data**, of the **MVL4_logic_vector** type, representing 32 individually resolved elements. The SIMM entity is instantiated with its data port connected to all 32 internal data elements. The ROM entity is instantiated with its data port connected to the rightmost eight elements of the internal data signal. When any of these elements is resolved, the resolution function is passed contributions from the corresponding elements of the SIMM and ROM data ports. When any of the remaining elements of the internal data signal are resolved, they have one less contribution, since they are not connected to any element of the ROM data port.

```
architecture detailed of memory_subsystem is

  signal internal_data : MVL4_logic_vector(31 downto 0);
  ...

begin

  boot_ROM : entity work.ROM(behavioral)
    port map ( a => internal_addr(15 downto 0),
               d => internal_data(7 downto 0),
               rd => ROM_select );

  main_mem : entity work.SIMM(behavioral)
    port map ( a => main_mem_addr, d => internal_data, ... );

  ...

end architecture detailed;
```

8.1.2   Summary of Resolved Subtypes

At this point, let us summarize the important points about resolved signals and their resolution functions. Resolved signals of resolved subtypes are the only means by which we may connect a number of sources together, since we need a resolution function to determine the final value of the signal or port from the contributing values. The resolution func-

tion must take a single parameter that is a one-dimensional unconstrained array of values
of the signal type, and must return a value of the signal type. The index type of the array
does not matter, so long as it contains enough index values for the largest possible collection of sources connected together. For example, an array type declared as follows is in-
adequate if the resolved signal has five sources:

```
type small_int is range 1 to 4;
type small_array is array (small_int range <>) of ... ;
```

The resolution function must be a pure function; that is, it must not have any side
effects. This requirement is a safety measure to ensure that the function always returns a
predictable value for a given set of source values. Furthermore, since the source values
may be passed in any order within the array, the function should be commutative; that is,
its result should be independent of the order of the values. When the design is simulated,
the resolution function is called whenever any of the resolved signal's sources is active.
The function is passed an array of all of the current source values, and the result it returns
is used to update the signal value. When the design is synthesized, the resolution function
specifies the way in which the synthesized hardware should combine values from multiple
sources for a resolved signal.

8.1.3   IEEE **std_logic_1164** Resolved Subtypes

In previous chapters we have used the IEEE standard multivalued logic package,
std_logic_1164. We are now in a position to describe all of the types and subtypes provided by the package. We defer a full description of the operations provided by the package to Chapter 9, in which we also describe other standard packages based on the
standard logic types. First, recall that the package provides the basic type **std_ulogic**, defined as

```
type std_ulogic is ('U', 'X', '0', '1', 'Z', 'W', 'L', 'H', '-');
```

and an array type **std_ulogic_vector**, defined as

```
type std_ulogic_vector is array ( natural range <> ) of std_ulogic;
```

We have not mentioned it before, but the "u" in "ulogic" stands for unresolved. These
types serve as the basis for the declaration of the resolved subtype **std_logic**, defined as
follows:

```
function resolved ( s : std_ulogic_vector ) return std_ulogic;

subtype std_logic is resolved std_ulogic;
```

The standard-logic package also declares an array subtype of standard-logic elements,
analogous to the **bit_vector** type, for use in declaring array signals:

```
subtype std_logic_vector (resolved) std_ulogic_vector;
```

The standard defines the resolution function **resolved** as follows:

```
type stdlogic_table is array (std_ulogic, std_ulogic) of std_ulogic;
constant resolution_table : stdlogic_table :=
  -- -------------------------------------------------
  -- 'U', 'X', '0', '1', 'Z', 'W', 'L', 'H', '-'
  -- -------------------------------------------------
  ( ( 'U', 'U', 'U', 'U', 'U', 'U', 'U', 'U', 'U' ),   -- 'U'
    ( 'U', 'X', 'X', 'X', 'X', 'X', 'X', 'X', 'X' ),   -- 'X'
    ( 'U', 'X', '0', 'X', '0', '0', '0', '0', 'X' ),   -- '0'
    ( 'U', 'X', 'X', '1', '1', '1', '1', '1', 'X' ),   -- '1'
    ( 'U', 'X', '0', '1', 'Z', 'W', 'L', 'H', 'X' ),   -- 'Z'
    ( 'U', 'X', '0', '1', 'W', 'W', 'W', 'W', 'X' ),   -- 'W'
    ( 'U', 'X', '0', '1', 'L', 'W', 'L', 'W', 'X' ),   -- 'L'
    ( 'U', 'X', '0', '1', 'H', 'W', 'W', 'H', 'X' ),   -- 'H'
    ( 'U', 'X', 'X', 'X', 'X', 'X', 'X', 'X', 'X' )    -- '-'
);

function resolved ( s : std_ulogic_vector ) return std_ulogic is
  variable result : std_ulogic := 'Z';   -- weakest state default
begin
  if s'length = 1 then
    return s(s'low);
  else
    for i in s'range loop
      result := resolution_table(result, s(i));
    end loop;
  end if;
  return result;
end function resolved;
```

VHDL tools are allowed to provide built-in implementations of this function to improve performance. The function uses the constant **resolution_table** to resolve the driving values. If there is only one driving value, the function returns that value unchanged. If the function is passed an empty array, it returns the value 'Z'. The value of **resolution_table** shows exactly what is meant by "forcing" driving values ('X', '0' and '1') and "weak" driving values ('W', 'L' and 'H'). If one driver of a resolved signal drives a forcing value and another drives a weak value, the forcing value dominates. On the other hand, if both drivers drive different values with the same strength, the result is the unknown value of that strength ('X' or 'W'). The high-impedance value, 'Z', is dominated by forcing and weak values. If a "don't care" value ('–') is to be resolved with any other value, the result is the unknown value 'X'. The interpretation of the "don't care" value is that the model has not made a choice about its output state. Finally, if an "uninitialized" value ('U') is to be resolved with any other value, the result is 'U', indicating that the model has not properly initialized all outputs.

In addition to this multivalued logic subtype, the package **std_logic_1164** declares a number of subtypes for more restricted multivalued logic modeling. The subtype declarations are

```
subtype X01 is
  resolved std_ulogic range 'X' to '1'; -- ('X','0','1')
subtype X01Z is
  resolved std_ulogic range 'X' to 'Z'; -- ('X','0','1','Z')
subtype UX01 is
  resolved std_ulogic range 'U' to '1'; -- ('U','X','0','1')
subtype UX01Z is
  resolved std_ulogic range 'U' to 'Z'; -- ('U','X','0','1','Z')
```

Each of these is a closed subtype; that is, the result of resolving values in each case is a value within the range of the subtype. The subtype **X01Z** corresponds to the type **MVL4** we introduced in Example 8.1.

8.2 Resolved Signals, Ports, and Parameters

In the previous discussion of resolved signals, we have limited ourselves to the simple case where a number of drivers or output ports of component instances drive a signal. Any input port connected to the resolved signal gets the final resolved value as the port value when a transaction is performed. We now look in more detail at the case of ports of mode **inout** being connected to a resolved signal. The question to answer here is, What value is seen by the input side of such a port? Is it the value driven by the component instance or the final value of the resolved signal connected to the port? In fact, it is the latter. An **inout** port models a connection in which the driver contributes to the associated signal's value, and the input side of the component senses the actual signal rather than using the driving value.

EXAMPLE 8.4 *Distributed synchronization using a wired-and signal*

Some asynchronous bus protocols use a distributed synchronization mechanism based on a wired-and control signal. This is a single signal driven by each module using active-low open-collector or open-drain drivers and pulled up by the bus terminator. If a number of modules on the bus need to wait until all are ready to proceed with some operation, they use the control signal as follows. Initially, all modules drive the signal to the '0' state. When each is ready to proceed, it turns off its driver ('Z') and monitors the control signal. So long as any module is not yet ready, the signal remains at '0'. When all modules are ready, the bus terminator pulls the signal up to the '1' state. All modules sense this change and proceed with the operation.

Following is an entity declaration for a bus module that has a port of the unresolved type **std_ulogic** for connection to such a synchronization control signal.

```
library ieee;  use ieee.std_logic_1164.all;

entity bus_module is
  port ( synch : inout std_ulogic;  ... );
end entity bus_module;
```

The architecture body for a system comprising several such modules is outlined below. The control signal is pulled up by a concurrent signal assignment statement, which acts as a source with a constant driving value of 'H'. This is a value having a weak strength, which is overridden by any other source that drives '0'. It can pull the signal high only when all other sources drive 'Z'.

```
architecture top_level of bus_based_system is

    signal synch_control : std_logic;
    ...

begin

    synch_control_pull_up : synch_control <= 'H';

    bus_module_1 : entity work.bus_module(behavioral)
        port map ( synch => synch_control, ... );

    bus_module_2 : entity work.bus_module(behavioral)
        port map ( synch => synch_control, ... );

    ...

end architecture top_level;
```

An outline of a behavioral architecture body for the bus module is:

```
architecture behavioral of bus_module is
begin

    behavior : process is
        ...
    begin
        synch <= '0'  after Tdelay_synch;
        ...
        -- ready to start operation
        synch <= 'Z' after Tdelay_synch;
        wait until synch = 'H';
        -- proceed with operation
        ...
    end process behavior;

end architecture behavioral;
```

Each instance initially drives its synchronization port with '0'. This value is passed up through the port and used as the contribution to the resolved signal from the entity instance. When an instance is ready to proceed with its operation, it changes its driving value to 'Z', modeling an open-collector or open-drain driver being turned off. The process then suspends until the value seen on the synchronization port changes to 'H'. If other instances are still driving '0', their contributions dominate, and the value of the signal stays '0'. When all other instances eventually change their contributions to 'Z', the value 'H' contributed by the pull-up statement dominates, and the value of the signal changes to 'H'. This value is passed back down through the ports of each instance, and the processes all resume.

8.2.1 Resolved Ports

Just as a signal declared with a signal declaration can be of a resolved subtype, so too can a port declared in an interface list of an entity. This is consistent with all that we have said about ports appearing just like signals to an architecture body. Thus if the architecture body contains a number of processes that must drive a port or a number of component instances that must connect outputs to a port, the port must be resolved. The final value driven by the resolved port is determined by resolving all of the sources within the architecture body. For example, we might declare an entity with a resolved port as follows:

```
library ieee;  use ieee.std_logic_1164.all;

entity IO_section is
  port ( data_ack : inout std_logic;  ... );
end entity IO_section;
```

The architecture body corresponding to this entity might instantiate a number of I/O controller components, each with their data acknowledge ports connected to the **data_ack** port of the entity. Each time any of the controllers updates its data acknowledge port, the standard-logic resolution function is invoked. It determines the driving value for the **data_ack** port by resolving the driving values from all controllers.

EXAMPLE 8.5   *A memory system with tristate buses*

We can write a model for a memory system composed of multiple memory devices with tristate data buses. The entity declaration for the memory devices is

```
library ieee; use ieee.std_logic_1164.all;
entity memory_256Kx8 is
  port ( ce_n, oe_n, we_n : in std_ulogic;
         a : in std_ulogic_vector(17 downto 0);
         d : inout std_ulogic_vector(7 downto 0) );
end entity memory_256Kx8;
```

The **d** port of the entity has unresolved elements because there is only one source for each element within the memory device. The entity declaration for the memory system is

```
library ieee; use ieee.std_logic_1164.all;
entity memory_1Mx8 is
  port ( ce_n, oe_n, we_n : in std_ulogic;
         a : in std_ulogic_vector(19 downto 0);
         d : inout std_logic_vector(7 downto 0) );
end entity memory_1Mx8;
```

In this case, the **d** port is of type **std_logic_vector** with resolved elements, since internally there are multiple sources, one per memory device. The structural architecture is

```
architecture struct of memory_1Mx8 is
  signal ce_decoded_n : std_ulogic_vector(3 downto 0);
begin

  with a(19 downto 18) select
    ce_decoded_n <= "1110" when "00",
                    "1101" when "01",
                    "1011" when "10",
                    "0111" when "11",
                    "XXXX" when others;

  chip0 : component memory_256Kx8
    port map ( ce_n => ce_decoded_n(0),
               oe_n => oe_n, we_n => we_n,
               a => a(17 downto 0), d => d );

  chip1 : component memory_256Kx8
    port map ( ce_n => ce_decoded_n(1),
               oe_n => oe_n, we_n => we_n,
               a => a(17 downto 0), d => d );

  ...

end architecture struct;
```

We can connect the **d** port of each memory-device instance directly to the **d** port of the memory system. The contributions of all of the instances are resolved to form the driving value of the memory system's **d** port. Had we inadvertently declared the **d** port of the memory system entity to be of type **std_ulogic_vector**, the analyzer would detect the error arising from multiple sources connected to the unresolved elements.

If it happens that the actual signal associated with a resolved port in an enclosing architecture body is itself a resolved signal, then the signal's resolution function will be called separately after the port's resolution function has determined the port's driving value. Note that the signal in the enclosing architecture body may use a different resolution function from the connected port, although in practice most designs use the one function for resolution of all signals of a given subtype.

An extension of the above scenario is a design in which there are several levels of hierarchy, with a process nested at the deepest level generating a value to be passed out through resolved ports to a signal at the top level. At each level, a resolution function is called to determine the driving value of the port at that level. The value finally determined for the signal at the top level is called the *effective value* of the signal. It is passed back down the hierarchy of ports as the effective value of each **in**-mode or **inout**-mode port. This value is used on the input side of each port.

EXAMPLE 8.6   *Hierarchical resolution in a computer system model*

Figure 8.1 shows the hierarchical organization for a single-board computer system, consisting of a frame buffer for a video display, an input/output controller section, a CPU/memory section and a bus expansion block. These are all sources for the resolved data bus signal. The CPU/memory section in turn comprises a memory block and a CPU/cache block. Both of these act as sources for the data port, so it must be a resolved port. The cache has two sections, both of which act as sources for the data port of the CPU/cache block. Hence, this port must also be resolved.

FIGURE 8.1
_____

A hierarchical block diagram of a single-board computer system, showing the hierarchical connections of the resolved data bus ports to the data bus signal.

Let us consider the case of one of the cache sections updating its data port. The new driving value is resolved with the current driving value from the other cache section to determine the driving value of the CPU/cache block data port. This result is then resolved with the current driving value of the memory block to determine the driving value of the CPU/memory section. Next, this driving value is resolved with the current driving values of the other top-level sections to determine the effective value of the data bus signal. The final step involves propagating this signal value back down the hierarchy for use as the effective value of each of the data ports. Thus, a module that reads the value of its data port will see the final resolved value of the data bus signal. This value is not necessarily the same as the driving value it contributes.

In Chapter 5, we indicated that we can read the value of a **buffer**-mode or **out**-mode port within an architecture of an entity. There is an important distinction between this and reading the value of an **inout**-mode port. As we mentioned above, the value seen internally for an **inout**-mode port is the effective value of the externally connected signal. Information is passed from the external connection into the architecture, as suggested by the "**in**" part of the **inout** port mode. In contrast, when we read a **buffer**-mode or **out**-

mode port, the value seen internally is the driving value of the port. There is no transmission of information into the architecture. We use a **buffer**-mode or **out**-mode port for designs that have buffered internal connections or that read the value of the port for internal verification, for example, using assertions.

EXAMPLE 8.7   *Verification of tristate disconnection timing*

Suppose we wish to verify that the outputs of a device are all 'Z' within a required interval of the device being disabled and remain all 'Z' until the device is enabled. The output values are not required internally to implement any functionality for the device. Hence, we declare the output ports using **out** mode, as follows:

```
entity device is
  port ( en : in std_ulogic;
          d_out : out std_ulogic_vector(7 downto 0); ... );
end entity device;
```

We can read the values driven onto the output ports in verification code in the architecture:

```
architecture verifying of device is
  constant T_z : delay_length := 200 ps;
begin
  d_out <= ... when en else
           ... when not en else
           "XXXXXXXX";
  assert en or (not en'delayed(T_z) and d_out ?= "ZZZZZZZZ");
end architecture verifying;
```

8.2.2 Driving Value Attribute

Since the value seen on a signal or on an **inout**-mode port may be different from the value driven by a process, VHDL provides an attribute, 'driving_value, that allows the process to read the value it contributes to the prefix signal. For example, if a process has a driver for a resolved signal s, it may be driving s with the value 'Z' from a previously executed signal assignment statement, but the resolution function for s may have given it the value '0'. The process can refer to s'driving_value to retrieve the value 'Z'. Note that a process can only use this attribute to determine its own contribution to a signal; it cannot directly find out another process's contribution.

VHDL-87

The 'driving_value attribute is not provided in VHDL-87.

8.2.3   Resolved Signal Parameters

Let us now return to the topic of subprograms with signal parameters and see how they behave in the presence of resolved signals. Recall that when a procedure with an **out**-mode signal parameter is called, the procedure is passed a reference to the caller's driver for the actual signal. Any signal assignment statements performed within the procedure body are actually performed on the caller's driver. If the actual signal parameter is a resolved signal, the values assigned by the procedure are used to resolve the signal value. No resolution takes place within the procedure. In fact, the procedure need not be aware that the actual signal is resolved.

In the case of reading a signal parameter to a function or procedure, a reference to the actual signal parameter is passed when the subprogram is called, and the subprogram uses the actual value of the signal. If the signal is resolved, the subprogram sees the value determined after resolution. In the case of an **inout** signal parameter, a procedure is passed references to both the signal and its driver, and no resolution is performed internally to the procedure.

EXAMPLE 8.8   *Procedures for distributed synchronization*

We can encapsulate the distributed synchronization protocol described in Example 8.4 in a set of procedures, each with a single signal parameter, as follows:

```
procedure init_synchronize ( signal synch : out std_logic ) is
begin
  synch <= '0';
end procedure init_synchronize;

procedure begin_synchronize ( signal synch : inout std_logic;
                              Tdelay : in delay_length := 0 fs ) is
begin
  synch <= 'Z' after Tdelay;
  wait until synch;
end procedure begin_synchronize;

procedure end_synchronize ( signal synch : inout std_logic;
                            Tdelay : in delay_length := 0 fs ) is
begin
  synch <= '0' after Tdelay;
  wait until not synch;
end procedure end_synchronize;
```

Suppose a process uses a resolved signal **barrier** of subtype **std_logic** to synchronize with other processes. The process can use the procedures to implement the protocol as follows:

```
synchronized_module : process is
  ...
begin
```

```
init_synchronize(barrier);
...
loop
  ...
  begin_synchronize(barrier);
  ...    -- perform operation, synchronized with other processes
  end_synchronize(barrier);

  ...
end loop;
end process synchronized_module;
```

The process has a driver for **barrier**, since the procedure calls associate the signal as an actual parameter with formal parameters of mode **out** and **inout**. A reference to this driver is passed to init_synchronize, which assigns the value '0' on behalf of the process. This value is used in the resolution of **barrier**. When the process is ready to start its synchronized operation, it calls **begin_synchronize**, passing references to its driver for **barrier** and to the actual signal itself. The procedure uses the driver to assign the value 'Z' on behalf of the process and then waits until the actual signal changes to 'H'. When the transaction on the driver matures, its value is resolved with other contributions from other processes and the result applied to the signal. This final value is used by the wait statement in the procedure to determine whether to resume the calling process. If the value is 'H', the process resumes, the procedure returns to the caller and the operation goes ahead. When the process completes the operation, it calls **end_synchronize** to reset **barrier** back to '0'.

Exercises

1. [❶ 8.1] Suppose there are four drivers connected to a resolved signal that uses the resolution function **resolve_tri_state_logic** shown on page 262. What is the resolved value of the signal if the four drivers contribute these values:

    a.   'Z', '1', 'Z', 'Z'?

    b.   '0', 'Z', 'Z, '0'?

    c.   'Z', '1', 'Z', '0'?

2. [❶ 8.1] Rewrite the following resolved signal declaration as a subtype declaration followed by a signal declaration using the subtype.

    ```
    signal synch_control : wired_and tri_state_logic := '0';
    ```

3. [❶ 8.1] What is the initial value of the following signal of the type **MVL4_logic** defined in Example 8.1? How is that value derived?

    ```
    signal int_req : MVL4_logic;
    ```

4. [❶ 8.1] Does the result of the resolution function defined in Example 8.1 depend on the order of contributions from drivers in the array passed to the function?

5. **[❶ 8.1]** Suppose we define a resolved array subtype **byte** that is a subtype of **word**, defined in Example 8.2, with 8 elements. We then declare a signal of type **byte** with three drivers. What is the resolved value of the signal if the three drivers contribute these values:

    a. "ZZZZZZZZ", "ZZZZ0011", "ZZZZZZZZ"?

    b. "XXXXZZZZ", "ZZZZZZZZ", "00000011"?

    c. "00110011", "ZZZZZZZZ", "ZZZZ1111"?

6. **[❶ 8.1]** Suppose a signal is declared as

    signal data_bus : MVL4_logic_vector(0 **to** 15);

    where **MVL4_logic_vector** is as described on page 268, and the following signal assignments are each executed in different processes:

    data_bus <= "ZZZZZZZZZZZZZZZZ";

    data_bus(0 **to** 7) <= "XXXXZZZZ";

    data_bus(8 **to** 15) <= "00111100";

    What is the resolved signal value after all of the transactions have been performed?

7. **[❶ 8.1]** Suppose there are four drivers connected to a signal of type **std_logic**. What is the resolved value of the signal if the four drivers contribute these values:

    a. 'Z', '0', 'Z', 'H'?

    b. 'H', 'Z', 'W', '0'?

    c. 'Z', 'W', 'L', 'H'?

    d. 'U', '0', 'Z', '1'?

    e. 'Z', 'Z', 'Z', '–'?

8. **[❶ 8.2]** Figure 8.2 is a timing diagram for the system with two bus modules using the wired-and synchronization signal described in Example 8.4. The diagram shows the driving values contributed by each of the bus modules to the **synch_control** signal. Complete the diagram by drawing the resolved waveform for **synch_control**. Indicate the times at which each bus module proceeds with its internal operation.

FIGURE 8.2

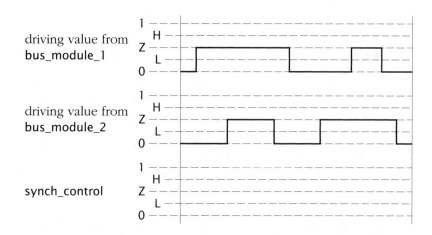

Timing diagram for wired-and synchronization

9. [❶ 8.2] Suppose all of the modules in the hierarchy of Figure 8.1 use resolved ports for their data connections. If the Mem, Cache, Serial and DMA modules all update their data drivers in the same simulation cycle, how many times is the resolution function invoked to determine the final resolved values of the data signals?

10. [❶ 8.2] Suppose a process in a model drives a bidirectional port **synch_T** of type **std_logic**. Write a signal assignment statement that inverts the process's contribution to the port.

11. [❷ 8.1] Develop a model that includes two processes, each of which drives a signal of the type **MVL4_logic** described in Example 8.1. Experiment with your simulator to see if it allows you to trace the invocation and execution of the resolution function.

12. [❷ 8.1] Develop a model of an inverter with an open-collector output of type **std_ulogic**, and a model of a pull-up resistor that drives its single **std_ulogic** port with the value 'H'. Test the models in a test bench that connects the outputs of a number of inverter instances to a signal of type **std_logic**, pulled up with a resistor instance. Verify that the circuit implements the active-low wired-or operation.

13. [❷ 8.1] Develop a behavioral model of an 8-bit-wide bidirectional transceiver, such as the 74245 family of components. The transceiver has two bidirectional data ports, **a** and **b**; an active-low output-enable port, **oe_n**; and a direction port, **dir**. When **oe_n** is low and **dir** is low, data is received from **b** to **a**. When **oe_n** is low and **dir** is high, data is transmitted from **a** to **b**. When **oe_n** is high, both **a** and **b** are high impedance. Assume a propagation delay of 5 ns for all output changes.

14. [❷ 8.1] Many combinatorial logic functions can be implemented in integrated circuits using pass transistors acting as switches. While a pass transistor is, in principle, a bidirectional device, for many circuits it is sufficient to model it as a unidirectional device. Develop a model of a unidirectional pass transistor switch, with an input port,

an output port and an enable port, all of type **std_ulogic**. When the enable input is 'H' or '1', the input value is passed to the output, but with weak drive strength. When the enable input is 'L' or '0', the output is high impedance. If the enable input is at an unknown level, the output is unknown, except that its drive strength is weak.

15. [❸ 8.1] Develop a behavioral model of a tristate buffer with data input, data output and enable ports, all of type **std_ulogic**. The propagation time from data input to data output when the buffer is enabled is 4 ns. The turn-on delay from the enable port is 3 ns, and the turn-off delay is 3.5 ns. Use the buffer and any other necessary gate models in a structural model of the 8-bit transceiver described in Exercise 13.

16. [❸ 8.1] Use the unidirectional pass transistor model of Exercise 14 in a structural model of a four-input multiplexer. The multiplexer has select inputs s0 and s1. Pass transistors are used to construct the multiplexer as shown in Figure 8.3.

FIGURE 8.3

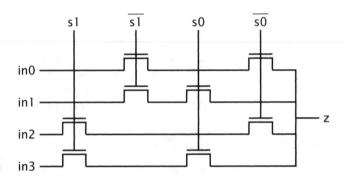

A multiplexer constructed of pass transistors.

17. [❸ 8.1] Develop a model of a distributed priority arbiter for a shared bus in a multiprocessor computer system. Each bus requester has a request priority, R, between 0 and 31, with 0 indicating the most urgent request and 31 indicating no request. Priorities are binary-encoded using 5-bit vectors, with bit 4 being the most-significant bit and bit 0 being the least-significant bit. The standard-logic values 'H' and '1' both represent the binary digit 1, and the standard-logic value '0' represents the binary digit 0. All requesters can drive and sense a 5-bit arbitration bus, A, which is pulled up to 'H' by the bus terminator. The requesters each use A and their own priority to compute the minimum of all priorities by comparing the binary digits of priorities as follows. For each bit position i:

- if $(R_{4...i+1} = A_{4...i+1})$ and $(R_i = 0)$: drive A_i with '0' after T_{pd}
- if $(R_{4...i+1} \neq A_{4...i+1})$ or $(R_i = 1)$: drive A_i with 'Z' after T_{pd}

T_{pd} is the propagation delay between sensing a value on A and driving a resulting value on A. When the value on A has stabilized, it is the minimum of all request priorities. The requester with $R = A$ wins the arbitration. If you are not convinced that the distributed minimization scheme operates as required, trace its execution for various combinations of priority values.

Chapter 9

Predefined and Standard Packages

In this chapter, we look at several predefined and standard packages, which provide types and operators for use in VHDL models. While we could define all of the data types and operations we need for a given model, we can greatly increase our productivity by reusing the standard packages. Moreover, simulation and synthesis tools often have optimized, built-in implementations of the operations from these packages.

9.1 The Predefined Packages **standard** and **env**

In previous chapters, we have introduced numerous predefined types and operators. We can use them in our VHDL models without having to write type declarations or subprogram definitions for them. These predefined items all come from a special package called standard, located in a special design library called **std**. A full listing of the standard package is included for reference in Appendix A.

Because nearly every model we write needs to make use of the contents of this library and package, as well as the library **work**, VHDL includes an implicit context clause of the form

```
library std, work;  use std.standard.all;
```

at the beginning of each design unit. Hence we can refer to the simple names of the predefined items without having to resort to their selected names. In the occasional case where we need to distinguish a reference to a predefined operator from an overloaded version, we can use a selected name, for example:

```
result := std.standard."<" ( a, b );
```

EXAMPLE 9.1 *A comparison operator for signed binary-coded integers*

A package that provides signed arithmetic operations on integers represented as bit vectors might include a relational operator, defined as follows:

```vhdl
function "<" ( a, b : bit_vector ) return boolean is
  variable tmp1 : bit_vector(a'range) := a;
  variable tmp2 : bit_vector(b'range) := b;
begin
  tmp1(tmp1'left) := not tmp1(tmp1'left);
  tmp2(tmp2'left) := not tmp2(tmp2'left);
  return std.standard."<" ( tmp1, tmp2 );
end function "<";
```

The function negates the sign bit of each operand, then compares the resultant bit vectors using the predefined relational operator from the package **standard**. The full selected name for the predefined operator is necessary to distinguish it from the function being defined. If the return expression were written as "tmp1 < tmp2", it would refer to the function in which it occurs, creating a circular definition.

VHDL-87, -93, and -2002

A number of new operations were added to VHDL in the 2008 revision. They are not available in earlier versions of the language. In summary, the changes are

- The types **boolean_vector**, **integer_vector**, **real_vector**, and **time_vector** are predefined (see Section 4.2.1). The predefined operations on **boolean_vector** are the same as those defined for **bit_vector**. The predefined operations on **integer_vector** include the relational operators ("=", "/=", "<", ">", "<=", and ">=") and the concatenation operator ("&"). The predefined operations on **real_vector** and **time_vector** include the equality and inequality operators ("=" and "/=") and the concatenation operator ("&").

- The array/scalar logic operations and logical reduction operations are predefined for **bit_vector** and **boolean_vector**, since they are arrays with **bit** and **boolean** elements, respectively.

- The matching relational operators "?=", "?/=", "?>", "?>=", "?<", and "?<=" are predefined for **bit**. Further, the operators "?=" and "?/=" are predefined for **bit_vector**.

- The operators **mod** and **rem** are predefined for **time**, since it is a physical type.

- The **maximum** and **minimum** operations are predefined for all of the predefined types.

- The functions **rising_edge** and **falling_edge** are predefined for **bit** and **boolean**. Prior to VHDL-2008, the **bit** versions of these functions were declared in the package **numeric_bit** (see Section 9.2.3). However, that was mainly to provide consistency with the **std_ulogic** versions defined in the **std_logic_1164** package. They rightly belong with the definition of the type on which they operate; hence, VHDL-2008 includes them in the package **standard**. The VHDL-2008 revision of the **numeric_bit** package redefines the operations there as aliases for the predefined versions. (We discuss aliases in Chapter 10.)

- The **to_string** operations are predefined for all scalar types and for **bit_vector**. Further, the **to_bstring**, **to_ostring**, and **to_hstring** operations and associated aliases are predefined for **bit_vector**.

VHDL also provided a second special package, called **env**, in the **std** library. The **env** package includes operations for accessing the simulation environment provided by a simulator. First, there are procedures for controlling the progress of a simulation:

```
procedure stop (status: integer);
procedure stop;

procedure finish (status: integer);
procedure finish;
```

When the procedure **stop** is called, the simulator stops and accepts further input from the user interface (if interactive) or command file (if running in batch mode). When the procedure **finish** is called, the simulator terminates; simulation cannot continue. The versions of the procedures that have the **status** parameter use the parameter value in an implementation-defined way. They might, for example, provide the value to a control script so that the script can determine what action to take next.

The **env** package also defines a function to access the resolution limit for the simulation:

```
function resolution_limit return delay_length;
```

We described the resolution limit in Section 2.2.4 when we introduced the predefined type **time**. One way in which we might use the **resolution_limit** function is to wait for simulation time to advance by one time step, as follows:

```
wait for env.resolution_limit;
```

Since the resolution limit, and hence the minimum time by which simulation advances, can vary from one simulation run to another, we cannot write a literal time value in such a wait statement. The use of the **resolution_limit** function allows us to write models that adapt to the resolution limit used in each simulation. We need to take care in using this function, however. It might be tempting to compare the return value with a given time unit, for example:

```
if env.resolution_limit > ns then   -- potentially illegal!
   ... -- do coarse-resolution actions
else
   ... -- do fine-resolution actions
end if;
```

The problem is that we are not allowed to write a time unit smaller than the resolution limit used in a simulation. If this code were simulated with a resolution limit greater than **ns**, the use of the unit name **ns** would cause an error; so the code can only succeed if the resolution limit is less than or equal to **ns**. We can avoid this problem by rewriting the example as:

```
if env.resolution_limit > 1.0E-9 sec then
    ... -- do coarse-resolution actions
else
    ... -- do fine-resolution actions
end if;
```

For resolution limits less than or equal to **ns**, the test returns false, so the "else" alternative is taken. For resolution limits greater than **ns**, the time literal 1.0E-9 sec is truncated to zero, and so the test returns true. Thus, even though the calculation is not quite what appears, it produces the result we want.

VHDL-87, -93, and -2002

These versions do not provide the **env** package. Some tools might provide equivalent functionality through implementation-defined mechanisms.

9.2   IEEE Standard Packages

When we design models, we can define types and operations using the built-in facilities of VHDL. However, the IEEE has published standards for packages that define commonly used data types and operations. Using these standards can save us development time. Furthermore, many tool vendors provide optimized implementations of the standard packages, so using them makes our simulations run faster. In this section, we outline the types and operations defined in a number of the IEEE standard packages. Complete details of the package declarations are included in Appendix A. Each of these packages is included in a library called **ieee**. Hence, to use one of the packages in a design, we name the library **ieee** in a library clause, and name the required package in a use clause. We have seen examples of how to do this for the IEEE standard package **std_logic_1164**; the same applies for the other IEEE standard packages.

9.2.1   Standard VHDL Mathematical Packages

The IEEE standard packages **math_real** and **math_complex** define constants and mathematical functions on real and complex numbers, respectively.

Real Number Mathematical Package

The constants defined in **math_real** are listed in Table 9.1. The functions, their operand types and meanings are listed in Table 9.2. In the figure, the parameters **x** and **y** are of type **real**, and the parameter **n** is of type **integer**.

TABLE 9.1   *Constants defined in the package* math_real

Constant	Value	Constant	Value
math_e	e	math_log_of_2	$\ln 2$
math_1_over_e	$1/e$	math_log_of_10	$\ln 10$
math_pi	π	math_log2_of_e	$\log_2 e$
math_2_pi	2π	math_log10_of_e	$\log_{10} e$
math_1_over_pi	$1/\pi$	math_sqrt_2	$\sqrt{2}$
math_pi_over_2	$\pi/2$	math_1_over_sqrt_2	$1/\sqrt{2}$
math_pi_over_3	$\pi/3$	math_sqrt_pi	$\sqrt{\pi}$
math_pi_over_4	$\pi/4$	math_deg_to_rad	$2\pi/360$
math_3_pi_over_2	$3\pi/2$	math_rad_to_deg	$360/2\pi$

TABLE 9.2   *Functions defined in the package* math_real

Function	Meaning	Function	Meaning
ceil(x)	Ceiling of x (least integer $\geq x$)	sign(x)	Sign of x (−1.0, 0.0 or +1.0)
floor(x)	Floor of x (greatest integer $\leq x$)	"mod"(x, y)	Floating-point modulus of x/y
round(x)	x rounded to nearest integer value (ties rounded away from 0.0)	realmax(x, y)	Greater of x and y
trunc(x)	x truncated toward 0.0	realmin(x, y)	Lesser of x and y
sqrt(x)	$\sqrt{x}$	log(x)	$\ln x$
cbrt(x)	$\sqrt[3]{x}$	log2(x)	$\log_2 x$
"**"(n, y)	n^y	log10(x)	$\log_{10} x$
"**"(x, y)	x^y	log(x, y)	$\log_y x$
exp(x)	e^x		
sin(x)	$\sin x$ (x in radians)	arcsin(x)	arcsin x
cos(x)	$\cos x$ (x in radians)	arccos(x)	arccos x
tan(x)	$\tan x$ (x in radians)	arctan(x)	arctan x
		arctan(y, x)	arctan of point (x, y)

Function	Meaning	Function	Meaning
sinh(x)	sinh x	arcsinh(x)	arcsinh x
cosh(x)	cosh x	arccosh(x)	arccosh x
tanh(x)	tanh x	arctanh(x)	arctanh x

In addition to the functions listed in Table 9.2, the **math_real** package defines the procedure **uniform** as follows:

```
procedure uniform ( variable seed1, seed2 : inout positive;
                    variable x : out real);
```

This procedure generates successive values between 0.0 and 1.0 (exclusive) in a pseudo-random number sequence. The variables **seed1** and **seed2** store the state of the generator and are modified by each call to the procedure. **Seed1** must be initialized to a value between 1 and 2,147,483,562, and **seed2** to a value between 1 and 2,147,483,398, before the first call to **uniform**.

EXAMPLE 9.2   *A random-stimulus test bench for an ALU*

Suppose we need to test a structural implementation of an ALU, whose entity is declared as follows:

```
use ieee.numeric_bit.all;
subtype ALU_func is unsigned(3 downto 0);
subtype data_word is unsigned(15 downto 0);
...

entity ALU is
  port ( a, b : in data_word;  func : in ALU_func;
         result : out data_word;  carry : out bit );
end entity ALU;
```

We can devise a test bench that stimulates an instance of the ALU with randomly generated data and function-code inputs:

```
architecture random_test of test_ALU is

  use ieee.numeric_bit.all;
  use ieee.math_real.uniform;

  signal a, b, result : data_word;
  signal func : ALU_func;
  signal carry : bit;

begin

  dut : entity work.ALU(structural)
    port map ( a, b, func, result, carry );
```

```
      stimulus : process is
        variable seed1, seed2 : positive := 1;
        variable a_real, b_real, func_real : real;
      begin
        wait for 100 ns;
        uniform ( seed1, seed2, a_real );
        uniform ( seed1, seed2, b_real );
        uniform ( seed1, seed2, func_real );
        a <= to_unsigned(
                natural(a_real
                        * real(2**integer'(data_word'length)) - 0.5),
                data_word'length );
        b <= to_unsigned(
                natural(b_real
                        * real(2**integer'(data_word'length)) - 0.5),
                data_word'length );
        func <= to_unsigned(
                natural(func_real
                        * real(2**integer'(ALU_func'length)) - 0.5),
                ALU_func'length );
      end process stimulus;

      ...   --verification process to check result and carry

    end architecture random_test;
```

The **stimulus** process generates new random stimuli for the ALU input signals every 100 ns. The process generates three random numbers in the range (0.0, 1.0) in the variables **a_real**, **b_real** and **func_real**. It then scales these values to get numbers in the range (–0.5, 65,635.5) for the data values and (–0.5, 15.5) for the function code value. These are rounded and converted to **unsigned** bit vectors for assignment to the ALU input signals.

Complex Number Mathematical Package

The **math_complex** package deals with complex numbers represented in Cartesian and polar form. The package defines types for these representations, as follows:

```
type complex is record
    re : real;     -- Real part
    im : real;     -- Imaginary part
  end record;

subtype positive_real is real range 0.0 to real'high;
subtype principal_value is real range -math_pi to math_pi;

type complex_polar is record
    mag : positive_real;     -- Magnitude
```

```
     arg : principal_value;   -- Angle in radians; -math_pi is illegal
  end record;
```

The constants defined in **math_complex** are

math_cbase_1 $1.0 + j0.0$

math_cbase_j $0.0 + j1.0$

math_czero $0.0 + j0.0$

The package defines a number of overloaded operators, listed in Table 9.3. The curly braces indicate that for each operator to the left of the brace, there are overloaded versions for all combinations of types to the right of the brace. Thus, there are six overloaded versions of each of the "+", "−", "*" and "/" operators.

TABLE 9.3   *Overloaded operators defined in* math_complex

Operator	Operation		Left operand	Right operand	Result
=	equality		complex_polar	complex_polar	boolean
/=	inequality		complex_polar	complex_polar	boolean
abs	magnitude			complex	positive_real
				complex_polar	positive_real
−	negation			complex	complex
				complex_polar	complex_polar
+	addition	⌠	complex	complex	complex
−	subtraction		real	complex	complex
*	multiplication		complex	real	complex
/	division	⟨	complex_polar	complex_polar	complex_polar
			real	complex_polar	complex_polar
		⌡	complex_polar	real	complex_polar

Overloaded versions of "=" and "/=" are necessary for numbers in polar form, since two complex numbers are equal if their magnitudes are both 0.0, even if their arguments are different. The predefined equality and inequality operators do not have this behavior. No overloaded versions of these operators are required for Cartesian form, since the predefined operators behave correctly.

In addition to the operators, the **math_complex** package defines a number of mathematical functions, listed in Table 9.4. In the table, the parameters **x** and **y** are real, the parameter **c** is **complex**, the parameter **p** is **complex_polar**, and the parameter **z** is either **complex** or **complex_polar**.

TABLE 9.4   *Functions defined in the package* math_complex

Function	Result type	Meaning
cmplx(x, y)	complex	$x + jy$
get_principal_value(x)	principal_value	$x + 2\pi k$ for some k, such that $-\pi < \text{result} \leq \pi$
complex_to_polar(c)	complex_polar	c in polar form
polar_to_complex(p)	complex	p in Cartesian form
arg(z)	principal_value	$\arg(z)$ in radians
conj(z)	same as z	complex conjugate of z
sqrt(z)	same as z	$\sqrt{z}$
exp(z)	same as z	e^z
log(z)	same as z	$\ln z$
log2(z)	same as z	$\log_2 z$
log10(z)	same as z	$\log_{10} z$
log(z, y)	same as z	$\log_y z$
sin(z)	same as z	$\sin z$
cos(z)	same as z	$\cos z$
sinh(z)	same as z	$\sinh z$
cosh(z)	same as z	$\cosh z$

9.2.2   The **std_logic_1164** Multivalue Logic System

The IEEE standard package **std_logic_1164** defines types and operations for models that need to deal with strong, weak and high-impedance strengths, and with unknown values. We have already described most of the types and operations in previous chapters and seen their use in examples. For completeness, we draw the information together in this section.

The types declared in **std_logic_1164** are

std_ulogic	The basic multivalued enumeration type (see page 48)
std_ulogic_vector	Array of **std_ulogic** elements (see page 107)
std_logic	Resolved multivalued enumeration subtype (see Section 8.1.3 on page 272)
std_logic_vector	Subtype of **std_ulogic_vector** with resolved elements (see Section 8.1.3 on page 272)

In addition, the package declares the subtypes X01, X01Z, UX01 and UX01Z for cases where we do not need to distinguish between strong and weak driving strengths. Each of these subtypes includes just the values listed in the subtype name.

Since the type **std_ulogic** and the subtype **std_logic** are scalar enumeration types, all of the predefined operations for such types are available. This includes the relational operators, **maximum**, **minimum**, and **to_string**. In addition, the matching relational operators "?=", "?/=", "?>", "?>=", "?<", and "?<=" are predefined for **std_ulogic** and **std_logic**. For the array type **std_ulogic_vector** and the subtype **std_logic_vector**, the predefined operations on one-dimensional arrays of discrete-type elements are available. This includes "&" and the relational operators. In addition, the matching equality ("?=") and inequality ("?/=") operators are defined for these types.

The operations provided by the **std_logic_1164** package include overloaded versions of the logical operators **and**, **nand**, **or**, **nor**, **xor**, **xnor** and **not**, operating on values of each of the scalar and vector types and subtypes listed above. It also includes overloaded versions of the shift operators **sll**, **srl**, **rol** and **ror** operating on the vector types. It does not overload the **sla** and **sra** operators on the premise that they assume a numeric interpretation of vectors. Instead, those operators are overloaded in separate packages, **numeric_std** and **numeric_std_unsigned**, that provide arithmetic operations assuming a numeric interpretation (see Section 9.2.3).

In Section 4.3.5 we described the **to_ostring** and **to_hstring** operations for converting **bit_vector** operands to strings in octal and hexadecimal form. The **std_logic_1164** package provides overloaded versions of these operations for **std_ulogic_vector** and **std_logic_vector** operands. The operations group elements into threes (octal) or fours (hexadecimal) for conversion into digits. However, if the vector needs to be extended on the left to make a multiple of three or four, the assumed value for the extra elements depends on the leftmost actual element. If the leftmost element is 'Z', then 'Z' elements are assumed; if it is 'X', then 'X' elements are assumed; otherwise, '0' elements are assumed.

Having grouped elements, they are converted to digits. If all of the elements in a group are '0', 'L', '1', or 'H', the group is converted to a normal digit character, with '0' and 'L' elements treated as '0', and '1' and 'H' elements treated as '1'. If all of the elements in a group are 'Z', then 'Z' is used as the digit character for the group. In all other cases, where a group contains one or more non-'0', -'L', -'1', -'H' or -'Z' elements, 'X' is used as the digit character for the group. Some examples are

```
to_ostring(B"01L_1H1") = "27"
to_ostring(B"011_ZZZ") = "3Z"
to_ostring(B"01U_UZZ") = "XX"

to_ostring(B"HH_000") = to_ostring(B"0HH_000") = "30"
to_ostring(B"ZZ_ZZZ") = to_ostring(B"ZZZ_ZZZ") = "ZZ"
to_ostring(B"X1_000") = to_ostring(B"XX1_000") = "X0"
to_ostring(B"1X_000") = to_ostring(B"01X_000") = "X0"
```

As well as providing the overloaded **to_ostring** and **to_hstring** operations, the **std_logic_1164** package provides all of the alternative names: **to_bstring**, **to_binary_string**, **to_octal_string**, and **to_hex_string**. Further, the package provides overloaded versions of the file read and write operations for text-based input/output. (File input/output is considered an advanced topic, and is not covered in this book.)

In addition to the overloaded operations, the package declares a number of functions for conversion between values of different types. In the following lists, the parameter **b** represents a bit value or bit vector, the parameter **s** represents a standard logic value or standard logic vector, and the parameter **x** represents a value of any of these types.

    To_Bit(s,xmap)   Convert a standard logic value to a bit value

    To_BitVector(s, xmap)
    To_Bit_Vector(s, xmap)
    To_BV(s, xmap)   Convert a standard logic vector to a bit vector

In these functions, the parameter **xmap** is a bit value that is used in the result when a bit to be converted is other than '0', '1', 'L' or 'H'. There are multiple alternative names for the second function, allowing us to choose based on consideration of coding style.

    To_StdULogic(b)   Convert a bit value to a standard logic value

    To_StdLogicVector(x)
    To_Std_Logic_Vector(x)
    To_SLV(x)   Convert to a **std_logic_vector**

    To_StdULogicVector(x)
    To_Std_ULogic_Vector(x)
    To_SULV(x)   Convert to a **std_ulogic_vector**

Note that the **To_StdLogicVector** and **To_StdULogicVector** function perform essentially the same operation. The fact that **std_logic_vector** has resolved elements is not relevant to the conversion. The two forms are provided for backward compatibility with previous versions of VHDL, where the distinction was relevant.

    To_01(x, xmap)   Strip strength

    To_X01(x)   Strip strength

    To_X01Z(x)   Strip strength

    To_UX01(x)   Strip strength

These strength-stripping functions remove the driving strength information from the parameter value. **To_01** convert 'L' and 'H' digits in a vector to '0' and '1' digits. The optional second parameter specifies the result value to produce if any digit in the first parameter is other than '0', '1', 'L' or 'H'. In that case, all digits of the result are set to the value specified in the second parameter. The default value of the second parameter is '0'. Some examples are

```
to_01( "LLHH01" ) = "001101"
to_01( "00X11U" ) = "000110"

to_01( "100LLL", 'X' ) = "100000"
to_01( "00W000", 'X' ) = "XXXXXX"
```

To_X01 converts 'U', 'X', 'Z', 'W' and '–' elements to 'X'. To_X01Z is similar, but leaves 'Z' elements intact. To_UX01 is similar to To_X01, but leaves 'U' elements intact.

Finally, the std_logic_1164 package contains the following utility functions:

rising_edge(s)	True when there is a rising edge on s, false otherwise
falling_edge(s)	True when there is a falling edge on s, false otherwise
is_X(s)	True if s contains an unknown value, false otherwise

The edge-detection functions detect changes between low and high values on a scalar signal, irrespective of the driving strengths of the values. The functions are true only during the simulation cycles on which such events occur. They serve the same purpose as the predefined functions of the same name operating on **bit** and **boolean** signals. The unknown-detection function determines whether there is a 'U', 'X', 'Z' or 'W' value in the scalar or vector value s.

VHDL-87, -93, and -2002

In the version of **std_logic_1164** for these versions of VHDL, **std_ulogic_vector** and **std_logic_vector** were declared as distinct array types, rather than one being a subtype of the other. This led to considerable inconvenience when both types were used in a design. The **std_logic_1164** package provided separate overloaded declarations for operations on each of the two types, and additional conversion functions between them were required.

Since VHDL-2008 adds numerous new predefined operations, the VHDL-2008 version of the package provides overloaded versions of them. They are not provided in the version of the package for earlier versions of VHDL.

VHDL-87

The overloaded versions of the **xnor** operator are not included in the VHDL-87 version of the standard-logic package.

9.2.3 Standard Integer Numeric Packages

The IEEE standard packages numeric_bit and numeric_std define arithmetic operations on integers represented using vectors of **bit** and **std_ulogic** elements respectively. Most synthesis tools accept models that use these types and operations for numeric computations. We discuss the topic of synthesis of VHDL models in more detail in Chapter 14. In this section, we outline the types and operations provided by the IEEE standard integer numeric packages. Full listings of the package declarations are included in Appendix A.

Each of the packages defines two types, **unsigned** and **signed**, to represent unsigned and signed integer values, respectively. In the case of the **numeric_bit** package, the types are unconstrained arrays of **bit** elements:

```
type unsigned is array ( natural range <> ) of bit;
type signed is array ( natural range <> ) of bit;
```

In the case of the numeric_std package, the types are defined similarly, but with resolved std_ulogic as the element type. This package also defines the types **unresolved_unsigned** and **unresolved_signed** (and the shorter aliases **u_unsigned** and **u_signed**) as arrays of unresolved std_ulogic elements. The declarations are

```
type unresolved_unsigned is array (natural range <>) of std_ulogic;
type unresolved_signed   is array (natural range <>) of std_ulogic;

alias u_unsigned is unresolved_unsigned;
alias u_signed   is unresolved_signed;

subtype unsigned is (resolved) unresolved_unsigned;
subtype signed   is (resolved) unresolved_signed;
```

Whichever package and type we use, the leftmost element is the most-significant digit, and the rightmost element is the least-significant digit. Signed numbers are represented using two's-complement encoding.

We declare objects of these types either directly or using a subtype to define the index range. For example:

```
signal head_position : signed ( 0 to 15 );

subtype address is unsigned ( 31 downto 0 );
signal next_PC : address;
constant PC_increment : unsigned := X"4";
```

The operations defined for **unsigned** and **signed** numbers are listed in Table 9.5. The curly braces indicate that for each operator to the left of the brace, there are overloaded versions for all combinations of types to the right of the brace. For example, there are six overloaded versions of each of the "+", "−", "*", "/", **rem** and **mod** operators. The notation "*element type*" refers to the element type (bit or std_ulogic) of the vector operand or operands.

The operands of arithmetic and relational operators need not be of the same length. The relational operators determine the result based on the numeric values represented by the operands, rather than using left-to-right lexicographic comparison. For those operators that produce a vector result, the length of the result depends on the length of the operands, as follows.

- **abs** and "−": the length of the operand

- Addition and subtraction of two vectors: the larger of the two operand lengths

- Addition and subtraction of a vector and an integer, natural number or scalar element: the length of the vector operand

- Multiplication of two vectors: the sum of the operand lengths

- Multiplication of a vector and an integer or natural number: twice the length of the vector operand

TABLE 9.5   *Operators defined in the IEEE standard synthesis packages*

Operator	Operation		Left operand	Right operand	Result
abs	absolute value			signed	signed
–	negation				
+	addition		unsigned	unsigned	unsigned
–	subtraction		unsigned	natural	unsigned
*	multiplication		natural	unsigned	unsigned
/	division		signed	signed	signed
rem	remainder		signed	integer	signed
mod	modulo		integer	signed	signed
+	addition		unsigned	*element type*	unsigned
–	subtraction		*element type*	unsigned	unsigned
			signed	*element type*	signed
			element type	signed	signed
=	equality		unsigned	unsigned	boolean
/=	inequality		unsigned	natural	boolean
<	less than		natural	unsigned	boolean
<=	less than or equal to		signed	signed	boolean
>	greater than		signed	integer	boolean
>=	greater than or equal to		integer	signed	boolean
?=	matching equality		unsigned	unsigned	*element type*
?/=	matching inequality		unsigned	natural	*element type*
?<	matching less than		natural	unsigned	*element type*
?<=	matching less than or equal to		signed	signed	*element type*
?>	matching greater than		signed	integer	*element type*
?>=	matching greater than or equal to		integer	signed	*element type*
sll	shift-left logical		unsigned	integer	unsigned
srl	shift-right logical		signed	integer	signed
sla	shift-left arithmetic				
sra	shift-right arithmetic				
rol	rotate left				
ror	rotate right				

Operator	Operation		Left operand	Right operand	Result
not	negation	{		unsigned	unsigned
				signed	signed
and	logical and		unsigned	unsigned	unsigned
or	logical or		unsigned	*element type*	unsigned
nand	negated logical and		*element type*	unsigned	unsigned
nor	negated logical or		signed	signed	signed
xor	exclusive or		signed	*element type*	signed
xnor	negated exclusive or		*element type*	signed	signed
and	logical and reduction			unsigned	*element type*
or	logical or reduction			signed	*element type*
nand	negated logical and reduction				
nor	negated logical or reduction				
xor	exclusive or reduction				
xnor	negated exclusive or reduction				

- Division of two vectors: the length of the left operand

- Remainder and modulo of two vectors: the length of the right operand

- Division, remainder and modulo of a vector and an integer or natural number: the length of the vector operand. If the result value is too large to fit in the result vector, the value is truncated and a warning issued during simulation.

- Shift and rotate operators: the length of the vector operand

- **not**: the length of the operand

- Binary logical operators: the length of the operands, whose lengths must be the same

EXAMPLE 9.3   *Addition with carry*

The addition operator that has two vector operands can be used to produce both the sum vector and a carry bit by extending the operands. For example, if we declare unsigned operand signals and a carry signal as

```
signal a, b, sum : unsigned(15 downto 0);
signal c_out : std_ulogic;
```

we can write an assignment that produces both the sum and the carry value:

```
(c_out, sum) <= ('0' & a) + ('0' & b);
```

The concatenations extend the operands by one bit, so the addition produces a 17-bit result. This is assigned to the aggregate of the carry signal (the leftmost bit of the result) and the sum signal (the rightmost 16 bits of the result).

The addition and subtraction operators that have an operand of the scalar element type allow us to describe an addition with carry in or a subtraction with borrow in. For example:

```
signal a, b : unsigned(15 downto 0);
signal sum  : unsigned(16 downto 0);
signal c_in;
...

sum <= ('0' & a) + ('0' & b) + c_in;
```

This can be synthesized as a single 16-bit adder with a carry input and a 17-bit result.

EXAMPLE 9.4   *A conditional incrementer*

We can use the "+" operator to treat a scalar control signal as an operand in a conditional incrementer. If the control signal is '0', an **unsigned** operand value is not incremented; if the control signal is '1", the value is incremented. The declarations and process are:

```
signal inc_en  : std_ulogic;
signal inc_reg : unsigned(7 downto 0);
...

inc_reg_proc : process (clk) is
begin
  if rising_edge(clk) then
    inc_reg <= inc_reg + inc_en;
  end if;
end process inc_reg_proc;
```

If we had written the if statement as follows:

```
if inc_en = '1' then
  inc_reg <= inc_reg + 1;
end if;
```

a synthesis tool might have generated an adder with the vector "00000001" as an input, connected to a regsiter with clock enable. By using the control signal as an operand, we more clearly imply an incrementer and a simple register without clock enable. We discuss coding styles for synthesis in more detail in Chapter 14.

For the division, remainder and modulo operators, if the right operand is zero, an assertion violation with severity level error is issued during simulation.

The logical shift operators **sll** and **srl** fill the vacated elements with '0'. Their behavior is the same as that of the predefined operators for bit_vector values. The behavior of the **sla** and **sra** operators, on the other hand, is different from the predefined versions, in that they assume a binary-coded numeric interpretation for a vector. The type of the left operand determines the kind of shift performed. If the operand is **unsigned**, a logical shift is performed, whereas if the parameter is **signed**, an arithmetic shift is performed. An arithmetic shift right (**sra** with a positive right operand or **sla** with a negative right operand) replicates the sign bit, giving the effect of division by a power of 2. An arithmetic shift left (**sra** with a negative right operand or **sla** with a positive right operand) fills the vacated bits on the right with '0', giving the effect of multiplication by a power of 2.

In addition to the overloaded operators, the **numeric_bit** and **numeric_std** packages define a number of functions, listed in Table 9.6. As in Table 9.5, the curly braces indicate that for each function to the left of the brace, there are overloaded versions for all combinations of types to the right of the brace.

TABLE 9.6 *Functions defined in the IEEE standard synthesis packages*

Function		First parameter	Second parameter	Result
minimum		unsigned	unsigned	unsigned
maximum		unsigned	natural	unsigned
		natural	unsigned	unsigned
		signed	signed	signed
		signed	integer	signed
		integer	signed	signed
shift_left		unsigned	natural	unsigned
shift_right		signed	natural	signed
rotate_left				
rotate_right				
find_leftmost		unsigned	*element type*	integer
find_rightmost		signed	*element type*	integer
resize		unsigned	natural	unsigned
		unsigned	unsigned	unsigned
		signed	natural	signed
		signed	signed	signed

Function		First parameter	Second parameter	Result
to_integer	{	unsigned		natural
		signed		integer
to_unsigned	{	natural	natural	unsigned
		natural	unsigned	unsigned
to_signed	{	integer	natural	signed
		integer	signed	signed
rising_edge[a]	{	**signal** bit		boolean
falling_edge[a]				
std_match[b]	{	unsigned	unsigned	boolean
		signed	signed	boolean
		std_ulogic	std_ulogic	boolean
		std_ulogic_vector	std_ulogic_vector	boolean
to_01[b]	{	unsigned	⟦ std_ulogic ⟧	unsigned
to_X01[b]		signed	⟦ std_ulogic ⟧	signed
to_X01Z[b]				
to_UX01[b]				
to_string to_bstring to_binary_string	{	unsigned		string
to_ostring to_octal_string		signed		string
to_hstring to_hex_string				

a. Provided in **numeric_bit** only.
b. Provided in **numeric_std** only.

The **maximum** and **minimum** functions are overloaded to compare their operands based on a numeric interpretation in the same way as the relational operators. For the versions that take two vector operands, the operands do not need to be of the same length.

The shift, rotate and **to_01** functions all produce a result that has the same length as the vector parameter. The shift and rotate functions perform similar operations to the overloaded shift and rotate operators. However, their second parameter is constrained to be a non-negative integer. Hence each of these functions can only shift or rotate elements in one direction. These functions were included in the package for earlier versions of VHDL that did not include the shift operators. They are maintained in the package for backward compatibility.

The **find_leftmost** function returns the index of the leftmost occurrence of the right-operand value in the left-operand vector. Similarly, the **find_rightmost** function returns the index of the rightmost occurrence of the right-operand value in the left-operand vector. If there is no such occurrence, the functions return −1. Since the index bound of an unsigned or signed vector are natural numbers, −1 is a clear indication that the value was not found. In both functions, search for the element value is performed using a matching equality test. We can use **find_leftmost** to gauge the magnitude of a number, since the leftmost occurrence of a 1 bit in an unsigned number is approximately $\log_2$ of the number. For a signed number, the leftmost bit that differs from the sign bit is likewise approximately $\log_2$ of the number.

The **resize** functions produce a result whose length is specified by the second parameter. For a second parameter of type natural, the parameter value specifies the number of bits in the result directly. For a second parameter of type unsigned or signed, the result has the same number of bits as the parameter value. Increasing the size of an **unsigned** number zero-extends to the left, whereas increasing the size of a **signed** number replicates the sign bit to the left. Truncating an **unsigned** number to length L keeps the rightmost L bits. Truncating a **signed** number to length L keeps the sign bit and the rightmost $L - 1$ bits.

The **to_integer** functions convert **unsigned** or **signed** values to **natural** or **integer** values, respectively. The **to_unsigned** and **to_signed** functions convert their first parameter to a vector whose length is given by the second parameter, either as a natural number directly, or as a vector whose length is used.

The edge-detection functions **rising_edge** and **falling_edge** are provided as aliases for the predefined edge-detection functions on type bit. They are included here for backward compatibility with earlier versions of VHDL, in which the edge-detection functions were not predefined. The **std_match** functions perform the same operations as the "?=" operator. Again, they are included for backward compatibility with earlier versions of VHDL that did not provide that operator.

The strength-stripping functions **to_01**, **to_X01**, **to_X01Z**, and **to_UX01** are overloaded for unsigned and signed operands, and perform the same operation as the corresponding functions for vectors in the **std_logic_1164** package.

Finally, the packages provide the string conversion operations. The **to_string** operation is actually predefined for **unsigned** and **signed**, since they are one-dimensional arrays of character elements in both packages. The **to_ostring** and **to_hstring** operations work in the same way as the corresponding operations in the **std_logic_1164** package. The only difference is that, when extending a **signed** value to form a complete group of three (for octal) or four (for hexadecimal) bits, the sign bit is replicated rather than '0' bits being added. The same aliases for all of the operations are also defined. Further, the packages provide overloaded versions of the file read and write operations for text-based input/output. (File input/output is considered an advanced topic, and is not covered in this book.)

VHDL-87, -93, and -2002

Since VHDL-2008 adds numerous new predefined operations, the VHDL-2008 version of the package provides overloaded versions of them. They are not provided in the version of the package for earlier versions of VHDL.

VHDL-87

Since VHDL-87 does not include the shift, rotate and **xnor** operators, they should be commented out of the standard synthesis packages when used with VHDL-87 tools. The shift and rotate functions can be used in VHDL-87 models. The **xnor** operator can be expressed as the negation (**not**) of the **xor** operator in VHDL-87.

As we have mentioned, the numeric_bit and numeric_std packages define new array types, **unsigned** and **signed**, to represent numbers in binary-coded form. Many designers, however, prefer to use the bit_vector and std_ulogic_vector types for numeric data. This approach is particularly useful in designs that include components, such as multiplexers, registers, and so on, that do not rely on numeric properties of data; they just store or manipulate arrays of bits. When such designs also include arithmetic elements, having to convert between the types for numeric interpretation and the plain vector type is a distraction. Historically, designers have adopted non-standard packages that provide arithmetic operations on bit_vector or std_ulogic_vector operands.

In the 2008 revision of VHDL, two new packages were added to library **ieee** for this purpose: numeric_bit_unsigned and numeric_std_unsigned. They are largely compatible with numeric_bit and numeric_std, respectively, and provide the corresponding unsigned operations. In summary, the similarities and differences among the packages are

- Numeric_bit_unsigned and numeric_std_unsigned provide the following operations corresponding to operations on unsigned in numeric_bit and numeric_std: arithmetic operators, shift operators, and relational operators; maximum, minimum, shift_left, shift_right, find_leftmost, find_rightmost, resize, and to_integer functions.

- Numeric_bit_unsigned provides a to_bitvector function (plus aliases to_bit_vector and to_bv) instead of to_unsigned.

- Numeric_std_unsigned provides to_stdulogicvector and to_stdlogicvector functions (plus aliases to_std_ulogic_vector, to_sulv, to_std_logic_vector, and to_slv) instead of to_unsigned.

- Numeric_bit_unsigned and numeric_std_unsigned do not provided other operations, since the normal bit_vector and std_ulogic_vector versions can be used. This includes overloaded logical operators; rising_edge, falling_edge, std_match and strength-stripping functions; to_ostring and to_hstring functions and the corresponding aliases; and read and write operations.

VHDL-87, -93, and -2002

These versions of VHDL do not provide the numeric_bit_unsigned and numeric_std_unsigned packages. Many tools for these versions provide a non-standard package, std_logic_unsigned, developed by Syopsys, Inc. It provides many of the same operations as numeric_std_unsigned.

9.2.4 Package Summary

In this section, we summarize the operations defined in the standard packages: std_logic_1164, numeric_std, numeric_bit, numeric_std_unsigned, and numeric_bit_unsigned.

Operator Overloading Summary

Table 9.7 summarizes the operand and result types for overloaded operations defined in the standard packages. The table does not include the predefined operations on the various types.

TABLE 9.7 *Operand and result types*

Operators	*Left*	*Right*	*Result*
Binary **and**, **or**, **nand**, **nor**, **xor**, **xnor**	std_ulogic	std_ulogic	std_ulogic
	LogicArrayType	*LogicArrayType*	*LogicArrayType*
	LogicArrayType	std_ulogic	*LogicArrayType*
	std_ulogic	*LogicArrayType*	*LogicArrayType*
not		std_ulogic	std_ulogic
		LogicArrayType	*LogicArrayType*
Unary reduction **and**, **or**, **nand**, **nor**, **xor**, **xnor**		*LogicArrayType*	std_ulogic
=, /=, <, <=, >, >=	*NumericArrayType*	*NumericArrayType*	boolean
	NumericArrayType	integer	boolean
	integer	*NumericArrayType*	boolean
?=, ?/=, ?<, ?<=, ?>, ?>=	*NumericArrayType*	*NumericArrayType*	*ArrayElementType*
	NumericArrayType	integer	*ArrayElementType*
	integer	*NumericArrayType*	*ArrayElementType*
rol, **ror**, **sll**, **srl**	*LogicArrayType*	integer	*LogicArrayType*
sla, **sra**	*NumericArrayType*	integer	*NumericArrayType*
Binary +, −, *, /, **mod**, **rem**	*NumericArrayType*	*NumericArrayType*	*NumericArrayType*
	NumericArrayType	integer	*NumericArrayType*
	integer	*NumericArrayType*	*NumericArrayType*

Operators	*Left*	*Right*	*Result*
Binary +, −	*NumericArrayType*	std_ulogic	*NumericArrayType*
	std_ulogic	*NumericArrayType*	*NumericArrayType*
Unary −, **abs**		signed, sfixed, float	signed, sfixed, float
maximum, minimum	*NumericArrayType*	*NumericArrayType*	*NumericArrayType*
	NumericArrayType	integer	*NumericArrayType*
	integer	*NumericArrayType*	*NumericArrayType*

Where overloaded operations are defined, the predefined operations are hidden. In the table, the notation use is as follows:

- *LogicArrayType*: arrays of **std_ulogic** elements

- *NumericArrayType*: **signed**, **unsigned**, **bit_vector** with operations in **numeric_bit_unsigned** visible, or **std_ulogic_vector** with operations in **numeric_std_unsigned** visible

- *ArrayElementType*: the element type of the operand array or arrays

Table 9.8 summarizes the result size for operations with array results. The notation for types is the same as that used in Table 9.7. In addition, L represents the left operand, R represents the right operand, A represents the array operand in the case where the other operand is scalar, and *Result* represents the result of the operation.

TABLE 9.8 *Result sizes and index ranges*

Operator	*Result type*	*Result size and/or range*
Array/array **and**, **or**, **nand**, **nor**, **xor**, **xnor**	*ArrayOfBits*	*Result*'length = L'length = R'length
Array/scalar **and**, **or**, **nand**, **nor**, **xor**, **xnor**	*ArrayOfBits*	*Result*'length = A'length
not	*ArrayOfBits*	*Result*'length = R'length
rol, **ror**, **sll**, **srl**, **sla**, **sra**	*ArrayOfBits*	*Result*'length = A'length
Binary +, −	unsigned, signed	maximum(L'length, R'length) − 1 down to 0
*	unsigned, signed	L'length + R'length − 1 down to 0
/	unsigned, signed	L'length − 1 down to 0

Operator	Result type	Result size and/or range
rem	unsigned, signed	R'length $-$ 1 down to 0
mod	unsigned, signed	R'length $-$ 1 down to 0
Unary $-$, **abs**	signed	R'length $-$ 1 down to 0
minimum, maximum	*DiscreteArrayType*	*Result*'length = A'length
	unsigned, signed	maximum(L'length, R'length) $-$ 1 down to 0

Conversion Function Summary

Next, we summarize the conversion functions defined in the standard packages. In order to present the information in more compact form, we have used some abbreviations for types and the packages in which the functions are defined: "bv" for **bit_vector**, "slv" for **std_logic_vector**, "sulv" for **std_ulogic_vector**, "1164" for **std_logic_1164**, "nbu" for **numeric_bit_unsigned**, "nsu" for **numeric_std_unsigned**, and "ns/b" for **numeric_std** and **numeric_bit**.

Table 9.9 shows the functions that convert between **bit** and **std_ulogic** scalar types, and between vectors of these types. We use the shorthand aliases for the functions here for brevity. The first parameter is the value to be converted. The **to_bit** and **to_bv** functions have a second parameter, **xmap**, as described in Section 9.2.2, to specify how metalogical values should be mapped. Those functions that convert from an abstract numeric value to a vector representation have a second parameter, either a natural value, **size**, specifying the size of the result or a value of the result type, **size_res**, whose size is used for the result.

TABLE 9.9   *Conversions between bit and standard-logic types*

Function	Result type	Parameter 1 type	Parameter 2	Package
to_bit	bit	std_ulogic	xmap	1164
to_std_ulogic	std_ulogic	bit		1164
to_bv	bit_vector	sulv	xmap	1164
		natural	size	nbu
		natural	size_res	nbu
to_sulv	sulv	bv		1164
		slv		1164
		natural	size	nsu
		natural	size_res	nsu

Function	Result type	Parameter 1 type	Parameter 2	Package
to_slv	slv	bv		1164
		sulv		1164
		natural	natural	nsu
		natural	size_res	nsu

Table 9.10 shows the functions that convert from the various numeric types to the **unsigned** and **signed** types defined in **numeric_std** and **numeric_bit**. The first parameter is the value to be converted, and the second parameter is either a natural value, **size**, specifying the size of the result or a value of the result type, **size_res**, whose size is used for the result.

TABLE 9.10   *Conversion functions yielding* unsigned *and* signed *values*

Function	Result type	Param 1 type	Param 2	Param 3	Param 4	Package
to_unsigned	unsigned	natural	size			ns/b
			size_res			
to_signed	signed	integer	size			ns/b
			size_res			

The final group of conversion functions is shown in Table 9.11. These functions convert from binary-coded vectors to abstract integer types. As in the preceding tables, the parameter is the value to be converted.

TABLE 9.11   *Conversion functions yielding* integer*values*

Function	Result type	Param 1 type	Package
to_integer	natural	bv	nbu
	natural	sulv	nsu
	natural	unsigned	ns/b
	integer	signed	

As we have mentioned, the packages provide aliases for the conversion functions for convenience and enhanced readability: for conversion to **bit_vector**, the names we can use are **to_bv**, **to_bitvector** and **to_bit_vector**; for conversion to **std_ulogic_vector**, the names are **to_sulv**, **to_stdulogicvector** and **to_std_ulogic_ vector**; and for conversion to **std_logic_vector**, the names are **to_slv**, **to_stdlogicvector** and **to_std_logic_vector**.

For each binary-coded numeric type, there is a **resize** function, shown in Table 9.12. The functions have a parameter **new_size** to specify the result size, or a parameter **size_res** for an object whose index range is used for that of the result.

Resizing an unsigned vector of type **bit_vector**, **std_ulogic_vector** or **unsigned** to produce a larger vector involves filling leftmost bits with '0'. Resizing these types to produce a smaller vector involves truncating the leftmost bits. For type **signed**, producing a larger vector involves filling the leftmost bits with copies of the operand's sign bit, and producing a smaller vector involves truncating the leftmost bits while retaining the sign bit.

TABLE 9.12   *Resizing functions*

Function	Result type	Param 1 type	Param 2	Package
resize	bv	bv	new_size	nbu
			size_res	
	sulv	sulv	new_size	nsu
			size_res	
	unsigned	unsigned	new_size	ns/b
			size_res	
	signed	signed	new_size	
			size_res	

Strength Reduction Function Summary

The strength reduction functions are defined for the entire family of types based on **std_ulogic**. Functions of the following form are defined:

```
function to_01   (s : Type; xmap : std_ulogic := '0') return Type;

function to_X01  (s : Type) return Type;

function to_X01Z (s : Type) return Type;

function to_UX01 (s : Type) return Type;
```

The type *Type* includes **std_ulogic**, **std_ulogic_vector**, **unresolved_unsigned**, **unresolved_signed**, and the subtypes of the vector types with resolved elements. The value returned by each function for each operand element value is shown in Table 9.13. The functions **to_X01**, **to_X01Z**, and **to_UX01**, when applied to vector operands, convert each operand element according to the table to yield the corresponding result element. The **to_01** function, however, behaves differently. Provided all of the elements are '0', '1', 'L', or 'H', they are converted according to the table. However, if any element is a metalogical value (a value other than '0', '1', 'L', or 'H'), all elements of the result are set to the value of the **xmap** parameter. Thus, we can test any element of the result to determine whether there were any metalogical elements in the operand.

The 'X' detection function is also defined for the entire family of types based on **std_ulogic**. The function definitions are of the form:

function is_X (S : *Type*) **return** boolean;

The version for **std_ulogic** returns true if the operand is a metalogical value, or false otherwise. The versions for vector types return true if any element of the operand is a metalogical value, or false otherwise.

TABLE 9.13   *Strength reduction mappings*

Function	'U'	'X'	'0'	'1'	'Z'	'W'	'L'	'H'	'–'
to_01	xmap	xmap	'0'	'1'	xmap	xmap	'0'	'1'	xmap
to_X01	'X'	'X'	'0'	'1'	'X'	'X'	'0'	'1'	'X'
to_X01Z	'X'	'X'	'0'	'1'	'Z'	'X'	'0'	'1'	'X'
to_UX01	'U'	'X'	'0'	'1'	'X'	'X'	'0'	'1'	'X'

EXAMPLE 9.5   *Unknown detection for a state-machine input*

We can use the **to_X01** function in behavioral models of ASIC and FPGA input cells to promote a resistive strength to a driving level as follows:

```
ncs_x01 <= to_X01(ncs);
```

We can use the **is_X** function to detect 'X' values in behavioral models and RTL code, for example, in the input to a state machine:

assert not is_X(ncs) **report** "ncs is X" **severity** error;

Exercises

1. [❶ 9.1] Write an assertion statement that verifies that the resolution limit is at most 1 ns.

2. [❶ 9.2] What string values are produced by **to_hstring** for the following **std_ulogic_vector** values: B"ZZZZ_0100", B"XX_L01H", B"01_00ZZ"?

3. [❶ 9.2] Write declarations for signals **a**, **b**, and **s** representing 24-bit unsigned numbers with **std_ulogic** elements. Write an assignment that adds **a**, **b**, and a **std_ulogic** signal **carry_in**, producing the sum in **s** and a **std_ulogic** signal **carry_out**.

4. [❶ 9.2] Write a process representing an edge-triggered D-flipflop with clock signal **clk**, enable signal **en**, data input **d**, and output **q**, all of type **std_ulogic**. The flipflop should store '0', '1', or 'X' values.

5. [❷ 9.1] Integers can be represented in *signed magnitude* form, in which the leftmost bit represents the sign ('0' for non-negative, '1' for negative), and the remaining bits are the absolute value of the number, represented in binary. If we wish to compare bit vectors containing numbers in signed magnitude form, we cannot use the predefined relational operators directly. We must first transform each number as follows: if the number is negative, complement all bits; if the number is non-negative, complement only the sign bit. Write a comparison function, overloading the operator "<", to compare signed-magnitude bit vectors using this method.

6. [❷ 9.2] Write a procedure that uses the uniform random number generator to generate a random value of an enumeration type named controller_state.

7. [❷ 9.2] In telephone systems, a signal is compressed before transmission. The formula for μ-law compression of a signal is

$$F(x) = \operatorname{sgn} x \frac{\ln(1 + \mu|x|)}{\ln(1 + \mu)} \qquad -1 \le x \le 1, \mu = 255$$

Develop a functional model of a compressor for values of type real.

8. [❷ 9.2] Develop a model of a decade counter with a 4-bit unsigned output.

Chapter 10

Aliases

Since the main purpose of a model written in VHDL is to describe a hardware design, it should be made as easy as possible to read and understand. In this chapter, we introduce *aliases* as a means of making a model clearer. As in everyday use, an alias is simply an alternate name for something. We see how we can use aliases in VHDL for both data objects and other kinds of items that do not represent data in a model.

10.1 Aliases for Data Objects

If we have a model that includes a data object, such as a constant, a variable, a signal or, as we see in a later chapter, a file, we can declare an alias for the object with an *alias declaration*. A simplified syntax rule for this is

> alias_declaration ⇐ **alias** identifier **is** name ;

An alias declaration in this form simply defines an alternate identifier to refer to the named data object. We can refer to the object using the new identifier, treating it as being of the type specified in the original object's declaration. Operations we perform using the alias are actually applied to the original object. (The only exceptions are reading the **'simple_name**, **'path_name** and **'instance_name** attributes and the attributes that provide information about the index ranges of an array. In these cases, the attributes refer to the alias name rather than the original object's name.)

> **EXAMPLE 10.1** *Aliases for package items*
>
> ---
>
> One use of alias declarations is to define simple names for objects imported from packages. Suppose, for example, that we need to use objects from two different packages, **alu_types** and **io_types**, and that each declares a constant named **data_width**, possibly with different values. If we include use clauses for these packages in our model, as follows:
>
> ```
> use work.alu_types.all, work.io_types.all;
> ```

neither of the versions of **data_width** becomes directly visible, since they have the same name. Hence we would have to refer to them as work.alu_types.data_width and work.io_types.data_width. However, we can avoid this long notation simply by introducing two alias declarations into our model, as shown in the following architecture body:

```
library ieee;  use ieee.std_logic_1164.all;
use work.alu_types.all, work.io_types.all;

architecture structural of controller_system is

  alias alu_data_width is work.alu_types.data_width;
  alias io_data_width is work.io_types.data_width;

  signal alu_in1, alu_in2,
         alu_result :
             std_ulogic_vector(0 to alu_data_width - 1);
  signal io_data : std_ulogic_vector(0 to io_data_width - 1);
  ...

begin

  ...

end architecture structural;
```

As well as denoting a whole data object, an alias can denote a single element from a composite data object, such as a record or an array. We write the element name, including a record element selector or an array index, as the name to be aliased. For example, given the following declarations of types and a variable:

```
type register_array is array (0 to 15) of bit_vector(31 downto 0);

type register_set is record
    general_purpose_registers : register_array;
    program_counter : bit_vector(31 downto 0);
    program_status : bit_vector(31 downto 0);
  end record;

variable CPU_registers : register_set;
```

we can declare aliases for the record elements:

```
alias PSW is CPU_registers.program_status;
alias PC is CPU_registers.program_counter;
alias GPR is CPU_registers.general_purpose_registers;
```

We can also declare aliases for individual registers in the register array, for example:

```
alias SP is CPU_registers.general_purpose_registers(15);
```

The name that we are aliasing can itself be an alias. Hence the alias declaration for SP can be written using the alias name GPR:

alias SP **is** GPR(15);

An alias can also be used to denote a slice of a one-dimensional array. For example, given the above declaration for **CPU_registers**, we can declare an alias for part of the program status register:

alias interrupt_level **is** PSW(30 **downto** 26);

This declares **interrupt_level** to denote a bit vector, with indices from 30 down to 26, being part of the bit vector denoted by **PSW**. In general, if we declare an alias for an array slice in this way, the alias denotes an array with index range and direction determined by the slice.

In many cases, it would be convenient to use an alias to take a slightly different view of the array being aliased. For example, we would like to view the interrupt_level alias as a bit vector indexed from four down to zero. We can do this by using an extended form of alias declaration, described by the following syntax rule:

alias_declaration ⇐
    alias identifier ⟦ : subtype_indication⟧ **is** name ;

This shows that we can indicate the subtype for the alias. The subtype determines how we view the original object that the alias denotes. We can include a subtype indication in aliases for scalar objects, but the bounds and direction specified must be the same as those of the original object. Hence this only serves as a form of documentation to restate the type information for the object. We can also include an unconstrained or partially constrained composite subtype as the alias subtype when aliasing an array or record object or an array slice. In this case, any index ranges that are unspecified in the subtype come from the corresponding index ranges of the original object. However, we can use the subtype indication to specify different index bounds and direction from the original object. The base type of the subtype indication must be the same as the base type of the original object. (This means that the subtype indication must refer to a composite type with the same element and index types as the original object.) Furthermore, there must be the same number of elements in the alias subtype and the original object. Elements in the alias denote the corresponding elements in the actual object, with array elements corresponding in left-to-right order. For example, if we were to declare the alias interrupt_level as follows:

alias interrupt_level : bit_vector(4 **downto** 0) **is** PSW(30 **downto** 26);

then **interrupt_level**(4) would denote **PSW**(30), **interrupt_level**(3) would denote **PSW**(29), and so on.

As another example, suppose we declare a register file as follows:

type register_array **is array** (natural **range** <>) **of** bit_vector;
signal register_file : register_array(0 **to** 15)(31 **downto** 0);

We can then declare an alias:

```
alias bigendian_register_file : register_array(open)(0 to 31) is
       register_file;
```

This alias views the register file as an array with the same top-level index range as the original, 0 to 15, since the subtype indication does not specify a top-level index range. Each element, however, is viewed with the index range 0 to 31 specified in the subtype indication.

EXAMPLE 10.2   *Normalization of array index ranges using aliases*

When we write subprograms that take parameters of unconstrained array types, the index bounds and direction of the parameter are not known until actual array objects are passed as arguments during a call. Without this knowledge, the body of the subprogram is difficult to write. For example, suppose we need to implement a function to perform addition on two bit vectors that represent two's-complement, signed integers. The function specification is

```
function "+" ( bv1, bv2 : bit_vector ) return bit_vector;
```

When the function is called it is possible that the first argument is indexed from 0 to 15, while the other argument is indexed from 31 down to 8. We must check that the arguments are of the same size and then index them in a loop running from the rightmost bit to the leftmost. The different ranges, directions and sizes make this difficult.

We can use aliases to make the task easier by viewing the objects as arrays with the same leftmost index and direction. The subprogram body is shown below. The alias declarations create views of the bit-vector arguments, indexed from one up to their length. The function, after checking that the arguments are of the same length, can then use the same index values for corresponding elements of the two arguments and the result.

```
function "+" ( bv1, bv2 : bit_vector ) return bit_vector is

  alias norm1 : bit_vector(1 to bv1'length) is bv1;
  alias norm2 : bit_vector(1 to bv2'length) is bv2;

  variable result : bit_vector(1 to bv1'length);
  variable carry : bit := '0';

begin
  if bv1'length /= bv2'length then
    report "arguments of different length" severity failure;
  else
    for index in norm1'reverse_range loop
      result(index) := norm1(index) xor norm2(index) xor carry;
      carry := ( norm1(index) and norm2(index) )
             or ( carry and ( norm1(index) or norm2(index) ) );
    end loop;
  end if;
```

```
   return result;
end function "+";
```

EXAMPLE 10.3   *Normalization of element array index ranges*

For subprograms that deal with arrays of arrays, both the top-level and lower-level index ranges may be undefined. Again, we can use aliases to view parameters with consistent index bounds and directions. However, we need to use the 'element attribute to refer to the actual index ranges of the parameter elements. For example, we can write a function that locates the first bit difference between two arrays of bit vectors as follows:

```
type bv_vector is array (natural range <>) of bit_vector;

function find_first_difference ( s1, s2 : in bv_vector)
                                     return natural is
  alias s1_norm : bv_vector(0 to s1'length - 1)
                           (0 to s1'element'length - 1) is s1;
  alias s2_norm : bv_vector(0 to s2'length - 1)
                           (0 to s2'element'length - 1) is s2;
  variable count : natural := 0;
begin
  assert s1'length = s2'length and
         s1'element'length = s2'element'length;
  for i in s1_norm'range loop
    for j in s1_norm'element'range loop
      exit when s1_norm(i)(j) /= s2_norm(i)(j);
      count := count + 1;
    end loop;
  end loop;
  return count;
end function find_first_difference;
```

The two parameters are of an unconstrained type, allowing the function to operate on arrays of various lengths and on arrays with various bit-vector element lengths. The function only requires that, on each call, the two actual parameters have the same shape. In order to deal with the differences, the function declares aliases for the parameters. It views each parameter with an index range starting at 0 and ascending to one less than the length. It views the elements similarly, with an index range starting at 0 and ascending to one less than length of each bit-vector element. The alias declaration uses the 'element attribute to get the constrained subtype for the actual parameter's elements. Within the function body, the inner for loop also uses the 'element attribute to get the index range for the elements of the aliases.

VHDL-87, -93, and -2002

These earlier versions of VHDL did not allow aliases of multidimensional array objects. For example, the following is illegal in earlier versions:

```
type bit_matrix is
  array (natural range <>, natural range <>) of bit;
signal s : bit_matrix(15 downto 0, 15 downto 0);
alias bigendian_s : bit_matrix(0 to 15, 0 to 15) is s;
```

VHDL-87

An alias declaration in VHDL-87 must include a subtype indication.

10.2 Aliases for Non-Data Items

We saw in the previous section that we can declare aliases for data objects such as constants, variables and signals. We can also declare aliases for other named items that do not represent stored data, such as types, subprograms, packages, entities and so on. In fact, the only kinds of items for which we cannot declare aliases are labels, loop parameters and generate parameters (see Chapter 13). The syntax rule for alias declarations for non-data items is

> alias_declaration ⇐
>   **alias** ⟮ identifier ⫾ character_literal ⫾ operator_symbol ⟯
>   **is** name ⟦ signature ⟧ ;

We can use character literals as aliases for enumeration literals, and operator symbols as aliases for function subprograms. We will return to the optional signature part shortly.

If we define an alias for a type, we can use the alias in any context where the original type name can be used. Furthermore, all of the predefined operations for values of the original type can be used without being declared. For example, if we define an alias:

```
alias binary_string is bit_vector;
```

we can declare objects to be of type **binary_string** and perform bit-vector operations on them; for example:

```
variable s1, s2 : binary_string(0 to 7);
...
s1 := s1 and not s2;
```

Declaring an alias for a type is different from declaring a new type. In the latter case, new overloaded versions of the operators would have to be declared. The alias, on the other hand, is simply another name for the existing type.

If we define an alias for an enumeration type, all of the enumeration literals of the original type are available for use. We do not need to define aliases for the literals, nor use fully selected names. For example, if a package system_types declares an enumeration type as follows:

type system_status **is** (idle, active, overloaded);

and a model defines an alias for this type:

alias status_type **is** work.system_types.system_status;

the model can simply refer to the literals idle, active and overloaded, instead of work.system_types.overloaded and so on. Similarly, if we declare an alias for a physical type, all of the unit names are available for use without aliasing or selection.

The optional signature part in an alias declaration is only used in aliases for subprograms and enumeration literals. These items can be overloaded, so it is possible that the name alone is not sufficient to identify which item is being aliased. The signature serves to identify one item uniquely. The syntax rule for a signature is

signature ⇐ [⟦ type_mark ⟦ , ... ⟧ ⟧ ⟦ **return** type_mark ⟧]

Note that the outer square bracket symbols ([...]) are a required part of the signature, whereas the hollow square brackets (⟦ ... ⟧) are part of the EBNF syntax and indicate optional parts of the signature.

When we declare an alias for a subprogram, the signature identifies which overloaded version of the subprogram name is aliased. The signature lists the types of each of the subprogram's parameters, in the same order that they appear in the subprogram's declaration. For example, if a package arithmetic_ops declares two procedures as follows:

procedure increment (bv : **inout** bit_vector; by : **in** integer := 1);

procedure increment (int : **inout** integer; by : **in** integer := 1);

we can declare aliases for the procedures as follows:

alias bv_increment **is**
  work.arithmetic_ops.increment [bit_vector, integer];

alias int_increment **is**
  work.arithmetic_ops.increment [integer, integer];

If the subprogram is a function, the signature also includes the type of the return value, after the keyword **return**. For example, we might alias the operator symbols "*", "+" and "–" to the bit operators **and**, **or** and **not**, as follows:

alias "*" **is** "and" [bit, bit **return** bit];

alias "+" **is** "or" [bit, bit **return** bit];

alias "–" **is** "not" [bit **return** bit];

We would then be able to express Boolean equations using these operators. For example, given bit signals s, a, b and c, we could write

```
s <= a * b + (-a) * c;
```

Note that when we alias an operator symbol to a function, the function overloads the operator symbol, so it must have the correct number of parameters for the operator. A binary operator symbol must be aliased to a function with two parameters, and a unary operator symbol must be aliased to a function with one parameter.

If we wish to alias an individual literal of an enumeration type, we must deal with the possibility that the literal may belong to several different enumeration types. We can use a signature to distinguish one particular meaning by noting that an enumeration literal is equivalent to a function with no parameters that returns a value of the enumeration type. For example, when we write the enumeration literal '1', we can think of this as a call to a function with no parameters, returning a value of type bit. We can write an alias for this literal as follows:

```
alias high is std.standard.'1' [ return bit ];
```

The signature distinguishes the literal as being of type bit, rather than of any other character type. Note that a selected name is required for a character literal, since a character literal by itself is not a syntactically valid name.

EXAMPLE 10.4 *Aliases for composing packages*

One useful application of aliases for non-data items is to compose a package by collecting together a number of items declared in other packages. The following package for use in a DMA controller design defines aliases for two types imported from the cpu_types package and for a function imported from a package that provides bit-vector arithmetic operations.

```
package DMA_controller_types_and_utilities is

  alias word is work.cpu_types.word;
  alias status_value is work.cpu_types.status_value;

  alias "+" is work.bit_vector_unsigned_arithmetic."+"
           [ bit_vector, bit_vector return bit_vector ];

  . . .

end package DMA_controller_types_and_utilities;
```

The DMA controller architecture body outlined below imports the aliases from the utility package. The reference to the name word denotes the type originally defined in the package cpu_types, and the operator "+" denotes the bit-vector operator originally defined in the package bit_vector_unsigned_arithmetic.

```
architecture behavioral of DMA_controller is

  use work.DMA_controller_types_and_utilities.all;
```

```
    begin

      behavior : process is

        variable address_reg0, address_reg1 : word;
        variable count_reg0, count_reg1 : word;
        ...

      begin

        ...
        address_reg0 := address_reg0 + X"0000_0004";

        ...
      end process behavior;

    end architecture behavioral;
```

VHDL-87

VHDL-87 does not allow aliases for non-data items. Aliases may only be declared for data objects.

Exercises

1. [❶ 10.1] Given the following declarations:

    ```
    subtype byte is bit_vector(0 to 7);
    type data_array is array (0 to 31) of byte;
    type network_packet is record
        source, dest, flags : byte;
        payload : data_array;
        checksum : byte;
      end record network_packet;
    variable received_packet : network_packet;
    ```

    write alias declarations for the individual elements of the variable.

2. [❶ 10.1] The layout of information within the **flags** element of a network packet described in Exercise 1 is shown in Figure 10.1. Write alias declarations for the individual fields of the **flags** element of the **received_packet** variable. The aliases for the ACKNO and SEQNO fields should view the fields as bit vectors indexed from two down to zero.

FIGURE 10.1

The layout of information within a network packet.

3. [❶ 10.2] Write an alias declaration that defines the name **cons** as an alias for the pre-defined operation "&" with a character left argument, a string right argument and a string result. Use the alias in a report statement that reports the string constructed from the value of the variable **grade_char** concatenated to the string "–grade".

4. [❷ 10.1] Develop a behavioral model of a bit-reversing module with the following entity interface:

```
entity reverser is
  port ( d_in : in std_ulogic_vector;
         d_out : out std_ulogic_vector );
end entity reverser;
```

When the entity is instantiated, the actual signals must be of the same length, but may differ in their index bounds and directions. The output is the input delayed by 500 ps using transport delay, and with the bits in reverse order from left to right.

Chapter 11

Generic Constants

The models that we have used as examples in preceding chapters all have fixed behavior and structure. In many respects, this is a limitation, and we would like to be able to write more general, or *generic*, models. VHDL provides us with a mechanism, called generics, for writing parameterized models. We discuss generics in this chapter and show how they may be used to write families of models with varying behavior and structure.

11.1 Generic Constants

The simplest form of generic model is parameterized by one or more *generic constants*. These are constants that cannot be changed within a design unit, but whose values are set when the design unit is initialized. We can write an entity with generic constants by including a *generic interface list* in its declaration, defining the *formal generic constants* that parameterize the entity. The extended syntax rule for entity declarations including generics is

> entity_declaration ⇐
>   **entity** identifier **is**
>   〚 **generic** (*generic*_interface_list) ; 〛
>   〚 **port** (*port*_interface_list) ; 〛
>   〚 entity_declarative_item 〛
>   〚 **begin**
>   〚 concurrent_assertion_statement
>   ⏐ *passive*_concurrent_procedure_call_statement
>   ⏐ *passive*_process_statement 〛 〛
>   **end** 〚 **entity** 〛 〚 identifier 〛 ;
>
> interface_list ⇐ interface_declaration 〚 ; ... 〛

The difference between this and the simpler rule we saw before is the inclusion of the optional generic interface list before the port interface list. The generic interface list is like any other interface list, but with restrictions on the kinds of interface items that we can include. In this book, we will just consider constant-class objects, which must be of mode **in**. Since these are the defaults for a generic interface list, we can use a simplified syntax rule for the interface declarations:

interface_declaration ⇐
    identifier ⦃ , ... ⦄ : subtype_indication ⟦ := expression ⟧

A simple example of an entity declaration including a generic interface list is

```
entity and2 is
  generic ( Tpd : time );
  port ( a, b : in bit;  y : out bit );
end entity and2;
```

This entity includes one generic constant, **Tpd**, of the predefined type **time**. The value of this generic constant may be used within the entity statements and any architecture body corresponding to the entity. In this example the intention is that the generic constant specify the propagation delay for the module, so the value should be used in a signal assignment statement as the delay. An architecture body that does this is

```
architecture simple of and2 is
begin

  and2_function :
    y <= a and b after Tpd;

end architecture simple;
```

The visibility of a generic constant extends from the end of the generic interface list to the end of the entity declaration and extends into any architecture body corresponding to the entity declaration.

A generic constant is given an actual value when the entity is used in a component instantiation statement. We do this by including a *generic map*, as shown by the extended syntax rule for component instantiations:

component_instantiation_statement ⇐
    *instantiation*_label :
            entity *entity*_name ⟦ (*architecture*_identifier) ⟧
            ⟦ **generic map** (*generic*_association_list) ⟧
            ⟦ **port map** (*port*_association_list) ⟧ ;

association_list ⇐ assiciation_element ⦃ , ... ⦄

The generic association list is like other forms of association lists, but since generic constants are always of class constant, the actual arguments we supply must be expressions. Thus the simplified syntax rule for generic associations limited to just generic constants is

association_element ⇐
        ⟦ *generic*_name => ⟧ ⦅ expression ∣ **open** ⦆

To illustrate this, let us look at a component instantiation statement that uses the **and2** entity shown above:

```
gate1 : entity work.and2(simple)
  generic map ( Tpd => 2 ns )
  port map ( a => sig1,   b => sig2,   y => sig_out );
```

The generic map specifies that this instance of the **and2** module uses the value 2 ns for the generic constant **Tpd**; that is, the instance has a propagation delay of 2 ns. We might include another component instantiation statement using **and2** in the same design but with a different actual value for **Tpd** in its generic map, for example:

```
gate2 : entity work.and2(simple)
  generic map ( Tpd => 3 ns )
  port map ( a => a1,   b => b1,   y => sig1 );
```

When the design is elaborated we have two processes, one corresponding to the instance **gate1** of **and2**, which uses the value 2 ns for **Tpd**, and another corresponding to the instance **gate2** of **and2**, which uses the value 3 ns.

EXAMPLE 11.1   *Generic constants in an entity for a control logic module*

As the syntax rule for the generic interface list shows, we may define a number of generic constants of different types and include default values for them. An entity declaration for a control logic module illustrates the possibilities:

```
entity control_unit is

  generic ( Tpd_clk_out, Tpw_clk : delay_length;
            debug : boolean := false );

  port ( clk : in bit;
         ready : in bit;
         control1, control2 : out bit );

end entity control_unit;
```

In this example, the generic interface list includes a list of two generic constants that parameterize the propagation delay of the module and a Boolean generic constant, **debug**, with a default value of false. The intention of this last generic constant is to allow a design that instantiates this entity to activate some debugging operation. This operation might take the form of report statements within if statements that test the value of **debug**.

We have the same flexibility in writing a generic map as we have in other association lists. We can use positional association, named association or a combination of both. We can omit actual values for generic constants that have default expressions, or we may explicitly use the default value by writing the keyword **open** in the generic map. To illustrate these possibilities, here are three different ways of writing a generic map for the control_unit entity:

generic map (200 ps, 1500 ps, false)

generic map (Tpd_clk_out => 200 ps, Tpw_clk => 1500 ps)

generic map (200 ps, 1500 ps, debug => **open**)

EXAMPLE 11.2   *Generic constants for specifying timing characteristics*

The entity declaration below for a D-flipflop includes generic constants: **Tpd_clk_q** to specify the propagation delay from clock rising edge to output, **Tsu_d_clk** to specify the setup time of data before a clock edge and **Th_d_clk** to specify the hold time of data after a clock edge.

```
entity D_flipflop is
  generic ( Tpd_clk_q, Tsu_d_clk, Th_d_clk : delay_length );
  port ( clk, d : in bit;  q : out bit );
end entity D_flipflop;
```

The values of these generic constants are used in the architecture body:

```
architecture basic of D_flipflop is
begin

  behavior : q <= d after Tpd_clk_q when rising_edge(clk);

  check_setup : process is
  begin
    wait until clk;
    assert d'last_event >= Tsu_d_clk
      report "setup violation";
  end process check_setup;

  check_hold : process is
  begin
    wait until clk'delayed(Th_d_clk);
    assert d'delayed'last_event >= Th_d_clk
      report "hold violation";
  end process check_hold;

end architecture basic;
```

The entity might be instantiated as follows, with actual values specified in the generic map for the generic constants:

```
request_flipflop : entity work.D_flipflop(basic)
  generic map ( Tpd_clk_q => 4 ns,
                Tsu_d_clk => 3 ns, Th_d_clk => 1 ns )
```

```
        port map ( clk => system_clock,
                   d => request, q => request_pending );
```

The second main use of generic constants in entities is to parameterize their structure. We can use the value of a generic constant to specify the size of an array port. To see why this is useful, let us look at an entity declaration for a register. A register entity that uses an unconstrained array type for its input and output ports can be declared as

```
entity reg is
  port ( d : in bit_vector;  q : out bit_vector;  ... );
end entity reg;
```

While this is a perfectly legal entity declaration, it does not include the constraint that the input and output ports **d** and **q** should be of the same size. Thus, we could write a component instantiation as follows:

```
signal small_data : bit_vector(0 to 7);
signal large_data : bit_vector(0 to 15);
...

problem_reg : entity work.reg
  port map ( d => small_data,  q => large_data, ... );
```

The model is analyzed and elaborated without the error being detected. It is only when the register tries to assign a small bit vector to a target bit vector of a larger size that the error is detected. We can avoid this problem by including a generic constant in the entity declaration to parameterize the size of the ports. We use the generic constant in constraints in the port declarations. To illustrate, here is the register entity declaration rewritten:

```
entity reg is
  generic ( width : positive );
  port ( d : in bit_vector(0 to width - 1);
         q : out bit_vector(0 to width - 1);
         ... );
end entity reg;
```

In this declaration we require that the user of the register specify the desired port width for each instance. The entity then uses the width value as a constraint on both the input and output ports, rather than allowing their size to be determined by the signals associated with the ports. A component instantiation using this entity might appear as follows:

```
signal in_data, out_data : bit_vector(0 to bus_size - 1);
...

ok_reg : entity work.reg
  generic map ( width => bus_size )
  port map ( d => in_data,  q => out_data, ... );
```

If the signals used as actual ports in the instantiation were of different sizes, the analyzer would signal the error early in the design process, making it easier to correct. As a matter of style, whenever the sizes of different array ports of an entity are related, generic constants should be considered to enforce the constraint.

EXAMPLE 11.3   *A register model with a generic constant for the port widths*

A complete model for the register, including the entity declaration and an architecture body, is

```
entity reg is
  generic ( width : positive );
  port ( d :   in  bit_vector(0 to width - 1);
         q :   out  bit_vector(0 to width - 1);
         clk, reset : in bit );
end entity reg;

-------------------------------------------------

architecture behavioral of reg is
begin

  behavior : process (clk, reset) is
    constant zero : bit_vector(0 to width - 1) := (others => '0');
  begin
    if reset then
      q <= zero;
    elsif rising_edge(clk) then
      q <= d;
    end if;
  end process behavior;

end architecture behavioral;
```

The generic constant is used to constrain the widths of the data input and output ports in the entity declaration. It is also used in the architecture body to determine the size of the constant bit vector **zero**. This bit vector is the value assigned to the register output when it is reset, so it must be of the same size as the register port. We can create instances of the register entity in a design, each possibly having different-sized ports. For example:

```
word_reg : entity work.reg(behavioral)
  generic map ( width => 32 )
  port map ( ... );
```

creates an instance with 32-bit-wide ports. In the same design, we might include another instance, as follows:

```
subtype state_vector is bit_vector(1 to 5);
...
```

```
state_reg : entity work.reg(behavioral)
  generic map ( width => state_vector'length )
  port map ( ... );
```

This register instance has 5-bit-wide ports, wide enough to store values of the subtype state_vector.

EXAMPLE 11.4   *An adder with generic constants for propagation delays*

Suppose we want to use generic constants to specify the propagation delays for an adder. The entity is declared with input and output ports that are arrays whose sizes are determined by a generic constant. We want to specify individual propagation delays for corresponding input and output port elements. The entity declaration is:

```
entity adder is
  generic ( width    : positive;
            Tpd_ab_s : time_vector(width - 1 downto 0) );
  port     ( a, b  : in  bit_vector(width - 1 downto 0);
             c_in  : in  bit;
             s     : out bit_vector(width - 1 downto 0);
             c_out : out bit );
end entity adder;
```

The generic constant width is used in the declaration of the second generic constant, Tpd_ab_s, to ensure that there is a matching propagation delay for each element of the input and output ports. We can instantiate the entity in a design as follows:

```
subtype byte is bit_vector(7 downto 0);
signal op1, op2, result : byte;
signal c_out : bit;
...

byte_adder : entity work.adder
  generic map ( width    => byte'length,
                Tpd_ab_s => (7 downto 1 => 120 ps,
                             0           => 80 ps) )
    port map   ( a => op1, b => op2, c_in => '0',
                 s => result, c_out => c_out );
```

In this instance, an actual value is given for width, and that is used to determine the index range for Tpd_ab_s, as well as for the ports. Note that we don't have to write the actual generics in this order. The values are determined for generics in the order of their occurrence in the generic list, not the generic map. Thus, we could have written the generic map as:

```
generic map ( Tpd_ab_s => (7 downto 1 => 120 ps,
                           0           => 80 ps),
              width    => byte'length )
```

though to do so might look a bit strange.

VHDL-87, -93, and -2002

These versions of VHDL do not allow the value of one generic constant to be used in the declarations of other generic constants in the same generic list. In the preceding example, we would have to declare the **Tpd_ab_s** generic as an unconstrained array and include an assertion in the entity statement part that the length of **Tpd_ab_s** is equal to **width**.

Exercises

1. [❶ 11.1] Add to the following entity interface a generic clause defining generic constants **Tpw_clk_h** and **Tpw_clk_l** that specify the minimum clock pulse width timing. Both generic constants have a default value of 3 ns.

   ```
   entity flipflop is
     port ( clk, d : in bit;   q, q_n : out bit );
   end entity flipflop;
   ```

2. [❶ 11.1] Write a component instantiation statement that instantiates the following entity from the current working library. The actual value for the generic constant should be 10 ns, and the **clk** signal should be associated with a signal called **master_clk**.

   ```
   entity clock_generator is
     generic ( period : delay_length );
     port ( clk : out std_ulogic );
   end entity clock_generator;
   ```

3. [❶ 11.1] Following is an incomplete entity interface that uses a generic constant to specify the sizes of the standard-logic vector input and output ports. Complete the interface by filling in the types of the ports.

   ```
   entity adder is
     generic ( data_length : positive );
     port ( a, b : in ...;   sum : out ... );
   end entity adder;
   ```

4. [❶ 11.1] A system has an 8-bit data bus declared as

   ```
   signal data_out : bit_vector(7 downto 0);
   ```

   Write a component instantiation statement that instantiates the **reg** entity defined in Example 11.3 to implement a 4-bit control register. The register data input connects to the rightmost four bits of **data_out**, the **clk** input to **io_write**, the **reset** input to **io_reset** and the data output bits to control signals **io_en**, **io_int_en**, **io_dir** and **io_mode**.

5. [❷ 11.1] Develop a behavioral model of a D-latch with separate generic constants for specifying the following propagation delays:

- rising data input to rising data output,

- falling data input to falling data output,

- rising enable input to rising data output and

- rising enable input to falling data output.

6. [❷ 11.1] Develop a behavioral model of a counter with output of type **natural** and clock and reset inputs of type **bit**. The counter has a Boolean generic constant, **trace_reset**. When this is true, the counter reports a trace message each time the reset input is activated.

7. [❷ 11.1] Develop a behavioral model of the adder described in Exercise 3.

8. [❷ 11.1] Develop a behavioral model of a multiplexer with n select inputs, 2^n data inputs and one data output.

9. [❸ 11.1] Develop a behavioral model of a RAM with generic constants governing the read access time, minimum write time, the address port width and the data port width.

Chapter 12

Components and Configurations

In Chapter 5 we saw how to write entity declarations and architecture bodies that describe the structure of a system. Within an architecture body, we can write component instantiation statements that describe instances of an entity and connect signals to the ports of the instances. This simple approach to building a hierarchical design works well if we know in advance all the details of the entities we want to use. However, that is not always the case, especially in a large design project. In this chapter we introduce an alternative way of describing the hierarchical structure of a design that affords significantly more flexibility at the cost of a little more effort in managing the design.

12.1 Components

The first thing we need to do to describe an interconnection of subsystems in a design is to describe the different kinds of components used. We have seen how to do this by writing entity declarations for each of the subsystems. Each entity declaration is a separate design unit and has corresponding architecture bodies that describe implementations. An alternative approach is to write *component declarations* in the declarative part of an architecture body or package interface. We can then create *instances* of the components within the statement part of the architecture body.

12.1.1 Component Declarations

A component declaration simply specifies the external interface to the component in terms of generic constants and ports. We do not need to describe any corresponding implementation, since all we are interested in is how the component is connected in the current level of the design hierarchy. This makes the architecture completely self-contained, since it does not depend on any other library units except its corresponding entity interface. Let us look at the syntax rule that governs how we write a component declaration.

component_declaration ⟸
    component identifier ⟦ **is** ⟧
        ⟦ **generic** (*generic*_interface_list) ; ⟧

⟦ **port** (*port*_interface_list) ; ⟧
  end component ⟦ identifier ⟧ ;

A simple example of a component declaration that follows this syntax rule is

```
component flipflop is
  generic ( Tprop, Tsetup, Thold : delay_length );
  port ( clk : in bit;  clr : in bit;  d : in bit;
         q : out bit );
end component flipflop;
```

This declaration defines a component type that represents a flipflop with clock, clear and data inputs, **clk**, **clr** and **d**, and a data output **q**. It also has generic constants for parameterizing the propagation delay, the data setup time and the data hold time.

Note the similarity between a component declaration and an entity declaration. This similarity is not accidental, since they both serve to define the external interface to a module. Although there is a very close relationship between components and entities, in fact, they embody two different concepts. This may be a source of confusion to newcomers to VHDL. Nevertheless, the flexibility afforded by having the two different constructs is a powerful feature of VHDL, so we will work through it carefully in this section and try to make the distinction clear.

One way of thinking about the difference between an entity declaration and a component declaration is to think of the modules being defined as having different levels of "reality." An entity declaration defines a "real" module: something that ultimately will have a physical manifestation. For example, it may represent a circuit board in a rack, a packaged integrated circuit or a standard cell included in a piece of silicon. An entity declaration is a separate design unit that may be separately analyzed and placed into a design library. A component declaration, on the other hand, defines a "virtual," or "idealized," module that is included within an architecture body. It is as though we are saying, "For this architecture body, we assume there is a module as defined by this component declaration, since such a module meets our needs exactly." We specify the names, types and modes of the ports on the virtual module (the component) and proceed to lay out the structure of the design using this idealized view.

Of course, we do not make these assumptions about modules arbitrarily. One possibility is that we know what real modules are available and customize the virtual reality based on that knowledge. The advantage here is that the idealization cushions us from the irrelevant details of the real module, making the design easier to manage. Another possibility is that we are working "top down" and will later use the idealized module as the specification for a real module. Either way, eventually a link has to be made between an instance of a virtual component and a real entity so that the design can be constructed. In the rest of this section, we look at how to use components in an architecture body, then come back to the question of the binding between component instances and entities.

VHDL-87

The keyword **is** may not be included in the header of a component declaration, and the component name may not be repeated at the end of the declaration.

12.1.2 Component Instantiation

If a component declaration defines a kind of module, then a component instantiation specifies a usage of the module in a design. We have seen how we can instantiate an entity directly using a component instantiation statement within an architecture body. Let us now look at an alternative syntax rule that shows how we can instantiate a declared component:

component_instantiation_statement $\Leftarrow$
    *instantiation*_label :
        ⟦ **component** ⟧ *component*_name
        ⟦ **generic map** (*generic*_association_list) ⟧
        ⟦ **port map** (*port*_association_list) ⟧ ;

This syntax rule shows us that we may simply name a component declared in the architecture body and, if required, provide actual values for the generics and actual signals to connect to the ports. The label is required to identify the component instance.

EXAMPLE 12.1 *A four-bit register using flipflop components*

We can construct a four-bit register using flipflops and an and gate, similar to the example in Chapter 5. The entity declaration is

```
entity reg4 is
  port ( clk, clr : in bit;  d : in bit_vector(0 to 3);
         q : out bit_vector(0 to 3) );
end entity reg4;
```

The architecture body describing the structure of this register uses the flipflop component shown on page 336.

```
architecture struct of reg4 is

  component flipflop is
    generic ( Tprop, Tsetup, Thold : delay_length );
    port ( clk : in bit;  clr : in bit;  d : in bit;
           q : out bit );
  end component flipflop;

begin
```

```
bit0 : component flipflop
    generic map ( Tprop => 2 ns, Tsetup => 2 ns, Thold => 1 ns )
    port map ( clk => clk, clr => clr, d => d(0), q => q(0) );

bit1 : component flipflop
    generic map ( Tprop => 2 ns, Tsetup => 2 ns, Thold => 1 ns )
    port map ( clk => clk, clr => clr, d => d(1), q => q(1) );

bit2 : component flipflop
    generic map ( Tprop => 2 ns, Tsetup => 2 ns, Thold => 1 ns )
    port map ( clk => clk, clr => clr, d => d(2), q => q(2) );

bit3 : component flipflop
    generic map ( Tprop => 2 ns, Tsetup => 2 ns, Thold => 1 ns )
    port map ( clk => clk, clr => clr, d => d(3), q => q(3) );

end architecture struct;
```

Note that all we have done here is specify the structure of this level of the design hierarchy, without having indicated how the flipflop is implemented. We will see how that may be done in the remainder of this chapter.

VHDL-87

The keyword **component** may not be included in a component instantiation statement in VHDL-87. The keyword is allowed in VHDL-93 and VHDL-2002 to distinguish between instantiation of a component and direct instantiation of an entity. In VHDL-87, the only form of component instantiation statement provided is instantiation of a declared component.

12.1.3 Packaging Components

Let us now turn to the issue of design management for large projects and see how we can make management of large libraries of entities easier using packages and components. Usually, work on a large design is partitioned among several designers, each responsible for implementing one or more entities that are used in the complete system. Each entity may need to have some associated types defined in a utility package, so that entity ports can be declared using those types. When the entity is used, other designers will need component declarations to instantiate components that will eventually be bound to the entity. It makes good sense to include a component declaration in the utility package, along with the types and other related items. This means that users of the entity do not need to rewrite the declarations, thus avoiding a potential source of errors and misunderstanding.

EXAMPLE 12.2 *Packaged component for a serial interface cell*

Suppose we are responsible for designing a serial interface cell for a microcontroller circuit. We can write a package specification that defines the interface to be used in the rest of the design:

```
library ieee;  use ieee.std_logic_1164.all;

package serial_interface_defs is

  subtype reg_address_vector is std_ulogic_vector(1 downto 0);

  constant status_reg_address : reg_address_vector := B"00";
  constant control_reg_address : reg_address_vector := B"01";
  constant rx_data_register : reg_address_vector := B"10";
  constant tx_data_register : reg_address_vector := B"11";

  subtype data_vector is std_ulogic_vector(7 downto 0);

  ...    -- other useful declarations

  component serial_interface is
    port ( clock_phi1, clock_phi2 : in std_ulogic;
           serial_select : in std_ulogic;
           reg_address : in reg_address_vector;
           data : inout data_vector;
           interrupt_request : out std_ulogic;
           rx_serial_data : in std_ulogic;
           tx_serial_data : out std_ulogic );
  end component serial_interface;

end package serial_interface_defs;
```

The component declaration in this package corresponds to our entity declaration for the serial interface:

```
library ieee;  use ieee.std_logic_1164.all;

use work.serial_interface_defs.all;

entity serial_interface is
  port ( clock_phi1, clock_phi2 : in std_ulogic;
         serial_select : in std_ulogic;
         reg_address : in reg_address_vector;
         data : inout data_vector;
         interrupt_request : out std_ulogic;
         rx_serial_data : in std_ulogic;
         tx_serial_data : out std_ulogic );
end entity serial_interface;
```

When other designers working on integrating the entire circuit need to instantiate the serial interface, they only need to import the items in the package, rather than re-writing all of the declarations. An outline of a design that does this is

```
library ieee;  use ieee.std_logic_1164.all;

architecture structure of microcontroller is

  use work.serial_interface_defs.serial_interface;

  ...      -- declarations of other components, signals, etc
begin

    serial_a : component serial_interface
      port map ( clock_phi1 => buffered_phi1,
                 clock_phi2 => buffered_phi2,
                 serial_select => serial_a_select,
                 reg_address => internal_addr(1 downto 0),
                 data => internal_data_bus,
                 interrupt_request => serial_a_int_req,
                 rx_serial_data => rx_data_a,
                 tx_serial_data => tx_data_a );

    ...      -- other component instances

end architecture structure;
```

12.2 Configuring Component Instances

Once we have described the structure of one level of a design using components and component instantiations, we still need to flesh out the hierarchical implementation for each component instance. We can do this by writing a *configuration declaration* for the design. In it, we specify which real entity interface and corresponding architecture body should be used for each of the component instances. This is called binding the component instances to design entities. Note that we do not specify any binding information for a component instantiation statement that directly instantiates an entity, since the entity and architecture body are specified explicitly in the component instantiation statement. Thus our discussion in this section only applies to instantiations of declared components.

12.2.1 Basic Configuration Declarations

We start by looking at a simplified set of syntax rules for configuration declarations, as the full set of rules is rather complicated. The simplest case arises when the entities to which component instances are bound are implemented with behavioral architectures. In this case, there is only one level of the hierarchy to flesh out. The simplified syntax rules are

configuration_declaration ⇐
      configuration identifier **of** *entity*_name **is**
          for *architecture*_name

⟦   **for** component_specification
                    binding_indication ;
            end for ; ⟧
        end for ;
    end ⟦ **configuration** ⟧ ⟦ identifier ⟧ ;

component_specification ⟸
    ⟦ *instantiation*_label ⟦ , ₀₀₀ ⟧ ⟦ **others** ⟧ **all** ⟧ : *component*_name

binding_indication ⟸ **use entity** *entity*_name ⟦ (*architecture*_identifier) ⟧

The identifier given in the configuration declaration identifies this particular specification for fleshing out the hierarchy of the named entity. There may be other configuration
declarations, with different names, for the same entity. Within the configuration declaration we write the name of the particular architecture body to work with (included after
the first **for** keyword), since there may be several corresponding to the entity. We then
include the binding information for each component instance within the architecture
body. The syntax rule shows that we can identify a component instance by its label and
its component name, as used in the component instantiation in the architecture body. We
bind it by specifying an entity name and a corresponding architecture body name. For example, we might bind instances **bit0** and **bit1** of the component **flipflop** as follows:

```
for bit0, bit1 : flipflop
  use entity work.edge_triggered_Dff(basic);
end for;
```

This indicates that the instances are each to be bound to the design entity
edge_triggered_Dff, found in the current working library, and that the architecture body
basic corresponding to that entity should be used as the implementation of the instances.
    Note that since we can identify each component instance individually, we have the
opportunity to bind different instances of a given component to different entity/architec-
ture pairs. After we have specified bindings for some of the instances in a design, we can
use the keyword **others** to bind any remaining instances of a given component type to
a given entity/architecture pair. Alternatively, if all instances of a particular component
type are to have the same binding, we can use the keyword **all** instead of naming individual instances. The syntax rules also show that the architecture name corresponding to
the entity is optional. If it is omitted, a default binding takes place when the design is elaborated for simulation or synthesis. The component instance is bound to whichever architecture body for the named entity has been most recently analyzed at the time of
elaboration. A further possibility is that we omit bindings for one or more component instances in the design. In this case, the default binding rule attempts to find an entity with
the same name as the component. The entity must be located in the same design library
as the design unit in which the instantiated component is declared. If no entity is found,
the component instance remains unbound (see Section 12.2.5). Relying on the default
binding rules to locate and bind the right entity can make a design difficult to understand
and reduces portability. The safest approach is to ensure that we bind all component instances explicitly.

A configuration declaration is a primary design unit, and as such, may be separately analyzed and placed into the working design library as a library unit. If it contains sufficient binding information so that the full design hierarchy is fleshed out down to behavioral architectures, the configuration may be used as the target unit of a simulation. The design is elaborated by substituting instances of the specified architecture bodies for bound component instances in the way described in Section 5.4. The only difference is that when component declarations are instantiated, the configuration must be consulted to find the appropriate architecture body to substitute.

EXAMPLE 12.3   *Configuration of a four-bit register*

Let us look at a sample configuration declaration that binds the component instances in the four-bit register of Example 12.1. Suppose we have a resource library for a project, **star_lib**, that contains the basic design entities that we need to use. Our configuration declaration might be written as follows:

```
library star_lib;
use star_lib.edge_triggered_Dff;

configuration reg4_gate_level of reg4 is

  for struct   -- architecture of reg4

    for bit0 : flipflop
      use entity edge_triggered_Dff(hi_fanout);
    end for;

    for others : flipflop
      use entity edge_triggered_Dff(basic);
    end for;

  end for;   -- end of architecture struct

end configuration reg4_gate_level;
```

The library clause preceding the design unit is required to locate the resource library containing the entities we need. The use clause following it makes the entity names we require directly visible in the configuration declaration. The configuration is called **reg4_gate_level** and selects the architecture **struct** of the **reg4** entity. Within this architecture, we single out the instance **bit0** of the **flipflop** component and bind it to the entity **edge_triggered_Dff** with architecture **hi_fanout**. This shows how we can give special treatment to particular component instances when configuring bindings. We bind all remaining instances of the **flipflop** component to the **edge_triggered_Dff** entity using the **basic** architecture.

VHDL-87

The keyword **configuration** may not be included at the end of a configuration dec-laration in VHDL-87.

12.2.2 Configuring Multiple Levels of Hierarchy

In the previous section, we saw how to write a configuration declaration for a design in which the instantiated components are bound to behavioral architecture bodies. Most re-alistic designs, however, have deeper hierarchical structure. The components at the top level have architecture bodies that, in turn, contain component instances that must be con-figured. The architecture bodies bound to these second-level components may also con-tain component instances, and so on. In order to deal with configuring these more complex hierarchies, we need to use an alternative form of binding indication in the con-figuration declaration. The alternative syntax rule is

binding_indication ⇐ **use configuration** *configuration*_name

This form of binding indication for a component instance allows us to bind to a precon-figured entity/architecture pair simply by naming the configuration declaration for the en-tity. For example, a component instance of **reg4** with the label **flag_reg** might be bound in a configuration declaration as follows:

```
for flag_reg : reg4
  use configuration work.reg4_gate_level;
end for;
```

EXAMPLE 12.4   *Hierarchical configuration of a counter*

In Chapter 5 we looked at a two-digit decimal counter, implemented using four-bit registers. We assume that the type **digit** is defined as follows in a package named counter_types:

```
subtype digit is bit_vector(3 downto 0);
```

The entity declaration for the counter is

```
use work.counter_types.digit;
```

```
entity counter is
  port ( clk, clr : in bit;
         q0, q1 : out digit );
end entity counter;
```

Now that we have seen how to use component declarations, we can rewrite the architecture body using component declarations for the registers, as follows:

```
architecture registered of counter is
```

```
component digit_register is
  port ( clk, clr : in bit;
         d : in digit;
         q : out digit );
end component digit_register;

signal current_val0, current_val1, next_val0, next_val1 : digit;

begin

val0_reg : component digit_register
  port map ( clk => clk, clr => clr, d => next_val0,
             q => current_val0 );

val1_reg : component digit_register
  port map ( clk => clk, clr => clr, d => next_val1,
             q => current_val1 );

-- other component instances
...

end architecture registered;
```

We can configure this implementation of the counter with the following configuration declaration:

```
configuration counter_down_to_gate_level of counter is

  for registered

    for all : digit_register
      use configuration work.reg4_gate_level;
    end for;

    ...      -- bindings for other component instances

  end for;   -- end of architecture registered

end configuration counter_down_to_gate_level;
```

This configuration specifies that each instance of the **digit_register** component is bound using the information in the configuration declaration named **reg4_gate_level** in the current design library, shown in Example 12.3. That configuration in turn specifies the entity to use (**reg4**), a corresponding architecture body (**struct**) and the bindings for each component instance in that architecture body. Thus the two configuration declarations combine to fully configure the design hierarchy down to the process level.

The example above shows how we can use separate configuration declarations for each level of a design hierarchy. As a matter of style this is good practice, since it prevents the configuration declarations themselves from becoming too complex. The alternative approach is to configure an entity and its hierarchy fully within the one configuration declaration. We look at how this may be done, as some models from other designers may take this approach. While this approach is valid VHDL, we recommend the practice of splitting up the configuration information into separate configuration declarations corresponding to the entities used in the design hierarchy.

To see how to configure multiple levels within one declaration, we need to look at a more complex form of syntax rule for configuration declarations. In fact, we need to split the rule into two parts, so that we can write a recursive syntax rule.

configuration_declaration ⇐
    configuration identifier **of** *entity*_name **is**
        block_configuration
    end ⟦ **configuration** ⟧ ⟦ identifier ⟧ ;

block_configuration ⇐
    for *architecture*_name
       ⦃   **for** component_specification
            binding_indication ;
            ⟦ block_configuration ⟧
        end for ; ⦄
    end for ;

The rule for a block configuration indicates how to write the configuration information for an architecture body and its inner component instances. (The reason for the name "block configuration" in the second rule is that it applies to block statements as well as architecture bodies. Block statements are considered an advanced topic and are not discussed in this book.) Note that we have included an extra part after the binding indication for a component instance. If the architecture that we bind to an instance also contains component instances, we can nest further configuration information for that architecture inside the enclosing block configuration.

EXAMPLE 12.5 *A complete configuration for the counter*

We can write a configuration declaration equivalent to that in Example 12.4 but containing all of the configuration information for the entire hierarchy, as follows:

```
library star_lib;
use star_lib.edge_triggered_Dff;

configuration full of counter is

  for registered  -- architecture of counter

    for all : digit_register
      use entity work.reg4(struct);

      for struct  -- architecture of reg4

        for bit0 : flipflop
          use entity edge_triggered_Dff(hi_fanout);
        end for;
```

```
      for others : flipflop
        use entity edge_triggered_Dff(basic);
      end for;

    end for;   -- end of architecture struct

  end for;

  ...   -- bindings for other component instances

  end for;   -- end of architecture registered

end configuration full;
```

The difference between this configuration declaration and the one in Example 12.4 is that the binding indication for instances of **digit_register** directly refers to the entity **reg4** and the architecture body **struct**, rather than using a separate configuration for the entity. The configuration then includes all of the binding information for component instances within **struct**. This relatively simple example shows how difficult it can be to read nested configuration declarations. Separate configuration declarations are easier to understand and provide more flexibility for managing alternative compositions of a design hierarchy.

12.2.3 Direct Instantiation of Configured Entities

As we have seen, a configuration declaration specifies the design hierarchy for a design entity. We can make direct use of a fully configured design entity within an architecture body by writing a component instantiation statement that directly names the configuration. The alternative syntax rule for component instantiation statements that expresses this possibility is

component_instantiation_statement ⇐
    *instantiation*_label :
        configuration *configuration*_name
        〖 **generic map** (*generic*_association_list) 〗
        〖 **port map** (*port*_association_list) 〗 ;

The configuration named in the statement includes a specification of an entity and a corresponding architecture body to use. We can include generic and port maps in the component instantiation to provide actual values for any generics of the entity and actual signals to connect to the ports of the entity. This is much like instantiating the entity directly, but with all of the configuration information for its implementation included.

EXAMPLE 12.6   *Direct instantiation of the counter configuration*

The following architecture body for an alarm clock directly instantiates the two-digit decimal counter entity. The component instantiation statement labeled **seconds** refers to the configuration **counter_down_to_gate_level**, shown in Example 12.4. That configuration, in turn, specifies the counter entity and architecture to use.

```
architecture top_level of alarm_clock is

    use work.counter_types.digit;

    signal reset_to_midnight, seconds_clk : bit;
    signal seconds_units, seconds_tens : digit;
    ...

begin

    seconds : configuration work.counter_down_to_gate_level
        port map ( clk => seconds_clk, clr => reset_to_midnight,
                        q0 => seconds_units, q1 => seconds_tens );

    ...

end architecture top_level;
```

VHDL-87

VHDL-87 does not allow direct instantiation of configured entities. Instead, we must declare a component, instantiate the component and write a separate configuration declaration that binds the instance to the configured entity.

12.2.4 Generic and Port Maps in Configurations

We now turn to a very powerful and important aspect of component configurations: the inclusion of generic maps and port maps in the binding indications. This facility provides a great deal of flexibility when binding component instances to design entities. However, the ideas behind the facility are somewhat difficult to grasp on first encounter, so we will work through them carefully. First, let us look at an extended syntax rule for a binding indication that shows how generic and port maps can be included:

binding_indication ⇐
      use ⟦   **entity** *entity*_name ⟦ (*architecture*_identifier) ⟧
              ⎮ **configuration** *configuration*_name ⟧
      ⟦ **generic map** (*generic*_association_list) ⟧
      ⟦ **port map** (*port*_association_list) ⟧

This rule indicates that after specifying the entity to which to bind (either directly or by naming a configuration), we may include a generic map or a port map or both. We show how this facility may be used by starting with some simple examples illustrating the more common uses. We then proceed to the general case.

One of the most important uses of this facility is to separate the specification of generic constants used for timing from the structure of a design. We can write component declarations in a structural description without including generic constants for timing. Later, when we bind each component instance to an entity in a configuration declaration, we can specify the timing values by supplying actual values for the generic constants of the bound entities.

EXAMPLE 12.7   *Timing generics in a configuration*

Suppose we are designing an integrated circuit for a controller, and we wish to use the register whose entity declaration includes generic constants for timing and port width, as follows:

```
library ieee;  use ieee.std_logic_1164.all;

entity reg is
  generic ( t_setup, t_hold, t_pd : delay_length;
            width : positive );
  port ( clock : in std_ulogic;
         data_in : in std_ulogic_vector(0 to width - 1);
         data_out : out std_ulogic_vector(0 to width - 1) );
end entity reg;
```

We can write a component declaration for the register without including the generic constants used for timing, as shown in the following architecture body for the controller:

```
architecture structural of controller is

  component reg is
    generic ( width : positive );
    port ( clock : in std_ulogic;
           data_in : in std_ulogic_vector(0 to width - 1);
           data_out : out std_ulogic_vector(0 to width - 1) );
  end component reg;

  ...

begin

  state_reg : component reg
    generic map ( width => state_type'length )
    port map ( clock => clock_phase1,
               data_in => next_state,
               data_out => current_state );

  ...

end architecture structural;
```

The component represents a virtual idealized module that has all of the structural characteristics we need, but ignores timing. The component instantiation statement specifies a value for the port width generic constant, but does not specify any timing parameters.

Since we are operating in the real world, we cannot ignore timing forever. Ultimately the values for the timing parameters will be determined from the physical layout of the integrated circuit. Meanwhile, during the design phase, we can use estimates for their values. When we write a configuration declaration for our design, we can configure the component instance as shown below, supplying the estimates in a generic map. Note that we also need to specify a value for the **width** generic of the bound entity. In this example, we supply the value of the **width** generic of the component instance. We discuss this in more detail on page 351.

```
configuration controller_with_timing of controller is

  for structural

    for state_reg : reg
      use entity work.reg(gate_level)
      generic map ( t_setup => 200 ps, t_hold => 150 ps,
                    t_pd => 150 ps, width => width );
    end for;

    ...

  end for;

end configuration controller_with_timing;
```

When we simulate the design, the estimated values for the generic constants are used by the real design entity to which the component instance is bound. Later, when the integrated circuit has been laid out, we can substitute, or *back annotate*, the actual timing values in the configuration declaration without having to modify the architecture body of the model. We can then resimulate to obtain test vectors for the circuit that take account of the real timing.

Another important use of generic and port maps in a configuration declaration arises when the entity to which we want to bind a component instance has different names for generic constants and ports. The maps in the binding indication can be used to make the link between component generics and ports on the one hand, and entity generics and ports on the other. Furthermore, the entity may have additional generics or ports beyond those of the component instance. In this case, the maps can be used to associate actual values or signals from the architecture body with the additional generics or ports.

EXAMPLE 12.8   *Remapping generics and ports in a configuration*

Suppose we need to use a two-input-to-four-output decoder in a design, as shown in the outline of an architecture body below. The component declaration for the decoder represents a virtual module that meets our needs exactly.

```
architecture structure of computer_system is
```

```
component decoder_2_to_4 is
  generic ( prop_delay : delay_length );
  port ( in0, in1 : in bit;
           out0, out1, out2, out3 : out bit );
end component decoder_2_to_4;

...

begin

interface_decoder : component decoder_2_to_4
  generic map ( prop_delay => 4 ns )
  port map ( in0 => addr(4), in1 => addr(5),
             out0 => interface_a_select,
             out1 => interface_b_select,
             out2 => interface_c_select,
             out3 => interface_d_select );

...

end architecture structure;
```

Now suppose we check in our library of entities for a real module to use for this instance and find a three-input-to-eight-output decoder. The entity declaration is:

```
entity decoder_3_to_8 is
  generic ( Tpd_01, Tpd_10 : delay_length );
  port ( s0, s1, s2 : in bit;
         enable : in bit;
         y0, y1, y2, y3, y4, y5, y6, y7 : out bit );
end entity decoder_3_to_8;
```

We could make use of this entity in our design if we could adapt to the different generic and port names and tie the unused ports to appropriate values. The following configuration declaration shows how this may be done.

```
configuration computer_structure of computer_system is

  for structure

    for interface_decoder : decoder_2_to_4
      use entity work.decoder_3_to_8(basic)
      generic map ( Tpd_01 => prop_delay, Tpd_10 => prop_delay )
      port map ( s0 => in0, s1 => in1, s2 => '0',
                 enable => '1',
                 y0 => out0, y1 => out1, y2 => out2, y3 => out3,
                 y4 => open, y5 => open, y6 => open, y7 => open );
    end for;

    ...

  end for;
```

end configuration computer_structure;

The generic map in the binding indication specifies the correspondence between entity generics and component generics. In this case, the component generic prop_delay is to be used for both entity generics. The port map in the binding indication similarly specifies which entity ports correspond to which component ports. Where the entity has extra ports, we can specify how those ports are to be connected. In this design, s2 is tied to '0', enable is tied to '1', and the remaining ports are left unassociated (specified by the keyword **open**).

The two preceding examples illustrate the most common uses of generic maps and port maps in configuration declarations. We now look at the general mechanism that underlies these examples, so that we can understand its use in more complex cases. We use the terms *local generics* and *local ports* to refer to the generics and ports of a component. Also, in keeping with previous discussions, we use the terms *formal generics* and *formal ports* to refer to the generics and ports of the entity to which the instance is bound.

When we write a component instantiation statement with a generic map and a port map, these maps associate actual values and signals with the *local* generics and ports of the component instance. Recall that the component is just a virtual module used as a template for a real module, so at this stage we have just made connections to the template. Next, we write a configuration declaration that binds the component instance to a real entity. The generic and port maps in the binding indication associate actual values and signals with the *formal* generics and ports of the entity. These actual values and signals may be the locals from the component instance, or they may be values and signals from the architecture body containing the component instance. Figure 12.1 illustrates the mappings. It is this two-stage association mechanism that makes configurations so powerful in mapping a design to real modules.

Figure 12.1 shows that the actual values and signals supplied in the configuration declaration may be local generics or ports from the component instance. This is the case for the formal generics Tpd_01 and Tpd_10 and for the formal ports s0, s1, y0, y1, y2 and y3 in Example 12.8. Every local generic and port of the component instance must be associated with a formal generic or port, respectively; otherwise the design is in error. The figure also shows that the configuration declaration may supply values or signals from the architecture body. Furthermore, they may be any other values or signals visible at the point of the component instantiation statement, such as the literals '0' and '1' shown in the example. Note that while it is legal to associate a signal in the architecture body with a formal port of the entity, it is not good practice to do so. This effectively modifies the structure of the circuit, making the overall design much more difficult to understand and manage. For example, in the configuration in Example 12.8, had we associated the formal port s2 with the signal addr(6) instead of the literal value '0', the operation of the circuit would be substantially altered.

The preceding examples show how we can use generic and port maps in binding indications to deal with differences between the component and the entity in the number and names of generics and ports. However, if the component and entity have similar interfaces, we can rely on a *default binding rule*. This rule is used automatically if we omit the generic map or the port map in a binding indication, as we did in the earlier examples

FIGURE 12.1

Values and signals
in architecture body

Association specified in
component instantiation
statement

Association specified in
configuration declaration

*The generic and port maps in the component instantiation and the configuration declaration
define a two-stage association. Values and signals in the architecture body are associated, via
the local generics and ports, with the formal generics and ports of the bound entity.*

in this section. The default rule causes each local generic or port of the component to be
associated with a formal generic or port of the same name in the entity interface. If the
entity interface includes further formal generics or ports, they remain open. If the entity
does not include a formal with the same name as one of the locals, the design is in error.
So, for example, if we declare a component as

```
component nand3 is
  port ( a, b, c : in bit := '1';  y : out bit );
end component nand3;
```

and instantiate it as

```
gate1 : component nand3
  port map ( a => s1, b => s2, c => open, y => s3 );
```

then attempt to bind to an entity declared as

```
entity nand2 is
  port ( a, b : in bit := '1';  y : out bit );
end entity nand2;
```

with a component configuration

```
for gate1 : nand3
  use entity work.nand2(basic);
end for;
```

an error occurs. The reason for the error is that there is no formal port named c to associate
with the local port of that name. The default rule requires that such a correspondence be
found, even though the local port is unconnected in the architecture body.

12.2.5 Deferred Component Binding

We have seen that we can specify the binding for a component instance either by naming
an entity and a corresponding architecture body, or by naming a configuration. A third
option is to leave the component instance unbound and to defer binding it until later in
the design cycle. The syntax rule for a binding indication that expresses this option is

binding_indication ⇐ **use open**

If we use this form of binding indication to leave a component instance unbound, we cannot include a generic map or port map. This makes sense: since there is no entity, there
are no formal generics or ports with which to associate actual values or signals.

A scenario in which we may wish to defer binding arises in complex designs that can
be partially simulated before all subsystems are complete. We can write an architecture
body for the system, including component declarations and instances as placeholders for
the subsystems. Initially, we write a configuration declaration that defers bindings of the
subsystems. Then, as the design of each subsystem is completed, the corresponding component configuration is updated to bind to the new entity. At intermediate stages it may
be possible to simulate the system with some of the components unbound. The effect of
the deferred bindings is simply to leave the corresponding ports unassociated when the
design is elaborated. Thus the inputs to the unbound modules are not used, and the outputs remain undriven.

EXAMPLE 12.9   *Deferred binding in a computer system model*

Following is an outline of a structural architecture for a single-board computer system.
The design includes all of the components needed to construct the system, including
a CPU, main memory and a serial interface.

```
architecture structural of single_board_computer is

  ...   -- type and signal declarations

  component processor is
    port ( clk : in bit;  a_d : inout word; ... );
  end component processor;

  component memory is
    port ( addr : in bit_vector(25 downto 0); ... );
  end component memory;
```

```
      component serial_interface is
        port ( clk : in bit;
               address : in bit_vector(3 downto 0); ... );
      end component serial_interface;

  begin

    cpu : component processor
      port map ( clk => sys_clk, a_d => cpu_a_d, ... );

    main_memory : component memory
      port map ( addr => latched_addr(25 downto 0), ... );

    serial_interface_a : component serial_interface
      port map ( clk => sys_clk,
                 address => latched_addr(3 downto 0), ... );

    ...

  end architecture structural;
```

However, if we have not yet designed an entity and architecture body for the serial interface, we cannot bind the component instance for the interface. Instead, we must leave it unbound, as shown in the following configuration declaration:

```
  library chips;

  configuration intermediate of single_board_computer is

    for structural

      for cpu : processor
        use entity chips.XYZ3000_cpu(full_function)
        port map ( clock => clk, addr_data => a_d, ... );
      end for;

      for main_memory : memory
        use entity work.memory_array(behavioral);
      end for;

      for all : serial_interface
        use open;
      end for;

      ...

    end for;

  end configuration intermediate;
```

We can proceed to simulate the design, using the implementations of the CPU and main memory, provided we do not try to exercise the serial interface. If the processor were to try to access registers in the serial interface, it would get no response. Since there is no entity bound to the component instance representing the interface, there is nothing to drive the data or other signals connected to the instance.

Exercises

1. [● 12.1] List some of the differences between an entity declaration and a component declaration.

2. [● 12.1] Write a component declaration for a binary magnitude comparitor, with two standard-logic vector data inputs, **a** and **b**, whose length is specified by a generic constant, and two standard-logic outputs indicating whether **a** = **b** and **a** < **b**. The component also includes a generic constant for the propagation delay.

3. [● 12.1] Write a component instantiation statement that instantiates the magnitude comparitor described in Exercise 2. The data inputs are connected to signals **current_position** and **upper_limit**, the output indicating whether **a** < **b** is connected to **position_ok** and the remaining output is open. The propagation delay of the instance is 12 ns.

4. [● 12.1] Write a package declaration that defines a subtype of natural numbers representable in eight bits and a component declaration for an adder that adds values of the subtype.

5. [● 12.2] Suppose we have an architecture body for a digital filter, outlined as follows:

```
architecture register_transfer of digital_filter is
  ...
  component multiplier is
    port ( ... );
  end component multiplier;
begin
  coeff_1_multiplier : component multiplier
    port map ( ... );
  ...
end architecture register_transfer;
```

Write a configuration declaration that binds the multiplier component instance to a multiplier entity called **fixed_point_mult** from the library **dsp_lib**, using the architecture **algorithmic**.

6. [● 12.2] Suppose the library **dsp_lib** referred to in Exercise 5 includes a configuration of the **fixed_point_mult** entity called **fixed_point_mult_std_cell**. Write an alternative configuration declaration for the filter described in Exercise 5, binding the multiplier instance using the **fixed_point_mult_std_cell** configuration.

7. [● 12.2] Modify the outline of the filter architecture body described in Exercise 5 to directly instantiate the **fixed_point_mult_std_cell** configuration described in Exercise 6, rather than using the multiplier component.

8. [❶ 12.2] Suppose we declare and instantiate a multiplexer component in an architecture body as follows:

```
component multiplexer is
  port ( s, d0, d1 : in bit; z : out bit );
end component multiplexer;

...

serial_data_mux : component multiplexer
  port map ( s => serial_source_select,
             d0 => rx_data_0, d1 => rx_data_1,
             z => internal_rx_data );
```

Write a binding indication that binds the component instance to the following entity in the current working library, using the most recently analyzed architecture and specifying a value of 3.5 ns for the propagation delay.

```
entity multiplexer is
  generic ( Tpd : delay_length := 3 ns );
  port ( s, d0, d1 : in bit; z : out bit );
end entity multiplexer;
```

9. [❶ 12.2] Draw a diagram, based on Figure 12.1, that shows the mapping between entity ports and generics, component ports and generics and other values in the configured computer system model of Example 12.8.

10. [❶ 12.2] Suppose we have an entity **nand4** with the following interface in a library gate_lib:

```
entity nand4 is
  generic ( Tpd_01, Tpd_10 : delay_length := 2 ns );
  port ( a, b, c, d : in bit := '1';  y : out bit );
end entity nand4;
```

We bind the entity to the component instance **gate1** described on page 352 using the following component configuration:

```
for gate1 : nand3
  use entity get_lib.nand4(basic);
end for;
```

Write the generic and port maps that comprise the default binding indication used in this configuration.

11. [❷ 12.1] Develop a structural model of a 32-bit bidirectional transceiver, implemented using a component based on the 8-bit transceiver described in Exercise 13 in Chapter 8.

12. [❷ 12.1] Develop a structural model for an 8-bit serial-in/parallel-out shift register, assuming you have available a 4-bit serial-in/parallel-out shift register. Include a com-

ponent declaration for the 4-bit register, and instantiate it as required for the 8-bit register. The 4-bit register has a positive-edge-triggered clock input, an active-low asynchronous reset input, a serial data input and four parallel data outputs.

13. [❷ 12.1] Develop a package of component declarations for two-input gates and an inverter, corresponding to the logical operators in VHDL. Each component has ports of type **bit** and generic constants for rising output and falling output propagation delays.

14. [❷ 12.2] Develop a configuration declaration for the 32-bit transceiver described in Exercise 11 that binds each instance of the 8-bit transceiver component to the 8-bit transceiver entity.

15. [❷ 12.2] Develop a behavioral model of a 4-bit shift register that implements the component interface described in Exercise 12. Write a configuration declaration for the 8-bit shift register, binding the component instances to the 4-bit shift register entity.

16. [❷ 12.2] Suppose we wish to use an XYZ1234A serial interface controller in the microcontroller described in Example 12.2. The entity interface for the XYZ1234A is

```
entity XYZ1234A is
  generic ( T_phi_out, T_d_z : delay_length;
            debug_trace : boolean := false );
  port ( phi1, phi2 : in std_ulogic;    -- 2 phase clock
         cs : in std_ulogic;            -- chip select
         a : in std_ulogic_vector(1 downto 0);    -- address
         d : inout std_ulogic_vector(1 downto 0);   -- data
         int_req : out std_ulogic;      -- interrupt
         rx_d : in std_ulogic;          -- rx serial data
         tx_d : out std_ulogic );       -- tx serial data
end entity XYZ1234A;
```

Write a configuration declaration that binds the **serial_interface** component instance to the **XYZ1234A** entity, using the most recently compiled architecture, setting both timing generics to 6 ns and using the default value for the **debug_trace** generic.

17. [❷ 12.1/12.2] Use the package described in Exercise 13 to develop a structural model of a full adder, described by the Boolean equations

$$S = (A \oplus B) \oplus C_{in}$$
$$C_{out} = A \cdot B + (A \oplus B) \cdot C_{in}$$

Write behavioral models of entities corresponding to each of the gate components and a configuration declaration that binds each component instance in the full adder to the appropriate gate entity.

18. [❸ 12.2] Develop a structural model of a 4-bit adder using instances of a full-adder component. Write a configuration declaration that binds each instance of the full-adder component, using the configuration declaration described in Exercise 17. For comparison, write an alternative configuration declaration that fully configures the 4-

bit adder hierarchy without using the configuration declaration described in Exercise 17.

19. [❸ 12.2] Develop a behavioral model of a RAM with bit-vector address, data-in and data-out ports. The size of the ports should be constrained by generics in the entity interface. Next, develop a test bench that includes a component declaration for the RAM without the generics and with fixed-sized address and data ports. Write a configuration declaration for the test bench that binds the RAM entity to the RAM component instance, using the component local port sizes to determine values for the entity formal generics.

Chapter 13

Generate Statements

Many digital systems can be implemented as regular iterative compositions of subsystems. Memories are a good example, being composed of a rectangular array of storage cells. Indeed, VLSI designers prefer to find such implementations, as they make it easier to produce a compact, area-efficient layout, thus reducing cost. If a design can be expressed as a repetition of some subsystem, we should be able to describe the subsystem once, then describe how it is to be repeatedly instantiated, rather than describe each instantiation individually. In this chapter, we look at the VHDL facility that allows us to generate such regular structures.

13.1 Generating Iterative Structures

We have seen how we can describe the implementation of a subsystem using concurrent statements such as processes and component instantiations. If we want to replicate a subsystem, we can use a *generate statement*. This is a concurrent statement containing further concurrent statements that are to be replicated during elaboration of a design. Generate statements are particularly useful if the number of times we want to replicate the concurrent statements is not fixed but is determined, for example, from the value of a generic constant. The syntax rule for writing *for-generate statements* is

> for_generate_statement ⇐
>   *generate*_label :
>   **for** identifier **in** discrete_range **generate**
>   generate_statement_body
>   **end generate** [*generate*_label] ;
>
> generate_statement_body ⇐
>   [{ block_declarative_item }
>   **begin**]
>   { concurrent_statement }
>   [**end** ;]

The generate label is required to identify the generated structure. The header of the for-generate statement looks very similar to that of a for loop and indeed serves a similar purpose. The discrete range specifies a set of values, and for each value, the block declarative items and concurrent statements in the body are replicated once. Within each replication, the value from the range is given by the identifier, called the *generate parameter*. It appears as a constant, with a type that is the base type of the discrete range. We can specify the discrete range using the same notations that we used in for loops. As a reminder, here is the syntax rule for a discrete range:

discrete_range ⇐
    *discrete*_subtype_indication
    ❘ *range*_attribute_name
    ❘ simple_expression ⟮ **to** ❘ **downto** ⟯ simple_expression

The kinds of declarations we can include in the generate statement body are the same kinds that we can declare in the declarative part of the architecture body, including constants, types, subtypes, subprograms and signals. These items are replicated once for each copy of the body and are local to that copy. Note that the syntax rule for a for-generate statement requires us to include the keyword **begin** if we include any declarations. However, if we have no declarations, we may omit the keyword. Also, we can include a closing **end** keyword at the end of the body before the **end generate** keywords. The syntax allows this for consistency with the more elaborate forms of generate statement that we will see in Section 13.2. In practice, we would not normally include the keyword in for-generate statements.

EXAMPLE 13.1   *A register consisting of replicated flipflop cells*

We can implement a register by replicating a flipflop cell. Let us look at how to do this for a register with tristate outputs, conforming to the following entity declaration:

```
library ieee;  use ieee.std_logic_1164.all;

entity register_tristate is
  generic ( width : positive );
  port ( clock : in std_ulogic;
         out_enable : in std_ulogic;
         data_in : in std_ulogic_vector(0 to width - 1);
         data_out : out std_ulogic_vector(0 to width - 1) );
end entity register_tristate;
```

The generic constant **width** specifies the width of the register in bits and is used to determine the size of the data input and output ports. The **clock** port enables data to be stored in the register, and the **out_enable** port controls the tristate data output port.

The architecture body for the register implements this register in terms of a D-flipflop component and a tristate buffer for each bit:

```
architecture cell_level of register_tristate is
```

```
    component D_flipflop is
      port ( clk : in std_ulogic;   d : in std_ulogic;
             q : out std_ulogic );
    end component D_flipflop;

    component tristate_buffer is
      port ( a : in std_ulogic;
             en : in std_ulogic;
             y : out std_ulogic );
    end component tristate_buffer;

begin

    cell_array : for bit_index in 0 to width - 1 generate

      signal data_unbuffered : std_ulogic;

    begin

      cell_storage : component D_flipflop
        port map ( clk => clock, d => data_in(bit_index),
                   q => data_unbuffered );

      cell_buffer : component tristate_buffer
        port map ( a => data_unbuffered, en => out_enable,
                   y => data_out(bit_index) );

    end generate cell_array;

end architecture cell_level;
```

The for-generate statement in this structural architecture body replicates the component instantiations labeled **cell_storage** and **cell_buffer**, with the number of copies being determined by **width**. For each copy, the generate parameter bit_index takes on successive values from 0 to **width** – 1. This value is used within each copy to determine which elements of the **data_in** and **data_out** ports are connected to the flipflop input and tristate buffer output. Within each copy there is also a local signal called **data_unbuffered**, which connects the flipflop output to the buffer input.

EXAMPLE 13.2   *Replication in a graphics transformation pipeline*

We can also use for-generate statements to describe behavioral models in which behavioral elements implemented using process statements are replicated. Suppose we are modeling part of a graphics transformation pipeline in which a stream of points representing vertices in a scene is to be transformed by matrix multiplication. The equation describing the transformation is

$$\begin{bmatrix} p'_1 \\ p'_2 \\ p'_3 \end{bmatrix} = \begin{bmatrix} a_{11} & a_{12} & a_{13} \\ a_{21} & a_{22} & a_{23} \\ a_{31} & a_{32} & a_{33} \end{bmatrix} \begin{bmatrix} p_1 \\ p_2 \\ p_3 \end{bmatrix}$$

where $[p_1, p_2, p_3]$ is the input point to the pipeline stage, and $[p'_1, p'_2, p'_3]$ is the transformed output three clock cycles later. We can implement the transformation with three identical cells, each producing one result element. The equation is

$$p'_i = a_{i1} \cdot p_1 + a_{i2} \cdot p_2 + a_{i3} \cdot p_3, \qquad i = 1, 2, 3$$

An outline of the architecture body implementing the pipeline with this stage is

```
architecture behavioral of graphics_engine is

    type point is array (1 to 3) of real;
    type transformation_matrix is array (1 to 3, 1 to 3) of real;

    signal p, transformed_p : point;
    signal a : transformation_matrix;
    signal clock : bit;
    ...

begin

    transform_stage : for i in 1 to 3 generate
    begin

        cross_product_transform : process is
            variable result1, result2, result3 : real := 0.0;
        begin
            wait until clock = '1';
            transformed_p(i) <= result3;
            result3 := result2;
            result2 := result1;
            result1 :=  a(i, 1) * p(1) + a(i, 2) * p(2) + a(i, 3) * p(3);
        end process cross_product_transform;

    end generate transform_stage;

    ...  -- other stages in the pipeline, etc

end architecture behavioral;
```

The for-generate statement replicates the process statement three times, once for each element of the transformed point signal. Each copy of the process uses its value of the generate parameter i to index the appropriate elements of the point and transformation matrix signals.

If we need to describe a regular two-dimensional structure, we can use nested for-generate statements. Nesting of generate statements is allowed in VHDL, since a generate statement is a kind of concurrent statement, and generate statements contain concurrent statements. Usually we write nested for-generate statements so that the outer statement creates the rows of the structure, and the inner statement creates the elements within each row. Of course, this is purely a convention relating to the way we might draw such a regular structure graphically. However, the convention does help to design and understand such structures.

EXAMPLE 13.3 *A two-dimensional memory structure*

We can use nested generate statements to describe a memory array, constructed from 4-bit-wide static memory (SRAM) circuits. Each SRAM stores 4M words (4×2^{20} words) of four bits each. We can construct a 16M $\times$ 32-bit memory array by generating a 4 $\times$ 8 array of SRAM circuits. An outline of the architecture body containing the memory array is shown below, and a schematic diagram is shown in Figure 13.1.

```
architecture generated of memory is

  component SRAM is
    port ( clk : in std_ulogic;
           a :  in std_ulogic_vector(0 to 10);
           d :  inout std_ulogic_vector(0 to 3);
           en, we : in std_ulogic );
  end component SRAM;

  signal buffered_address : std_ulogic_vector(0 to 10);
  signal SRAM_data : std_ulogic_vector(0 to 31);
  signal bank_select : std_ulogic_vector(0 to 3);
  signal buffered_we : std_ulogic;

  ...  -- other declarations

begin

  bank_array : for bank_index in 0 to 3 generate
  begin

    nibble_array : for nibble_index in 0 to 7 generate

      constant data_lo : natural := nibble_index * 4;
      constant data_hi : natural := nibble_index * 4 + 3;

    begin

      an_SRAM : component SRAM
        port map ( clk => clk,
                   a => buffered_address,
                   d => SRAM_data(data_lo to data_hi),
                   en => bank_select(bank_index),
                   we => buffered_we );
```

FIGURE 13.1

A schematic for a 16M × 32-bit memory array composed of 4M × 4-bit SRAM circuits.

```
        end generate nibble_array;
    end generate bank_array;
    ...   -- other component instances, etc
  end architecture generated;
```

VHDL-87, -93, and -2002

These versions do not allow us to include a closing **end** keyword before the **end generate** keywords in a for-generate statement.

VHDL-87

A generate statement may not include a declarative part or the keyword **begin** in VHDL-87. The syntax for a for-generate statement is

> for_generate_statement ⇐
>   *generate*_label :
>   **for** identifier **in** discrete_range **generate**
>   〈 concurrent_statement 〉
>   **end generate** 〚 *generate*_label 〛 ;

Since it is not possible to declare objects locally within a generate statement, we must declare them in the architecture body containing the generate statement. We can declare an array of objects indexed by the same range as the generate parameter. For example, the signal **data_unbuffered** declared in the generate statement in Example 13.1 can be replaced by an array in the declarative part of the architecture body:

> **signal** data_unbuffered : std_ulogic_vector(0 **to** width - 1);

Each reference to **data_unbuffered** within the generate statement is replaced by a reference to the element **data_unbuffered(bit_index)**.

13.2 Conditionally Generating Structures

In the examples in the previous section, each cell in an iterative structure was connected identically. In some designs, however, there are particular cells that need to be treated differently. This often occurs where cells are connected to their neighbors. The cells at each end do not have neighbors on both sides, but instead are connected to signals or ports in the enclosing architecture body. We can deal with these special cases within an iterative structure using a conditional forms of generate statement. The first of these is an *if-generate statement*, with the syntax rule:

> if_generate_statement ⇐
>   *generate*_label :
>   **if** condition **generate**
>   generate_statement_body
>   〈 **elsif** condition **generate**
>   generate_statement_body 〉
>   〚 **else generate**
>   generate_statement_body 〛
>   **end generate** 〚 *generate*_label 〛 ;

This is like a sequential if statement, except that the conditions control how declarations and concurrent statements are copied in the design, rather than controlling selection of sequential statements for execution. When the model is elaborated, the conditions in the if-generate statement are tested from first to last until one is found that is true. The declarations (if any) and concurrent statements in the corresponding body are then included in the elaborated model. If no condition is true and there is an **else generate** alternative, the declarations and statements from that alternative are included. The **else generate** alternative is optional, allowing for the possibility of no declarations or statements being included if none of the conditions is true. The generate label in an if-generate statement is required to identify the structure that is generated, if any.

When we write an if-generate statement within an enclosing for-generate statement to deal with boundary conditions, we can refer to the values of generic constants or the generate parameter of the enclosing statement in the conditions of the if-generate statement.

EXAMPLE 13.4   *A shift register composed of flipflop cells*

We can construct a serial-to-parallel shift register from master/slave flipflop cells, as follows:

```
library ieee;  use ieee.std_logic_1164.all;

entity shift_reg is
  port ( phi1, phi2 : in std_ulogic;
         serial_data_in : in std_ulogic;
         parallel_data : out std_ulogic_vector );
end entity shift_reg;

-------------------------------------------------

architecture cell_level of shift_reg is

  alias normalized_parallel_data :
          std_ulogic_vector(0 to parallel_data'length - 1)
        is parallel_data;

  component master_slave_flipflop is
    port ( phi1, phi2 : in std_ulogic;
           d : in std_ulogic;
           q : out std_ulogic );
  end component master_slave_flipflop;

begin
  reg_array : for index in normalized_parallel_data'range generate
  begin
      reg : if index = 0 generate
        cell : component master_slave_flipflop
          port map ( phi1, phi2,
                     d => serial_data_in,
                     q => normalized_parallel_data(index) );
      else generate
        cell : component master_slave_flipflop
          port map ( phi1, phi2,
                     d => normalized_parallel_data(index - 1),
```

```
                            q => normalized_parallel_data(index) );
        end generate other_cell;

    end generate reg_array;

end architecture cell_level;
```

The architecture contains a component declaration for the flipflop, then makes multiple instantiations using a for-generate statement. Within the for-generate statement, an if-generate statement is used to treat the first flipflop cell differently from the other cells. The condition "**index** = 0" identifies this first cell, which takes its input data from the **serial_data_in** port. The remaining cells take their input from the neighboring cell's output.

EXAMPLE 13.5 *A ripple-carry adder composed of full adders and a half adder*

A ripple-carry adder has a half adder at the least-significant end and has different carry in and out connections for the cells at the ends and in the middle. We can use a nested if-generate with three alternatives to deal with the differences:

```
adder: for i in width-1 downto 0 generate

    signal carry_chain : unsigned(width-1 downto 1);

begin

    adder_cell: if i = width-1 generate  -- most-significant cell

        add_bit: component full_adder
            port map (a => a(i), b => b(i), s => s(i),
                      c_in => carry_chain(i), c_out => c_out);

    elsif i = 0 generate  -- least-significant cell

        add_bit: component half_adder
            port map (a => a(i), b => b(i), s => s(i),
                      c_out => carry_chain(i+1));

    else generate  -- middle cell

        add_bit: component full_adder
            port map (a => a(i), b => b(i), s => s(i),
                      c_in => carry_chain(i),
                      c_out => carry_chain(i+1));

    end generate adder_cell;

end generate adder;
```

Another important use of if-generate statements is to conditionally include or omit part of a design, usually depending on the value of a generic constant. A good example is the inclusion or otherwise of *instrumentation*: additional processes or component instances that trace or debug the operation of a design during simulation. When the design is sufficiently tested, a generic constant can be changed to exclude the instrumentation so that it does not slow down a large simulation and is not included when the design is synthesized.

EXAMPLE 13.6   *Conditional inclusion of instrumentation code*

Suppose we wish to measure the relative frequencies of instruction fetches, data reads and data writes made by a CPU accessing memory in a computer system. This information may be important when considering how to optimize a design to improve performance. An entity declaration for the computer system is

```
entity computer_system is
  generic ( instrumented : boolean := false );
  port ( ... );
end entity computer_system;
```

The generic constant **instrumented** is used to determine whether to include the instrumentation to measure relative frequencies of each kind of memory access. An outline of the architecture body is

```
architecture block_level of computer_system is

  ...  -- type and component declarations for cpu and memory, etc

  signal clock : bit;      -- the system clock
  signal mem_req : bit;    -- cpu access request to memory
  signal ifetch : bit;     -- indicates access is
                           --    to fetch an instruction
  signal write : bit;      -- indicates access is a write
  ...                      -- other signal declarations

begin

  ...  -- component instances for cpu and memory, etc

  instrumentation : if instrumented generate

    signal ifetch_freq, write_freq, read_freq : real := 0.0;

  begin

    access_monitor : process is
      variable access_count, ifetch_count,
               write_count, read_count : natural := 0;
    begin
      wait until mem_req = '1';
      if ifetch then
        ifetch_count := ifetch_count + 1;
      elsif write then
        write_count := write_count + 1;
```

```
      else
        read_count := read_count + 1;
      end if;
      access_count := access_count + 1;
      ifetch_freq <= real(ifetch_count) / real(access_count);
      write_freq <= real(write_count) / real(access_count);
      read_freq <= real(read_count) / real(access_count);
    end process access_monitor;

  end generate instrumentation;

end architecture block_level;
```

The signals ifetch_freq, write_freq and read_freq and the process access_monitor are only included in the design if the generic constant **instrumented** is true. The process resumes each time the CPU requests access to the memory and keeps count of the number of each kind of access, as well as the total access count. It uses these values to update the relative frequencies. We can trace these signals using our simulator to see how the relative frequencies converge over the lifetime of a simulation.

We can control whether the instrumentation is included or not when we write a configuration declaration for the design. To include the instrumentation, we configure an instance of the computer system as follows:

```
for system_under_test : computer_system
  use entity work.computer_system(block_level)
  generic map ( instrumented => true )
  ...
end for;
```

To exclude the instrumentation, we change the value of the generic constant in the generic map to false.

VHDL-87, -93, and -2002

These versions do not allow us to include **elsif** or **else** alternatives in an if-generate statement. Instead, we must write each alternative as a separate if-generate statement. For example, the if-generate statement in Example 13.5 would be written as:

```
msb_cell: if i = width-1 generate -- most-significant cell
  ...
end generate msb_cell;

lsb_cell: if i = 0 generate -- least-significant cell
  ...
end generate lsb_cell;

mid_cell: if i > 0 and i < width-1 generate -- middle cell
  ...
end generate lsb_cell;
```

Also, these versions do not permit a closing **end** keyword in each alternative of an if-generate statement.

VHDL-87

A generate statement may not include a declarative part or the keyword **begin** in VHDL-87. The syntax for a conditional generate statement is

generate_statement ⟸
    *generate*_label :
    if condition **generate**
        〔 concurrent_statement 〕
    end generate 〖 *generate*_label 〗 ;

Any objects required by the generate statement must be declared in the declarative part of the enclosing architecture body.

The second conditional form of generate statement is a *case-generate statement*, in which we specify alternatives in a similar way to a case statement. We specify a static expression (one whose value can be computed during elaboration), and choice values for each alternative. The syntax rule is:

case_generate_statement ⟸
    *generate*_label :
    case expression **generate**
    〔 **when** choices =>
        generate_statement_body 〕
    〔 ... 〕
    end generate 〖 *generate*_label 〗 ;

This is like a sequential case statement, except that the expression and choices control how declarations and concurrent statements are copied in the design. When the model is elaborated, the expression is evaluated (which explains why it must be static) and a matching choice is selected. The declarations (if any) and concurrent statements in the corresponding body are then included in the elaborated model. The rules governing sequential case statement expressions and choices also apply to the expression and choices in a case-generate statement, with the further stipulation that the expression be static.

EXAMPLE 13.7   *Selection among alternative implementations*

Multiplication of complex numbers in Cartesian form involves four scalar multiplications, a subtraction, and an addition. Depending on the constraints that apply to a design, these operations can be implemented in one clock cycle using multiple function units, in multiple clock cycles using fewer function units, or in a pipeline. Suppose we have an enumeration type, defined as follows, for specifying the implementation to use:

```vhdl
type implementation_type is
        (single_cycle, multicycle, pipelined);
```

An entity declaration for a complex multiplier has a generic constant of this type controlling the implementation:

```vhdl
entity complex_multiplier is
  generic ( implementation : implementation_type; ... );
  port ( ... );
end entity complex_multiplier;
```

Within the architecture, we use the value of the generic constant in a case-generate statement to determine what components to instantiate and how to interconnect them:

```vhdl
architecture rtl of complex_multiplier is
  ...
begin

  mult_structure : case implementation generate
    when single_cycle =>
        signal real_pp1, real_pp2 : ...;
        ...
      begin
        real_mult1 : component multiplier
          port map ( ... );
        ...
      end;
    when multicycle =>
        signal real_pp1, real_pp2 : ...;
        ...
      begin
        mult : component multiplier
          port map ( ... );
        ...
      end;
    when pipelined =>
        signal real_pp1, real_pp2 : ...;
        ...
      begin
        mult1 : component multiplier
          port map ( ... );
        ...
      end;
```

```
    end generate mutl_structure;

  end architecture rtl;
```

The case-generate statement includes three alternatives, one for each possible implementation style. Each alternative can have local declarations and concurrent statements with the same names and labels as those in other alternatives, as well as differently named declarations and differently labeled statements.

VHDL-87, -93, and -2002

These versions do not provide case-generate statements. Instead, we must write each alternative as a separate if-generate statement in which the condition compares the selector expression with a choice value.

Exercises

1. [❶ 13.1] Draw a diagram illustrating the circuit described by the following generate statement:

   ```
   synch_delay_line : for stage in 1 to 4 generate
     delay_ff : component d_ff
       port map ( clk => sys_clock,
                  d => delayed_data(stage - 1),
                  q => delayed_data(stage) );
   end generate synch_delay_line;
   ```

2. [❶ 13.1] Write a generate statement that instantiates an inverter component for each element of an input bit-vector signal **data_in** to derive an inverted bit-vector output signal **data_out_n**. Use the index range of **data_in** to determine the number of inverters required, and assume that **data_out_n** has the same index range as **data_in**.

3. [❶ 13.2] Write a conditional generate statement that connects a signal external_clock directly to a signal **internal_clock** if a Boolean generic constant **positive_clock** is true. If the generic is false, the statement should connect **external_clock** to **internal_clock** via an instance of an inverter component.

4. [❷ 13.1] Develop a structural model for an *n*-bit-wide two-input multiplexer composed of single-bit-wide two-input multiplexer components. The width *n* is a generic constant in the entity interface.

5. [❷ 13.1] A first-in/first-out (FIFO) queue can be constructed from the register component shown in Figure 13.2. The bit width of the component is a generic constant in the component interface. The FIFO is constructed by chaining cells together and connecting their **reset** inputs in parallel. The depth of the FIFO is specified by a generic constant in the entity interface. Develop a structural model for a FIFO implemented in this manner.

FIGURE 13.2

A register component used to construct a FIFO.

6. [❷ 13.1/13.2] Develop a structural model for a binary ripple counter implemented using D-flipflops as shown in Figure 13.3. The width n is a generic constant in the entity interface.

FIGURE 13.3

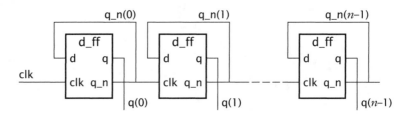

A binary ripple counter.

7. [❷ 13.1/13.2] Develop a structural model for an n-bit-wide ripple-carry adder. The least-significant bits are added using a half-adder component, and the remaining bits are added using full-adder components.

8. [❸ 13.1/13.2] Exercises 33 and 37 in Chapter 5 describe the components needed to implement a 16-bit carry-look-ahead adder. The same components can be used to implement a 64-bit carry-look-ahead adder as shown in Figure 13.4. The 64-bit addition is split into four identical 16-bit groups, each implemented with a 16-bit carry-look-ahead adder. The carry-look-ahead generator is augmented to include generate and propagate outputs, calculated in the same way as those calculated by each 4-bit adder. An additional carry-look-ahead generator is used to calculate the carry inputs to each 16-bit group. Develop a structural model of a 64-bit carry-look-ahead adder using nested generate statements to describe the two-level iterative structure of the circuit.

FIGURE 13.4

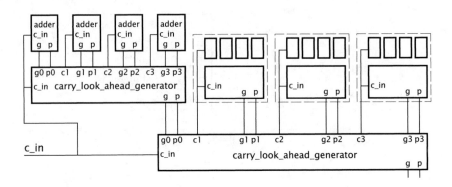

A 64-bit carry-look-ahead adder.

Chapter 14

Design for Synthesis

In this book we have discussed many aspects of VHDL and looked at examples of its use. One very strong motivation for using VHDL is hardware synthesis. The idea behind synthesis is to allow us to think of our design in abstract terms. We need not be so concerned about how best to implement the design in hardware logic—that is the job of the synthesis tool. It converts our abstract description into a structural description at a lower level of abstraction.

This chapter offers a brief introduction to synthesis, based on the IEEE standards that cover synthesis of VHDL models. A full coverage of the topic warrants a complete book in its own right. We refer the interested reader to the large number of books on hardware synthesis (for example, [1]).

14.1 Synthesizable Subsets

There are several synthesis tools available from different design automation tool vendors. While many of them perform the same general process, they differ in their command sets and the way in which we specify synthesis constraints. Hence we discuss synthesis tools only in very general terms. More important, synthesis tools differ in the subsets of VHDL that they accept as input. The majority only accept designs described at the register-transfer level and synthesize to circuits composed of gates, flipflops, registers, and other basic components. A small number of *behavioral synthesis* tools accept designs described at a higher level of abstraction. However, developing behavioral synthesis technology that is usable in practice has proven to be very difficult, so the techniques are not widely adopted. They are most successful in certain specialized application areas, such as digital signal processing.

The disparity between synthesis tools motivated the development of IEEE Standard 1076.6, *Standard for VHDL Register Transfer Level Synthesis*. The first version of this standard, published in 1999, specified a "level-1" lowest common denominator subset of VHDL that was acceptable to most synthesis tools. The intention was to assist designers in writing models that were portable between synthesis tools and to ensure that the behavior of the synthesized designs matched simulation results.

In 2004, a revision of the standard was published, specifying a level-2 synthesis subset of VHDL. The intention of this subset, as described in the Introduction to the standard, is "to include a maximum subset of VHDL that could be used to describe synthesizable RTL logic." It provides considerably more flexibility in the way models can be written. It is much closer to the subsets now implemented by synthesis tools. Nonetheless, there remains variation among tools, so we need to consult the documentation for any particular tool that we might use to find out what forms of input it accepts.

There are two aspects of synthesis subsets of VHDL. The first is the collection of language features that are included in the subset. This comprises the types that can be used to represent data and the declarations, specifications, and statements that can be included in models. The second aspect is the way in which we write code to represent different hardware elements. The task of a synthesis tool is to analyze a VHDL description and infer what hardware elements are represented and how they are connected. A tool cannot infer hardware from any arbitrarily written VHDL model. Instead, we need to write models in a *synthesis style* that is recognized by the tool. Style guidelines include templates for process statements from which various kinds of hardware elements can be inferred, and restrictions on the way in which we write and combine statements. We will look at both of these aspects, as specified by the IEEE 1076.6-2004 standard.

One further point to note about synthesis subsets is that they have historically lagged behind revisions of the VHDL standard. As an illustration, the 1999 version of the IEEE 1076.6 standard specified that models use the VHDL-87 version of the language, despite VHDL-93 having been published six years earlier. In 1999, many synthesis tools still only supported VHDL-87; now, VHDL-93 is widely supported. The changes between VHDL-93 and VHDL-2002 were relatively minor, apart from the addition of protected types. Since these are not supported for synthesis, synthesis tools effectively support VHDL-2002. That is the version of the language referenced in IEEE 1076.6-2004. The changes between VHDL-2002 and VHDL-2008 are much more significant. If past experience is an indicator, it may be some time before synthesis vendors implement the changes in their tools. Again, we should consult the documentation for any particular tool to see whether it supports VHDL-2008 features. The notes throughout this book describing differences between earlier versions of VHDL and VHDL-2008 will also be helpful as we write synthesizable models.

14.2 Use of Data Types

The synthesis standard allows us to use the following data types:

- enumeration types, including the predefined types **boolean**, **bit** and **character**

- integer types, including the predefined type **integer** and the subtypes **natural** and **positive**

- arrays of scalar elements, including the predefined types **bit_vector** and **string**

- **std_ulogic**, **std_ulogic_vector**, **std_logic** and **std_logic_vector**, defined in package **std_logic_1164**

- **unsigned** and **signed**, defined in package **numeric_bit**

- **unsigned** and **signed**, defined in package **numeric_std**

The synthesis standard allows us to use these types for constants, signals, and variables. When we declare a constant, we must include an initial value expression to give the constant a value. We cannot declare a deferred constant in a package. The synthesis standard specifies that any initial value expression in a signal or variable declaration is ignored. This makes sense in some circuits, such as ASICs, where the initial value of a storage location is indeterminate. In FPGAs, however, the storage can be initialized to specified values. Tools for synthesizing to FPGAs may allow an initial value expression in a signal or variable declaration for this purpose.

14.2.1 Scalar Types

Models conforming with the synthesis standard may define and use enumeration types, with some restrictions. The predefined types **boolean** and **bit** and the standard logic types **std_ulogic** and **std_logic** are implemented in hardware as individual bits. Most of the time, we use **std_ulogic** and **std_logic**, since that allows us to represent high-impedance and unknown states, as well as low and high logic levels. User-defined enumeration types may be implemented by tool-dependent encoding. Alternatively, we may specify the encoding by decorating the type with a string attribute, **enum_encoding**, described in Section 14.7.

Models conforming with the synthesis standard may also define and use integer types. Values of these types are implemented in the synthesized design as vectors of bits. If an integer type includes only non-negative values, the synthesized vector uses unsigned binary encoding. If the type includes negative values, two's-complement signed encoding is used. The number of bits in the encoding is determined by the range of values in the type. For example, given the following declarations in a model:

```
type sample is range -64 to 63;
subtype table_index is natural range 0 to 1023;
```

values of type **sample** should be implemented using 7-bit two's-complement encoding, and values of subtype **table_index** should be implemented using 10-bit unsigned encoding. Types that don't include 0 are encoded as though 0 were allowed. For example, the type

```
type index_type is range 4 to 15;
```

would be represented using 4-bit unsigned encoding. Synthesis tools conforming with the standard should support integers within the range -2^{31} to $+2^{31} - 1$, mapping to 32-bit two's-complement encoding.

The synthesis standard also allows use of other predefined enumeration types, including **character**, but they may not be supported by tools. The remaining classes of scalar types, namely, physical and floating-point types, are not supported by the synthesis standard. Definition and use of such types in a model are either ignored or treated as an error.

14.2.2 Composite and Other Types

Models conforming with the synthesis standard may define and use array and record types, but there are some significant restrictions on the use of array types. They must be indexed by an integer range, and the index bounds must be static, so that the synthesis tool can determine how much storage or how many bits of data are required in the hardware. The element type can only be an allowed scalar type, as described above, or a one-dimensional vector of an enumeration type representing individual bits. Thus, for example, the following array types are permissible:

```
type coeffs is array (3 downto 0) of integer;

type channel_states is array (0 to 7) of state;
  -- state is an enumeration type

subtype word is bit_vector(31 downto 0);
type reg_file is array (0 to 15) of word;
```

whereas the following are not:

```
type color is (red, green, blue);
type plane_status is array (color) of boolean;
  -- non-integer index type

type matrix is array (1 to 3, 1 to 3) of real;
  -- 2D, and floating-point elements

type reg_file_set is array (0 to 3) of reg_file;
  -- elements are vectors of non-bits
```

In addition, some tools limit arrays to be one-dimensional. Such tools would not allow the **matrix** type shown above.

The types **unsigned** and **signed** defined in **numeric_bit** and **numeric_std** are array types that meet the requirements for synthesizability, since they are one-dimensional arrays of elements that represent bits. The synthesis standard requires that we use these types if we need to represent unsigned or signed numbers at the bit level. We cannot use array types that we define in our model.

Historically, many designers have used the non-standard packages **std_logic_arith**, **std_logic_signed**, and **std_logic_unsigned**. These packages provide types and operations similar to those now provided by **numeric_std** and **numeric_std_unsigned**. With VHDL-2008, the standard packages incorporate all the operations provided by the non-standard packages. Nonetheless, synthesis tools still support use of the non-standard packages for representing numeric data at the bit level.

The synthesis standard does not support use of access types, file types or incomplete type declarations. Synthesis tools should ignore their declarations and are not required to accept models that use access-type values or file operations. In particular, dynamic allocation of objects using the **new** allocator and deallocation of objects using the **deallocate** procedure are not supported. The synthesis standard does support declaration of subtypes, but ignores user-defined resolution functions within subtype indications.

14.3 Interpretation of Standard Logic Values

If we use the standard logic types **std_ulogic** or **std_logic** in our models, we need to consider how a synthesis tool interprets values of different driving strength and unknown values. The synthesized hardware deals only with logic 0 and 1 values. We use standard logic values other than 0 and 1 to simulate the effects of weak driving strength and indeterminate logic values. We use the term *metalogical* to refer to the values 'U', 'X', 'W', and '–' that do not represent logic levels.

When our model assigns to a signal a value calculated by an expression from other signal values, the synthesis tool generates a hardware circuit that implements the logic of the expression. However, when our model uses a literal standard logic value, the synthesis tool must represent the value as either a logic 0 or a logic 1. The synthesis standard specifies that the standard logic values '0' and 'L', like the bit value '0' and the Boolean value false, are represented as a logic 0. Similarly, the standard logic values '1' and 'H', like the bit value '1' and the Boolean value true, are represented as a logic 1. Thus the synthesis tool does not attempt to interpret the strength information associated with the standard logic value.

When our model assigns the standard logic value 'Z' to a signal, the synthesis tool generates a tristate buffer for the signal. Usually such an assignment is nested within a conditional statement. In that case, hardware generated for the condition is used to enable or disable the tristate buffer. For example, the if statement

```
if request_enable = '1' then
  request <= ready;
else
  request <= 'Z';
end if;
```

would result in synthesis of a tristate buffer driving **request**. The input to the buffer would be connected to **ready**, and the control signal to enable the buffer would be connected to **request_enable**. When our model uses 'Z' in contexts other than a signal assignment (for example, in a comparison expression), the synthesis tool treats it in the same way as a metalogical value.

Use of metalogical values in a model is either ignored or not accepted by the synthesis tool, depending on the context. When values are tested for equality with metalogical values, the result is deemed to be false. Similarly, a test for inequality with metalogical values is deemed to be true. The rationale is that real hardware values are known to be either logic 0 or logic 1, so it does not make sense to synthesize hardware to compare with any other values. Thus any statements controlled by an equality comparison with a metalogical value, such as statements nested in an if statement or a case statement, can be ignored by the synthesis tool. They exist in the model purely for simulation purposes. In the cases of metalogical values appearing as operands of other relational operators and of arithmetic, logical and shift operators, the synthesis tool should not accept the model.

The **std_match** function defined in the **numeric_std** package can be used to compare standard logic values and vectors. It has the advantage of producing the same results in simulation and synthesis, unlike comparison using the "=" operator. Synthesis tools represent the use of **std_match** by an equivalence test. Simulation tools perform the comparison ignoring the driving strength of the parameters. If both values represent the same logic level, the comparison returns true. If either value is a metalogical value other than '–', the comparison returns false. The value '–' is interpreted as "don't care", so comparison with it returns true. Synthesis of a comparison using **std_match** with a literal vector containing "don't care" elements results in comparison hardware that excludes the "don't care" bits from the comparison. VHDL-2008 defines the matching relational operators, including "?=", which has the same behavior for **std_ulogic** and **std_ulogic_vector** values as **std_match**. As synthesis tools evolve to implement VHDL-2008 features, we should expect to see them treat the matching relational operators in a similar way to **std_match**.

14.4 Modeling Combinational Logic

Combinational circuits are those in which the outputs are determined solely by the current values of inputs; the circuit does not maintain any internal state. The simplest way to model combinational logic in synthesizable VHDL is using concurrent signal assignment statements. For example, we can model a Boolean function of inputs as follows:

```
status <= '1' when ready and sample < limit else '0';
```

A synthesis tool would generate hardware composed of a comparator for the input signals **sample** and **limit**, and a gate to combine the comparison output with the signal **ready**. It may optimize the hardware to meet timing and area constraints, but the result would perform the same function. Note that we have written the statement in this way to be compatible with VHDL-2002. As tools include VHDL-2008 features, we can rewrite the statement as

```
status <= ready and sample ?< limit;
```

EXAMPLE 14.1   *Modeling arithmetic circuits*

We can model a combinational arithmetic circuit using a concurrent assignment with an arithmetic expression on the right-hand side. For example, the following assignment in an architecture represents an adder for **unsigned** operands **a** and **b**, producing an unsigned result, **sum**, of the same size:

```
sum <= a + b;
```

If we also need to include a carry input to an addition, we can write the following in VHDL-2008:

```
sum <= a + b + carry_in;
```

In earlier versions of the **numeric_bit** and **numeric_std** packages, there was no overloaded addition operator with a scalar operand. We would have to write this as

```
sum <= a + b + unsigned'(0 => carry_in);
```

to create a one-element vector from the **carry_in** scalar. Alternatively, if we are using a synthesis tool that supports the **std_logic_arith** package, we could use the vector/scalar operator defined there.

If we want the carry result of the addition, we need to extend the operands by one bit, so that the result is one bit longer than the operands. We can then use the extra result bit as the carry:

```
tmp_sum <= ('0' & a) + ('0' & b);
sum <= tmp_sum(7 downto 0);
carry <= tmp_sum(8);
```

In VHDL-2008, we can write this as:

```
(carry, sum) <= ('0' & a) + ('0' & b);
```

EXAMPLE 14.2   *Modeling a multiplexer*

We can use a selected signal assignment statement to describe a multiplexer, for example:

```
with addr(1 downto 0) select
  request <=  request_a when "00",
              request_b when "01",
              request_c when "10",
              request_d when "11";
```

This assumes **bit_vector** signals. If we are using **std_ulogic_vector** signals, the choices do not cover all possible values. We would have to include a further alternative as follows:

```
with addr(1 downto 0) select
  request <=  request_a when "00",
              request_b when "01",
              request_c when "10",
              request_d when "11",
              'X' when others;
```

A synthesis tool would interpret the choices covering valid logic levels as implying hardware, and the **others** choice as representing metalogical values for simulation purposes, to be ignored.

We could also have expressed this behavior using a conditional signal assignment statement, as follows:

```
request <= request_a when addr(1 downto 0) = "00" else
           request_b when addr(1 downto 0) = "01" else
           request_c when addr(1 downto 0) = "10" else
           request_d when addr(1 downto 0) = "11" else
           'X';
```

However, in a conditional signal assignment, the conditions need not be mutually exclusive, so the synthesis tool would infer a priority-encoded chain of multiplexers to conform with the language semantics. This structure would be slower than a simple multiplexer. The tool may be able to optimize the hardware, but it is safer to use a selected signal assignment to imply a multiplexer function if that is our design intent.

One situation in which a conditional signal assignment statement is appropriate is combinational logic with a tristate buffered output, for example:

```
data_bus <= resize(sample_byte, 16)
            when std_match(sample_enable, '1') else
            "ZZZZZZZZZZZZZZZZ";
```

We can also use a process statement to describe combinational logic. The process must be sensitive to all of the inputs, and the combinational outputs must be assigned values in all possible executions of the process. This form of process is most useful when there are multiple outputs.

EXAMPLE 14.3   *A combinational process for multiple outputs*

Suppose we need to model a block of logic that has multiple outputs with tristate drivers all controlled by the same condition. We could use separate conditional signal assignment statements, but that would require us to repeat the condition in each one. Instead, we use a process to represent the logic block, as follows:

```
read_sample : process ( read_enable,
                             sample, limit_exceeded, ready )
begin
  if std_match(read_enable, '1') then
    data <= sample;
    parity <= calc_parity(sample);
    status <= ready and not limit_exceeded;
  else
    data <= "ZZZZZZZZ";
    parity <= 'Z';
    status <= 'Z';
  end if;
end process read_sample;
```

In this process, any change in any of the inputs results in new values being determined for all of the outputs. Thus the design is purely combinational. A synthesis tool would infer combinational network with tristate drivers on the outputs.

When we write a process that declares and uses a variable, a synthesis tool may infer a need for storage in the synthesized hardware. However, if all possible executions of the model in response to input changes involve the variable being assigned a value before being read, no storage is needed.

EXAMPLE 14.4   *Intermediate variables in combinational processes*

Consider the following process containing a variable assignment:

```
adder : process ( sel, a, b, c )
  variable operand : integer;
begin
  if sel = '1' then
    operand := a;
  else
    operand := b;
  end if;
  sum <= operand + c;
end process adder;
```

The process is sensitive to all of the inputs. There are two possible execution paths when an input changes. If **sel** is '1', the value of **a** is assigned to **operand** and subsequently added with **c** to determine the output **sum**. Alternatively, if **sel** is '0', the value of **b** is assigned to **operand** and added with **c**. Thus we can think of **operand** as representing the intermediate node in a combinational network consisting of a multiplexer and an adder. The value assigned to **operand** need not be stored.

Note the importance of including in the sensitivity list all inputs that are read by a combinational process. A synthesis tool will typically issue a warning if an input is read in the process but not mentioned in the sensitivity list. The difficulty in maintaining consistency between the sensitivity list and the set of signals read is the main motivation for allowing the reserved word **all** in sensitivity lists in VHDL-2008. Since this is a relatively minor extension for synthesis vendors to implement, we would hope to see it introduced quickly.

14.5 Modeling Sequential Logic

Sequential circuits are those that maintain an internal state. The outputs they produce in response to given inputs depend on the history of inputs received previously. Most sequential circuits we design are *synchronous*, or *clocked*. They use a rising or falling edge of a clock, or a level of an enable signal, to control advance of state or storage of data. The synthesis standard supports descriptions of these kinds of circuits. Most current design methodologies prefer edge-triggered sequential design, since achieving correct timing is more straightforward. Occasionally we might design an *asynchronous* circuit: a sequential circuit without a clock or enable input. Such circuits store state using combinational feedback loops. The synthesis standard and most synthesis tools do not support synthesis of these kinds of circuits. If we must include them, we must describe them using structural models and instantiate them as components within a synthesizable model.

Unlike signals used for data, which can be of a fairly wide variety of types, clock signals are restricted to be of type **bit**, **std_ulogic** or a subtype such as **std_logic**. A clock signal need not necessarily be a single scalar signal; it may be a scalar element of an array of **bit** or **std_ulogic** values.

14.5.1 Modeling Edge-Triggered Logic

We model edge-triggered sequential logic using processes. The synthesis standard allows considerable flexibility in modeling edge-triggered sequential logic, though not all synthesis tools implement the full generality. The premise is that a signal or variable assignment executed under control of a clock-edge condition implies edge-triggered storage. Clock-edge conditions are expressions of the following forms, for rising clock-edges:

* rising_edge(*clock_signal*_name)
* *clock_signal*_name'event **and** *clock_signal*_name = '1'
* *clock_signal*_name = '1' **and** *clock_signal*_name'event
* **not** *clock_signal*_name'stable **and** *clock_signal*_name = '1'
* *clock_signal*_name = '1' **and not** *clock_signal*_name'stable

and for falling clock-edges:

* falling_edge(*clock_signal*_name)
* *clock_signal*_name'event **and** *clock_signal*_name = '0'
* *clock_signal*_name = '0' **and** *clock_signal*_name'event
* **not** *clock_signal*_name'stable **and** *clock_signal*_name = '0'
* *clock_signal*_name = '0' **and not** *clock_signal*_name'stable

We can write an expression of one of these forms in the condition of an if statement within a process. The process must also have the clock signal name in its sensitivity list. Any signal or variable assignments within the if statement are then said to be *synchronous assignments*, controlled by the clock-edge condition. We can also include assignments in if statements controlled by other conditions involving asynchronous control signals. We must also include the control signals in the sensitivity list of the process. The assignments within such if statements are called *asynchronous assignments*, as they are not controlled by a clock-edge condition. The operators in expressions on the right-hand sides of assignments, whether synchronous or asynchronous, imply combinational logic connected to register inputs. As well as assignments, we can include other sequential statements within the process. These statements govern the flow of control leading to assignments. Thus, they imply combination logic, such as multiplexers, that feed the inputs of registers implied by the assignments. There are some restrictions, however. For example, we cannot arbitrarily include wait statements, nor can we refer to clock-edge expressions in assignments.

EXAMPLE 14.5 *Edge-triggered register*

One of the simplest forms of process represents an edge-triggered register:

```
simple_reg : process ( clk ) is
begin
  if clk'event and clk = '1' then
    reg_out <= data_in;
  end if;
end process simple_reg;
```

In this process, the assignment to **reg_out** is a synchronous assignment, controlled by the rising clock-edge condition. The process represents a register with **clk** as the clock signal, **data_in** as the input, and **reg_out** as the output.

EXAMPLE 14.6 *Edge-triggered register with synchronous control inputs*

We can include more involved statements within the controlling if statement to model registers with synchronous control signals. For example, the following process models a register with synchronous reset and enable controlling storage for two output signals:

```
dual_reg : process ( clk ) is
begin
  if rising_edge(clk) then
    if reset = '1' then
      q1 <= X"00";
      q2 <= X"0000";
    elsif en = '1' then
      q1 <= d1;
      q2 <= d2;
    end if;
  end if;
end process dual_reg;
```

In this case, all of the assignments are synchronous, governed by the rising clock-edge condition. The nested if statement chooses between resetting the outputs, updating them, or leaving them unchanged. A synthesis tool could infer a register, updated on every clock-edge, with a multiplexer at the input selecting between the hardwired 0 values, the data inputs, and the fed-back outputs. Alternatively, if the target technology supports registers with separate reset and enable control signals, the tool may infer use of them. We will see in Section 14.7 how we can use attributes to select the implementation.

EXAMPLE 14.7   *Counters as registers combined with arithmetic*

We can combine computational logic and storage in the one process. The computational logic is represented by the expressions in assignments. Counters are a good illustration of this approach. The following process represents an up/down counter wtih synchronous reset, load and count enable:

```
signal d_in, count : unsigned(11 downto 0);
...

up_down_counter : process (clk) is
begin
  if rising_edge(clk) then
    if reset = '1' then
      count <= X"000";
    elsif load_en = '1' then
      count <= d_in;
    elsif count_en = '1' then
      if dir = '1' then
        count <= count + 1;
      else
        count <= count - 1;
      end if;
    end if;
  end if;
end process up_down_counter;
```

We could augment this with a concurrent assignment statement to derive a terminal count signal:

```
tc <= '1' when std_match(count, X"111") else '0';
```

EXAMPLE 14.8   *Register wtih asynchronous control signals*

If our implementation technology provides registers with asynchronous control signals, we can represent them with processes containing asynchronous assignments. For example, the following process represents a register with asynchronous reset:

```
reg : process (clk, reset) is
begin
  if reset = '1' then
    q <= "0000";
  elsif rising_edge(clk) then
    q <= d;
  end if;
end process reg;
```

In this process, the first assignment is not controlled by a clock-edge condition; hence, it is asynchronous, and the **reset** control signal must be included in the sensitivity list of the process. The second assignment is synchronous and models the edge-triggered behavior of the register.

EXAMPLE 14.9 *Shift register with asynchronous and synchronous control*

We can combine asynchronous and synchronous control in a single process. For example, the we could model a shift register with asyncrhnous reset and synchronous parallel load as follows:

```
shift_reg : process (clk, reset) is
begin
  if reset = '1' then
    q <= "00000000";
  elsif rising_edge(clk) then
    if load_en = '1' then
      q <= d_in
    else
      q <= q(6 downto 0) & d_s;
    end if;
  end if;
end process reg;
```

Note that we do not include the **load_en** signal in the sensitivity list, as it is a synchronous control signal.

The synthesis standard allows more involved structures than those demonstrated by the preceding examples. For example, it lists the following as a legal synthesizable process:

```
RegProc5 : process( clk, reset )
begin
  if (en = '1' and rising_edge(clk)) or reset = '1' then
    if reset = '1' then
      Q <= '0'; -- async assignment
    elsif en = '1' and rising_edge(clk) then -- sync condition
      Q <= D; -- sync assignment
    end if;
  end if ;
end process ;
```

While it is, in principle, possible to analyze the control flow in such a process and determine whether each of the assignments is synchronous or asynchronous, synthesis tools are generally more restrictive in what they will accept. It is often clearer to write processes in the forms illustrated by the preceding examples than in more convoluted forms.

Recall that a process with signals listed in the sensitivity list is equivalent to a process containing a wait statement that is sensitive to the signals. Synthesis tools allow us to express edge-sensitive behavior using explicit wait statements in a process, with some restrictions. The synthesis standard specifies quite complicated rules for the structure of such wait statements, covering the signals that can be listed in the **on** clause and the form of condition that can be written in the **until** clause. (A **for** clause is not allowed, as that would imply specific timing.) Current synthesis tools are more restrictive, since inferring control logic for the general cases allowed by the standard could be arbitrarily complicated.

The simplest case allowed by synthesis tools is a wait statement as the first statement in the process, with a clock-edge condition in the until clause. There must not be any other wait statements or references to clock-edges in the process, nor in any procedures called from the process.

EXAMPLE 14.10   *Edge-triggered register with explicit wait statement*

We can represent and edge-triggered register with synchronous reset as follows:

```
reg : process is
begin
  wait until rising_edge(clk);
  if reset = '1' then
    q <= X"00";
  elsif en = '1' then
    q <= d;
  end if;
end process dual_reg;
```

The assignments to **q** only occur after a rising edge occurs on the **clk** signal. Hence, both **reset** and **en** are synchronous control signals.

EXAMPLE 14.11   *Explicit wait and asynchronous control*

The synthesis standard allows us to write the following process to express asynchronous control using an explicit wait statement.

```
reg : process is
begin
  wait until reset = '1' or rising_edge(clk);
  if reset = '1' then
    q <= X"00";
  elsif rising_edge(clk) then
    if en = '1' then
      q <= d;
    end if;
```

```
  end if;
end process dual_reg;
```

The asynchronous condition is included in the wait statement. The wait statement is followed immediately by an if statement that tests both the asynchronous condition and the clock-edge condition. Thus, in this example, **reset** is an asynchronous control signal and **en** is a synchronous control signal. While this is acceptable according to the synthesis standard, not all tools accept it, instead limiting conditions in wait statements to just clock-edge conditions.

The synthesis standard allows a process to include multiple explicit wait statements, though some tools do not support it. In general, the hardware inferred for such a process includes some form of state machine, since the hardware must keep track of progress through the statements from one cycle to the next. Compare this with a process containing only one wait statement (explicit or implied), which always performs one complete pass through the process statement body for each clock-edge.

The rules for processes with multiple wait statements require that each statement must wait for the same condition, and in particular, must wait for the same edge of a single clock signal. This makes sense, as the wait statements correspond to transitions in the controlling state machine in the inferred hardware. If the wait statements include asynchronous conditions, as in Example 14.11, then each wait statement must be followed by identical tests for those conditions. Again, this corresponds to the control hardware implementation. The asynchronous behavior is that of the state machine.

EXAMPLE 14.12 *Sequential multiplier*

We can describe a multiplier that takes multiple clock cycles to compute its result using a shift-and-add method. The following process, based on an example in the IEEE 1076.6 standard, describes the behavior:

```
MultProc : process is
begin
  wait until rising_edge(clk);
  if start = '1' then
    done <= '0';
    P <= (others => '0');
    for i in A'range loop
      wait until rising_edge(clk);
      if A(i) = '1' then
        P <= (P(6 downto 0) & '0') + B;
      else
        P <= P(6 downto 0) & '0';
      end if;
    end loop;
    done <= '1';
```

```
    end if;
  end process;
```

This process implies an edge-triggered state machine that controls registers for the **done** and P output signals. The state machine tests the **start** signal on each clock-edge. When it is '0', it leaves P unchanged and sets **done**. Otherwise, it resets **done** and P, then sequences through a number of cycles (determined by **A'range**) to update P with successive partial products. On completion of the sequence, it sets **done** again.

Where wait statements appear in a loop that implements sequential behavior, we can use an exit or next statement after each wait statement to describe reset behavior. For asynchronous reset, this is a case of each wait statement being followed by identical tests for asynchronous conditions.

EXAMPLE 14.13   *Reset in a loop*

The following process from the IEEE 1076.6 synthesis standard models a UART serializer for data transmission:

```
UartTxFunction : process is
begin
  TopLoop : loop
    if nReset = '0' then
      SerialDataOut <= '1';
      TxRdyReg <= '1';
    end if;

    wait until nReset = '0' or
                (rising_edge(UartTxClk) and DataRdy = '1');
    next TopLoop when nReset = '0';
    SerialDataOut <= '0';
    TxRdyReg <= '0';

    -- Send 8 Data Bits
    for i in 0 to 7 loop
      wait until nReset = '0' or rising_edge(UartTxClk);
      next TopLoop when nReset = '0';
      SerialDataOut <= DataReg(i);
      TxRdyReg <= '0';
    end loop;

    -- Send Parity Bit
    wait until nReset = '0' or rising_edge(UartTxClk);
    next TopLoop when nReset = '0';
    SerialDataOut <=
      DataReg(0) xor DataReg(1) xor DataReg(2) xor
      DataReg(3) xor DataReg(4) xor DataReg(5) xor
```

```
          DataReg(6) xor DataReg(7);
      TxRdyReg <= '0';

      -- Send Stop Bit
      wait until nReset = '0' or rising_edge(UartTxClk);
      next TopLoop when nReset = '0';
      SerialDataOut <= '1';
      TxRdyReg <= '1';
    end loop;
end process;
```

Each wait statement in the process includes a test for a rising edge of the
UartTxClk signal, as well as for the the asynchronous nReset signal. The identical next
statements all restart the outer loop when the asynchronous reset condition is true.
We can rewrite this process to describe synchronous reset, as follows:

```
UartTxFunction : process is
begin
  TopLoop : loop
    wait until rising_edge(UartTxClk);
    if nReset = '0' then
      SerialDataOut <= '1';
      TxRdyReg <= '1';
    elsif DataRdy = '1' then
      SerialDataOut <= '0';
      TxRdyReg <= '0';

      -- Send 8 Data Bits
      for i in 0 to 7 loop
        wait rising_edge(UartTxClk);
        exit TopLoop when nReset = '0';
        SerialDataOut <= DataReg(i);
        TxRdyReg <= '0';
      end loop;

      -- Send Parity Bit
      wait rising_edge(UartTxClk);
      exit TopLoop when nReset = '0';
      SerialDataOut <=
        DataReg(0) xor DataReg(1) xor DataReg(2) xor
        DataReg(3) xor DataReg(4) xor DataReg(5) xor
        DataReg(6) xor DataReg(7);
      TxRdyReg <= '0';

      -- Send Stop Bit
      wait until rising_edge(UartTxClk);
      exit TopLoop when nReset = '0';
      SerialDataOut <= '1';
      TxRdyReg <= '1';
```

```
      end if;
    end loop;
  end process;
```

In this case we have used exit statements instead of next statements, though the latter would work just as well.

The until clause in a wait statement can also be an expression of the following forms, in addition to those listed on page 384:

- *clock_signal*_name = '1'

- *clock_signal*_name = '0'

Since the wait statement waits until the signal changes value, a change to '1' must represent a rising edge, and a change to '0' must represent a falling edge. Thus, we could write the wait statement in Example 14.10 as:

```
wait until clk = '1';
```

While this is allowed, the form using **rising_edge** is a preferred style, since it is more descriptive and deals correctly with weak driving strengths ('L' and 'H') during simulation.

14.5.2 Level-Sensitive Logic and Inferring Storage

Level-sensitive sequential logic maintains state, but does not respond to clock-edges. Instead, state is usually updated under control of an enable signal. While the enable signal is asserted, the state can change according to data inputs. While the enable signal is negated, changes on the data inputs are ignored and the circuit maintains its current state.

EXAMPLE 14.14   *A transparent latch*

Consider the following model for a transparent latch:

```
latch : process ( enable, d )
begin
  if enable = '1' then
    q <= d;
  end if;
end process latch;
```

This process is sensitive to changes on the **enable** and **d** inputs. If **enable** is '1' when either input changes, the data value is used to update the output **q**. If **enable** is '0', the current value is maintained on **q**. This behavior is implied by the semantics of signals and signal assignment in VHDL. When the synthesis tool implements the model as a hardware circuit, it must provide some storage to maintain the value for the output. The tool must infer the need for storage from the model semantics.

In general, a synthesis tool must infer storage if there are possible executions of the process that do not involve assignment to a given signal or variable. If the process does not include clock-edge conditions, then level-sensitive storage is inferred. The process must then include in its sensitivity list all signals that the process reads. The latch example illustrates storage inference due to existence of paths on which a signal is not updated. If the process executes when **enable** is '0', the assignment to **q** is bypassed, so storage is inferred for **q**.

EXAMPLE 14.15   *Transparent latch with reset*

The following process is another example of a latch, in this case involving storage inference for a variable:

```
latch_with_reset : process ( enable, reset, d )
  variable stored_value : bit;
begin
  if reset = '1' then
    stored_value := '0';
  elsif enable = '1' then
    stored_value := d;
  end if;
  q <= stored_value;
end process latch_with_reset;
```

The output signal **q** is assigned on every execution of the process, so no storage is inferred for it. However, the variable **stored_value** is not assigned when **reset** and **enable** are both '0'; hence storage is inferred for the variable.

In principle, storage is also inferred for a process that does not include a reference to a clock-edge expression if there are possible executions in which a signal or variable is read before being assigned. However, such a process represents an asynchronous sequential circuit and is not supported by synthesis tools. Consider the following erroneous process intended to describe a counter with reset:

```
counter : process ( count_en )
  variable count : natural range 0 to 15;
begin
  q <= (q + 1) mod 16;
end process counter;
```

The process is sensitive to changes of **count_en**. Whenever that signal changes, the old value of **q** is read and incremented to determine the new value. The value must be maintained until the next change of **count_en**, implying the need for storage for **q**, even though it is assigned in all possible executions of the process.

The synthesis standard recommends against writing level-sensitive processes in which signals or variables are read before being assigned. Usually such processes are not what we intend, and the inference of storage is inadvertent. On the other hand, a process in which a variable is first assigned and then read in all possible execution paths is legal and useful. Such a process simply models combinational logic, as we discussed in Section 14.4, with the variable denoting an intermediate node in the combinational network.

14.5.3 Modeling State Machines

Many designs expressed at the register-transfer level consist of combinational data paths controlled by finite-state machines. Hence it is important to be able to describe a finite-state machine in such a way that it can be synthesized. The preferred style is to separate the implementation into two processes, one describing the combinational logic that calculates the next state and output values, and the other being a register that stores the state. This style is accepted by all synthesis tools, whereas finite-state machines implied by multiple wait statements in a process, as described in Section 14.5.1, are not uniformly supported.

EXAMPLE 14.16   *Finite-state machine with Mealy and Moore outputs*

The following architecture body represents a finite state machine described using two processes:

```
architecture rtl of state_machine is
  type state is (ready, ack, err);
  signal current_state, next_state : state;
begin

  next_state_and_output : process ( current_state, in1, in2 )
  begin
    case current_state is
      when ready =>
        out1 <= '0';
        if in1 = '1' then
          out2 <= '1';
          next_state <= ack;
        else
          out2 <= '0';
          next_state <= ready;
        end if;
      when ack =>
        out1 <= '0';
        if in2 = '1' then
          out2 <= '0';
          next_state <= ready;
        else
          out2 <= '0';
          next_state <= err;
        end if;
```

```
      when err =>
        out1 <= '1';
        out2 <= '0';
        next_state <= err;
    end case;
  end process next_state_and_output;

  state_reg : process ( clk, reset )
  begin
    if reset = '1' then
      current_state <= ready;
    elsif rising_edge(clk) then
      current_state <= next_state;
    end if;
  end process state_reg;

end rtl;
```

The architecture body defines an enumeration type for the state values. We can either rely on the synthesis tool to determine the encoding for the state or use the **enum_encoding** attribute to define our own encoding, as described in Section 14.7. The signal **current_state** represents the output of the state register, and the signal **next_state** is the state to be assumed by the state machine on the next clock-edge. The process **next_state_and_output** describes the combinational logic. It uses a case statement to determine the next state and output values, depending on the current state value. Note that the output **out1** is uniquely determined by the current state. It is a Moore machine output. The output **out2**, on the other hand, depends on both the current state and the current inputs to the machine. It is a Mealy machine output. The process **state_reg** describes the state register. It has an asynchronous reset control input that forces the machine into the ready state. When **reset** is inactive, the process updates the current state on each rising clock-edge.

In the process representing the combinational logic, we have included assignments for both output signals in all states. An alternative way of writing the process is:

```
  next_state_and_output : process ( current_state, in1, in2 )
  begin
    out1 <= '0'; out2 <= '0';
    case current_state is
      when ready =>
        if in1 = '1' then
          out2 <= '1';
          next_state <= ack;
        else
          next_state <= ready;
        end if;
      when ack =>
        if in2 = '1' then
          next_state <= ready;
```

```
        else
          next_state <= err;
        end if;
      when err =>
        out1 <= '1';
        next_state <= err;
    end case;
  end process next_state_and_output;
```

In this version, we include "default" assignments to the outputs before the case statement. Then, in the case statement, we only assign to each output when the value differs from the default. This is a much more succinct form, especially when there are many outputs. Moreover, it helps us avoid missing an assignment and inadvertently implying level-sensitive storage for an output. For these reasons, we recommend this style.

14.6 Modeling Memories

Many designs include memories, and many implementation technologies, such as FPGAs, include memory resources that can be used as RAMs and ROMs. Synthesis tools can infer memory hardware for processes written in certain ways. The IEEE 1076.6 synthesis standard specifies that a RAM be modeled in much the same way as a register, but with the storage represented by an array of bits, vectors, or integers. An address vector, converted to integer, is used to index the array for reading or writing.

A RAM model typically includes declaration of an array type and a signal of that type, for example:

```
type mem_array is array (0 to 2**depth - 1) of
                    std_ulogic_vector(width - 1 downto 0);
signal RAM : mem_array;
```

The way we write the process modeling the memory determines what kind of RAM inferred.

EXAMPLE 14.17   *Asynchronous RAM*

An asynchronous RAM is essentially a level-sensitive storage device. Thus, we can model it in a similar way to a latch. Assuming the type and signal declaration given above, the behavior is modeled as follows:

```
asynch_RAM : process (addr, d_in, we) is
begin
  if we = '1' then
    RAM(to_integer(addr)) <= d_in;
  end if;
end process asynch_RAM;
```

```
d_out <= RAM(to_integer(addr));
```

The process represents the writing part of the behavior; it updates the RAM signal while the **we** input is '1'. The assignment represents the reading part of the behavior. Note that not all implementation technologies provide asynchronous memories, since they do not interface well with clocked synchronous designs.

EXAMPLE 14.18 *Synchronous RAM with asynchronous read*

Most implementation technologies provide RAMs that perform write operations synchronously. They have embedded registers that store the address and data for a write. In some technologies, the read operation is done asynchronously. A model for such a RAM is

```
synch_RAM : process (clk) is
begin
  if rising_edge(clk) then
    if we = '1' then
      RAM(to_integer(addr)) <= d_in;
    end if;
  end if;
end process synch_RAM;

d_out <= RAM(to_integer(addr));
```

EXAMPLE 14.19 *Synchronous RAM with synchronous read*

If a RAM has embedded registers for the read control signals, read operations are also performed synchronously. RAMs differ in the data they read when a write is also performed in the same cycle. One form of RAM reads the old content of the memory location before updating it with the new data. We can model this as follows:

```
synch_RAM : process (clk) is
begin
  if rising_edge(clk) then
    d_out <= RAM(to_integer(addr));
    if we = '1' then
      RAM(to_integer(addr)) <= d_in;
    end if;
  end if;
end process synch_RAM;
```

We could interchange the assignment to **d_out** with the inner if statement without affecting the behavior, since the assignments do not affect the RAM content until after the process suspends. A synthesis tool would infer the same behavior with the statements in either order.

Another form provides the newly written data, modeled as follows:

```
synch_RAM : process (clk) is
begin
  if rising_edge(clk) then
    if we = '1' then
      RAM(to_integer(addr)) <= d_in;  d_out <= d_in;
    else
      d_out <= RAM(to_integer(addr));
    end if;
  end if;
end process synch_RAM;
```

In both cases, we can add an enable input controlling reading and writing at a new address. For example, the first version above, augmented with an enable input, is

```
synch_RAM : process (clk) is
begin
  if rising_edge(clk) then
    if en = '1' then
      d_out <= RAM(to_integer(addr));
      if we = '1' then
        RAM(to_integer(addr)) <= d_in;
      end if;
    end if;
  end if;
end process synch_RAM;
```

EXAMPLE 14.20   *Pipelined synchronous RAM*

The RAMs with synchronous read in the preceding examples start a read access on a clock-edge and provide the data after a read-access delay. In some designs, the data may arrive too late in a clock cycle to be used for further computation. We can add a storage register on the RAM output so that the data can be used in the subsequent clock cycle. This amounts to pipelining the RAM access. We can combine the RAM and pipeline registers into a single process representing a pipelined RAM:

```
pipelined_RAM : process (clk) is
  variable pipelined_en : std_ulogic;
  variable pipelined_d_out :
             std_ulogic_vector(width - 1 downto 0);
begin
  if rising_edge(clk) then
    if pipelined_en = '1' then
      d_out <= pipelined_d_out;
    end if;
    pipelined_en := en;
```

```
      if en = '1' then
        pipelined_d_out := RAM(to_integer(addr));
        if we = '1' then
          RAM(to_integer(addr)) <= d_in;
        end if;
      end if;
    end if;
  end process pipelined_RAM;
```

If we are synthesizing to an implementation technology, such as an FPGA, in which a RAM can be loaded with initial contents on system reset, we may be able to specify the initial content as part of the synthesizable model. Some tools allow us to specify initial contents in an initial value aggregate in the signal declaration, for example:

```
signal RAM : RAM_array := (X"0020", X"FC01", X"101E", X"C000",
                           . . .
                           others => X"0000");
```

Some tools also allow us to write a function that loads data from a file and returns an array of values to assign as the initial value for the signal. The IEEE 1076.6 synthesis standard, however, does not specify either of these approaches. We would need to consult our tool vendor's documentation to see how a memory can be initialized, and we should recognize that the approach used may not be portable among different tools.

We can model ROMs using similar techniques to those used for RAMs, but omitting the code representing the write operations. Since ROM content does not change, we can use a constant instead of a signal to model the storage. We specify the ROM content in the form of an array aggregate, for example:

```
constant ROM : mem_array := (X"0020", X"FC01", X"101E", X"C000",
                             . . .
                             others => X"0000");
```

Reading the ROM asynchronously can then be modeled using a concurrent assignment:

```
d_out <= ROM(to_integer(addr));
```

For a small ROM, a synthesis tool could optimize this as combinational logic.

Another way to model a small ROM is using a case statement. We use the address as the selector expression and assign different literal values to the output signal based on the address.

EXAMPLE 14.21   *A small ROM modeled using a case statement*

We can model a lookup ROM giving 7-segment display codes for BCD digits as follows:

```
decoder : process ( bcd ) is
begin
  case bcd is
    when X"0" =>    seg <= "0111111";
    when X"1" =>    seg <= "0000110";
    when X"2" =>    seg <= "1011011";
    when X"3" =>    seg <= "1001111";
    when X"4" =>    seg <= "1100110";
    when X"5" =>    seg <= "1101101";
    when X"6" =>    seg <= "1111101";
    when X"7" =>    seg <= "0000111";
    when X"8" =>    seg <= "1111111";
    when X"9" =>    seg <= "1101111";
    when others => seg <= "1000000";
  end case;
end process decoder;
```

Alternatively, we could use a selected assignment:

```
with bcd select
  seg <= "0111111" when X"0", "0000110" when X"1",
         "1011011" when X"2", "1001111" when X"3",
         "1100110" when X"4", "1101101" when X"5",
         "1111101" when X"6", "0000111" when X"7",
         "1111111" when X"8", "1101111" when X"9",
         "1000000" when others
```

If we want to use a block RAM resource as a ROM, we can use the same form of process as for a RAM, but omit the statements that update the array. For example, we can adapt the first process in Example 14.19 to model a ROM as follows:

```
block_ROM : process (clk) is
begin
  if rising_edge(clk) then
    d_out <= ROM(to_integer(addr));
  end if;
end process block_ROM;
```

14.7 Synthesis Attributes

When we use a synthesis tool to infer a hardware implementation for a design, we can direct it to optimize either the speed or area of the generated circuit. In some applications, that general directive may be sufficient, resulting in an implementation that meets our constraints. Often, however, we need to take finer control of the synthesis process. One way in which we can do so is by including *attribute specifications* in our models to direct a synthesis tool to infer hardware in particular ways.

In order to add attributes to a model, we first need to declare an attribute, giving it a type. The syntax rule for an attribute declaration is

attribute_declaration ⇐ **attribute** identifier : type_mark ;

An attribute declaration simply defines the identifier as an attribute that can take on values from the specified type. The type can be almost any VHDL type, but we will only consider attributes of type **boolean** and **string** here. Some examples of attribute declarations are

```
attribute KEEP : boolean;
attribute BUFFERED : string;
```

Once we have defined an attribute name and type, we then use attribute specifications to decorate items within a design with particular values. The simplified syntax rules for an attribute specification are

attribute_specification ⇐
    attribute identifier **of** identifier 〖 , ... 〗 : entity_class **is** expression ;

entity_class ⇐
    entity   ⫿ **procedure**   ⫿ **function**
    ⫿ **type**   ⫿ **subtype**
    ⫿ **constant**   ⫿ **signal**   ⫿ **variable**
    ⫿ **component** ⫿ **label**

The first identifier in an attribute specification is the name of a previously declared attribute. The items to be decorated with this attribute are then listed by name after the reserved word **of**. Only those named items of the particular kind specified by the "entity" class are decorated. Note that we use the term "entity" here to refer to any item in the design, not to be confused with an entity interface defined in an entity declaration. We adopt this terminology to remain consistent with the *VHDL Language Reference Manual*, since you may need to refer to it occasionally. However, we use the term as little as possible, preferring instead to refer to "items" in the design, to avoid confusion. The list of classes shown here covers those kinds of items relevant to our discussion of synthesis attributes. Other classes are allowed, but we omit them here for simplicity's sake. Finally, the actual value for the attribute of the decorated items is the result of the expression included in the attribute specification. Here are some examples of attribute specifications using the attributes defined earlier:

```
attribute KEEP of multiplier : entity is true;
attribute BUFFERED of reset : signal is "RESET_BUF";
```

There are a number of rules governing the way in which we write attribute delarations and specifications in a model. First, the attribute declaration must precede the attribute specification, so that the attribute name is visible in the specification. If we are going to use several attributes in many places in a model, we can include the attribute declarations in a package, and then include a use clause for the package in each design unit. That way, we only need to write the attribute specifications in each design unit, instead of repeating the attribute declarations.

The second rule is that an attribute specification must occur in the same declarative part as the item that it decorates. We cannot write it nested inside an inner declarative part. For example, the following is legal:

```
signal reset : std_ulogic;
attribute BUFFERED of reset : signal is "RESET_BUF";
```

whereas the following is not:

```
signal reset : std_ulogic;

procedure do_action is
  attribute BUFFERED of reset : signal is "RESET_BUF";
  ...
begin
  ...
end procedure do_action;
```

The only exception to this rule is that, since an entity is not declared within a declarative part, we write an attribute specification for an entity immediately within the declarative part of the entity, for example:

```
entity controller is
  port ( ... );

  attribute KEEP : boolean;
  attribute KEEP of controller : entity is true;

end entity controller;
```

The third rule is that to decorate a concurrent statement, such as a process, a concurrent signal assignment, or a component instance, we decorate the label of the statement. For example:

```
architecture rtl of system is

  component controller is ...

  attribute KEEP : boolean;
  attribute KEEP of control_section : label is true;
  ...

begin

  control_section : component controller
    port map ( ... );

  ...

end architecture rtl;
```

Different synthesis tools support different attributes to specify different aspects of hardware inference and different aspects of target technologies. This is possibly an aspect in which tools most widely diverge, since the attributes a given tool supports reflect the particular capabilities and synthesis algorithms implemented by the tool. We need to refer to a tool's documentation to discover what attributes are supported and how to use them.

In an effort to create at least a small amount of harmony, the IEEE 1076.6 synthesis standard defines a minimal set of synthesis attributes. We describe them here, as they are indicative of the kinds of attributes supported by tools. The standard specifies a package of attribute declaration to be analyzed into the **ieee** library. While we could declare the attributes ourselves in each design, using the standard package is more convenient. Synthesis tools usually include similar packages for their implementation-defined attributes. The standard package is

```
package RTL_ATTRIBUTES is
  attribute KEEP : boolean;
  attribute CREATE_HIERARCHY : boolean;
  attribute DISSOLVE_HIERARCHY : boolean;
  attribute SYNC_SET_RESET : boolean;
  attribute ASYNC_SET_RESET : boolean;
  attribute ONE_HOT : boolean;
  attribute ONE_COLD : boolean;
  attribute FSM_STATE : string;
  attribute FSM_COMPLETE : boolean;
  attribute BUFFERED : string;
  attribute INFER_MUX : boolean;
  attribute IMPLEMENTATION : string;
  attribute RETURN_PORT_NAME : string;
  attribute ENUM_ENCODING : string;
  attribute ROM_BLOCK : string;
  attribute RAM_BLOCK : string;
  attribute LOGIC_BLOCK : string;
  attribute GATED_CLOCK : boolean;
  attribute COMBINATIONAL : boolean;
end package RTL_ATTRIBUTES;
```

If we need to use any of these attributes, we can include a use clause in our model to make them directly visible. Several of these attributes are boolean. Decorating an item with the value true for one of these attributes directs a tool to synthesize in a particular way. Decorating with the value false is the same as not decorating the item. Attributes of type string allow us to specify further information for use by the synthesis tool. The meaning of each attribute is described below.

KEEP : boolean

Decorates: entity, component declaration, component instantiation, signal, variable

This attribute directs the tool to preserve the hardware represented by the decorated item in the inferred hardware. The item should not be deleted or replicated during optimization of the design. We can use this attribute for parts of a design that we have previously synthesized and are re-using.

CREATE_HIERARCHY : boolean

Decorates: entity, block, subprogram, process

This attribute directs the tool to maintain the decorated item as a distinct hierarchical construct in the inferred hardware. It should not be subsumed into an enclosing construct during optimization.

DISSOLVE_HIERARCHY : boolean

Decorates: entity, component declaration, component instantiation

This attribute directs the tool to merge the construct into the hardware in which the item is instantiated. The tool can then globally optimize the construct in the context of its instantiation.

SYNC_SET_RESET : boolean

Decorates: signal, process, block, entity

This attribute is used to identify edge-sensitive storage devices that have separate synchronous set/reset inputs in the target technology. Using those inputs is more efficient than multiplexing the data inputs. We use the attribute to decorate a set/reset signal connected to storage devices or the construct that represents a storage device. For example, in the following:

```
attribute SYNC_SET_RESET of reset : signal is true;
...

reg : process ( clk ) is
begin
  if rising_edge(clk) then
    if reset = '1' then
      q <= (others => '0');
    else
      q <= d;
    end if;
  end if;
end process reg;
```

the tool infers hardware with **reset** connected to the separate synchronous reset input of the register. Without the attribute, the tool could infer a register whose input comes from a multiplexer with **reset** as the select input, a zero vector as one data input, and **d** as the other data input.

ASYNC_SET_RESET : boolean

Decorates: signal, process, block, entity

This attribute is used to identify level-sensitive storage devices that have separate asynchronous set/reset inputs in the target technology. It is used in a similar way to SYNC_SET_RESET.

ONE_HOT : boolean

Decorates: signal

This attribute specifies that, in a collection of signals, each of which is decorated with true for this attribute, at most one scalar value is '1' at any time. The directive allows a synthesis tool to avoid inferring priority logic based on the signals in the collection. For example, if we write

```
ff : process ( clk, reset, set ) is
begin
  if reset = '1' then
    q <= '0';
  elsif set = '1' then
    q <= '1';
  elsif rising_edge(clk) then
    q <= d;
  end if;
end process ff;
```

we are specifying that reset has priority over set. If the target technology includes flipflops with set and reset, but requires that only one be active at a time, the tool would infer a connection to the set input driven with set and not reset. If we add the following attribute specification:

attribute ONE_HOT **of** set, reset : **signal is** true;

we are telling the tool that only one of set and reset is active at a time, so it can make direct connections to the set and reset input of the flipflop. Of course, we must ensure separately that our statement is valid. We might include an assertion to that effect in the model.

ONE_COLD : boolean

Decorates: signal

This attribute specifies that, in a collection of signals, each of which is decorated with true for this attribute, at most one scalar value is '0' at any time. It is used in a similar way to **ONE_HOT**.

FSM_STATE : string

Decorates: type, subtype, signal, variable

This attribute directs the tool to encode the state vector of a finite-state machine in a specified way. The allowed attribute values are:

- "BINARY": unsigned binary encoding with the minimal number of bits

- "GRAY": Gray coding, in which exactly one bit value changes on each tansition

- "ONE_HOT": an encoding in which each code value has exactly one '1' bit

- "ONE_COLD": an encoding in which each code value has exactly one '0' bit

- "AUTO" or empty string: the tool selects an encoding

- A string of the same form as the **ENUM_ENCODING** attribute, described on page 408

If both the **FSM_STATE** and **ENUM_ENCODING** attributes are specified for a given state machine, the **FSM_STATE** attribute takes precedence.

FSM_COMPLETE : boolean

Decorates: type, subtype, signal, variable

This attribute directs the tool to include default transitions in the finite-state machine that uses the decorated item for its state vector. We typically describe the default transitions with an others clause in a case statement, dealing with state encodings not explicitly described. For example, given the following declarations and attribute specifications:

```
type state_type is (idle, state1, state2);
signal state, next_state : state_type;
attribute FSM_STATE of state, next_state : signal is
          "ONE_HOT";
attribute FSM_COMPLETE of state, next_state : signal is
          true;
...
```

we can write a process for the state machine's combinational logic as follows:

```
fsm_logic : process (state, ...) is
begin
  case state is
    when idle   =>  next_state <= ...;
    when state1 =>  next_state <= ...;
    when state2 =>  next_state <= ...;
    when others =>  next_state <= idle;
  end case;
end process fsm_logic;
```

According to the rules of VHDL, all alternatives for the state value are covered by the first three choices in the case statement. However, there are several synthesized encoding values that are not covered, since one-hot encoding is specified. Given the **FSM_COMPLETE** attribute, the synthesis tool includes additional transitions based on the **others** clause, as this would be the alternative selected for an illegal state value.

BUFFERED : string

Decorates: signal

This attribute directs the tool to use a particular library cell to buffer the driver for the decorated signal. The attribute value specifies the name of the library cell to use, for example:

attribute BUFFERED **of** clk : **signal is** "BUFG";

Alternatively, the attribute value can be one of the following special strings:

- "HIGH_DRIVE": use a high-drive buffer from the synthesis library
- "CLOCK_BUF": use a clock buffer from the synthesis library
- "RESET_BUF": use a reset buffer from the synthesis library

INFER_MUX : boolean

Decorates: case statement label, selected assignment statement label
This attribute directs the tool to infer a multiplexer implementation for the statement instead of random logic or ROM implementation.

IMPLEMENTATION : string

Decorates: procedure, function, signal or variable assignment label
This attribute directs the tool to use a specified synthesis library cell to implement calls to a subprogram or an assigment to a signal or variable, rather than inferring hardware from the subprogram body or assignment expression. The attribute value specifies the library cell name. We use this attribute when we have a VHDL implementation that we wish to simulate, but want to synthesize using the library cell. For example:

```
procedure multiplier
            ( signal clk, start : in std_ulogic;
              signal a, b : in unsigned(15 downto 0);
              signal done : out std_ulogic;
              signal p : out unsigned(31 downto 0) is
begin
  ...
end procedure multiplier;

attribute IMPLEMENTATION of multiplier : procedure is
            "MULTSEQ_16X16;
...

multiplier(clk, start, data1, data2, done, product);
```

When we simulate this model, the body of the procedure is called. When we synthesize, the procedure body is ignored, and the MULTSEQ_16X16 library cell is included in the inferred hardware.

RETURN_PORT_NAME : string

Decorates: function

This attribute is used in conjunction with the **IMPLEMENTATION** attribute for a function. The **RETURN_PORT_NAME** attribute value specifies the name of the port on the library cell that corresponds to the return value of the function. For example:

```
function and_or_invert (a, b, c, d : in std_ulogic)
                              return std_ulogic is
begin
  return not ( (a and b) or (c and d) );
end function and_or_invert;

attribute IMPLEMENTATION of and_or_invert : function is
          "AOI";
attribute RETURN_PORT_NAME of and_or_invert : function is
          "O";
...

q <= and_or_invert(w, x, y, z);
```

The **IMPLEMENTATION** attribute specifies that the **AOI** library cell be used for the function. The **RETURN_PORT_NAME** attribute specifies that the **O** port of that cell is the output port.

ENUM_ENCODING : string

Decorates: type, subtype

This attribute directs the tool to use a specified binary encoding for values of the enumeration type or subtype decorated by the attribute. The value of the attribute is a sequence of bit-vector literals, representing the encoding for the enumeration values in the type. For example, given an enumeration type for states in a finite-state machine:

```
type state is (idle, preamble, data, crc, ok, error);
```

we can define the state encoding as follows:

```
attribute enum_encoding of state : type is
          "000 001 010 011 100 111";
```

The bit vectors correspond in order to the enumeration values in the type definition. All of the literals must contain the same number of bits, and underscore characters may be included to enhance readability. Note that we should ensure that the enumeration values are listed in ascending order of their encodings. Otherwise synthesized relational operations may not produce the same results as relational operators evaluated during simulation.

ROM_BLOCK : string

Decorates: constant, variable, signal

This attribute directs the tool to implement the decorated item as a ROM. The attribute value specifies the library cell to use for the ROM. For example:

```
            constant ROM : mem_array := (X"0020", X"FC01",
                                         ...
                                         others => X"0000");

            attribute ROM_BLOCK of ROM : constant is "ROM_SYNCH";
```

RAM_BLOCK : string

> *Decorates*: variable, signal
> This attribute directs the tool to implement the decorated item as a RAM.
> The attribute value specifies the library cell to use for the RAM. For example:

```
            signal RAM : mem_array;

            attribute RAM_BLOCK of RAM : signal is "RAM_PIPELINED";
```

LOGIC_BLOCK : string

> *Decorates*: constant, variable, signal
> This attribute directs the tool to implement the decorated item as a combinational logic block (instead of a ROM) or discrete sequential logic (for example, using flipflops and registers, instead of a RAM).

GATED_CLOCK : boolean

> *Decorates*: signal, process
> This attribute directs the tool to use clock gating rather than separate enable inputs for edge-triggered storage devices. Use of clock gating can reduce power consumption considerably. However, we must ensure that the enable signal used to gate the clock is glitch free and has appropriate timing.
> We can use this attribute to decorate a gated clock signal, in which case all storage devices connected to the clock use clock gating. For example:

```
            attribute GATED_CLOCK of gclk : signal is true;
            ...

            gclk <= clk and enable;

            reg : process (gclk) is
            begin
              if rising_edge(gclk) then
                q <= d;
              end if;
            end process;
```

Alternatively, we can use the attribute to decorate specific processes that are to use clock gating. For example:

```
            attribute GATED_CLOCK of reg : label is true;

            reg : process(clk) is
            begin
              if rising_edge(clk) then
```

```
        if enable = '1' then
            q <= d;
        end if;
    end if;
end process;
```

Without gated clocking, the register inferred for this process would be active on each clock-edge. The internal logic transitions would involve dynamic power consumption. By decorating the process with the attribute, we direct the tool to use clock gating instead of using the **enable** signal to select the input to be stored. The register is only active on those clock-edges where **enable** is '1'.

COMBINATIONAL : boolean

Decorates: process, signal assignment label

This attribute directs the tool to infer purely combinational logic for the decorated item. It is an error if the decorated item represents sequential logic. We can use this attribute to force the synthesis tool to issue an error if we inadvertently imply level sensitive storage by omitting an assignment to an object on some path through a process.

14.8 Metacomments

Normally, comments in a model are not interpreted by a tool. We include comments as documentation for the human reader. However, the synthesis standard defines two *metacomments*, that is, comments that are to be interpreted by a synthesis tool. They are

```
-- rtl_synthesis off
```

and

```
-- rtl_synthesis on
```

The metacomments are not case sensitive; they can be in lowercase, uppercase or a combination of the two. Any VHDL code following an **rtl_synthesis off** metacomment and before a subsequent **rtl_synthesis on** metacomment is ignored by the synthesis tool. It is as though the code were also comments. Thus the model, excluding the ignored parts, must still be a valid VHDL model. Other tools, such as simulators, do not ignore the code. We would normally use the metacomments to exclude from synthesis parts of the model that are only intended for simulation. Examples are processes that check timing or that use file input/output for instrumentation.

EXAMPLE 14.22   *Omitting monitoring code from synthesis*

Suppose we include code in an architecture body to monitor operation of the design during simulation. We can exclude the code from analysis by the synthesis tool by surrounding it in metacomments, as follows:

```
architecture rtl of subsystem is
  ...
begin
  ... -- synthesizable processes and assignments
  -- rtl_synthesis off
  monitor : process is
    use std.textio.all;
    file monitor_file : text open write_mode is "monitor.txt";
    variable L : line;
    ...
  begin
    ...
  end process monitor;
  -- rtl_synthesis on
end architecture rtl;
```

Use of files and file operations is not allowed in synthesizable code, so the synthesis tool would produce errors if it tried to interpret the **monitor** process.

We must take care when excluding part of a model from synthesis to ensure that we don't inadvertently omit part of the model that should be synthesized to hardware. Otherwise we can get a mismatch between simulation results and operation of the synthesized hardware.

Exercises

1. [❶ 14.2] Which of the following types does the IEEE 1076.6 standard allow as the type of a variable?

    ```
    type temp is range -60 to 150;
    type temp_vec is array (natural range <>) of temp;
    type location is (inside, outside, buried);
    type local_temp_vec is array (location) of temp;
    type location_vec is array (natural range <>) of location;
    type word_vec is array (natural range <>) of
            std_ulogic_vector(31 downto 0);
    ```

2. [❶ 14.3] What hardware, if any, would be inferred for the following statement?

    ```
    if sel = '0' or sel = 'L' then
      z <= in0;
    elsif sel = '1' or sel = 'H' then
      z <= in1;
    elsif sel = 'U' then
    ```

```
          z <= 'U';
      else
          z <= 'X';
      end if;
```

3. **[❶ 14.4]** What hardware would be inferred for the following assignment?

    ```
    with fn select
        z <= a + b        when "00",
             a - b        when "01",
             a and b      when "10",
             a and not b when "11";
    ```

4. **[❶ 14.4]** Write a synthesizable process that represents a logic block with tristate outputs. If **enable_n** is '0', an 8-bit output **dat_o** is driven with the value of either **reg1** (if **adr** is '0') or **reg2** (if **adr** is '1'), and a single-bit output **ack_o** is driven with '1'. If **enable_n** is '1', both outputs are 'Z'.

5. **[❶ 14.4/14.5]** Why would a synthesis tool infer storage for the following process?

    ```
    mux_adder : process ( sel, x, y, z, carry_in )
      variable operand : unsigned(15 downto 0);
    begin
      case sel is
        when "00" => operand := x;
        when "01" => operand := y;
        when "10" => operand := z;
        when others =>
          report "Illegal value for sel." severity error;
      end case;
      sum <= operand + carry_in;
    end process mux_adder;
    ```

6. **[❶ 14.5]** Write a process representing an edge-triggered register with no reset but with synchronous enable.

7. **[❶ 14.6]** Write declarations for the storage of an 8K × 16-bit RAM storing values of type **signed**, with all locations initialized to zero.

8. **[❶ 14.6]** Rewrite the 7-segment decoder of Example 14.21 using a constant to represent the ROM storage.

9. **[❶ 14.7]** Write an attribute specification for inclusion in the state machine model of Example 14.16 specifying an encoding of "00" for **ready**, "01" for **ack**, and "11" for **err**.

Chapter 15

Case Study: System Design Using the Gumnut Core

In this case study we develop a synthesizable model of a digital alarm clock using the *Gumnut* 8-bit microcontroller core, described in *Digital Design: An Embedded Systems Approach Using VHDL* [2]. We treat the processor core model as an IP (intellectual property) block that we intantiate in the system as a black box, and synthesize the system into an FPGA target. In order to understand how to include the Gumnut in a design, we describe the external interface and bus protocol. We also describe the instruction set so that we can develop the embedded software for the system.

15.1 Overview of the Gumnut

The Gumnut is an 8-bit processor core intended for educational purposes. (A gumnut is a small seedpod of an Australian eucalyptus tree. It is something small from which large things grow.) The Gumnut is similar to 8-bit microcontrollers for small embedded applications, but has an instruction set architecture more similar to RISC processors. We use it as the subject of this case study to show how we might develop high-level models of complex devices such as a CPU. We start by describing the view of the processor as seen by the machine language programmer and by the hardware designer interfacing the processor with the rest of a computer system.

15.1.1 Instruction Set Architecture

The Gumnut has separate instruction and data memories. The instruction memory stores up to 4,096 instructions (using 12-bit addresses), and the data memory stores 256 bytes (using 8-bit addresses). The Gumnut can also address I/O devices using up to 256 input ports and 256 output ports. Within the core, there are eight general-purpose registers, named r0 through r7, that can hold data to be operated upon by instructions. Register r0 is special, in that it is hardwired to have the value 0, and any updates to it are ignored. The processor also has two single-bit condition-code registers called Z (zero) and C (carry). They are set to 1 or cleared to 0 depending on the result of certain instructions, and can be tested to decide among alternative courses of action in the program.

Table 15.1 lists the complete Gumnut instruction set in assembly-language format. In the table, *rd* and *rs* are registers, *op2* is a register (*rs2*) or an immediate value (*immed*), *count* is count of number of places to shift or rotate, *disp* is a displacement from the next-instruction address, and *addr* is a jump target address.

TABLE 15.1   *The Gumnut instruction set*

Arithmetic and logical instructions	
add *rd, rs, op2*	Add *rs* and *op2*, result in *rd*
addc *rd, rs, op2*	Add *rs* and *op2* with carry, result in *rd*
sub *rd, rs, op2*	Subtract *op2* from *rs*, result in *rd*
subc *rd, rs, op2*	Subtract *op2* from *rs* with carry, result in *rd*
and *rd, rs, op2*	Logical AND of *rs* and *op2*, result in *rd*
or *rd, rs, op2*	Logical OR of *rs* and *op2*, result in *rd*
xor *rd, rs, op2*	Logical XOR of *rs* and *op2*, result in *rd*
mask *rd, rs, op2*	Logical AND of *rs* and NOT *op2*, result in *rd*
Shift instructions	
shl *rd, rs, count*	Shift *rs* value left *count* places, result in *rd*
shr *rd, rs, count*	Shift *rs* value right *count* places, result in *rd*
rol *rd, rs, count*	Rotate *rs* value left *count* places, result in *rd*
ror *rd, rs, count*	Rotate *rs* value right *count* places, result in *rd*
Memory and I/O instructions	
ldm *rd, (rs)±offset*	Load to *rd* from memory
stm *rd, (rs)±offset*	Store to memory from *rd*
inp *rd, (rs)±offset*	Input to *rd* from input controller register
out *rd, (rs)±offset*	Output to output controller register from *rd*
Branch instructions	
bz ±*disp*	Branch if Z is set
bnz ±*disp*	Branch is Z is not set
bc ±*disp*	Branch if C is set
bnc ±*disp*	Branch if C is not set

Jump instructions	
jmp *addr*	Jump to *addr*
jsb *addr*	Jump to subroutine at *addr*
Miscellaneous instructions	
ret	Return from subroutine
reti	Return from interrupt
enai	Enable interrupts
disi	Disable interrupts
wait	Wait for interrupts
stby	Enter low-power standby mode

The arithmetic and logical instructions operate on 8-bit data values stored in the core's general-purpose registers and store the result in the destination register, *rd*. For each instruction, one value is taken from a source register, *rs*. The other value, *op2*, either comes from a second source register (*rs2*) or is an immediate value (*immed*) specified as part of the instruction.

The addition and subtraction instructions treat the data values as 8-bit unsigned integers. The **addc** instruction includes the value of the C condition code as a carry-in bit, and the **subc** instruction includes the C value as a borrow-in bit. All of the instructions in this group modify the Z and the C bits. They set Z to 1 if the instruction result is 0, and they clear Z to 0 if the result is non-zero. The **add** and **addc** instructions set C to the carry-out bit of the addition, the **sub** and **subc** instruction set C to the borrow out of the subtraction, and the remaining logical instructions clear C to 0.

The shift instructions shift or rotate 8-bit values taken from the general purpose register *rs* and store the result in register *rd*. The number of places to shift or rotate is specified in the instruction as *count*. The shift-left and shift-right instructions discard the bits shifted past the end of the 8-bit byte and fill the vacated bit positions with 0s. The rotate-left and rotate-right instructions copy the bits shifted past the end of the byte around to the other end. All of these instructions set Z to 1 if the instruction result is 0, and they clear Z to 0 if the result is non-zero. They set the C bit to the value of the last bit shifted past the end of the byte.

The Gumnut has separate instructions and separate 8-bit address spaces for accessing data memory and I/O controllers. For all of the Gumnut's memory and I/O instructions, the address to access is computed by adding the current value in *rs* and an *offset* value specified in the instruction. The load from memory instruction reads from the data memory at the computed address and puts the read value in register *rd*. The store to memory writes the value from register *rd* to the data memory at the computed address. The input and output instructions perform similar operations, but read or write to the I/O controller registers at the computed address. None of these instructions affect the values of the Z and C bits.

If we want to specify a particular address to access, we can use r0 as the register for *rs*. Recall that r0 always contains 0, so adding it to the offset value specified in the instruction just gives the offset value. In this case, we usually interpret the offset value as an unsigned 8-bit address. Our assembler tool allows us to imply the specification "(r0)" by omission and just write the address value, for example,

```
inp r3, 156
```

which reads from the I/O controller register at address 156 into r3. Similarly, if a register contains the address we want to access, we can use an offset of 0. Again, our assembler allows us to imply a 0 offset by omission, as in the instruction

```
out r3, (r7)
```

The branch instructions modify the sequential flow of execution by changing value of the program counter (PC) in the Gumnut core. Each form of branch tests a condition, and if the condition is true, adds a signed 8-bit displacement value to the PC. The displacement, specified in the instruction, indicates how many locations forward or backward the next instruction to execute is from the current instruction. (A displacement of 0 refers to the instruction after the branch, since the PC has already been incremented after fetching the branch instruction.) If the condition is false, the PC is unchanged, and execution continues sequentially. The different branch instructions allow us to test each of the Z and C condition code bits for being set to 1 or not set to 1. Since these bits are affected by arithmetic, logical and shift instructions, we often deliberately precede a branch instruction with one of these instructions to compare data values. In other cases, the condition code setting occurs as a serendipitous side effect of data operations that we need to perform anyway. Execution of a branch instruction does not affect the values of the Z and C bits.

The first of the jump instructions, **jmp**, unconditionally breaks the sequential flow of execution by setting the PC to the address specified in the instruction. The second of the jump instructions, **jsb**, allows us to call a subroutine. It is used in tandem with the **ret** instruction, which returns from the subroutine to the place of the call. The **jsb** instruction pushes the incremented PC value (the return address) onto an internal stack and then updates the PC with the subroutine address specified in the instruction. The **ret** instruction pops the saved return address from the stack to the PC. The return-address stack can hold up to eight entries. The **jmp** and **jsb** instructions do not affect the values of the Z and C bits.

The remaining miscellaneous instructions deal with interrupts. The enable-interrupt (**enai**) instruction allows the processor to respond to interrupt events, and the disable-interrupt (**disi**) instruction prevents the processor from responding. When the processor responds to an interrupt event, it saves the incremented PC value and the values of the Z and C condition codes in special registers, disables further interrupts, and then transfers control to the interrupt handler at address 1. The interrupt handler finishes with a return-from-interrupt (**reti**) instruction rather than an **ret** instruction. The **reti** instruction restores the saved PC and condition code values and re-enables interrupts. The **wait** instruction suspends execution until an interrupt occurs, and the **stby** instruction enters a low-power standby mode until an interrupt occurs. The difference is that the CPU would normally be able to respond to an interrupt immediately when suspended using a **wait** instruction, whereas it could take some time to power up from a **stby** instruction. The instructions in this group, apart from the **reti** instruction, do not affect the values of the Z and C bits.

Instructions in the Gumnut are all 18 bits long, and are encoded in several formats, shown in Figure 15.1. The leftmost bits, together with the function code (*fn*), form the opcode. The encoding used for function codes is shown in Table 15.2. Those instructions that specify register numbers have the numbers encoded in 3-bit binary form in the *rd*, *rs*, and *rs2* fields of the instruction word. Similarly, instructions that specify immediate values, offsets, or displacements have those values binary encoded in the rightmost 8 bits of the instruction word. The shaded parts of the instruction word in each format represent bits that are ignored.

FIGURE 15.1

Gumnut instruction formats.

TABLE 15.2   *Function code values*

add	000	addc	001	sub	010	subc	011
and	100	or	101	xor	110	mask	111
shl	00	shr	01	rol	10	ror	11
ldm	00	stm	01	inp	10	out	11
bz	00	bnz	01	bc	10	bnc	11
jmp	0	jsb	1				
ret	000	reti	001	enai	010	disi	011
wait	100	stby	101				

15.1.2 External Interface

The Gumnut interfaces to the rest of the system in which it is embedded via a number of external signals. These are shown in Figure 15.2. Each of the instruction memory, data memory, and I/O ports connect to the core using a simplified version of the Wishbone bus, an open bus specification published by the OpenCores Organization [5]. The **clk_i** signal is the master clock for the Gumnut. All other signals are sampled or set synchronously with the clock. The **rst_i** signal re-initializes the Gumnut to its reset state. When **rst_i** is negated, the Gumnut commences instruction execution, starting from address 0 in the instruction memory.

The **int_req** signal is used to request an interrupt of the Gumnut. When this signal is active and the Gumnut interrupts are enabled, the Gumnut will save state and transfer to the interrupt service code. It asserts the **int_ack** signal for one cycle to indicate start of interrupt service. The I/O port controller must negate **int_req** before the service code returns and re-enables interrupts; otherwise a second spurious interrupt will be received. Usually, an I/O port controller would negate the interrupt request in response to **int_ack** or to the Gumnut reading or writing an I/O port register.

We will describe the bus timing for read and write operations on the data memory bus. The timing for reads and writes on the port bus and for reads on the instruction memory bus is identical. The timing of read operations is shown in Figure 15.3. The Gumnut starts a read operation by driving the **data_adr_o** signals with the address and setting **data_cyc_o** and **data_stb_o** to 1. It also sets **data_we_o** to 0 to indicate that the operation is a read. The memory decodes the address to access the data and drives the data onto the **data_dat_i** signal. If the memory is able to provide the data within the first clock cycle, it sets the **data_ack_i** signal to 1 in that cycle, as shown in Figure 15.3(a). On the next rising clock-edge, the Gumnut sees **data_ack_i** at 1 and completes the operation by setting **data_cyc_o**, **data_stb_o** and **data_we_o** all to 0. If, on the other hand, the memory is slow and is not able to provide the data within the cycle, it leaves **data_ack_i** at 0, as shown in

FIGURE 15.2
_____

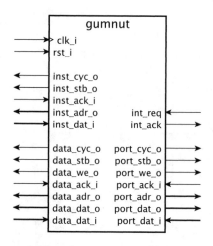

Gumnut core external interface.

FIGURE 15.3

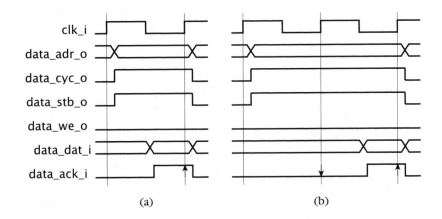

Gumnut data memory read operation: without wait cycles (a), and with one wait cycle (b).

Figure 15.3(b). The Gumnut sees **data_ack_i** at 0 on the rising clock-edge, and extends the operation for a further cycle. The memory can keep **data_ack_i** at 0 for as long as it needs to access the data. Eventually, when it is ready, it drives **data_ack_i** to 1 to complete the operation.

The timing of write operations is similar, shown in Figure 15.4. Again, the Gumnut starts a write operation by driving the **data_adr_o** signal with the address and setting **data_cyc_o** and **data_stb_o** to 1. It sets **data_we_o** to 1 to indicate that the operation is a write and drives the data to be written into the **data_dat_o** signal. The memory decodes the address and updates the selected location with the data. If the memory is able to complete the write within the first clock cycle, it sets the **data_ack_i** signal to 1 in that cycle, as shown in Figure 15.4(a), and the handshake completes as for the read operation. Oth-

FIGURE 15.4

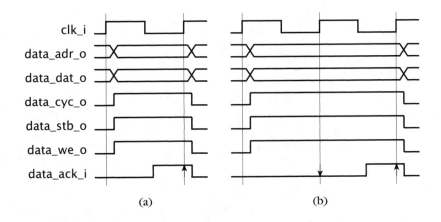

Gumnut data memory write operation: without wait cycles (a), and with one wait cycle (b).

erwise, if the memory is slow, it leaves **data_ack_i** at 0, as shown in Figure 15.4(b), and the operation is extended, as for a read operation.

At first sight, it might appear that the **data_cyc_o** and **data_stb_o** signals are duplicates of each other. However, the Wishbone bus specification defines other more involved operations in which the two control signals serve distinct purposes. While the Gumnut does not use those operations, it includes the signals in order to maintain compatibility with the Wishbone specification. The additional signal is a small cost to pay for compatibility with a large pool of third-party components.

The Gumnut Entity Declaration

We can now write the entity declaration for the Gumnut core, as shown below. The generic constant **debug** controls whether the model writes debugging messages to the standard output stream. The ports of the entity correspond to those shown in Figure 15.2.

```
library ieee;
use ieee.std_logic_1164.all, ieee.numeric_std.all;

entity gumnut is
  generic ( debug : boolean := false );
  port ( clk_i : in std_ulogic;
         rst_i : in std_ulogic;
         -- Instruction memory bus
         inst_cyc_o : out std_ulogic;
         inst_stb_o : out std_ulogic;
         inst_ack_i : in std_ulogic;
         inst_adr_o : out unsigned(11 downto 0);
         inst_dat_i : in std_ulogic_vector(17 downto 0);
         -- Data memory bus
         data_cyc_o : out std_ulogic;
         data_stb_o : out std_ulogic;
         data_we_o : out std_ulogic;
         data_ack_i : in std_ulogic;
         data_adr_o : out unsigned(7 downto 0);
         data_dat_o : out std_ulogic_vector(7 downto 0);
         data_dat_i : in std_ulogic_vector(7 downto 0);
         -- I/O port bus
         port_cyc_o : out std_ulogic;
         port_stb_o : out std_ulogic;
         port_we_o : out std_ulogic;
         port_ack_i : in std_ulogic;
         port_adr_o : out unsigned(7 downto 0);
         port_dat_o : out std_ulogic_vector(7 downto 0);
         port_dat_i : in std_ulogic_vector(7 downto 0);
         -- Interrupts
         int_req : in std_ulogic;
```

```
                  int_ack : out std_ulogic );
    end entity gumnut;
```

Instruction and Data Memories

In systems that use the Gumnut core, we need to provide instruction and data memories. We can provide them as further IP blocks to be instantiated in designs. The entity declaration for the instruction memory is

```
library ieee;
use ieee.std_logic_1164.all, ieee.numeric_std.all;

entity inst_mem is
  generic ( IMem_file_name : string := "gasm_text.dat" );
  port ( clk_i : in std_ulogic;
         cyc_i : in std_ulogic;
         stb_i : in std_ulogic;
         ack_o : out std_ulogic;
         adr_i : in unsigned(11 downto 0);
         dat_o : out std_ulogic_vector(17 downto 0) );
end entity inst_mem;
```

The generic constant IMem_file_name specifies the name of a file from which program is loaded. The default file name used by gasm is **gasm_text.dat**, so we use the same default name for the generic constant. The ports of the entity mirror those of the Gumnut entity.

The entity declaration for the data memory is similar:

```
library ieee;
use ieee.std_logic_1164.all, ieee.numeric_std.all;

entity data_mem is
  generic ( DMem_file_name : string := "gasm_data.dat" );
  port ( clk_i : in std_ulogic;
         cyc_i : in std_ulogic;
         stb_i : in std_ulogic;
         we_i : in std_ulogic;
         ack_o : out std_ulogic;
         adr_i : in unsigned(7 downto 0);
         dat_i : in std_ulogic_vector(7 downto 0);
         dat_o : out std_ulogic_vector(7 downto 0) );
end entity data_mem;
```

Again, the entity has a generic for specifying the file name for the initial memory contents, and ports that mirror those of the Gumnut entity. We don't show the architecture bodies for the memories here, in the interest of brevity. They are available on the companion website for the book.

Next, we provide a subsystem model that includes an instance of the core and each of the memories. This subsystem can then be instantiated in a larger design and connected to the required I/O controllers. The subsystem entity declaration is

```vhdl
library ieee;
use ieee.std_logic_1164.all, ieee.numeric_std.all;

entity gumnut_with_mem is
  generic ( IMem_file_name : string := "gasm_text.dat";
            DMem_file_name : string := "gasm_data.dat";
            debug : boolean := false );
  port ( clk_i : in std_ulogic;
         rst_i : in std_ulogic;
         -- I/O port bus
         port_cyc_o : out std_ulogic;
         port_stb_o : out std_ulogic;
         port_we_o : out std_ulogic;
         port_ack_i : in std_ulogic;
         port_adr_o : out unsigned(7 downto 0);
         port_dat_o : out std_ulogic_vector(7 downto 0);
         port_dat_i : in std_ulogic_vector(7 downto 0);
         -- Interrupts
         int_req : in std_ulogic;
         int_ack : out std_ulogic );
end entity gumnut_with_mem;
```

The structural architecture body is shown below. It uses component declarations for the Gumnut core and the memories, allowing alternative architecture bodies to be bound using a separate configuration declaration.

```vhdl
library ieee;
use ieee.std_logic_1164.all, ieee.numeric_std.all;

architecture struct of gumnut_with_mem is

  -- Instruction memory bus
  signal inst_cyc_o : std_ulogic;
  signal inst_stb_o : std_ulogic;
  signal inst_ack_i : std_ulogic;
  signal inst_adr_o : unsigned(11 downto 0);
  signal inst_dat_i : std_ulogic_vector(17 downto 0);
  -- Data memory bus
  signal data_cyc_o : std_ulogic;
  signal data_stb_o : std_ulogic;
  signal data_we_o : std_ulogic;
  signal data_ack_i : std_ulogic;
  signal data_adr_o : unsigned(7 downto 0);
  signal data_dat_o : std_ulogic_vector(7 downto 0);
  signal data_dat_i : std_ulogic_vector(7 downto 0);
```

```vhdl
component gumnut is
  generic ( debug : boolean );
  port ( clk_i : in std_ulogic;
         rst_i : in std_ulogic;
         -- Instruction memory bus
         inst_cyc_o : out std_ulogic;
         inst_stb_o : out std_ulogic;
         inst_ack_i : in std_ulogic;
         inst_adr_o : out unsigned(11 downto 0);
         inst_dat_i : in std_ulogic_vector(17 downto 0);
         -- Data memory bus
         data_cyc_o : out std_ulogic;
         data_stb_o : out std_ulogic;
         data_we_o : out std_ulogic;
         data_ack_i : in std_ulogic;
         data_adr_o : out unsigned(7 downto 0);
         data_dat_o : out std_ulogic_vector(7 downto 0);
         data_dat_i : in std_ulogic_vector(7 downto 0);
         -- I/O port bus
         port_cyc_o : out std_ulogic;
         port_stb_o : out std_ulogic;
         port_we_o : out std_ulogic;
         port_ack_i : in std_ulogic;
         port_adr_o : out unsigned(7 downto 0);
         port_dat_o : out std_ulogic_vector(7 downto 0);
         port_dat_i : in std_ulogic_vector(7 downto 0);
         -- Interrupts
         int_req : in std_ulogic;
         int_ack : out std_ulogic );
end component gumnut;

component inst_mem is
  generic ( IMem_file_name : string );
  port ( clk_i : in std_ulogic;
         cyc_i : in std_ulogic;
         stb_i : in std_ulogic;
         ack_o : out std_ulogic;
         adr_i : in unsigned(11 downto 0);
         dat_o : out std_ulogic_vector(17 downto 0) );
end component inst_mem;

component data_mem is
  generic ( DMem_file_name : string );
  port ( clk_i : in std_ulogic;
         cyc_i : in std_ulogic;
         stb_i : in std_ulogic;
         we_i : in std_ulogic;
         ack_o : out std_ulogic;
```

```vhdl
          adr_i : in unsigned(7 downto 0);
          dat_i : in std_ulogic_vector(7 downto 0);
          dat_o : out std_ulogic_vector(7 downto 0) );
  end component data_mem;

begin

  core : component gumnut
    generic map ( debug => debug )
    port map ( clk_i      => clk_i,
               rst_i      => rst_i,
               inst_cyc_o => inst_cyc_o,
               inst_stb_o => inst_stb_o,
               inst_ack_i => inst_ack_i,
               inst_adr_o => inst_adr_o,
               inst_dat_i => inst_dat_i,
               data_cyc_o => data_cyc_o,
               data_stb_o => data_stb_o,
               data_we_o  => data_we_o,
               data_ack_i => data_ack_i,
               data_adr_o => data_adr_o,
               data_dat_o => data_dat_o,
               data_dat_i => data_dat_i,
               port_cyc_o => port_cyc_o,
               port_stb_o => port_stb_o,
               port_we_o  => port_we_o,
               port_ack_i => port_ack_i,
               port_adr_o => port_adr_o,
               port_dat_o => port_dat_o,
               port_dat_i => port_dat_i,
               int_req    => int_req,
               int_ack    => int_ack );

  core_inst_mem : component inst_mem
    generic map ( IMem_file_name => IMem_file_name )
    port map ( clk_i => clk_i,
               cyc_i => inst_cyc_o,
               stb_i => inst_stb_o,
               ack_o => inst_ack_i,
               adr_i => inst_adr_o,
               dat_o => inst_dat_i );

  core_data_mem : component data_mem
    generic map ( DMem_file_name => DMem_file_name )
    port map ( clk_i => clk_i,
               cyc_i => data_cyc_o,
               stb_i => data_stb_o,
               we_i  => data_we_o,
               ack_o => data_ack_i,
```

```
                        adr_i => data_adr_o,
                        dat_i => data_dat_o,
                        dat_o => data_dat_i );

    end architecture struct;
```

15.2 A Digital Alarm Clock

In this section we design a digital alarm clock based on the Gumnut as an illustration of a design flow for a complete embedded processor system. We will focus on the hardware design aspects using VHDL, and refer to details of the embedded software design on the companion website. We start with a statement of functional requirements.

Our alarm clock shall have four 7-segment LED digits for displaying the clock time and the alarm time in 24-hour format. The clock shall have four push-button switches:

- Alarm set: When this button is held on, the alarm time can be advanced.

- Time set: When this button is held on, the clock time can be advance.

- Hours advance: When this button is pressed once, the hours of the alarm time or clock time are advanced by one. Whe the button is pressed and held, the hours of the alarm time or clock time are advanced at a a rate of four per second.

- Minutes advance: This button is similar to the hours advance button, but advances the minutes of the alarm time or clock time instead of the hours.

When both the hours advance and minutes advance buttons are pressed while the alarm set or time set button is held on, the alarm time or clock time, respectively, is reset to midnight. When neither the alarm set nor the time set button is held on, the hours advance and minutes advance buttons have no effect.

The clock shall have a two-position switch that enables or disables the alarm, and a LED indicator that shows whether the alarm is enabled. The clock shall also have an output that activates a sounder when the alarm is triggered. (The output could also activate an alternate device, such as a radio or CD player.) The alarm is triggered when the clock time equals the alarm time, provided that the alarm is enabled and neither the clock time nor the alarm time is being set.

These requirements may appear to be quite precise and complete, but as we will see as we proceed through the design, there are some details that are unspecified. We will need to make assumptions based on our common sense and understanding of what a digital alarm clock should do. This is not unusual in system design.

15.2.1 System Design

For the purpose of this case study, we will describe an implementation of the digital alarm clock using an FPGA development board. The author used a Xilinx Spartan-3 starter board with four 7-segment displays, four push buttons, eight 2-position slider switches and eight discrete LEDs. One of the slider switches serves as the alarm enable switch, and one discrete LED serves for the alarm enable indicator. Another discrete LED serves in place of the alarm sounder output.

We start our system design by considering the hardware/software trade-off. We could implement the design entirely in hardware. However, that may not be the most effective, since the clock would need numerous counters, multiplexers and comparators. Since an FPGA includes block memories that can be used for program and data storage, we may be able to fit an implementation based on an embedded processor into a smaller FPGA than would be needed for a hardware implementation. Moreover, developing and maintaining software can be simpler than hardware, so there may be non-technical benefits to an embedded processor implementation. For this case study, we will focus on an implementation that uses an embedded Gumnut core for nearly all of the functionality, and leave comparison with a hardware implementation to an exercise.

Figure 15.5 shows a block diagram of the alarm clock system. It includes

- The Gumnut core, driven by an externally generated 50MHz clock.

- An input port for the push buttons (pb(3 **downto** 0)).

- An input button for the slider switches (sw(7 **downto** 0)).

- A registered output port for the digit anode drivers (digit(3 **downto** 0)).

- A register output port for the digit segment drivers (seg(7 **downto** 0)). Seg(0) is segment *a*, seg(1) is segment *b*, etc., and seg(7) is the decimal point.

- A registered output port for the discrete LEDs (led(7 **downto** 0)).

- An output port for a programmable timer for generating periodic interrupts. The timer is driven by a 1 MHz clock divided down from the external clock and has a register to store the divisor written by the processor. The timer repeatedly counts down from the divisor value and generates an interrupt upon reaching 0.

FIGURE 15.5

A block diagram of the digital alarm clock using an embedded Gumnut core.

An entity declaration for the alarm clock is shown below. It includes a debug generic constant for use in simulation and ports corresponding to the external connection shown in the block diagram.

```vhdl
library ieee;
use ieee.std_logic_1164.all;

entity alarm_clock is
  generic ( debug : boolean := false );
  port ( clk : in std_ulogic;
         pb : in std_ulogic_vector(3 downto 0);
         sw : in std_ulogic_vector(7 downto 0);
         led : out std_ulogic_vector(7 downto 0);
         digit : out std_ulogic_vector(3 downto 0);
         seg : out std_ulogic_vector(7 downto 0) );
end entity alarm_clock ;
```

The synthesizable architecture body for the alarm clock is based on the block diagram:

```vhdl
library ieee; use ieee.numeric_std.all;

architecture synth of alarm_clock is

  component gumnut_with_mem is
    generic ( debug : boolean := false );
    port ( clk_i : in std_ulogic;
           rst_i : in std_ulogic;
           port_cyc_o : out std_ulogic;
           port_stb_o : out std_ulogic;
           port_we_o : out std_ulogic;
           port_ack_i : in std_ulogic;
           port_adr_o : out unsigned(7 downto 0);
           port_dat_o : out std_ulogic_vector(7 downto 0);
           port_dat_i : in std_ulogic_vector(7 downto 0);
           int_req : in std_ulogic;
           int_ack : out std_ulogic );
  end component gumnut_with_mem;

  signal reset : std_ulogic;

  signal port_cyc_o : std_ulogic;
  signal port_stb_o : std_ulogic;
  signal port_we_o : std_ulogic;
  signal port_ack_i : std_ulogic;
  signal port_adr_o : unsigned(7 downto 0);
  signal port_dat_o : std_ulogic_vector(7 downto 0);
  signal port_dat_i : std_ulogic_vector(7 downto 0);
  signal int_req : std_ulogic;
  signal int_ack : std_ulogic;
```

```vhdl
  signal pb_synch : std_ulogic_vector(pb'range);
  signal sw_synch : std_ulogic_vector(sw'range);
  signal clk_1MHz : std_ulogic;
begin

  -- reset generation

  reset_gen : reset <= '0';

  -- processor core

  core : gumnut_with_mem
    generic map ( debug => debug )
    port map ( clk_i => clk,
               rst_i => reset,
               port_cyc_o => port_cyc_o,
               port_stb_o => port_stb_o,
               port_we_o => port_we_o,
               port_ack_i => port_ack_i,
               port_adr_o => port_adr_o,
               port_dat_o => port_dat_o,
               port_dat_i => port_dat_i,
               int_req => int_req,
               int_ack => int_ack );

  port_ack_i <= '1';

  -- input port:
  --    push buttons 1 and 0 when port_addr = "-------0"
  --    switches when port_addr = "-------1"

  synch : process ( clk )
    variable pb_tmp : std_ulogic_vector(pb'range);
    variable sw_tmp : std_ulogic_vector(sw'range);
  begin
    if rising_edge(clk) then
      pb_synch <= pb_tmp;
      sw_synch <= sw_tmp;
      pb_tmp := pb;
      sw_tmp := sw;
    end if;
  end process synch;

  with port_adr_o(0) select
    port_dat_i <= "0000" & pb_synch when '0',
                  sw_synch when '1',
                  "XXXXXXXX" when others;

  -- digit output port register (port_addr = "-------1")
```

```vhdl
digit_reg : process (clk)
begin
  if rising_edge(clk) then
    if reset = '1' then
      digit <= "1111";
    elsif port_cyc_o = '1' and port_stb_o = '1'
          and port_we_o = '1' and port_adr_o(0) = '1' then
      digit <= not port_dat_o(3 downto 0);
    end if;
  end if;
end process digit_reg;

-- segment output port register (port_addr = "------1-")

seg_reg : process (clk)
begin
  if rising_edge(clk) then
    if reset = '1' then
      seg <= "11111111";
    elsif port_cyc_o = '1' and port_stb_o = '1'
          and port_we_o = '1' and port_adr_o(1) = '1' then
      seg <= not port_dat_o;
    end if;
  end if;
end process seg_reg;

-- led output port register (port_addr = "-----1--")

led_reg : process (clk, reset)
begin
  if rising_edge(clk) then
    if reset = '1' then
      led <= "00000000";
    elsif port_cyc_o = '1' and port_stb_o = '1'
          and port_we_o = '1' and port_adr_o(2) = '1' then
      led <= port_dat_o;
    end if;
  end if;
end process led_reg;

-- divide 50MHz clock down to 1MHz

div_50 : process (clk)
  variable count : integer range 0 to 49;
begin
  if rising_edge(clk) then
    if reset = '1' then
      clk_1MHz <= '0';
      count := 49;
    elsif count = 0 then
```

```
              count := 49;
              clk_1Mhz <= '1';
          else
              count := count - 1;
              clk_1Mhz <= '0';
          end if;
        end if;
    end process div_50;

    -- timer (port_addr = "----1---")
    timer : process (clk)
      variable divisor, count : unsigned(7 downto 0);
    begin
      if rising_edge(clk) then
        if reset = '1' then
          divisor := X"00";
          count   := X"00";
          int_req <= '0';
        elsif port_cyc_o = '1' and port_stb_o = '1'
              and port_we_o = '1' and port_adr_o(3) = '1' then
          divisor := unsigned(port_dat_o);
          count := divisor;
        elsif clk_1MHz = '1' then
          if count = 0 then
            int_req <= '1';
            count := divisor;
          else
            count := count - 1;
          end if;
        end if;
        if int_ack = '1' then
          int_req <= '0';
        end if;
      end if;
    end process timer;

  end architecture synth;
```

The architecture includes a component declaration for the Gumnut core with instruction and data memories, described in Section 15.1.2, and an instance of the component. We will rely on the default binding rules to bind the Gumnut entity and architecture to the instance, rather than using a configuration, since not all synthesis tools support use of configurations. The **reset** input to the core is tied to '0', since we don't need an external reset in this design. The **port_ack_i** input is tied high, since all input/output ports transfer data in a single cycle.

The input ports are represented by the process **synch** and the combinational assignment statement. The process synchronizes the push button and switch inputs with the system clock to avoid problems with metastability that might arise from input changes close to a clock-edge. The combinational assignment simply selects between the synchronized push button and switch inputs, based on the port address bus from the Gumnut. The registered output ports for the digit, segment and LED drivers are represented by the processes digit_reg, seg_reg and led_reg, respectively. The digit and segment registers both invert the data, since the circuits on the development board illuminate the display when the driver outputs are low. The circuits for the discrete LEDs, on the other hand, illuminate the LEDs when the driver outputs are high, so the LED register does not not invert the data.

The div_50 process represents the clock divider. It generates a one-cycle pulse on clk_1MHz whenever the count variable reaches 0. The timer process represents the programmable timer. It has variables for the divisor written by the processor and for the down counter. When the clk_1MHz signal is pulsed, the timer decrements the counter. Upon reaching 0, the int_req signal is activated and the counter reloaded with the divisor. When the int_ack signal is activated, the int_req signal is cleared.

While the alarm clock entity and architecture body describe the main hardware required for the system, they do not deal with the specific electrical interface for the FPGA pins. We describe that information in a top-level entity and architecture, as follows:

```vhdl
library ieee;
use ieee.std_logic_1164.all;

entity alarm_clock_top is
  generic ( debug : boolean := false );
  port ( clk50in : in std_ulogic;
         pb_in : in std_ulogic_vector(3 downto 0);
         sw_in : in std_ulogic_vector(7 downto 0);
         led_out : out std_ulogic_vector(7 downto 0);
         digit_out : out std_ulogic_vector(3 downto 0);
         seg_out : out std_ulogic_vector(7 downto 0) );
end entity alarm_clock_top ;

-- ------------------------------------------------------------------

library unisim;
use unisim.vcomponents.all ;

architecture struct of alarm_clock_top is

  signal clkint : std_ulogic;
  signal clk : std_ulogic;

  signal pb : std_ulogic_vector(pb_in'range);
  signal sw : std_ulogic_vector(sw_in'range);
  signal led : std_ulogic_vector(led_out'range);
  signal digit : std_ulogic_vector(digit_out'range);
  signal seg : std_ulogic_vector(seg_out'range);

  component alarm_clock is
    generic ( debug : boolean := false );
    port ( clk : in std_ulogic;
```

```vhdl
        pb : in std_ulogic_vector(3 downto 0);
        sw : in std_ulogic_vector(7 downto 0);
        led : out std_ulogic_vector(7 downto 0);
        digit : out std_ulogic_vector(3 downto 0);
        seg : out std_ulogic_vector(7 downto 0) );
  end component alarm_clock ;

begin

  -- input/output and clock buffers

  clkin_ibuf : component ibufg_lvcmos33
    port map ( i => clk50in, o => clkint );

  clk_bufg : component bufg
    port map ( i => clkint, o => clk ) ;

  pb_buf_gen : for i in 0 to 3 generate
    pb_buf : component ibuf_lvcmos33
      port map ( i => pb_in(i), o => pb(i) );
  end generate pb_buf_gen;

  sw_buf_gen : for i in 0 to 7 generate
    sw_buf : component ibuf_lvcmos33
      port map ( i => sw_in(i), o => sw(i) );
  end generate sw_buf_gen;

  led_buf_gen : for i in 0 to 7 generate
    led_buf : component obuf_lvcmos33
      port map ( i => led(i),   o => led_out(i) );
  end generate led_buf_gen;

  digit_buf_gen : for i in 0 to 3 generate
    digit_buf : component obuf_lvcmos33
      port map ( i => digit(i), o => digit_out(i) );
  end generate digit_buf_gen;

  seg_buf_gen : for i in 0 to 7 generate
    seg_buf : component obuf_lvcmos33
      port map ( i => seg(i),   o => seg_out(i) );
  end generate seg_buf_gen;

  -- the alarm clock core

  alarm_clock_core : alarm_clock
    generic map ( debug => debug )
    port map ( clk => clk, pb => pb, sw => sw,
               led => led, digit => digit, seg => seg );

end architecture struct;
```

The entity is much the same as that described earlier. The architecture declares a component for the alarm clock internal hardware and instantiates it. The main purpose of the architecture, however, is to instantiate pin buffers connected between the internal hardware signals and the FPGA pins. The component declarations for the buffers are drawn from the package **vcomponents** in library **unisim**, supplied by the FPGA vendor. The pins are programmed to use 3.3V low-voltage CMOS electrical levels, specified using the **ibuf_lvcmos33** input buffer components and the **obuf_lvcmos33** components. The buffered clock signal, **clkint**, is further buffered using a **bufg** component, which drives a global clock tree on the FPGA. These buffer components are all recognized by the FPGA vendor's synthesis and mapping tools. Documentation on use of the buffers and sample models illustrating their use are provided by the vendor.

The hardware we have described so far simply provides an interface to the alarm clock's "user interface." Most of the functionality of the alarm clock is implemented by the embedded software that runs on the Gumnut core. Since we are focusing on the hardware using VHDL in this book, we do not describe the software here. The complete design suite, including the software source code, documentation and tools, is available on the companion website.

15.2.2 Synthesizing and Implementing the Alarm Clock

Now that we have a synthesizable description of the alarm clock, we outline the steps needed to implement it in our FPGA development board. We make use of a number of tools provided by the FPGA vendor, and an assembler for the Gumnut. The basic tool flow is illustrated in Figure 15.6. The inputs to the tool flow are the assembler source code for the emedded software, the VHDL source files, and a constraints file created using a constraints editor program. The constraints include a requirement that the clock frequency be 50 MHz. They also include placement of input and output pins based on the physical connections of FPGA pins to circuits on the development board. These connections are described in the documentation for the development board.

Implementation commences with assembly of the software code. The Gumnut assembler produces two memory data files, one for the program memory image and one for the data memory image. Next, the VHDL files are used by the synthesis tool to generate a low-level representation of the system. The representation also makes use of specialized hardware resources provided by the target FPGA, such as block memories and carry-chains. The mapping tool allocates each of the elements in the low-level representation to specific hardware resources in the target FPGA. The place and route tool then decides which logic blocks, memories and routing connections in the FPGA are used for the hardware resources. This tool makes use of the constraints to ensure that the inputs and outputs are properly connected and that delays do not exceed the maximum specified. The output of the place and route tool is a database (the .ncd file) containing detailed information about how the design is implemented in the FPGA.

Two tools use the database to generate further information. The static timing analysis tool uses a timing model of the internal paths of the FPGA to determine the delays in the placed and routed design. It predicts that the mimimum clock period for correct operation is 16.989 ns, corresponding to a maximum clock frequency of 58.862 MHz. This is well within the specified clock constraint, so no tuning of the implementation is needed. Were the constraint violated, we could use the tools to identify critical paths and add constraints to guide the tools toward a faster implementation. Alternatively, we could modify the

FIGURE 15.6

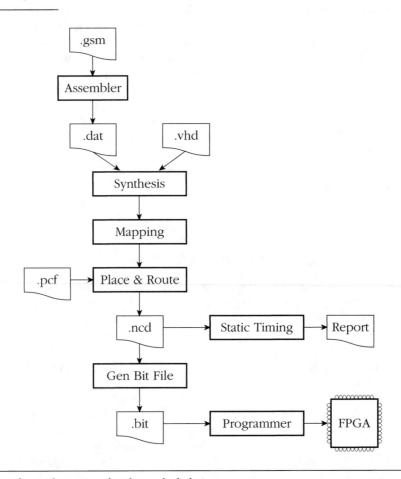

Tool flow for implementing the alarm clock design.

VHDL code to avoid implying hardware with long delays. For example, we could reduce the complexity of combinational logic that processes data between clock-edges.

The second tool that uses the database is the bit-file generator. It creates a file containing information needed to program the target FPGA. In a manufactured design, the bit file would be stored in a flash memory and used to configure the FPGA upon power-up. For our development board, the programmer tool uses a JTAG interface to configure the FPGA from the bit file. Once the FPGA is configured, it commences operation, with the Gumnut executing the embedded software. The development board becomes a digital alarm clock.

Of course, it is unrealistic to expect to write the VHDL code and embedded software, implement it and have it work correctly first time. For that reason, the flow described above is idealized. In practice, the author developed the alarm clock model and the embedded software incrementally. First, the hardware was developed and simulated using a simple test bench that verified correct operation of the timer. Development of the software started with the interrupt service routine and the periodic task dispatcher. That was followed by code to drive each of the input and output interfaces. The tasks for scanning digits, debouncing buttons and switches, setting the alarm and time values using the buttons, counting the clock time, and managing the alarm function were each added and tested in turn. The behavior of this system is sufficiently simple that debugging could be done by careful code review and by deduction from details of malfunction. An alternative would be to use embedded monitoring hardware that can be automatically inserted into the design using the FPGA vendor's tools.

Exercises

1. [❶ 15.1] Determine the encoding for the following Gumnut instructions:

    a.   sub r2, r1, r0

    b.   and r4, r4, 0x30

    c.   ror r1, r1, 2

    d.   ldm r6, (r2)−1

    e.   out r4, 0x10

    f.   bz +7

    g.   jsb 0xD0

2. [❶ 15.1] What Gumnut instructions are encoded by the following 18-bit hexadecimal values?

    a.   0DBC0

    b.   38326

    c.   33D63

    d.   25906

    e.   3EC11

    f.   3DC70

    g.   3F200

3. [❹ 15.2] Synthesize and implement the alarm clock design using an FPGA development board.

4. [❹] Develop I/O controllers to interface with the Gumnut core. Possibilities include a serial input/output UART, parallel input/output, USB interface, I^{2}C interface, analog-to-digital and digital-to-analog converters, real-time clock/calendar, and so on. You may wish to contribute your designs to the OpenCores repository at www.opencores.org.

Appendix A

Standard Packages

The package declarations for the IEEE standard packages described in this book are listed in this appendix.[1] The IEEE standard also includes package bodies defining the detailed meaning of each of the operators and functions provided by the packages. However, simulator vendors are allowed to substitute accelerated implementations of the packages rather than compiling the package bodies into simulations. The IEEE standard requires the packages **standard**, **env**, and **textio** to be in a library called **std**, and the remaining packages to be in a library named **ieee**.

A.1 The Predefined Package **standard**

The predefined types, subtypes and functions of VHDL are defined in the package **standard**. Each design unit in a design is automatically preceded by the following context clause:

```
library std, work;  use std.standard.all;
```

so the predefined items are directly visible in the design. The package **standard** is listed here. The comments indicate which operators are implicitly defined for each explicitly defined type. These operators are also automatically made visible in design units. The types *universal_integer* and *universal_real* are anonymous types. They cannot be referred to explicitly.

```
package standard is

  type boolean is (false, true);

    -- implicitly declared for boolean operands:
    -- "and", "or", "nand", "nor", "xor" , "xnor", "not"
    -- "=", "/=", "<", "<=", ">", ">="
    -- minimum, maximum, rising_edge, falling_edge, to_string

  type bit is ('0', '1');
```

---

1. The material in this appendix is derived from IEEE Draft Std 1076-2008/D4.1, Draft Standard VHDL Language Reference Manual.

```
    -- implicitly declared for bit operands:
    -- "and", "or", "nand", "nor", "xor" , "xnor", "not"
    -- "=", "/=", "<", "<=", ">", ">="
    -- "?=", "?/=", "?<", "?<=", "?>", "?>=", "??"
    -- minimum, maximum, rising_edge, falling_edge, to_string

type character is (
    nul,    soh,    stx,    etx,    eot,    enq,    ack,    bel,
    bs,     ht,     lf,     vt,     ff,     cr,     so,     si,
    dle,    dc1,    dc2,    dc3,    dc4,    nak,    syn,    etb,
    can,    em,     sub,    esc,    fsp,    gsp,    rsp,    usp,
    ' ',    '!',    '"',    '#',    '$',    '%',    '&',    ''',
    '(',    ')',    '*',    '+',    ',',    '-',    '.',    '/',
    '0',    '1',    '2',    '3',    '4',    '5',    '6',    '7',
    '8',    '9',    ':',    ';',    '<',    '=',    '>',    '?',
    '@',    'A',    'B',    'C',    'D',    'E',    'F',    'G',
    'H',    'I',    'J',    'K',    'L',    'M',    'N',    'O',
    'P',    'Q',    'R',    'S',    'T',    'U',    'V',    'W',
    'X',    'Y',    'Z',    '[',    '\',    ']',    '^',    '_',
    '`',    'a',    'b',    'c',    'd',    'e',    'f',    'g',
    'h',    'i',    'j',    'k',    'l',    'm',    'n',    'o',
    'p',    'q',    'r',    's',    't',    'u',    'v',    'w',
    'x',    'y',    'z',    '{',    '|',    '}',    '~',    del,
    c128,   c129,   c130,   c131,   c132,   c133,   c134,   c135,
    c136,   c137,   c138,   c139,   c140,   c141,   c142,   c143,
    c144,   c145,   c146,   c147,   c148,   c149,   c150,   c151,
    c152,   c153,   c154,   c155,   c156,   c157,   c158,   c159,
    ' ',    '¡',    '¢',    '£',    '¤',    '¥',    '¦',    '§',
    '¨',    '©',    'ª',    '«',    '¬',    '',    '®',    '¯',
    '°',    '±',    '²',    '³',    '´',    'µ',    '¶',    '·',
    '¸',    '¹',    'º',    '»',    '¼',    '½',    '¾',    '¿',
    'À',    'Á',    'Â',    'Ã',    'Ä',    'Å',    'Æ',    'Ç',
    'È',    'É',    'Ê',    'Ë',    'Ì',    'Í',    'Î',    'Ï',
    'Ð',    'Ñ',    'Ò',    'Ó',    'Ô',    'Õ',    'Ö',    '×',
    'Ø',    'Ù',    'Ú',    'Û',    'Ü',    'Ý',    'Þ',    'ß',
    'à',    'á',    'â',    'ã',    'ä',    'å',    'æ',    'ç',
    'è',    'é',    'ê',    'ë',    'ì',    'í',    'î',    'ï',
    'ð',    'ñ',    'ò',    'ó',    'ô',    'õ',    'ö',    '÷',
    'ø',    'ù',    'ú',    'û',    'ü',    'ý',    'þ',    'ÿ');

    -- implicitly declared for character operands:
    -- "=", "/=", "<", "<=", ">", ">="
    -- minimum, maximum, to_string

type severity_level is (note, warning, error, failure);

    -- implicitly declared for severity_level operands:
    -- "=", "/=", "<", "<=", ">", ">="
    -- minimum, maximum, to_string

-- type universal_integer is range implementation_defined;

    -- implicitly declared for universal_integer operands:
    -- "=", "/=", "<", "<=", ">", ">="
    -- unary "+", "-", "abs"
    -- "+", "-", "*", "/", "mod", "rem"
    -- minimum, maximum, to_string

-- type universal_real is range implementation_defined;
```

```
      -- implicitly declared for universal_real operands:
      -- "=", "/=", "<", "<=", ">", ">="
      -- unary "+", "-", "abs"
      -- "+", "-", "*", "/", "mod", "rem"
      -- minimum, maximum, to_string

  type integer is range implementation_defined;

      -- implicitly declared for integer operands:
      -- "=", "/=", "<", "<=", ">", ">="
      -- unary "+", "-", "abs"
      -- "**", "+", "-", "*", "/", "mod", "rem"
      -- minimum, maximum, to_string

  subtype natural is integer range 0 to integer'high;
  subtype positive is integer range 1 to integer'high;

  type real is range implementation_defined;

      -- implicitly declared for real operands:
      -- "=", "/=", "<", "<=", ">", ">="
      -- unary "+", "-", "abs"
      -- "**", "+", "-", "*", "/"
      -- minimum, maximum, to_string

  type time is range implementation_defined
    units
        fs;
        ps  = 1000 fs;
        ns  = 1000 ps;
        us  = 1000 ns;
        ms  = 1000 us;
        sec = 1000 ms;
        min = 60 sec;
        hr  = 60 min;
    end units;

      -- implicitly declared for time operands:
      -- "=", "/=", "<", "<=", ">", ">="
      -- unary "+", "-", "abs"
      -- "+", "-", "*", "/", "mod", "rem"
      -- minimum, maximum, to_string

  subtype delay_length is time range 0 fs to time'high;

  impure impure function now return delay_length;

  type string is array (positive range <>) of character;

      -- implicitly declared for string operands:
      -- "=", "/=", "<", "<=", ">", ">=", "&"
      -- minimum, maximum

  type boolean_vector is array (natural range <>) of boolean;

      -- implicitly declared for boolean_vector operands:
      -- "and", "or", "nand", "nor", "xor" , "xnor", "not"
      -- "sll", "srl", "sla", "sra", "rol", "ror"
      -- "=", "/=", "<", "<=", ">", ">=", "&"
      -- minimum, maximum

  type bit_vector is array (natural range <>) of bit;
```

```
    -- implicitly declared for bit_vector operands:
    -- "and", "or", "nand", "nor", "xor" , "xnor", "not"
    -- "sll", "srl", "sla", "sra", "rol", "ror"
    -- "=", "/=", "<", "<=", ">", ">=", "?=", "?/=", "&"
    -- minimum, maximum
    -- to_string, to_bstring, to_binary_string
    -- to_ostring, to_octal_string, to_hstring, to_hex_string

  type integer_vector is array (natural range <>) of integer;

    -- implicitly declared for integer_vector operands:
    -- "=", "/=", "<", "<=", ">", ">=", "&"
    -- minimum, maximum

  type real_vector is array (natural range <>) of real;

    -- implicitly declared for real_vector operands:
    -- "=", "/=", "&"
    -- minimum, maximum

  type time_vector is array (natural range <>) of time;

    -- implicitly declared for time_vector operands:
    -- "=", "/=", "&"
    -- minimum, maximum

  type file_open_kind is (read_mode, write_mode, append_mode);

    -- implicitly declared for file_open_kind operands:
    -- "=", "/=", "<", "<=", ">", ">="
    -- minimum, maximum, to_string

  type file_open_status is
        (open_ok, status_error, name_error, mode_error);

    -- implicitly declared for file_open_status operands:
    -- "=", "/=", "<", "<=", ">", ">="
    -- minimum, maximum, to_string

  attribute foreign: string;

end STANDARD;
```

VHDL-87, -93, and -2002

The following items are not included in standard for these earlier versions: the matching relational operators; the "??" operator; array/scalar and reducing logical operators; the operators **mod** and **rem** on **time** operands; the functions **maximum, minimum, rising_edge,** and **falling_edge**; the functions **to_string, to_ostring, to_hstring** and associated aliases; the types **boolean_vector, integer_vector, real_vector,** and **time_vector** and associated operations.

VHDL-87

The following items are not included in standard in VHDL-87: the types **file_open_kind** and **file_open_status**; the subtype **delay_length**; the attribute **foreign;**

the operators **xnor**, **sll**, **srl**, **sla**, **sra**, **rol** and **ror**. The result time of the function now is time. The type character includes only the first 128 values, corresponding to the ASCII character set.

A.2   The Predefined Package env

```
package env is

  procedure stop (status: integer);
  procedure stop;

  procedure finish (status: integer);
  procedure finish;

  function resolution_limit return delay_length;

end package env;
```

VHDL-87, -93, and -2002

The env package is not provided in these versions.

A.3   The Predefined Package textio

```
package textio is

  type line is access string;

    -- implicitly declared for line operands:
    -- "=", "/=", deallocate

  type text is file of string;

    -- implicitly declared for text operands:
    -- file_open, file_close, read, write, flush, endfile

  type side is (right, left);

    -- implicitly declared for side operands:
    -- "=", "/=", "<", "<=", ">", ">="
    -- minimum, maximum, to_string

  subtype width is natural;

  file input : text open read_mode is "STD_INPUT";
  file output : text open write_mode is "STD_OUTPUT";

  procedure readline(file F: text; L: inout line);

  procedure read ( L : inout line;  value: out bit;
                                    good : out boolean );
  procedure read ( L : inout line;  value: out bit );

  procedure read ( L : inout line;  value: out bit_vector;
                                    good : out boolean );
  procedure read ( L : inout line;  value: out bit_vector );
```

```
    procedure read ( L : inout line;  value: out boolean;
                                      good : out boolean );
    procedure read ( L : inout line;  value: out boolean );

    procedure read ( L : inout line;  value: out character;
                                      good : out boolean );
    procedure read ( L : inout line;  value: out character );

    procedure read ( L : inout line;  value: out integer;
                                      good : out boolean );
    procedure read ( L : inout line;  value: out integer );

    procedure read ( L : inout line;  value: out real;
                                      good : out boolean );
    procedure read ( L : inout line;  value: out real );

    procedure read ( L : inout line;  value: out string;
                                      good : out boolean );
    procedure read ( L : inout line;  value: out string );

    procedure read ( L : inout line;  value: out time;
                                      good : out boolean );
    procedure read ( L : inout line;  value: out time );

    procedure sread ( L: inout line;  value : out string;
                                      strlen: out natural);

    alias string_read is sread [line, string, natural];

    alias bread is read [line, bit_vector, boolean];
    alias bread is read [line, bit_vector];
    alias binary_read is read [line, bit_vector, boolean];
    alias binary_read is read [line, bit_vector];

    procedure oread ( L: inout line;  value: out bit_vector;
                                      good : out boolean );
    procedure oread ( L: inout line;  value: out bit_vector );

    alias octal_read is oread [line, bit_vector, boolean];
    alias octal_read is oread [line, bit_vector];

    procedure hread ( L: inout line;  value: out bit_vector;
                                      good : out boolean );
    procedure hread ( L: inout line;  value: out bit_vector );

    alias hex_read is hread [line, bit_vector, boolean];
    alias hex_read is hread [line, bit_vector];

    procedure writeline ( file F : text;  L : inout line );

    procedure tee ( file F: text;  L: inout line );

    function justify ( value: string;
                       justified: side := right;
                       field: width := 0 ) return string;

    procedure write ( L : inout line;  value : in bit;
                      justified: in side := right; field: in width := 0 );

    procedure write ( L : inout line;  value : in bit_vector;
                      justified: in side := right;  field: in width := 0 );
```

```
        procedure write ( L : inout line;  value : in boolean;
                           justified: in side := right;  field: in width := 0 );

        procedure write ( L : inout line;  value : in character;
                           justified: in side := right;  field: in width := 0 );

        procedure write ( L : inout line;  value : in integer;
                           justified: in side := right;  field: in width := 0 );

        procedure write ( L : inout line;  value : in real;
                           justified: in side := right;  field: in width := 0;
                           digits: in natural := 0 );

        procedure write ( L: inout line;  value: in real;
                           format: in string);

        procedure write ( L : inout line;  value : in string;
                           justified: in side := right;  field: in width := 0 );

        procedure write ( L : inout line;  value : in time;
                           justified: in side := right;  field: in width := 0;
                           unit: in time := ns );

    alias swrite is write [line, string, side, width];
    alias string_write is write [line, string, side, width];

    alias bwrite is write [line, bit_vector, side, width];
    alias binary_write is write [line, bit_vector, side, width];

        procedure owrite ( L: inout line;  value: in bit_vector;
                           justified: in side := right;  field: in width := 0 );

    alias octal_write is owrite [line, bit_vector, side, width];

        procedure hwrite ( L: inout line;  value: in bit_vector;
                           justified: in side := right;  field: in width := 0 );

    alias hex_write is hwrite [line, bit_vector, side, width];

end package textio;
```

VHDL-87, -93, and -2002

The **textio** package in these versions does not provide the following items: the **flush** operation on **text**; the **maximum**, **minimum**, and **to_string** operations on **side**; the **justify** and **tee** operations; the **sread**, **oread**, **hread**, **swrite**, **owrite**, and **hwrite** operations and associated aliases; the **write** operation with C-style formatting.

A.4 Standard VHDL Mathematical Packages

A.4.1 The **math_real** Package

```
package math_real is

constant copyrightnotice: string
        := "Copyright 1996, 2008 IEEE. All rights reserved.";
```

```
constant  math_e : real := 2.71828_18284_59045_23536;
constant  math_1_over_e : real := 0.36787_94411_71442_32160;
constant  math_pi : real := 3.14159_26535_89793_23846;
constant  math_2_pi : real := 6.28318_53071_79586_47693;
constant  math_1_over_pi : real := 0.31830_98861_83790_67154;
constant  math_pi_over_2 : real := 1.57079_63267_94896_61923;
constant  math_pi_over_3 : real := 1.04719_75511_96597_74615;
constant  math_pi_over_4 : real := 0.78539_81633_97448_30962;
constant  math_3_pi_over_2 : real := 4.71238_89803_84689_85769;
constant  math_log_of_2 : real := 0.69314_71805_59945_30942;
constant  math_log_of_10 : real := 2.30258_50929_94045_68402;
constant  math_log2_of_e : real := 1.44269_50408_88963_4074;
constant  math_log10_of_e: real := 0.43429_44819_03251_82765;
constant  math_sqrt_2: real := 1.41421_35623_73095_04880;
constant  math_1_over_sqrt_2: real := 0.70710_67811_86547_52440;
constant  math_sqrt_pi: real := 1.77245_38509_05516_02730;
constant  math_deg_to_rad: real := 0.01745_32925_19943_29577;
constant  math_rad_to_deg: real := 57.29577_95130_82320_87680;

function sign  (x : in real) return real;
function ceil  (x : in real) return real;
function floor (x : in real) return real;
function round (x : in real) return real;
function trunc (x : in real) return real;

function "mod" (x, y : in real) return real;

function realmax (x, y : in real) return real;
function realmin (x, y : in real) return real;

procedure uniform (variable seed1,seed2 : inout positive;
                   variable x : out real);

function sqrt (x : in real) return real;
function cbrt (x : in real) return real;

function "**" (x : in integer;  y : in real) return real;
function "**" (x : in real;     y : in real) return real;

function exp   (x : in rea) return real;
function log   (x : in rea) return real;
function log2  (x : in rea) return real;
function log10 (x : in rea) return real;
function log   (x : in real; base: in real) return real;

function sin (x : in real) return real;
function cos (x : in real) return real;
function tan (x : in real) return real;

function arcsin (x : in real) return real;
function arccos (x : in real) return real;
function arctan (y : in real) return real;
function arctan (y : in real;  x : in real ) return real;

function sinh (x : in real) return real;
function cosh (x : in real) return real;
function tanh (x : in real) return real;

function arcsinh (x : in real) return real;
function arccosh (x : in real) return real;
function arctanh (x : in real) return real;

end math_real;
```

A.4.2   The **math_complex** Package

```
use work.math_real.all;
package math_complex is

  constant copyrightnotice: string
            := "Copyright 1996, 2008 IEEE. All rights reserved.";

  type complex is
    record
      re : real;
      im : real;
    end record;

  subtype positive_real is real range 0.0 to real'high;
  subtype principal_value is real range -math_pi to math_pi;

  type complex_polar is
    record
      mag : positive_real;
      arg : principal_value;   -- -math_pi is illegal
    end record;

  constant math_cbase_1 : complex := complex'(1.0, 0.0);
  constant math_cbase_j : complex := complex'(0.0, 1.0);
  constant math_czero   : complex := complex'(0.0, 0.0);

  function "="  (l : in complex_polar;  r : in complex_polar) return boolean;
  function "/=" (l : in complex_polar;  r : in complex_polar) return boolean;

  function cmplx (x : in real;  y: in real:= 0.0) return complex;

  function get_principal_value (x : in real) return principal_value;

  function complex_to_polar (z : in complex)       return complex_polar;
  function polar_to_complex (z : in complex_polar) return complex;

  function "abs" (z: in complex      ) return positive_real;
  function "abs" (z: in complex_polar) return positive_real;

  function arg  (z: in complex      ) return principal_value;
  function arg  (z: in complex_polar) return principal_value;

  function "-"  (z: in complex      ) return complex;
  function "-"  (z: in complex_polar) return complex_polar;

  function conj (z: in complex      ) return complex;
  function conj (z: in complex_polar) return complex_polar;

  function sqrt (z: in complex      ) return complex;
  function sqrt (z: in complex_polar) return complex_polar;

  function exp  (z: in complex      ) return complex;
  function exp  (z: in complex_polar) return complex_polar;

  function log   (z: in complex      ) return complex;
  function log2  (z: in complex      ) return complex;
  function log10 (z: in complex      ) return complex;
  function log   (z: in complex_polar) return complex_polar;
  function log2  (z: in complex_polar) return complex_polar;
  function log10 (z: in complex_polar) return complex_polar;
  function log   (z: in complex;       base: in real) return complex;
  function log   (z: in complex_polar; base: in real) return complex_polar;

  function sin  (z : in complex      ) return complex;
  function sin  (z : in complex_polar) return complex_polar;
  function cos  (z : in complex      ) return complex;
  function cos  (z : in complex_polar) return complex_polar;
```

```vhdl
    function sinh (z : in complex     ) return complex;
    function sinh (z : in complex_polar) return complex_polar;
    function cosh (z : in complex     ) return complex;
    function cosh (z : in complex_polar) return complex_polar;

    function "+" (l: in complex;  r: in complex) return complex;
    function "+" (l: in real;     r: in complex) return complex;
    function "+" (l: in complex;  r: in real   ) return complex;
    function "+" (l: in complex_polar;  r: in complex_polar) return complex_polar;
    function "+" (l: in real;            r: in complex_polar) return complex_polar;
    function "+" (l: in complex_polar;  r: in real          ) return complex_polar;

    function "-" (l: in complex;  r: in complex) return complex;
    function "-" (l: in real;     r: in complex) return complex;
    function "-" (l: in complex;  r: in real   ) return complex;
    function "-" (l: in complex_polar;  r: in complex_polar) return complex_polar;
    function "-" (l: in real;            r: in complex_polar) return complex_polar;
    function "-" (l: in complex_polar;  r: in real          ) return complex_polar;

    function "*" (l: in complex;  r: in complex) return complex;
    function "*" (l: in real;     r: in complex) return complex;
    function "*" (l: in complex;  r: in real   ) return complex;
    function "*" (l: in complex_polar;  r: in complex_polar) return complex_polar;
    function "*" (l: in real;            r: in complex_polar) return complex_polar;
    function "*" (l: in complex_polar;  r: in real          ) return complex_polar;

    function "/" (l: in complex;  r: in complex) return complex;
    function "/" (l: in real;     r: in complex) return complex;
    function "/" (l: in complex;  r: in real   ) return complex;
    function "/" (l: in complex_polar;  r: in complex_polar) return complex_polar;
    function "/" (l: in real;            r: in complex_polar) return complex_polar;
    function "/" (l: in complex_polar;  r: in real          ) return complex_polar;

end math_complex;
```

A.5   The **std_logic_1164** Multivalue Logic System Package

```vhdl
use std.textio.all;

package std_logic_1164 is

    type std_ulogic is ( 'U',    -- Uninitialized
                         'X',    -- Forcing  Unknown
                         '0',    -- Forcing  0
                         '1',    -- Forcing  1
                         'Z',    -- High Impedance
                         'W',    -- Weak     Unknown
                         'L',    -- Weak     0
                         'H',    -- Weak     1
                         '-'     -- Don't care
                        );

    type std_ulogic_vector is array (natural range <>) of std_ulogic;

    function resolved (s : std_ulogic_vector) return std_ulogic;

    subtype std_logic is resolved std_ulogic;
    subtype std_logic_vector is (resolved) std_ulogic_vector;

    subtype X01 is resolved std_ulogic range 'X' to '1';
    subtype X01Z is resolved std_ulogic range 'X' to 'Z';
    subtype UX01 is resolved std_ulogic range 'U' to '1';
    subtype UX01Z is resolved std_ulogic range 'U' to 'Z';
```

```
function "and"  (l : std_ulogic; r : std_ulogic) return UX01;
function "nand" (l : std_ulogic; r : std_ulogic) return UX01;
function "or"   (l : std_ulogic; r : std_ulogic) return UX01;
function "nor"  (l : std_ulogic; r : std_ulogic) return UX01;
function "xor"  (l : std_ulogic; r : std_ulogic) return UX01;
function "xnor" (l : std_ulogic; r : std_ulogic) return ux01;
function "not"  (l : std_ulogic) return UX01;

function "and"  (l, r : std_ulogic_vector) return std_ulogic_vector;
function "nand" (l, r : std_ulogic_vector) return std_ulogic_vector;
function "or"   (l, r : std_ulogic_vector) return std_ulogic_vector;
function "nor"  (l, r : std_ulogic_vector) return std_ulogic_vector;
function "xor"  (l, r : std_ulogic_vector) return std_ulogic_vector;
function "xnor" (l, r : std_ulogic_vector) return std_ulogic_vector;
function "not"  (l    : std_ulogic_vector) return std_ulogic_vector;

function "and"  (l : std_ulogic_vector;
                 r : std_ulogic)        return std_ulogic_vector;
function "and"  (l : std_ulogic;
                 r : std_ulogic_vector) return std_ulogic_vector;
function "nand" (l : std_ulogic_vector;
                 r : std_ulogic)        return std_ulogic_vector;
function "nand" (l : std_ulogic;
                 r : std_ulogic_vector) return std_ulogic_vector;
function "or"   (l : std_ulogic_vector;
                 r : std_ulogic)        return std_ulogic_vector;
function "or"   (l : std_ulogic;
                 r : std_ulogic_vector) return std_ulogic_vector;
function "nor"  (l : std_ulogic_vector;
                 r : std_ulogic)        return std_ulogic_vector;
function "nor"  (l : std_ulogic;
                 r : std_ulogic_vector) return std_ulogic_vector;
function "xor"  (l : std_ulogic_vector;
                 r : std_ulogic)        return std_ulogic_vector;
function "xor"  (l : std_ulogic;
                 r : std_ulogic_vector) return std_ulogic_vector;
function "xnor" (l : std_ulogic_vector;
                 r : std_ulogic)        return std_ulogic_vector;
function "xnor" (l : std_ulogic;
                 r : std_ulogic_vector) return std_ulogic_vector;

function "and"  (l : std_ulogic_vector) return std_ulogic;
function "nand" (l : std_ulogic_vector) return std_ulogic;
function "or"   (l : std_ulogic_vector) return std_ulogic;
function "nor"  (l : std_ulogic_vector) return std_ulogic;
function "xor"  (l : std_ulogic_vector) return std_ulogic;
function "xnor" (l : std_ulogic_vector) return std_ulogic;

function "sll" (l : std_ulogic_vector; r : integer) return std_ulogic_vector;
function "srl" (l : std_ulogic_vector; r : integer) return std_ulogic_vector;
function "rol" (l : std_ulogic_vector; r : integer) return std_ulogic_vector;
function "ror" (l : std_ulogic_vector; r : integer) return std_ulogic_vector;

function To_bit       (s : std_ulogic;
                       xmap : bit := '0') return bit;
function To_bitvector (s : std_ulogic_vector;
                       xmap : bit := '0') return bit_vector;

function To_StdULogic       (b : bit)                return std_ulogic;
function To_StdLogicVector   (b : bit_vector)         return std_logic_vector;
function To_StdLogicVector   (s : std_ulogic_vector)  return std_logic_vector;
function To_StdULogicVector  (b : bit_vector)         return std_ulogic_vector;
function To_StdULogicVector  (s : std_logic_vector)   return std_ulogic_vector;
```

```vhdl
alias To_Bit_Vector is
        To_bitvector[std_ulogic_vector, bit return bit_vector];
alias To_BV is
        To_bitvector[std_ulogic_vector, bit return bit_vector];

alias To_Std_Logic_Vector is
        To_StdLogicVector[bit_vector return std_logic_vector];
alias To_SLV is
        To_StdLogicVector[bit_vector return std_logic_vector];

alias To_Std_Logic_Vector is
        To_StdLogicVector[std_ulogic_vector return std_logic_vector];
alias To_SLV is
        To_StdLogicVector[std_ulogic_vector return std_logic_vector];

alias To_Std_ULogic_Vector is
        To_StdULogicVector[bit_vector return std_ulogic_vector];
alias To_SULV is
        To_StdULogicVector[bit_vector return std_ulogic_vector];

alias To_Std_ULogic_Vector is
        To_StdULogicVector[std_logic_vector return std_ulogic_vector];
alias To_SULV is
        To_StdULogicVector[std_logic_vector return std_ulogic_vector];

function To_01 (s : std_ulogic_vector;
                xmap : std_ulogic := '0') return std_ulogic_vector;
function To_01 (s : std_ulogic;
                xmap : std_ulogic := '0') return std_ulogic;
function To_01 (s : bit_vector;
                xmap : std_ulogic := '0') return std_ulogic_vector;
function To_01 (s : bit;
                xmap : std_ulogic := '0') return std_ulogic;

function To_X01 (s : std_ulogic_vector) return std_ulogic_vector;
function To_X01 (s : std_ulogic)        return X01;

function To_X01 (b : bit_vector) return std_ulogic_vector;
function To_X01 (b : bit)        return X01;

function To_X01Z (s : std_ulogic_vector) return std_ulogic_vector;
function To_X01Z (s : std_ulogic)        return X01Z;

function To_X01Z (b : bit_vector) return std_ulogic_vector;
function To_X01Z (b : bit)        return X01Z;

function To_UX01 (s : std_ulogic_vector) return std_ulogic_vector;
function To_UX01 (s : std_ulogic)        return UX01;

function To_UX01 (b : bit_vector) return std_ulogic_vector;
function To_UX01 (b : bit)        return UX01;

function "??" (l : std_ulogic) return boolean;

function rising_edge  (signal s : std_ulogic) return boolean;
function falling_edge (signal s : std_ulogic) return boolean;

function Is_X (s : std_ulogic_vector) return boolean;
function Is_X (s : std_ulogic)        return boolean;

-- the following operations are predefined

--   function "?=" (l, r : std_ulogic)        return std_ulogic;
--   function "?=" (l, r : std_ulogic_vector) return std_ulogic;

--   function "?/=" (l, r : std_ulogic)        return std_ulogic;
--   function "?/=" (l, r : std_ulogic_vector) return std_ulogic;
```

```
--  function "?<"  (1, r : std_ulogic) return std_ulogic;
--  function "?<=" (1, r : std_ulogic) return std_ulogic;
--  function "?>"  (1, r : std_ulogic) return std_ulogic;
--  function "?>=" (1, r : std_ulogic) return std_ulogic;

-- the following operations are predefined

--  function to_string (value : std_ulogic)        return string;
--  function to_string (value : std_ulogic_vector) return string;

alias to_bstring        is to_string [std_ulogic_vector return string];
alias to_binary_string is to_string [std_ulogic_vector return string];

function to_ostring (value : std_ulogic_vector) return string;
alias to_octal_string is to_ostring [std_ulogic_vector return string];

function to_hstring (value : std_ulogic_vector) return string;
alias to_hex_string is to_hstring [std_ulogic_vector return string];

procedure read (1 : inout line; value : out std_ulogic;
                                good : out boolean);
procedure read (1 : inout line; value : out std_ulogic);

procedure read (1 : inout line; value : out std_ulogic_vector;
                                good : out boolean);
procedure read (1 : inout line; value : out std_ulogic_vector);

procedure write (1 : inout line; value : in std_ulogic;
                justified : in side := right; field : in width := 0);

procedure write (1 : inout line; value : in std_ulogic_vector;
                justified : in side := right; field : in width := 0);

alias bread is read [line, std_ulogic_vector, boolean];
alias bread is read [line, std_ulogic_vector];
alias binary_read is read [line, std_ulogic_vector, boolean];
alias binary_read is read [line, std_ulogic_vector];

procedure oread (1 : inout line; value : out std_ulogic_vector;
                                 good : out boolean);
procedure oread (1 : inout line; value : out std_ulogic_vector);
alias octal_read is oread [line, std_ulogic_vector, boolean];
alias octal_read is oread [line, std_ulogic_vector];

procedure hread (1 : inout line; value : out std_ulogic_vector;
                                 good : out boolean);
procedure hread (1 : inout line; value : out std_ulogic_vector);
alias hex_read is hread [line, std_ulogic_vector, boolean];
alias hex_read is hread [line, std_ulogic_vector];

alias bwrite is write [line, std_ulogic_vector, side, width];
alias binary_write is write [line, std_ulogic_vector, side, width];

procedure owrite (1 : inout line; value : in std_ulogic_vector;
                justified : in side := right; field : in width := 0);
alias octal_write is owrite [line, std_ulogic_vector, side, width];

procedure hwrite (1 : inout line; value : in std_ulogic_vector;
                justified : in side := right; field : in width := 0);
alias hex_write is hwrite [line, std_ulogic_vector, side, width];

end package std_logic_1164;
```

VHDL-87, -93, and -2002

In the std_logic_1164 package for these versions, std_logic_vector is declared as a distinct type, not as a subtype of std_ulogic_vector. Operations provided by the package for std_ulogic_vector are also overloaded for std_logic_vector.

The package for these versions does not provide the following items: array/scalar and reduction logical operators; shift operators; aliases for the conversion functions; the To_01 function; the "??" operator; the matching relational operators; the to_string, to_bstring, to_ostring, and to_hstring functions and associated aliases; the read, oread, hread, write, owrite, and hwrite operations and associated aliases.

VHDL-87

The overloaded versions of the xnor operator are not included in the VHDL-87 version of the standard-logic package.

A.6 Standard Integer Numeric Packages

A.6.1 The numeric_bit Package

```
use std.textio.all;
package numeric_bit is

   constant CopyRightNotice : string
     := "Copyright © 1997, 2008 IEEE. All rights reserved.";

   type unsigned is array (natural range <>) of bit;
   type signed   is array (natural range <>) of bit;

   function "abs" (arg : signed) return signed;
   function "-"   (arg : signed) return signed;

   function "+" (l, r : unsigned)                return unsigned;
   function "+" (l : unsigned; r : bit)          return unsigned;
   function "+" (l : bit;      r : unsigned)     return unsigned;
   function "+" (l : unsigned; r : natural)      return unsigned;
   function "+" (l : natural;  r : unsigned)     return unsigned;
   function "+" (l, r : signed)                  return signed;
   function "+" (l : signed;   r : bit)          return signed;
   function "+" (l : bit;      r : signed)       return signed;
   function "+" (l : integer;  r : signed)       return signed;
   function "+" (l : signed;   r : integer)      return signed;

   function "-" (l, r : unsigned)                return unsigned;
   function "-" (l : unsigned; r : bit)          return unsigned;
   function "-" (l : bit;      r : unsigned)     return unsigned;
   function "-" (l : unsigned; r : natural)      return unsigned;
   function "-" (l : natural;  r : unsigned)     return unsigned;
   function "-" (l, r : signed)                  return signed;
   function "-" (l : signed;   r : bit)          return signed;
   function "-" (l : bit;      r : signed)       return signed;
   function "-" (l : signed;   r : integer)      return signed;
   function "-" (l : integer;  r : signed)       return signed;
```

```
function "*" (l, r : unsigned)                return unsigned;
function "*" (l : unsigned; r : natural)  return unsigned;
function "*" (l : natural;  r : unsigned) return unsigned;
function "*" (l, r : signed)                  return signed;
function "*" (l : signed;   r : integer)  return signed;
function "*" (l : integer;  r : signed)   return signed;

function "/" (l, r : unsigned)                return unsigned;
function "/" (l : unsigned; r : natural)  return unsigned;
function "/" (l : natural;  r : unsigned) return unsigned;
function "/" (l, r : signed)                  return signed;
function "/" (l : signed;   r : integer)  return signed;
function "/" (l : integer;  r : signed)   return signed;

function "rem" (l, r : unsigned)                return unsigned;
function "rem" (l : unsigned; r : natural)  return unsigned;
function "rem" (l : natural;  r : unsigned) return unsigned;
function "rem" (l, r : signed)                  return signed;
function "rem" (l : signed;   r : integer)  return signed;
function "rem" (l : integer;  r : signed)   return signed;

function "mod" (l, r : unsigned)                return unsigned;
function "mod" (l : unsigned; r : natural)  return unsigned;
function "mod" (l : natural;  r : unsigned) return unsigned;
function "mod" (l, r : signed)                  return signed;
function "mod" (l : signed;   r : integer)  return signed;
function "mod" (l : integer;  r : signed)   return signed;

function find_leftmost  (arg : unsigned; y : bit) return integer;
function find_leftmost  (arg : signed;   y : bit) return integer;

function find_rightmost (arg : unsigned; y : bit) return integer;
function find_rightmost (arg : signed;   y : bit) return integer;

function "=" (l, r : unsigned)                return boolean;
function "=" (l : unsigned; r : natural)  return boolean;
function "=" (l : natural;  r : unsigned) return boolean;
function "=" (l, r : signed)                  return boolean;
function "=" (l : signed;   r : integer)  return boolean;
function "=" (l : integer;  r : signed)   return boolean;

function "/=" (l, r : unsigned)                return boolean;
function "/=" (l : unsigned; r : natural)  return boolean;
function "/=" (l : natural;  r : unsigned) return boolean;
function "/=" (l, r : signed)                  return boolean;
function "/=" (l : signed;   r : integer)  return boolean;
function "/=" (l : integer;  r : signed)   return boolean;

function "<" (l, r : unsigned)                return boolean;
function "<" (l : unsigned; r : natural)  return boolean;
function "<" (l : natural;  r : unsigned) return boolean;
function "<" (l, r : signed)                  return boolean;
function "<" (l : signed;   r : integer)  return boolean;
function "<" (l : integer;  r : signed)   return boolean;

function "<=" (l, r : unsigned)                return boolean;
function "<=" (l : unsigned; r : natural)  return boolean;
function "<=" (l : natural;  r : unsigned) return boolean;
function "<=" (l, r : signed)                  return boolean;
function "<=" (l : signed;   r : integer)  return boolean;
function "<=" (l : integer;  r : signed)   return boolean;

function ">" (l, r : unsigned)                return boolean;
function ">" (l : unsigned; r : natural)  return boolean;
function ">" (l : natural;  r : unsigned) return boolean;
function ">" (l, r : signed)                  return boolean;
```

```
function ">"  (l : signed;   r : integer)  return boolean;
function ">"  (l : integer;  r : signed)   return boolean;

function ">=" (l, r : unsigned)            return boolean;
function ">=" (l : unsigned; r : natural)  return boolean;
function ">=" (l : natural;  r : unsigned) return boolean;
function ">=" (l, r : signed)              return boolean;
function ">=" (l : signed;   r : integer)  return boolean;
function ">=" (l : integer;  r : signed)   return boolean;

function minimum (l, r : unsigned)            return unsigned;
function minimum (l : unsigned; r : natural)  return unsigned;
function minimum (l : natural;  r : unsigned) return unsigned;
function minimum (l, r : signed)              return signed;
function minimum (l : signed;   r : integer)  return signed;
function minimum (l : integer;  r : signed)   return signed;

function maximum (l, r : unsigned)            return unsigned;
function maximum (l : unsigned; r : natural)  return unsigned;
function maximum (l : natural;  r : unsigned) return unsigned;
function maximum (l, r : signed)              return signed;
function maximum (l : signed;   r : integer)  return signed;
function maximum (l : integer;  r : signed)   return signed;

function "?="  (l, r : unsigned)            return bit;
function "?="  (l : unsigned; r : natural)  return bit;
function "?="  (l : natural;  r : unsigned) return bit;
function "?="  (l, r : signed)              return bit;
function "?="  (l : signed;   r : integer)  return bit;
function "?="  (l : integer;  r : signed)   return bit;

function "?/=" (l, r : unsigned)            return bit;
function "?/=" (l : unsigned; r : natural)  return bit;
function "?/=" (l : natural;  r : unsigned) return bit;
function "?/=" (l, r : signed)              return bit;
function "?/=" (l : signed;   r : integer)  return bit;
function "?/=" (l : integer;  r : signed)   return bit;

function "?<"  (l, r : unsigned)            return bit;
function "?<"  (l : unsigned; r : natural)  return bit;
function "?<"  (l : natural;  r : unsigned) return bit;
function "?<"  (l, r : signed)              return bit;
function "?<"  (l : signed;   r : integer)  return bit;
function "?<"  (l : integer;  r : signed)   return bit;

function "?<=" (l, r : unsigned)            return bit;
function "?<=" (l : unsigned; r : natural)  return bit;
function "?<=" (l : natural;  r : unsigned) return bit;
function "?<=" (l, r : signed)              return bit;
function "?<=" (l : signed;   r : integer)  return bit;
function "?<=" (l : integer;  r : signed)   return bit;

function "?>"  (l, r : unsigned)            return bit;
function "?>"  (l : unsigned; r : natural)  return bit;
function "?>"  (l : natural;  r : unsigned) return bit;
function "?>"  (l, r : signed)              return bit;
function "?>"  (l : signed;   r : integer)  return bit;
function "?>"  (l : integer;  r : signed)   return bit;

function "?>=" (l, r : unsigned)            return bit;
function "?>=" (l : unsigned; r : natural)  return bit;
function "?>=" (l : natural;  r : unsigned) return bit;
function "?>=" (l, r : signed)              return bit;
function "?>=" (l : signed;   r : integer)  return bit;
function "?>=" (l : integer;  r : signed)   return bit;
```

```
function shift_left   (arg : unsigned; count : natural) return unsigned;
function shift_left   (arg : signed;   count : natural) return signed;

function shift_right  (arg : unsigned; count : natural) return unsigned;
function shift_right  (arg : signed;   count : natural) return signed;

function rotate_left  (arg : unsigned; count : natural) return unsigned;
function rotate_left  (arg : signed;   count : natural) return signed;

function rotate_right (arg : unsigned; count : natural) return unsigned;
function rotate_right (arg : signed;   count : natural) return signed;

function "sll" (arg : unsigned; count : integer) return unsigned;
function "sll" (arg : signed;   count : integer) return signed;
function "srl" (arg : unsigned; count : integer) return unsigned;
function "srl" (arg : signed;   count : integer) return signed;
function "rol" (arg : unsigned; count : integer) return unsigned;
function "rol" (arg : signed;   count : integer) return signed;
function "ror" (arg : unsigned; count : integer) return unsigned;
function "ror" (arg : signed;   count : integer) return signed;
function "sla" (arg : unsigned; count : integer) return unsigned;
function "sla" (arg : signed;   count : integer) return signed;
function "sra" (arg : unsigned; count : integer) return unsigned;
function "sra" (arg : signed;   count : integer) return signed;

function resize (arg : unsigned; new_size : natural) return unsigned;
function resize (arg : signed;   new_size : natural) return signed;
function resize (arg, size_res : unsigned) return unsigned;
function resize (arg, size_res : signed) return signed;

function to_integer  (arg : unsigned) return natural;
function to_integer  (arg : signed)   return integer;

function to_unsigned (arg : natural; size     : natural)  return unsigned;
function to_unsigned (arg : natural; size_res : unsigned) return unsigned;
function to_signed   (arg : integer; size     : natural)  return signed;
function to_signed   (arg : integer; size_res : signed)   return signed;

function "and"  (l, r : unsigned) return unsigned;
function "and"  (l, r : signed)   return signed;
function "nand" (l, r : unsigned) return unsigned;
function "nand" (l, r : signed)   return signed;
function "or"   (l, r : unsigned) return unsigned;
function "or"   (l, r : signed)   return signed;
function "nor"  (l, r : unsigned) return unsigned;
function "nor"  (l, r : signed)   return signed;
function "xor"  (l, r : unsigned) return unsigned;
function "xnor" (l, r : unsigned) return unsigned;
function "xnor" (l, r : signed)   return signed;
function "xor"  (l, r : signed)   return signed;
function "not"  (l : unsigned)    return unsigned;
function "not"  (l : signed)      return signed;

function "and"  (l : bit;      r : unsigned) return unsigned;
function "and"  (l : unsigned; r : bit)      return unsigned;
function "and"  (l : bit;      r : signed)   return signed;
function "and"  (l : signed;   r : bit)      return signed;
function "nand" (l : bit;      r : unsigned) return unsigned;
function "nand" (l : unsigned; r : bit)      return unsigned;
function "nand" (l : bit;      r : signed)   return signed;
function "nand" (l : signed;   r : bit)      return signed;
function "or"   (l : bit;      r : unsigned) return unsigned;
function "or"   (l : unsigned; r : bit)      return unsigned;
function "or"   (l : bit;      r : signed)   return signed;
function "or"   (l : signed;   r : bit)      return signed;
```

```vhdl
function "nor"  (l : bit;       r : unsigned) return unsigned;
function "nor"  (l : unsigned; r : bit)      return unsigned;
function "nor"  (l : bit;       r : signed)   return signed;
function "nor"  (l : signed;   r : bit)      return signed;
function "xor"  (l : bit;       r : unsigned) return unsigned;
function "xor"  (l : unsigned; r : bit)      return unsigned;
function "xor"  (l : bit;       r : signed)   return signed;
function "xor"  (l : signed;   r : bit)      return signed;
function "xnor" (l : bit;       r : unsigned) return unsigned;
function "xnor" (l : unsigned; r : bit)      return unsigned;
function "xnor" (l : bit;       r : signed)   return signed;
function "xnor" (l : signed;   r : bit)      return signed;

function "and"  (l : unsigned) return bit;
function "and"  (l : signed)   return bit;
function "nand" (l : unsigned) return bit;
function "nand" (l : signed)   return bit;
function "or"   (l : unsigned) return bit;
function "or"   (l : signed)   return bit;
function "nor"  (l : unsigned) return bit;
function "nor"  (l : signed)   return bit;
function "xor"  (l : unsigned) return bit;
function "xor"  (l : signed)   return bit;
function "xnor" (l : unsigned) return bit;
function "xnor" (l : signed)   return bit;

alias rising_edge is std.standard.rising_edge
                    [std.standard.bit return std.standard.boolean];
alias falling_edge is std.standard.falling_edge
                    [std.standard.bit return std.standard.boolean];

-- the following operations are predefined

-- function to_string (value : unsigned) return string;
-- function to_string (value : signed)   return string;

alias to_bstring is to_string [unsigned return string];
alias to_bstring is to_string [signed   return string];

alias to_binary_string is to_string [unsigned return string];
alias to_binary_string is to_string [signed   return string];

function to_ostring (value : unsigned) return string;
function to_ostring (value : signed)   return string;

alias to_octal_string is to_ostring [unsigned return string];
alias to_octal_string is to_ostring [signed   return string];

function to_hstring (value : unsigned) return string;
function to_hstring (value : signed)   return string;

alias to_hex_string is to_hstring [unsigned return string];
alias to_hex_string is to_hstring [signed   return string];

procedure read(l : inout line; value : out unsigned; good : out boolean);
procedure read(l : inout line; value : out unsigned);
procedure read(l : inout line; value : out signed;   good : out boolean);
procedure read(l : inout line; value : out signed);

alias bread is read [line, unsigned, boolean];
alias bread is read [line, unsigned];
alias bread is read [line, signed,   boolean];
alias bread is read [line, signed];

alias binary_read is read [line, unsigned, boolean];
alias binary_read is read [line, unsigned];
```

```
    alias binary_read is read [line, signed,   boolean];
    alias binary_read is read [line, signed];

    procedure oread (l : inout line; value : out unsigned; good : out boolean);
    procedure oread (l : inout line; value : out unsigned);
    procedure oread (l : inout line; value : out signed;   good : out boolean);
    procedure oread (l : inout line; value : out signed);

    alias octal_read is oread [line, unsigned, boolean];
    alias octal_read is oread [line, unsigned];
    alias octal_read is oread [line, signed,   boolean];
    alias octal_read is oread [line, signed];

    procedure hread (l : inout line; value : out unsigned; good : out boolean);
    procedure hread (l : inout line; value : out unsigned);
    procedure hread (l : inout line; value : out signed;   good : out boolean);
    procedure hread (l : inout line; value : out signed);

    alias hex_read is hread [line, unsigned, boolean];
    alias hex_read is hread [line, unsigned];
    alias hex_read is hread [line, signed,   boolean];
    alias hex_read is hread [line, signed];

    procedure write (l : inout line; value : in unsigned;
                     justified : in side := right; field : in width := 0);
    procedure write (l : inout line; value : in signed;
                     justified : in side := right; field : in width := 0);

    alias bwrite is write [line, unsigned, side, width];
    alias bwrite is write [line, signed,   side, width];

    alias binary_write is write [line, unsigned, side, width];
    alias binary_write is write [line, signed,   side, width];

    procedure owrite (l : inout line; value : in unsigned;
                      justified : in side := right; field : in width := 0);
    procedure owrite (l : inout line; value : in signed;
                      justified : in side := right; field : in width := 0);

    alias octal_write is owrite [line, unsigned, side, width];
    alias octal_write is owrite [line, signed,   side, width];

    procedure hwrite (l : inout line; value : in unsigned;
                      justified : in side := right; field : in width := 0);
    procedure hwrite (l : inout line; value : in signed;
                      justified : in side := right; field : in width := 0);

    alias hex_write is hwrite [line, unsigned, side, width];
    alias hex_write is hwrite [line, signed,   side, width];

end package numeric_bit;
```

VHDL-87, -93, and -2002

The numeric_bit package for these versions does not provide the following items: the array/bit addition and subtraction operators; the find_leftmost, find_rightmost, maximum, and minimum operations; the matching relational operators; the **sla** and **sra** operators; the resize, to_unsigned, and to_signed functions with size_res parameter; the array/scalar and reduction logical operators; the to_string, to_bstring, to_ostring, and to_hstring functions and associated aliases; the read, oread, hread, write, owrite, and hwrite operations and associated aliases.

VHDL-87

The overloaded versions of the shift, rotate and **xnor** operators must be commented out of the numeric_bit package if VHDL-87 compatibility is required.

A.6.2 The numeric_std Package

```vhdl
use std.textio.all;
library ieee; use ieee.std_logic_1164.all;

package numeric_std is

    constant CopyRightNotice : string
      := "Copyright © 1997, 2008 IEEE. All rights reserved.";

    type unresolved_unsigned is array (natural range <>) of std_ulogic;
    type unresolved_signed   is array (natural range <>) of std_ulogic;

    alias u_unsigned is unresolved_unsigned;
    alias u_signed   is unresolved_signed;

    subtype unsigned is (resolved) unresolved_unsigned;
    subtype signed   is (resolved) unresolved_signed;

    -- The declaration of all operators and functions is exactly the same
    -- as in numeric_bit, but with parameters of types unresolved_unsigned
    -- and unresolved_signed instead of unsigned and signed, respectively.

    -- In addition, the following functions are declared:
    function std_match (l, r : std_ulogic)            return boolean;
    function std_match (l, r : unresolved_unsigned)   return boolean;
    function std_match (l, r : unresolved_signed)     return boolean;
    function std_match (l, r : std_ulogic_vector)     return boolean;

    function To_01 (s : unresolved_unsigned;
                    xmap : std_ulogic := '0') return unresolved_unsigned;
    function To_01 (s : unresolved_signed;
                    xmap : std_ulogic := '0') return unresolved_signed;

    function To_X01 (s : unresolved_unsigned) return unresolved_unsigned;
    function To_X01 (s : unresolved_signed)   return unresolved_signed;

    function To_X01Z (s : unresolved_unsigned) return unresolved_unsigned;
    function To_X01Z (s : unresolved_signed)   return unresolved_signed;

    function To_UX01 (s : unresolved_unsigned) return unresolved_unsigned;
    function To_UX01 (s : unresolved_signed)   return unresolved_signed;

    function Is_X   (s : unresolved_unsigned) return boolean;
    function Is_X   (s : unresolved_signed)   return boolean;

end package numeric_std;
```

VHDL-87, -93, and -2002

In the numeric_std package for these versions, **unsigned** and **signed** are declared as separate array types with **std_logic** as the element types. There are no declarations of **unresolved_unsigned**, **unresolved_signed**, or the corresponding aliases. The operations provided by the package are declared for the **unsigned** and **signed** types.

As for the **numeric_bit** package, the **numeric_std** package for these versions does not provide the following items: the array/bit addition and subtraction operators; the **find_leftmost**, **find_rightmost**, **maximum**, and **minimum** operations; the matching relational operators; the **sla** and **sra** operators; the **resize**, **to_unsigned**, and **to_signed** functions with **size_res** parameter; the array/scalar and reduction logical operators; the **to_string**, **to_bstring**, **to_ostring**, and **to_hstring** functions and associated aliases; the **read**, **oread**, **hread**, **write**, **owrite**, and **hwrite** operations and associated aliases. In addition, the package does not provide the **To_X01**, **To_X01Z**, **To_UX01**, and **Is_X** functions.

VHDL-87

The overloaded versions of the shift, rotate and **xnor** operators must be commented out of the **numeric_std** package if VHDL-87 compatibility is required.

A.6.3   The **numeric_bit_unsigned** Package

```
package numeric_bit_unsigned is

  constant CopyRightNotice : STRING :=
    "Copyright 2008 IEEE. All rights reserved.";

  function "+" (l, r : bit_vector)           return bit_vector;
  function "+" (l : bit_vector; r : bit)     return bit_vector;
  function "+" (l : bit;        r : bit_vector) return bit_vector;
  function "+" (l : bit_vector; r : natural)  return bit_vector;
  function "+" (l : natural;    r : bit_vector) return bit_vector;

  function "-" (l, r : bit_vector)           return bit_vector;
  function "-" (l : bit_vector; r : bit)     return bit_vector;
  function "-" (l : bit;        r : bit_vector) return bit_vector;
  function "-" (l : bit_vector; r : natural)  return bit_vector;
  function "-" (l : natural;    r : bit_vector) return bit_vector;

  function "*" (l, r : bit_vector)           return bit_vector;
  function "*" (l : bit_vector; r : natural)  return bit_vector;
  function "*" (l : natural;    r : bit_vector) return bit_vector;

  function "/" (l, r : bit_vector)           return bit_vector;
  function "/" (l : bit_vector; r : natural)  return bit_vector;
  function "/" (l : natural;    r : bit_vector) return bit_vector;

  function "rem" (l, r : bit_vector)           return bit_vector;
  function "rem" (l : bit_vector; r : natural)  return bit_vector;
  function "rem" (l : natural;    r : bit_vector) return bit_vector;

  function "mod" (l, r : bit_vector)           return bit_vector;
  function "mod" (l : bit_vector; r : natural)  return bit_vector;
  function "mod" (l : natural;    r : bit_vector) return bit_vector;

  function find_leftmost  (arg : bit_vector; y : bit) return integer;
  function find_rightmost (arg : bit_vector; y : bit) return integer;

  function "=" (l, r : bit_vector)           return boolean;
  function "=" (l : bit_vector; r : natural)  return boolean;
  function "=" (l : natural;    r : bit_vector) return boolean;
```

```
function "/=" (l, r : bit_vector)              return boolean;
function "/=" (l : bit_vector; r : natural)    return boolean;
function "/=" (l : natural;     r : bit_vector) return boolean;

function "<"  (l, r : bit_vector)              return boolean;
function "<"  (l : bit_vector; r : natural)    return boolean;
function "<"  (l : natural;     r : bit_vector) return boolean;

function "<=" (l, r : bit_vector)              return boolean;
function "<=" (l : bit_vector; r : natural)    return boolean;
function "<=" (l : natural;     r : bit_vector) return boolean;

function ">"  (l, r : bit_vector)              return boolean;
function ">"  (l : bit_vector; r : natural)    return boolean;
function ">"  (l : natural;     r : bit_vector) return boolean;

function ">=" (l, r : bit_vector)              return boolean;
function ">=" (l : bit_vector; r : natural)    return boolean;
function ">=" (l : natural;     r : bit_vector) return boolean;

function minimum (l, r : bit_vector)           return bit_vector;
function minimum (l : bit_vector; r : natural) return bit_vector;
function minimum (l : natural;     r : bit_vector) return bit_vector;

function maximum (l, r : bit_vector)           return bit_vector;
function maximum (l : bit_vector; r : natural) return bit_vector;
function maximum (l : natural;     r : bit_vector) return bit_vector;

function "?="  (l, r : bit_vector)             return bit;
function "?="  (l : bit_vector; r : natural)   return bit;
function "?="  (l : natural;     r : bit_vector) return bit;

function "?/=" (l, r : bit_vector)             return bit;
function "?/=" (l : bit_vector; r : natural)   return bit;
function "?/=" (l : natural;     r : bit_vector) return bit;

function "?<"  (l, r : bit_vector)             return bit;
function "?<"  (l : bit_vector; r : natural)   return bit;
function "?<"  (l : natural;     r : bit_vector) return bit;

function "?<=" (l, r : bit_vector)             return bit;
function "?<=" (l : bit_vector; r : natural)   return bit;
function "?<=" (l : natural;     r : bit_vector) return bit;

function "?>"  (l, r : bit_vector)             return bit;
function "?>"  (l : bit_vector; r : natural)   return bit;
function "?>"  (l : natural;     r : bit_vector) return bit;

function "?>=" (l, r : bit_vector)             return bit;
function "?>=" (l : bit_vector; r : natural)   return bit;
function "?>=" (l : natural;     r : bit_vector) return bit;

function shift_left   (arg : bit_vector; count : natural) return bit_vector;
function shift_right  (arg : bit_vector; count : natural) return bit_vector;
function rotate_left  (arg : bit_vector; count : natural) return bit_vector;
function rotate_right (arg : bit_vector; count : natural) return bit_vector;

function "sll" (arg : bit_vector; count : integer) return bit_vector;
function "srl" (arg : bit_vector; count : integer) return bit_vector;
function "rol" (arg : bit_vector; count : integer) return bit_vector;
function "ror" (arg : bit_vector; count : integer) return bit_vector;
function "sla" (arg : bit_vector; count : integer) return bit_vector;
function "sra" (arg : bit_vector; count : integer) return bit_vector;

function resize (arg : bit_vector; new_size : natural)    return bit_vector;
function resize (arg : bit_vector; size_res : bit_vector) return bit_vector;

function to_integer  (arg : bit_vector) return natural;
```

```
function to_bitvector (arg : natural;
                       size     : natural)     return bit_vector;
function to_bitvector (arg : natural;
                       size_res : bit_vector) return bit_vector;

alias to_bit_vector is
      to_bitvector[natural, natural return bit_vector];
alias to_bv is
      to_bitvector[natural, natural return bit_vector];

alias to_bit_vector is
      to_bitvector[natural, bit_vector return bit_vector];
alias to_bv is
      to_bitvector[natural, bit_vector return bit_vector];

end package numeric_bit_unsigned;
```

VHDL-87, -93, and -2002

The numeric_bit_unsigned package is not provided in these versions.

A.6.4   The **numeric_std_unsigned** Package

```
library ieee; use ieee.std_logic_1164.all;

package numeric_std_unsigned is

  constant CopyRightNotice : string :=
    "Copyright 2008 IEEE. All rights reserved.";

  -- The declaration of the following operators and functions is exactly
  -- the same as in numeric_bit_unsigned, but with parameters of type
  -- std_ulogic_vector instead of bit_vector:
  --   Operators "+", "-", "*", "/", "rem", "mod"
  --   Functions find_leftmost, find_rightmost, minimum, maximum
  --   Operators "=", "/=", "<", "<=", ">", ">="
  --   Operators "?=", "?/=", "?<", "?<=", "?>", "?>="
  --   Functions shift_left, shift_right, rotate_left, rotate_right

  -- Operators "sll", "srl", "rol", "ror" are not declared in this package,
  -- as the versions in std_logic_1164 perform the required operations.
  -- The following shift operators are declared:

  function "sla" (arg : std_ulogic_vector;
                  count : integer) return std_ulogic_vector;
  function "sra" (arg : std_ulogic_vector;
                  count : integer) return std_ulogic_vector;

  -- In addition, the following functions are declared:

  function to_integer (arg : std_ulogic_vector) return natural;

  function To_StdLogicVector (arg : natural; size : natural)
                             return std_logic_vector;
  function To_StdLogicVector (arg : natural; size_res : std_ulogic_vector)
                             return std_logic_vector;

  alias To_Std_Logic_Vector is
        To_StdLogicVector[natural, natural return std_logic_vector];
  alias To_SLV is
        To_StdLogicVector[natural, natural return std_logic_vector];
  alias To_Std_Logic_Vector is
```

```
                    To_StdLogicVector[natural, std_ulogic_vector return std_logic_vector];
alias To_SLV is
                    To_StdLogicVector[natural, std_ulogic_vector return std_logic_vector];

function To_StdULogicVector (arg : natural; size : natural)
                            return std_ulogic_vector;
function To_StdULogicVector (arg : natural; size_res : std_ulogic_vector)
                            return std_ulogic_vector;

alias To_Std_ULogic_Vector is
                    To_StdULogicVector[natural, natural return std_ulogic_vector];
alias To_SULV is
                    To_StdULogicVector[natural, natural return std_ulogic_vector];
alias To_Std_ULogic_Vector is
                    To_StdULogicVector[natural, std_ulogic_vector
                            return std_ulogic_vector];
alias To_SULV is
                    To_StdULogicVector[natural, std_ulogic_vector
                            return std_ulogic_vector];

end package numeric_std_unsigned;
```

VHDL-87, -93, and -2002

The numeric_std_unsigned package is not provided in these versions.

Appendix B

VHDL Syntax

In this appendix we present the full set of syntax rules for VHDL using the EBNF notation introduced in Chapter 1. Those aspects of the language not covered in this book are described in *The Designer's Guide to VHDL* [1]. The form of EBNF used in this book differs from that of the VHDL Language Reference Manual (LRM) in order to make the syntax rules more intelligible to the VHDL user. The LRM includes a separate syntax rule for each minor syntactic category. In this book, we condense the grammar into a smaller number of rules, each of which defines a larger part of the grammar. We introduce the EBNF symbols "(", ")" and "￿₀₀" as part of this simplification. Our aim is to avoid the large amount of searching required when using the LRM rules to resolve a question of grammar.

Those parts of the syntax rules that were introduced in VHDL-2008 are underlined in this appendix. A model written using earlier versions of the language may not use these features. In addition, there are some entirely new rules introduced in VHDL-2008 that have no predecessors in earlier versions. We identify these rules by underlining the rule name on the left-hand side of the "⇐"symbol.

Some of the rules refer to the syntax rules for the PSL. Such references are identified by the italicized prefix "*PSL_*". The PSL syntax rules are not included here. The interested reader should refer to the PSL standard or to books on PSL for details.

Index to Syntax Rules

B.1 Design File

design_file ⇐ design_unit 〔 ••• 〕

design_unit ⇐
   〔 library_clause I use_clause I <u>context_reference</u> 〕
   library_unit

library_unit ⇐
   entity_declaration   Ɩ architecture_body
   Ɩ package_declaration   Ɩ package_body
   Ɩ <u>package_instantiation_declaration</u>
   Ɩ configuration_declaration   Ɩ <u>context_declaration</u>
   Ɩ *PSL_*<u>Verification_Unit</u>

library_clause ⇐ **library** identifier 〔 , ••• 〕 ;

<u>context_reference</u> ⇐ **context** selected_name 〔 , ••• 〕 ;

B.2 Library Unit Declarations

entity_declaration ⇐
   entity identifier **is**
      〚 **generic** (*generic*_interface_list) ; 〛
      〚 **port** (*port*_interface_list) ; 〛
      〔 entity_declarative_item 〕
   〚 **begin**
      〔 concurrent_assertion_statement
      Ɩ *passive*_concurrent_procedure_call_statement
      Ɩ *passive*_process_statement 〕 〛
      Ɩ *PSL_*<u>PSL_Directive</u>
   end 〚 **entity** 〛 〚 identifier 〛 ;

entity_declarative_item ⇐
    subprogram_declaration   ❘ subprogram_body
    ❘ subprogram_instantiation_declaration
    ❘ package_declaration   ❘ package_body
    ❘ package_instantiation_declaration
    ❘ type_declaration   ❘ subtype_declaration
    ❘ constant_declaration   ❘ signal_declaration
    ❘ *shared*_variable_declaration   ❘ file_declaration
    ❘ alias_declaration
    ❘ attribute_declaration   ❘ attribute_specification
    ❘ disconnection_specification   ❘ use_clause
    ❘ group_template_declaration   ❘ group_declaration
    ❘ *PSL*_Property_Declaration   ❘ *PSL*_Sequence_Declaration
    ❘ *PSL*_Clock_Declaration

architecture_body ⇐
    architecture identifier **of** *entity*_name **is**
        { block_declarative_item }
    begin
        { concurrent_statement }
    end [**architecture**] [identifier] ;

configuration_declaration ⇐
    configuration identifier **of** *entity*_name **is**
        { use_clause ❘ attribute_specification ❘ group_declaration }
        { **use vunit** *verification_unit*_name { , … } ; }
        block_configuration
    end [**configuration**] [identifier] ;

block_configuration ⇐
    for (*architecture*_name
        ❘ *block_statement*_label
        ❘ *generate_statement*_label
            [((*static*_discrete_range ❘ *static*_expression ❘ *alternative*_label))])
        { use_clause }
        { block_configuration ❘ component_configuration }
    end for ;

component_configuration ⇐
    for component_specification
        [binding_indication ;]
        { **use vunit** *verification_unit*_name { , … } ; }
        [block_configuration]
    end for ;

context_declaration ⇐
    context identifier **is**
        { library_clause ❘ use_clause ❘ context_reference }
    end [**context**] [identifier] ;

B.3 Declarations and Specifications

package_declaration ⟸
    package identifier is
        ⟦ **generic** (*generic*_interface_list) ;
        ⟦ **generic map** (*generic*_association_list) ; ⟧ ⟧
        ❴ package_declarative_item ❵
    end ⟦ **package** ⟧ ⟦ identifier ⟧ ;

package_declarative_item ⟸
    subprogram_declaration
    ❘ subprogram_instantiation_declaration
    ❘ package_declaration
    ❘ package_instantiation_declaration
    ❘ type_declaration   ❘ subtype_declaration
    ❘ constant_declaration   ❘ signal_declaration
    ❘ variable_declaration   ❘ file_declaration
    ❘ alias_declaration   ❘ component_declaration
    ❘ attribute_declaration   ❘ attribute_specification
    ❘ disconnection_specification   ❘ use_clause
    ❘ group_template_declaration   ❘ group_declaration
    ❘ *PSL*_Property_Declaration   ❘ *PSL*_Sequence_Declaration

package_body ⟸
    package body identifier **is**
        ❴ package_body_declarative_item ❵
    end ⟦ **package body** ⟧ ⟦ identifier ⟧ ;

package_body_declarative_item ⟸
    subprogram_declaration   ❘ subprogram_body
    ❘ subprogram_instantiation_declaration
    ❘ package_declaration   ❘ package_body
    ❘ package_instantiation_declaration
    ❘ type_declaration   ❘ subtype_declaration
    ❘ constant_declaration   ❘ variable_declaration
    ❘ file_declaration   ❘ alias_declaration
    ❘ attribute_declaration   ❘ attribute_specification
    ❘ use_clause
    ❘ group_template_declaration   ❘ group_declaration

package_instantiation_declaration ⟸
    package identifier **is new** *uninstantiated_package*_name
        ⟦ **generic map** (*generic*_association_list) ⟧ ;

subprogram_specification ⟸
    procedure_specification ❘ function_specification

procedure_specification ⇐
    procedure identifier
        ⟦ **generic** (*generic*_interface_list)
        ⟦ **generic map** (*generic*_association_list) ⟧ ⟧
        ⟦ ⟦ **parameter** ⟧ (*parameter*_interface_list) ⟧

function_specification ⇐
    ⟦ **pure** ⎮ **impure** ⟧ **function** ⟨ identifier ⎮ operator_symbol ⟩
        ⟦ **generic** (*generic*_interface_list)
        ⟦ **generic map** (*generic*_association_list) ⟧ ⟧
        ⟦ ⟦ **parameter** ⟧ (*parameter*_interface_list) ⟧ **return** type_mark

subprogram_declaration ⇐ subprogram_specification ;

subprogram_body ⇐
    subprogram_specification **is**
        { subprogram_declarative_item }
    begin
        { sequential_statement }
    end ⟦ **procedure** ⎮ **function** ⟧ ⟦ identifier ⎮ operator_symbol ⟧ ;

subprogram_declarative_item ⇐
    subprogram_declaration   ⎮ subprogram_body
    ⎮ subprogram_instantiation_declaration
    ⎮ package_declaration   ⎮ package_body
    ⎮ package_instantiation_declaration
    ⎮ type_declaration   ⎮ subtype_declaration
    ⎮ constant_declaration   ⎮ variable_declaration
    ⎮ file_declaration   ⎮ alias_declaration
    ⎮ attribute_declaration   ⎮ attribute_specification
    ⎮ use_clause
    ⎮ group_template_declaration   ⎮ group_declaration

subprogram_instantiation_declaration ⇐
    ⟨ **procedure** ⎮ **function** ⟩ identifier **is**
        new *uninstantiated_subprogram*_name ⟦ signature ⟧
            ⟦ **generic map** (*generic*_association_list) ⟧ ;

type_declaration ⇐
    type identifier **is** type_definition ;
    ⎮ **type** identifier ;

type_definition ⇐
    enumeration_type_definition   ⎮ integer_type_definition
    ⎮ floating_type_definition   ⎮ physical_type_definition
    ⎮ array_type_definition   ⎮ record_type_definition
    ⎮ access_type_definition   ⎮ file_type_definition
    ⎮ protected_type_declaration   ⎮ protected_type_body

constant_declaration ⇐
    constant identifier { , ... } : subtype_indication ⟦ := expression ⟧ ;

signal_declaration ⇐
    signal identifier ⟦ , ₒₒₒ ⟧ : subtype_indication ⟦ **register** ⎮ **bus** ⟧
                            ⟦ := expression ⟧ ;

variable_declaration ⇐
    ⟦ **shared** ⟧ **variable** identifier ⟦ , ₒₒₒ ⟧ : subtype_indication ⟦ := expression ⟧ ;

file_declaration ⇐
    file identifier ⟦ , ₒₒₒ ⟧ : subtype_indication
            ⟦ ⟦ **open** *file_open_kind*_expression ⟧ **is** *string*_expression ⟧ ;

alias_declaration ⇐
    alias (identifier ⎮ character_literal ⎮ operator_symbol)
            ⟦ : subtype_indication⟧ **is** name ⟦ signature ⟧ ;

component_declaration ⇐
    component identifier ⟦ **is** ⟧
            ⟦ **generic** (*generic*_interface_list) ; ⟧
            ⟦ **port** (*port*_interface_list) ; ⟧
    end component ⟦ identifier ⟧ ;

attribute_declaration ⇐ **attribute** identifier : type_mark ;

attribute_specification ⇐
    attribute identifier **of** entity_name_list : entity_class **is** expression ;

entity_name_list ⇐
    ((identifier ⎮ character_literal ⎮ operator_symbol) ⟦ signature ⟧) ⟦ , ₒₒₒ ⟧
    ⎮ **others**
    ⎮ **all**

entity_class ⇐
    entity   ⎮ **architecture**   ⎮ **configuration**   ⎮ **package**
    ⎮ **procedure**   ⎮ **function**   ⎮ **type**   ⎮ **subtype**
    ⎮ **constant**   ⎮ **signal**   ⎮ **variable**   ⎮ **file**
    ⎮ **component**   ⎮ **label**   ⎮ **literal**   ⎮ **units**
    ⎮ **group**   ⎮ **property**   ⎮ **sequence**

configuration_specification ⇐
    for component_specification
        binding_indication ;
            ⟦ **use vunit** *verification_unit*_name ⟦ , ₒₒₒ ⟧ ; ⟧
    ⟦ **end for** ; ⟧

component_specification ⇐
    (*instantiation*_label ⟦ , ₒₒₒ ⟧ ⎮ **others** ⎮ **all**) : *component*_name

binding_indication ⟸
    use ⟨   **entity** *entity*_name ⟦ (*architecture*_identifier) ⟧
           Ⅰ **configuration** *c*onfiguration_name
           Ⅰ **open** ⟩
    ⟦ **generic map** (*generic*_association_list) ⟧
    ⟦ **port map** (*port*_association_list) ⟧

disconnection_specification ⟸
    disconnect ⟦ *signal*_name { , ... } Ⅰ **others** Ⅰ **all** ⟩ : type_mark
        after *time*_expression ;

group_template_declaration ⟸
    group identifier **is** (⟦ entity_class ⟦ <> ⟧ ⟧ { , ... }) ;

group_declaration ⟸
    group identifier : *group_template*_name (⟦ name Ⅰ character_literal ⟧ { , ... }) ;

use_clause ⟸ **use** selected_name { , ... } ;

B.4 Type Definitions

enumeration_type_definition ⟸ (⟦ identifier Ⅰ character_literal ⟧ { , ... })

integer_type_definition ⟸
    range ⟨ *range*_attribute_name
        Ⅰ simple_expression ⟨ **to** Ⅰ **downto** ⟩ simple_expression ⟩

floating_type_definition ⟸
    range ⟨ *range*_attribute_name
        Ⅰ simple_expression ⟨ **to** Ⅰ **downto** ⟩ simple_expression ⟩

physical_type_definition ⟸
    range ⟨ *range*_attribute_name
        Ⅰ simple_expression ⟨ **to** Ⅰ **downto** ⟩ simple_expression ⟩
      units
        identifier ;
        { identifier – physical_literal ; }
      end units ⟦ identifier ⟧

array_type_definition ⟸
    array (⟦ type_mark **range** <> ⟧ { , ... }) **of** *element*_subtype_indication
    Ⅰ **array** (discrete_range { , ... }) **of** *element*_subtype_indication

record_type_definition ⟸
    record
        ⟦ identifier { , ... } : subtype_indication ; ⟧
        { ... }
    end record ⟦ identifier ⟧

access_type_definition ⟸ **access** subtype_indication

file_type_definition ⟸ **file of** type_mark

protected_type_declaration ⇐
   protected
      ⦃ protected_type_declarative_item ⦄
   end protected ⟦ identifier ⟧

protected_type_declarative_item ⇐
   subprogram_declaration   ⎪ subprogram_instantiation_declaration
   ⎪ attribute_specification   ⎪ use_clause

protected_type_body ⇐
   protected body
      ⦃ protected_type_body_declarative_item ⦄
   end protected body ⟦ identifier ⟧

protected_type_body_declarative_item ⇐
   subprogram_declaration   ⎪ subprogram_body
   ⎪ subprogram_instantiation_declaration
   ⎪ package_declaration   ⎪ package_body
   ⎪ package_instantiation_declaration
   ⎪ type_declaration   ⎪ subtype_declaration
   ⎪ constant_declaration   ⎪ variable_declaration
   ⎪ file_declaration   ⎪ alias_declaration
   ⎪ attribute_declaration   ⎪ attribute_specification
   ⎪ use_clause
   ⎪ group_template_declaration   ⎪ group_declaration

subtype_declaration ⇐ **subtype** identifier **is** subtype_indication ;

subtype_indication ⇐
   ⟦ resolution_indication ⟧ type_mark ⟦ constraint ⟧

resolution_indication ⇐
   *resolution_function*_name
   ⎪ (resolution_indication
         ⎪ ⦅ *record_element*_identifier resolution_indication ⦆ ⦃ , ⦁⦁⦁ ⦄)

constraint ⇐
   range ⦅ *range*_attribute_name
         ⎪ simple_expression ⦅ **to** ⎪ **downto** ⦆ simple_expression ⦆
   ⎪ array_constraint
   ⎪ record_constraint

array_constraint ⇐
   (discrete_range ⦃ , ... ⦄) ⟦ array_constraint ⎪ record_constraint ⟧
   ⎪ (**open**) ⟦ array_constraint ⎪ record_constraint ⟧

record_constraint ⇐
   (⦅ *record_element*_identifier ⦅ array_constraint ⎪ record_constraint ⦆ ⦆ ⦃ , ⦁⦁⦁ ⦄)

discrete_range ⇐
   *discrete*_subtype_indication
   ⫿ *range*_attribute_name
   ⫿ simple_expression ⫲ **to** ⫿ **downto** ⫳ simple_expression

type_mark ⇐ *type*_name ⫿ *subtype*_name

B.5 Concurrent Statements

concurrent_statement ⇐
   block_statement
   ⫿ process_statement
   ⫿ concurrent_procedure_call_statement
   ⫿ concurrent_assertion_statement
   ⫿ concurrent_signal_assignment_statement
   ⫿ component_instantiation_statement
   ⫿ generate_statement
   ⫿ *PSL*_PSL_Directive

block_statement ⇐
   *block*_label :
   block ⟦ (*guard*_expression) ⟧ ⟦ **is** ⟧
      ⟦ **generic** (*generic*_interface_list) ;
      ⟦ **generic map** (*generic*_association_list) ; ⟧ ⟧
      ⟦ **port** (*port*_interface_list) ;
      ⟦ **port map** (*port*_association_list) ; ⟧ ⟧
      ⦃ block_declarative_item ⦄
   begin
      ⦃ concurrent_statement ⦄
   end block ⟦ *block*_label ⟧ ;

block_declarative_item ⇐

subprogram_declaration	⫿ subprogram_body
⫿ subprogram_instantiation_declaration	
⫿ package_declaration	⫿ package_body
⫿ package_instantiation_declaration	
⫿ type_declaration	⫿ subtype_declaration
⫿ constant_declaration	⫿ signal_declaration
⫿ *shared*_variable_declaration	⫿ file_declaration
⫿ alias_declaration	⫿ component_declaration
⫿ attribute_declaration	⫿ attribute_specification
⫿ configuration_specification	⫿ disconnection_specification
⫿ use_clause	
⫿ group_template_declaration	⫿ group_declaration
⫿ *PSL*_Property_Declaration	⫿ *PSL*_Sequence_Declaration
⫿ *PSL*_Clock_Declaration	

process_statement ⇐
    ⟦ *process*_label : ⟧
    ⟦ **postponed** ⟧ **process** ⟦ ((*signal*_name ⟨ , ... ⟩) ∣ **all**) ⟧ ⟦ **is** ⟧
        ⟨ process_declarative_item ⟩
    begin
        ⟨ sequential_statement ⟩
    end ⟦ **postponed** ⟧ **process** ⟦ *process*_label ⟧ ;

process_declarative_item ⇐
    subprogram_declaration   I subprogram_body
    <u>I subprogram_instantiation_declaration</u>
    <u>I package_declaration</u>   <u>I package_body</u>
    <u>I package_instantiation_declaration</u>
    I type_declaration   I subtype_declaration
    I constant_declaration   I variable_declaration
    I file_declaration   I alias_declaration
    I attribute_declaration   I attribute_specification
    I use_clause
    I group_template_declaration   I group_declaration

concurrent_procedure_call_statement ⇐
    ⟦ label : ⟧ ⟦ **postponed** ⟧ *procedure*_name ⟦ (*parameter*_association_list) ⟧ ;

concurrent_assertion_statement ⇐
    ⟦ label : ⟧ ⟦ **postponed** ⟧ **assert** condition
                    ⟦ **report** expression ⟧ ⟦ **severity** expression ⟧ ;

concurrent_signal_assignment_statement ⇐
    ⟦ label : ⟧ ⟦ **postponed** ⟧ concurrent_simple_signal_assignment
    I ⟦ label : ⟧ ⟦ **postponed** ⟧ concurrent_conditional_signal_assignment
    I ⟦ label : ⟧ ⟦ **postponed** ⟧ concurrent_selected_signal_assignment

concurrent_simple_signal_assignment ⇐
    target <= ⟦ **guarded** ⟧ ⟦ delay_mechanism ⟧ waveform ;

concurrent_conditional_signal_assignment ⇐
    target <= ⟦ **guarded** ⟧ ⟦ delay_mechanism ⟧
        waveform **when** condition
        ⟨ **else** waveform **when** condition ⟩
        ⟦ **else** waveform ⟧ ;

concurrent_selected_signal_assignment ⇐
    with expression **select** ⟦ ? ⟧
        target <= ⟦ **guarded** ⟧ ⟦ delay_mechanism ⟧
            ⟨ waveform **when** choices , ⟩
        waveform **when** choices ;

component_instantiation_statement ⇐
    *instantiation*_label :
            ([**component**] *component*_name
            | **entity** *entity*_name [(*architecture*_identifier)]
            | **configuration** *configuration*_name)
        [**generic map** (*generic*_association_list)]
        [**port map** (*port*_association_list)] ;

generate_statement ⇐
    for_generate_statement | if_generate_statement | case_generate_statement

for_generate_statement ⇐
    *generate*_label :
    for identifier **in** discrete_range **generate**
        generate_statement_body
    end generate [*generate*_label] ;

if_generate_statement ⇐
    *generate*_label :
    if [*alternative*_label :] condition **generate**
        generate_statement_body
    { **elsif** [*alternative*_label :] condition **generate**
        generate_statement_body }
    [**else** [*alternative*_label :] **generate**
        generate_statement_body]
    end generate [*generate*_label] ;

case_generate_statement ⇐
    *generate*_label :
    case expression **generate**
        (**when** [*alternative*_label :] choices =>
            generate_statement_body)
        { ... }
    end generate [*generate*_label] ;

generate_statement_body ⇐
        [{ block_declarative_item }
    begin]
        { concurrent_statement }
    [**end** [*alternative*_label] ;]

B.6   Sequential Statements

sequential_statement ⇐
    wait_statement | assertion_statement
    | report_statement | signal_assignment_statement
    | variable_assignment_statement | procedure_call_statement
    | if_statement | case_statement
    | loop_statement | next_statement

⟦ exit_statement   ⟦ return_statement
⟦ null_statement

wait_statement ⟸
    ⟦ label : ⟧ **wait** ⟦ **on** *signal*_name ⟨ , ∘∘∘ ⟩ ⟧
                 ⟦ **until** condition ⟧
                 ⟦ **for** *time*_expression ⟧ ;

assertion_statement ⟸
    ⟦ label : ⟧ **assert** condition
                 ⟦ **report** expression ⟧ ⟦ **severity** expression ⟧ ;

report_statement ⟸
    ⟦ label : ⟧ **report** expression ⟦ **severity** expression ⟧ ;

signal_assignment_statement ⟸
    ⟦ label : ⟧ simple_signal_assignment
    ⟦ ⟦ label : ⟧ conditional_signal_assignment
    ⟦ ⟦ label : ⟧ selected_signal_assignment

simple_signal_assignment ⟸
    (name ⟦ aggregate) <= ⟦ delay_mechanism ⟧ waveform ;
    ⟦ name <= **force** ⟦ **in** ⟦ **out** ⟧ expression ;
    ⟦ name <= **release** ⟦ **in** ⟦ **out** ⟧ ;

conditional_signal_assignment ⟸
    conditional_waveform_assignment ⟦ conditional_force_assignment

conditional_waveform_assignment ⟸
    ⟦ label : ⟧
    (name ⟦ aggregate) <= ⟦ delay_mechanism ⟧
        waveform **when** condition
        ⟨ **else** waveform **when** condition ⟩
        ⟦ **else** waveform ⟧ ;

conditional_force_assignment ⟸
    ⟦ label : ⟧
    name <= **force** ⟦ **in** ⟦ **out** ⟧
        expression **when** condition
        ⟨ **else** expression **when** condition ⟩
        ⟦ **else** expression ⟧ ;

selected_signal_assignment ⟸
    selected_waveform_assignment ⟦ selected_force_assignment

selected_waveform_assignment ⟸
    ⟦ label : ⟧
    with expression **select** ⟦ **?** ⟧
        (name ⟦ aggregate) <= ⟦ delay_mechanism ⟧
            ⟨ waveform **when** choices , ⟩
        waveform **when** choices ;

selected_signal_assignment ⇐
    〚 label : 〛
    with expression **select** 〚 ? 〛
        name <= **force** 〚 **in** ▯ **out** 〛
                { expression **when** choices , }
                expression **when** choices ;

delay_mechanism ⇐ **transport** ▯ 〚 **reject** *time*_expression 〛 **inertial**

waveform ⇐
    (*value*_expression 〚 **after** *time*_expression 〛
       ▯ **null** 〚 **after** *time*_expression 〛) { , ∘∘∘ }
    ▯ **unaffected**

variable_assignment_statement ⇐
    〚 label : 〛 simple_variable_assignment
    <u>▯ 〚 label : 〛 conditional_variable_assignment</u>
    <u>▯ 〚 label : 〛 selected_variable_assignment</u>

simple_variable_assignment ⇐
    (name ▯ aggregate) := expression ;

<u>conditional_variable_assignment</u> ⇐
    (name ▯ aggregate) :=
        expression **when** condition
        { **else** expression **when** condition }
        〚 **else** expression 〛 ;

<u>selected_variable_assignment</u> ⇐
    with expression **select** 〚 ? 〛
        (name ▯ aggregate) :=
        { expression **when** choices , }
        expression **when** choices ;

procedure_call_statement ⇐
    〚 label : 〛 *procedure*_name 〚 (*parameter*_association_list) 〛 ;

if_statement ⇐
    〚 *if*_label : 〛
    if condition **then**
        { sequential_statement }
    { **elsif** condition **then**
        { sequential_statement } }
    〚 **else**
        { sequential_statement } 〛
    end if 〚 *if*_label 〛 ;

case_statement ⇐
   ⟦ *case*_label : ⟧
   case ⟦ ? ⟧ expression **is**
      (**when** choices => { sequential_statement })
      { ₀₀₀ }
   end case ⟦ ? ⟧ ⟦ *case*_label ⟧ ;

loop_statement ⇐
   ⟦ *loop*_label : ⟧
   ⟦ **while** condition ⏐ **for** identifier **in** discrete_range ⟧ **loop**
      { sequential_statement }
   end loop ⟦ *loop*_label ⟧ ;

next_statement ⇐ ⟦ label : ⟧ **next** ⟦ *loop*_label ⟧ ⟦ **when** condition ⟧ ;

exit_statement ⇐ ⟦ label : ⟧ **exit** ⟦ *loop*_label ⟧ ⟦ **when** condition ⟧ ;

return_statement ⇐ ⟦ label : ⟧ **return** ⟦ expression ⟧ ;

null_statement ⇐ ⟦ label : ⟧ **null** ;

B.7   Interfaces and Associations

interface_list ⇐
   (interface_constant_declaration
   ⏐ interface_signal_declaration
   ⏐ interface_variable_declaration
   ⏐ interface_file_declaration
   ⏐ interface_type_declaration
   ⏐ interface_subprogram_declaration
   ⏐ interface_package_declaration) { ; ₀₀₀ }

interface_constant_declaration ⇐
   ⟦ **constant** ⟧ identifier { , ₀₀₀ } : ⟦ **in** ⟧ subtype_indication
                                   ⟦ := *static*_expression ⟧

interface_signal_declaration ⇐
   ⟦ **signal** ⟧ identifier { , ₀₀₀ } : ⟦ mode ⟧ subtype_indication ⟦ **bus** ⟧
                                   ⟦ := *static*_expression ⟧

interface_variable_declaration ⇐
   ⟦ **variable** ⟧ identifier { , ₀₀₀ } : ⟦ mode ⟧ subtype_indication
                                   ⟦ := *static*_expression ⟧

mode ⇐ **in** ⏐ **out** ⏐ **inout** ⏐ **buffer** ⏐ **linkage**

interface_file_declaration ⇐
   file identifier { , ₀₀₀ } : subtype_indication

interface_type_declaration ⇐ **type** identifier

interface_subprogram_declaration ⇐
    ⟨   **procedure** identifier
        ⟦ ⟦ **parameter** ⟧ (*parameter*_interface_list) ⟧
    | ⟦ **pure** | **impure** ⟧ **function** ⟨ identifier | operator_symbol ⟩
        ⟦ ⟦ **parameter** ⟧ (*parameter*_interface_list) ⟧ **return** type_mark
    ⟩ ⟦ **is** ⟨ *subprogram*_name | <> ⟩ ⟧

interface_package_declaration ⇐
    package identifier **is new** *uninstantiated_package*_name
        generic map (⟨ *generic*_association_list | <> | **default** ⟩)

association_list ⇐ ⟨ ⟦ formal_part => ⟧ actual_part ⟩ ⟨ , ... ⟩

formal_part ⇐
    *generic*_name
    | *port*_name
    | *parameter*_name
    | *function*_name (⟨ *generic*_name | *port*_name | *parameter*_name ⟩)
    | type_mark (⟨ *generic*_name | *port*_name | *parameter*_name ⟩)

actual_part ⇐
    ⟦ **inertial** ⟧ expression
    | *signal*_name
    | *variable*_name
    | *file*_name
    | subtype_indication
    | *subprogram*_name
    | *package*_name
    | **open**
    | *function*_name (⟨ *signal*_name | *variable*_name ⟩)
    | type_mark (⟨ *signal*_name | *variable*_name ⟩)

B.8 Expressions and Names

condition ⇐ expression

expression ⇐ ⟨ **??** primary ⟩ | logical_expression

logical_expression ⇐
    relation ⟨ **and** relation ⟩ | relation ⟦ **nand** relation ⟧
    | relation ⟨ **or** relation ⟩ | relation ⟦ **nor** relation ⟧
    | relation ⟨ **xor** relation ⟩ | relation ⟨ **xnor** relation ⟩

relation ⇐
    shift_expression
        ⟦ ⟨ = | /= | < | <= | > | >= | ?= | ?/= | ?< | ?<= | ?> | ?>= ⟩ shift_expression ⟧

shift_expression ⇐
    simple_expression ⟦ ⟨ **sll** | **srl** | **sla** | **sra** | **rol** | **ror** ⟩ simple_expression ⟧

simple_expression ⇐ ⟦ + ▯ − ⟧ term { (+ ▯ − ▯ &) term }

term ⇐ factor { (* ▯ / ▯ **mod** ▯ **rem**) factor }

factor ⇐
    primary ⟦ ** primary ⟧
    ▯ **abs** primary
    ▯ **not** primary
    ▯ **and** primary
    ▯ **nand** primary
    ▯ **or** primary
    ▯ **nor** primary
    ▯ **xor** primary
    ▯ **xnor** primary

primary ⇐
    name   ▯ literal
    ▯ aggregate   ▯ function_call
    ▯ qualified_expression   ▯ type_mark (expression)
    ▯ **new** subtype_indication   ▯ **new** qualified_expression
    ▯ (expression)

function_call ⇐ *function*_name ⟦ (*parameter*_association_list) ⟧

qualified_expression ⇐ type_mark ' (expression) ▯ type_mark ' aggregate

name ⇐
    identifier
    ▯ operator_symbol
    ▯ character_literal
    ▯ selected_name
    ▯ (name ▯ function_call) (expression { , ... })
    ▯ (name ▯ function_call) (discrete_range)
    ▯ attribute_name
    ▯ external_name

selected_name ⇐
    (name ▯ function_call) . (identifier ▯ character_literal ▯ operator_symbol ▯ **all**)

operator_symbol ⇐ " { graphic_character } "

attribute_name ⇐
    (name ▯ function_call) ⟦ signature ⟧ ' identifier ⟦ (expression) ⟧

signature ⇐ [⟦ type_mark { , ... } ⟧ ⟦ **return** type_mark ⟧]

external_name ⇐
      << **constant** external_pathname : subtype_indication >>
    ▯ << **signal** external_pathname : subtype_indication >>
    ▯ << **variable** external_pathname : subtype_indication >>

external_pathname ⇐
    absolute_pathname ▯ relative_pathname ▯ package_pathname

absolute_pathname ⇐ . ⦃ pathname_element . ⦄ *object*_identifier

relative_pathname ⇐ ⦃ ∧ . ⦄ ⦃ pathname_element . ⦄ *object*_identifier

pathname_element ::=
    *entity*_identifier
    ⫾ *component_instantiation*_label
    ⫾ *block*_label
    ⫾ *generate_statement*_label ⟦ (*static*_expression) ⟧
    ⫾ *package*_identifier

package_pathname ⇐ @ *library*_identifier . { *package*_identifier . } *object*_identifier

literal ⇐
    decimal_literal   ⫾ based_literal
    ⫾ physical_literal   ⫾ identifier
    ⫾ character_literal   ⫾ string_literal
    ⫾ bit_string_literal   ⫾ **null**

physical_literal ⇐ ⟦ decimal_literal ⫾ based_literal ⟧ *unit*_name

decimal_literal ⇐ integer ⟦ . integer ⟧ ⟦ E ⟦ + ⟧ integer ⫾ E − integer ⟧

based_literal ⇐
    integer # based_integer ⟦ . based_integer ⟧ # ⟦ E ⟦ + ⟧ integer ⫾ E − integer ⟧

integer ⇐ digit ⦃ ⟦ _ ⟧ ₒₒₒ ⦄

based_integer ⇐ (digit ⫾ letter) ⦃ ⟦ _ ⟧ ₒₒₒ ⦄

character_literal ⇐ ' graphic_character '

string_literal ⇐ " ⦃ graphic_character ⦄ "

bit_string_literal ⇐
    ⟦ integer ⟧ (B ⫾ O ⫾ X ⫾ UB ⫾ UO ⫾ UX ⫾ SB ⫾ SO ⫾ SX ⫾ D)
    " ⟦ graphic_character ⦃ ⟦ _ ⟧ ₒₒₒ ⦄ ⟧ "

aggregate ⇐ ((⟦ choices => ⟧ expression) ⦃ , ₒₒₒ ⦄)

choices ⇐ (simple_expression ⫾ discrete_range ⫾ identifier ⫾ **others**) ⦃ | ₒₒₒ ⦄

label ⇐ identifier

identifier ⇐ letter ⦃ ⟦ _ ⟧ (letter ⫾ digit) ⦄ ⫾ \ graphic_character ⦃ ₒₒₒ ⦄ \

tool_directive ⇐ ` identifier ⦃ graphic_character ⦄

Appendix C

Answers to Exercises

In this appendix, we provide sample answers to the quiz-style exercises marked with the symbol "❶". Readers are encouraged to test their answers to the other, more involved, exercises by running the models on a VHDL simulator.

Chapter 1

1. Entity declaration: defines the interface to a module, in terms of its ports, their data transfer direction and their types. Behavioral architecture body: defines the function of a module in terms of an algorithm. Structural architecture body: defines an implementation of a module in terms of an interconnected composition of sub-modules. Process statement: encapsulates an algorithm in a behavioral description, contains sequential actions to be performed. Signal assignment statement: specifies values to be applied to signals at some later time. Port map: specifies the interconnection between signals and component instance ports in a structural architecture.

2.
```
apply_transform : process is
begin
  d_out <= transform(d_in) after 200 ps;
  -- debug_test <= transform(d_in);
  wait on enable, d_in;
end process apply_transform;
```

3. Basic identifiers: last_item. Reserved words: **buffer**. Invalid: prev item, value−1 and element#5 include characters that may not occur within identifiers; _control starts with an underscore; 93_999 starts with a digit; entry_ ends with an underscore.

4. 16#1#   16#22#   16#100.0#   16#0.8#

5. 12   132   44   250000   32768   0.625

6. The literal 16#23DF# is an integer expressed in base 16, whereas the literal X"23DF" is a string of 16 bits.

7. O"747" = B"111_100_111"
    O"377" = B"011_111_111"
    O"1_345" = B"001_011_100_101"

    X"F2" = B"1111_0010"
    X"0014" = B"0000_0000_0001_0100"
    X"0000_0001" = B"0000_0000_0000_0000_0000_0000_0000_0001"

8. 10UO"747" = B"0_111_100_111"
    10UO"377" = B"0_011_111_111"
    10UO"1_345" = B"1_011_100_101"

    10SO"747" = B"1_111_100_111"
    10SO"377" = B"0_011_111_111"
    10SO"1_345" = B"1_011_100_101"

    12UX"F2" = B"0000_1111_0010"
    12SX"F2" = B"1111_1111_0010"
    10UX"F2" *is illegal due to truncation of leading 1 bits*
    10SX"F2" = B"11_1111_0010"

9. D"24" = B"11000"
    12D"24" = B"0000_0001_1000"
    4D"24" *is illegal due to truncation of a leading 1 bit*

Chapter 2

1. **constant** bits_per_word : integer := 32;
    constant pi : real := 3.14159;

2. **variable** counter : integer := 0;
    variable busy_status : boolean;
    variable temp_result : std_ulogic;

3. counter := counter + 1;
    busy_status := true;
    temp_result := 'W';

4. **package** misc_types **is**
        type small_int **is range** 0 **to** 255;
        type fraction **is range** -1.0 **to** +1.0;
        type current **is range** integer'low **to** integer'high
          units nA;
            uA = 1000 nA;
            mA = 1000 uA;
            A = 1000 mA;
          end units;
        type colors **is** (red, yellow, green);
    end package misc_types;

5. a. Legal

    b. Illegal, should be: a = '1' **and** b = '0' **and** state = idle

    c. Illegal, should be: a = '0' **and** b = '1' **and** state = idle

    d. Legal

6. pulse_range'left = pulse_range'low = 1 ms
    pulse_range'right = pulse_range'high = 100 ms
    pulse_range'ascending = true

    word_index'left = 31word_index'right = 0
    word_index'low = 0word_index'high = 31
    word_index'ascending = false

7. state'pos(standby) = 1   state'val(2) = active1
    state'succ(active2) *is undefined*   state'pred(active1) = standby
    state'leftof(off) *is undefined*   state'rightof(off) = standby

8. 2 * 3 + 6 / 4 = 7
    3 + -4 *is syntactically incorrect*
    "cat" & character'('0') = "cat0"
    true **and** x **and** **not** y **or** z *is syntactically incorrect*
    B"101110" **sll** 3 = B"110000"
    (B"100010" **sra** 2) & X"2C"= B"11100000101100"

Chapter 3

1. **if** n **mod** 2 = 1 **then**
       odd := '1';
    else
       odd := '0';
    end if;

2. **if** year **mod** 400 = 0 **then**
       days_in_February := 29;
    elsif year **mod** 100 = 0 **then**
       days_in_February := 28;
    elsif year **mod** 4 = 0 **then**
       days_in_February := 29;
    else
       days_in_February := 28;
    end if;

3. **case** x **is**
       when '0' | 'L' => x := '0';
       when '1' | 'H' => x := '1';

```
      when others => x := 'X';
   end case;
```

4.
```
   case ch is
      when 'A' to 'Z' | 'a' to 'z' |
           'À' to 'Ö' | 'Ø' to 'ß' | 'à' to 'ö' | 'ø' to 'ÿ' =>
         character_class := 1;
      when '0' to '9' =>  character_class := 2;
      when nul to usp | del | c128 to c159 =>  character_class := 4;
      when others => character_class := 3;
   end case;
```

5.
```
   loop
      wait until clk;
      exit when d;
   end loop;
```

6.
```
   sum := 1.0;
   term := 1.0;
   n := 0;
   while abs term > abs (sum / 1.0E5) loop
     n := n + 1;
     term := term * x / real(n);
     sum := sum + term;
   end loop;
```

7.
```
   sum := 1.0;
   term := 1.0;
   for n in 1 to 7 loop
     term := term * x / real(n);
     sum := sum + term;
   end loop;
```

8.
```
   assert to_X01(q) = not to_X01(q_n)
      report "flipflop outputs are not complementary";
```

9. Insert the statement after the comment "-- *at this point, reset = '1'*":

```
      report "counter is reset";
```

Chapter 4

1.
```
   type num_vector is array (1 to 30) of integer;
   variable numbers : num_vector;
   ...

   sum := 0;
   for i in numbers'range loop
```

```vhdl
      sum := sum + numbers(i);
    end loop;
    average := sum / numbers'length;
```

2.
```vhdl
   type std_ulogic_to_bit_array is array (std_ulogic) of bit;
   constant std_ulogic_to_bit : std_ulogic_to_bit_array
      := ( 'U' => '0', 'X' => '0', '0' => '0', '1' => '1', 'Z' => '0',
           'W' => '0', 'L' => '0', 'H' => '1', '-' => '0' );
   ...

   for index in 0 to 15 loop
     v2(index) := std_ulogic_to_bit(v1(index));
   end loop;
```

3.
```vhdl
   type free_map_array is array (0 to 1, 0 to 79, 0 to 17) of bit;
   variable free_map : free_map_array;
   ...

   found := false;
   search_loop : for side in 0 to 1 loop
     for track in 0 to 79 loop
       for sector in 0 to 17 loop
         if free_map(side, track, sector) then
           found := true;   free_side := side;
           free_track := track;   free_sector := sector;
           exit search_loop;
         end if;
       end loop;
     end loop;
   end loop;
```

4.
```vhdl
   subtype std_ulogic_byte is std_ulogic_vector(7 downto 0);
   constant Z_byte : std_ulogic_byte := "ZZZZZZZZ";
```

5.
```vhdl
   type times_array is array (positive range <>) of time_vector;
   subtype times4_array is times_array(1 to 4);
   variable times4_10 : times4_array(open)(0 to 9);
```

6.
```vhdl
   count := 0;
   for index in v'range loop
     if v(index) then
       count := count + 1;
     end if;
   end loop;
```

7. Assuming the declarations

```
    variable v1 : bit_vector(7 downto 0);
    variable v2 : bit_vector(31 downto 0);
    ...

    v2(31 downto 24) := v1;
    v2 := v2 sra 24;
```

8.
```
type test_record is record
    stimulus : bit_vector(0 to 2);
    delay : delay_length;
    expected_response : bit_vector(0 to 7);
end record test_record;
```

Chapter 5

1.
```
entity lookup_ROM is
    port ( address : in lookup_index;  data : out real );

    type lookup_table is array (lookup_index) of real;
    constant lookup_data : lookup_table
            := ( real'high, 1.0, 1.0/2.0, 1.0/3.0, 1.0/4.0, ... );

end entity lookup_ROM;
```

2.
```
architecture functional of lookup_ROM is
begin
    data <= lookup_data(address) after 200 ps;
end architecture functional;
```

3. Transactions are 'Z' at 0 ns, '0' at 10 ns, '1' at 30 ns, '1' at 55 ns, 'H' at 65 ns and 'Z' at 100 ns. The signal is active at all of these times. Events occur at each time except 55 ns, since the signal already has the value '1' at that time.

4. **s'delayed(5 ns):** 'Z' at 5 ns, '0' at 15 ns, '1' at 35 ns, 'H' at 70 ns, 'Z' at 105 ns. **s'stable(5 ns):** false at 0 ns, true at 5 ns, false at 10 ns, true at 15 ns, false at 30 ns, true at 35 ns, false at 65 ns, true at 70 ns, false at 100 ns, true at 105 ns. **s'quiet(5 ns):** false at 0 ns, true at 5 ns, false at 10 ns, true at 15 ns, false at 30 ns, true at 35 ns, false at 55 ns, true at 60 ns, false at 65 ns, true at 70 ns, false at 100 ns, true at 105 ns. **s'transaction** (assuming an initial value of '0'): '1' at 0 ns, '0' at 10 ns, '1' at 30 ns, '0' at 55 ns, '1' at 65 ns, '0' at 100 ns. At time 60 ns, **s'last_event** is 30 ns, **s'last_active** is 5 ns, and **s'last_value** is '0'.

5. **wait on** s **until not** s **and** en;

6. **wait until** ready **for** 5 ms;

7. The variable v1 is assigned **false**, since s is not updated until the next simulation cycle. The variable v2 is assigned **true**, since the wait statement causes the process to resume after s is updated with the value '1'.

8. At 0 ns: schedule '1' for 6 ns. At 3 ns: schedule '0' for 7 ns. At 8 ns: schedule '1' for 14 ns. At 9 ns: delete transaction scheduled for 14 ns, schedule '0' for 13 ns. The signal **z** takes on the values '1' at 6 ns and '0' at 7 ns. The transaction scheduled for 13 ns does not result in an event on **z**.

9. At 0 ns: schedule 1 for 7 ns, 23 for 9 ns, 5 for 10 ns, 23 for 12 ns and –5 for 15 ns. At 6 ns: schedule 23 for 13 ns, delete transactions scheduled for 15 ns, 10 ns and 9 ns. The signal **x** takes on the values 1 at 7 ns and 23 at 12 ns.

10. The process is sensitive to **current_state** and in1, as these are the signals read by the process.

11. ```
mux_logic : process is
begin
  if enable and sel then
    z <= a and not b after 5 ns;
  elsif enable and sel then
    z <= x or y after 6 ns;
  else
    z <= '0' after 4 ns;
  end if;
  wait on a, b, enable, sel, x, y;
end process mux_logic;
```

12. ```
process is
begin
  case bit_vector'(s, r) is
    when "00"        =>  q <= unaffected;
    when "01"        =>  q <= '0';
    when "10" | "11" =>  q <= '1';
  end case;
  wait on s, r;
end process;
```

13. ```
assert (not clk'event) or clk'delayed'last_event >= T_pw_clk
    report "interval between changes on clk is too small";
```

14. ```
bit_0 : entity work.ttl_74x74(basic)
    port map ( pr_n => '1', d => q0_n, clk => clk, clr_n => reset,
               q => q0, q_n => q0_n );

bit_1 : entity work.ttl_74x74(basic)
  port map ( pr_n => '1', d => q1_n, clk => q0_n, clr_n => reset,
             q => q1, q_n => q1_n );
```

15.

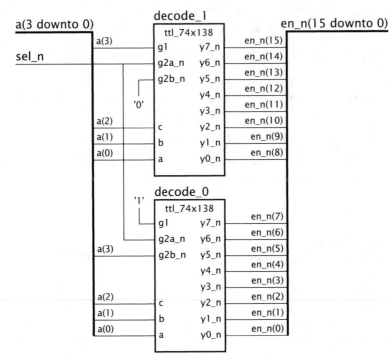

16. One possible order is suggested: analyzing all entity declarations first, followed by all architecture bodies:

    entity **edge_triggered_Dff**
    entity **reg4**
    entity **add_1**
    entity **buf4**
    entity **counter**
    architecture **behav** of **edge_triggered_Dff**
    architecture **struct** of **reg4**
    architecture **boolean_eqn** of **add_1**
    architecture **basic** of **buf**
    architecture **registered** of **counter**

An alternative is

    entity **counter**
    entity **buf4**
    entity **add_1**
    entity **reg4**
    architecture **registered** of **counter**
    architecture **basic** of **buf**
    architecture **boolean_eqn** of **add_1**
    entity **edge_triggered_Dff**

```
architecture struct of reg4
architecture behav of edge_triggered_Dff
```

17. **library** company_lib, project_lib;
    use company_lib.in_pad, company_lib.out_pad, project_lib.**all**;

18. **context** phantom_context **is**
      library ieee, IP_worx, phantom_lib;
      use ieee.std_logic_1164.**all**;
      use IP_worx.**all**, phantom_lib.**all**;
    end context phantom_context;

Chapter 6

1. **constant** operand1 : **in** integer
   operand1 : integer
   constant tag : **in** bit_vector(31 **downto** 16)
   tag : bit_vector(31 **downto** 16)
   constant trace : **in** boolean := false
   trace : boolean := false

2. **variable** average : **out** real
   average : **out** real
   variable identifier : **inout** string
   identifier : **inout** string

3. **signal** clk : **out** bit
   signal data_in : **in** std_ulogic_vector
   signal data_in : std_ulogic_vector

4. Some alternatives are

   ```
   stimulate ( s, 5 ns, 3 );
   stimulate ( target => s, delay => 5 ns, cycles => 3 );

   stimulate ( s, 10 ns, 1 );
   stimulate ( s, 10 ns );
   stimulate ( target => s, delay => 10 ns, cycles => open );
   stimulate ( target => s, cycles => open, delay => 10 ns );
   stimulate ( target => s, delay => 10 ns );

   stimulate ( s, 1 ns, 15 );
   stimulate ( target => s, delay => open, cycles => 15 );
   stimulate ( target => s, cycles => 15 );
   stimulate ( s, cycles => 15 );
   ```

5. swapper : **process is**
   begin
     shuffle_bytes (ext_data, int_data, swap_control, Tpd_swap);

```
        wait on ext_data, swap_control;
    end process swapper;
```

6. product_size := approx_log_2(multiplicand)
                      + approx_log_2(multiplier);

7. **assert** now <= 20 ms
        report "simulation time has exceeded 20 ms";

8. The third, first, none and third, respectively.

9.
```
        architecture behavioral of computer system is
            signal internal_data : bit_vector(31 downto 0);
            interpreter : process is
                variable opcode : bit_vector(5 downto 0);
                procedure do_write is
                    variable aligned_address : natural;
                begin
                    ...
                end procedure do_write;
            begin
            ...
            end process interpreter;
        end architecture behavioral;
```

Chapter 7

1. **package** EMS_types **is**
        type engine_speed **is range** 0 **to** integer'high
            units rpm;
            end units engine_speed;
        constant peak_rpm : engine_speed := 6000 rpm;
        type gear **is** (first, second, third, fourth, reverse);
    end package EMS_types;

```
    work.EMS_types.engine_speed
    work.EMS_types.rpm              work.EMS_types.peak_rpm
    work.EMS_types.gear            work.EMS_types.first
    work.EMS_types.second          work.EMS_types.third
    work.EMS_types.fourth          work.EMS_types.reverse
```

2. **procedure** increment (num : **inout** integer);

3. **function** odd (num : integer) **return** boolean;

4. **constant** e : real;

5. No. The package does not contain any subprogram declarations or deferred constant declarations.

6. **use** work.EMS_types.engine_speed;

7. **library** DSP_lib;
   use DSP_lib.systolic_FFT, DSP_lib.DSP_types.**all**;

Chapter 8

1. a. '1'.

   b. '0'.

   c. Either '1' or '0'. The order of contributions within the array passed to the resolution function is not defined. This particular resolution function returns the leftmost non-'Z' value in the array, so the result depends on the order in which the simulator assembles the contributions.

2. **subtype** wired_and_logic **is** wired_and tri_state_logic;
   signal synch_control : wired_and_logic := '0';

3. The initial value is 'X'. The default initial value of type **MVL4**, 'X', is used as the initial value of each driver of **int_req**. These contributions are passed to the resolution function, which returns the value 'X'.

4. No, since the operation represented by the table in the resolution function is commutative and associative, with 'Z' as its identity.

5. a. "ZZZZ0011"

   b. "XXXX0011"

   c. "0011XX11"

6. "XXXXZZZZ00111100"

7. a. '0'

   b. '0'

   c. 'W'

   d. 'U'

   e. 'X'

8.

driving value from
bus_module_1

driving value from
bus_module_2

synch_control

Both bus modules proceed when
synch_control changes to 'H'.

9. The resolution function is invoked seven times: for the Mem port, the Cache port, the CPU/Mem Section port, the Serial port, the DMA port, the I/O Section port and the Data Bus signal.

10. We cannot simply invert the value read from the port, since the value may differ from that driven by the process. Instead, we use the **'driving_value** attribute:

```
synch_T <= not synch_T'driving_value;
```

Chapter 9

1. **assert** std.env.resolution_limit < 1.0E-9 sec;

2. to_hstring(B"ZZZZ_0100") = "Z4"
    to_hstring(B"XX_L01H") = to_hstring(B"XXXX_L01H") = "X3"
    to_hstring(B"01_00ZZ") = to_hstring(B"0001_00ZZ") = "1X"

3. **use** ieee.numeric_std.**all**;
    ...
    signal a, b, s : unsigned(23 **downto** 0);
    signal carry_in, carry_out : std_ulogic;
    ...
    (carry_out, s) <= a + b + carry_in;

4. One approach, using implicit conversion of **en** to **boolean**, is

```
D_ff : process (clk) is
begin
  if rising_edge(clk) then
    if en then
```

```
            q <= To_X01(d);
          end if;
        end if;
      end process D_ff;
```

Alternatively:

```
    D_ff : process (clk) is
    begin
      if rising_edge(clk) and To_X01(en) = '1' then
        q <= To_X01(d);
      end if;
    end process D_ff;
```

Chapter 10

1. ```
   alias received_source is received_packet.source;
   alias received_dest is received_packet.dest;
   alias received_flags is received_packet.flags;
   alias received_payload is received_packet.payload;
   alias received_checksum is received_packet.checksum;
   ```

2. ```
   alias received_AK is received_packet.flags(0);
   alias received_ACKNO : bit_vector(2 downto 0)
           is received_packet.flags(1 to 3);
   alias received_SEQNO : bit_vector(2 downto 0)
           is received_packet.flags(4 to 6);
   alias received_UD is received_packet.flags(7);
   ```

3. ```
   alias cons is "&" [ character, string return string ];

   report cons ( grade_char, "-grade" );
   ```

Chapter 11

1. ```
   entity flipflop is
     generic ( Tpw_clk_h, T_pw_clk_l : delay_length := 3 ns );
     port ( clk, d : in bit;  q, q_n : out bit );
   end entity flipflop;
   ```

2. ```
   clk_gen : entity work.clock_generator
     generic map ( period => 10 ns )
     port map ( clk => master_clk );
   ```

3. ```
   entity adder is
     generic ( data_length : positive );
     port ( a, b : in std_ulogic_vector(data_length - 1 downto 0);
   ```

```
              sum : out std_ulogic_vector(data_length - 1 downto 0) );
       end entity adder;
```

4.  ```
    io_control_reg : entity work.reg
       generic map ( width => 4 )
       port map ( d => data_out(3 downto 0),
                  q(0) => io_en, q(1) => io_int_en,
                  q(2) => io_dir, q(3) => io_mode,
                  clk => io_write, reset => io_reset );
    ```

Chapter 12

1. An entity declaration uses the keyword **entity** where a component declaration uses the keyword **component**. An entity declaration is a design unit that is analyzed and placed into a design library, whereas a component declaration is simply a declaration in an architecture body or a package. An entity declaration has a declarative part and a statement part, providing part of the implementation of the interface, whereas a component declaration simply declares an interface with no implementation information. An entity declaration represents the interface of a "real" electronic circuit, whereas a component declaration represents a "virtual" or "template" interface.

2.  ```
    component magnitude_comparator is
       generic ( width : positive;  Tpd : delay_length );
       port ( a, b : in std_ulogic_vector(width - 1 downto 0);
              a_equals_b, a_less_than_b : out std_ulogic );
    end component magnitude_comparator;
    ```

3.  ```
    position_comparator : component magnitude_comparator
       generic map ( width => current_position'length, Tpd => 12 ns )
       port map ( a => current_position, b => upper_limit,
                  a_less_than_b => position_ok, a_equals_b => open );
    ```

4.  ```
    package small_number_pkg is
       subtype small_number is natural range 0 to 255;
       component adder is
          port ( a, b : in small_number;  s : out small_number );
       end component adder;
    end package small_number_pkg;
    ```

5.  ```
    library dsp_lib;
    configuration digital_filter_rtl of digital_filter is
       for register_transfer
          for coeff_1_multiplier : multiplier
             use entity dsp_lib.fixed_point_mult(algorithmic);
          end for;
       end for;
    end configuration digital_filter_rtl;
    ```
    ```

6. ```
   library dsp_lib;
   configuration digital_filter_std_cell of digital_filter is
     for register_transfer
       for coeff_1_multiplier : multiplier
         use configuration dsp_lib.fixed_point_mult_std_cell;
       end for;
     end for;
   end configuration digital_filter_std_cell;
   ```

7. ```
   library dsp_lib;
   architecture register_transfer of digital_filter is
     ...
   begin
     coeff_1_multiplier :
       configuration dsp_lib.fixed_point_mult_std_cell
         port map ( ... );
     ...
   end architecture register_transfer;
   ```

8. ```
   use entity work.multiplexer
     generic map ( Tpd => 3.5 ns );
   ```

9.

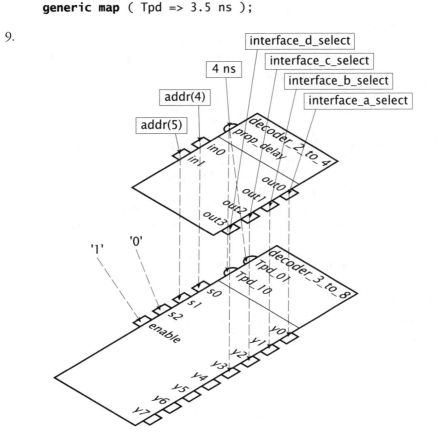
   ```

10. **generic map** (Tpd_01 => **open**, Tpd_10 => **open**)
    port map (a => a, b => b, c => c, d => **open**, y => y)

Chapter 13

1.
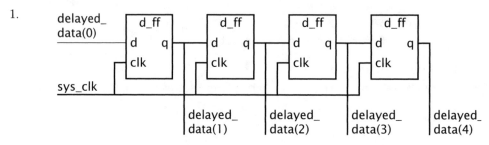

2. inverter_array : **for** index **in** data_in'range **generate**
       inv : **component** inverter
         port map (i => data_in(index), y_n => data_out_n(index));
     end generate inverter_array;

3. direct_clock : **if** positive_clock **generate**
       internal_clock <= external_clock;
     else generate
       clock_inverter : **component** inverter
         port map (i => external_clock, y => internal_clock);
     end generate inverting_clock;

Chapter 14

1. **Temp** is allowed, as it is an integer type. **Temp_vec** is allowed, as it is an array type indexed by an integer type and has an integer element type. **Location** is allowed, as it is an enumeration type. **Local_temp_vec** is not allowed, as its index type is not an integer type. **Location_vec** is allowed, as it is an array type indexed by an integer type and has an enumeration element type. **Word_vec** is allowed, as it is an array type indexed by an integer type and has as its element type a one-dimensional array of an enumeration type representing bits.

2. A 2-to-1 multiplexer with **sel** as its select input, **in0** and **in1** as the data inputs, and **z** as the data output. The tests for 'U' and other metalogical values would be ignored by the synthesis tool.

3. A synthesis tool might infer the hardware shown at the left below. This might subsequently be optimized as shown at the right.

4.
```
logic_block : process (enable_n, adr, reg1, reg2) is
begin
  if std_match(enable_n, '0') then
    if std_match(adr, '0') then
      dat_o <= reg1;
    else
      dat_o <= reg2;
    end if;
    ack_o <= '1';
  else
    dat_o <= "ZZZZZZZZ";
    ack_o <= 'Z';
  end if;
end process logic_block;
```

5. The process makes no assignment to **operand** on the path in which **sel** is "11". Hence, the previous value of operand must be stored when **sel** changes to "11". The storage takes the form of a transparent latch enabled by **sel** being other than "11". We can eliminate this storage by adding an assignment of a default value to **operand** in the **others** alternative of the case statement.

6.
```
en_reg : process ( clk ) is
begin
  if rising_edge(clk) then
    if en = '1' then
      reg_out <= data_in;
    end if;
  end if;
end process en_reg;
```

7.
```
type RAM_type is array (0 to 8191) of signed(15 downto 0);
signal RAM : RAM_type := (others => X"0000");
```

8.
```
type decoder_array is array (0 to 15) of std_ulogic_vector(1 to 7);
constant decoder_ROM : decoder_array :=
  ( 0 => "0111111", 1 => "0000110",
    2 => "1011011", 3 => "1001111",
    4 => "1100110", 5 => "1101101",
```

```
        6 => "1111101", 7 => "0000111",
        8 => "1111111", 9 => "1101111",
        others => "1000000" );
...

decoder : seg <= decoder_ROM(to_integer(bcd));
```

9. We can decorate the type **state** with the **enum_encoding** attribute as follows:

```
        attribute enum_encoding of state : type is "00 01 11";
```

Alternatively, we could decorate **state** with the **fsm_state** attribute:

```
        attribute fsm_state of state : type is "00 01 11";
```

or we could decorate the signals **current_state** and **next_state**:

```
        attribute fsm_state of
          current_state, next_state : signal is "00 01 11";
```

Chapter 15

1. a. sub r2, r1, r0: 11 1001 0001 0000 0010 = 0x39102

    b. and r4, r4, 0x30: 01 0010 0100 0011 0000 = 0x12430

    c. ror r1, r1, 2: 11 0000 1001 0100 0011 = 0x30943

    d. ldm r6, (r2)–1: 10 0011 0010 1111 1111 = 0x232FF

    e. out r4, 0x10: 10 1110 0000 0000 1010 = 0x2E00A

    f. bz +7: 11 1110 0000 0000 0111 = 3E007

    g. jsb 0xD0: 11 1101 0000 1101 0000 = 3D0D0

2. a. 0DBC0 = 00 1101 1011 1100 0000: subc r3, r3, 0xC0

    b. 38326 = 11 1000 0011 0010 0110: xor r0, r3, r1

    c. 33D63 = 11 0011 1101 0110 0011: ror r7, r5, 3

    d. 25906 = 10 0101 1001 0000 0110: stm r3, (r1)+6

    e. 3EC11 = 11 1110 1100 0001 0001: bnc +17

    f. 3DC70 = 11 1101 1100 0111 0000: jsb 0xC70

    g. 3F200 = 11 1111 0010 0000 0000: enai

References

[1] P. J. Ashenden, *The Designer's Guide to VHDL, 3rd edition*, Morgan Kaufmann Publishers, Boston, MA, 2008.

[2] P. J. Ashenden, *Digital Design: An Embedded Systems Approach Using VHDL*, Morgan Kaufmann Publishers, Boston, MA, 2008.

[3] C. G. Bell and A. Newell, *Computer Structures: Readings and Examples*, McGraw-Hill, New York, 1971.

[4] D. D. Gajski and R. H. Kuhn, "New VLSI Tools," IEEE Computer, Vol. 16, no. 12 (December 1983), pp. 11–14.

[5] OpenCores Organization, *WISHBONE System-on-Chip (SoC) Interconnection Architecture for Portable IP Cores, Revision B.3*, 2002, www.opencores.org/projects.cgi/web/wishbone/wbspec_b3.pdf.

Index

Page numbers in bold face denote whole sections and subsections that address a topic.

Operators and Symbols

". *See* string literal; bit string literal
&. *See* concatenation operator (&)
'. *See* character literal; attribute name
**. *See* exponentiation operator (**)
*. *See* multiplication operator (*)
+. *See* identity operator (+); addition operator (+)
–. *See* negation operator (–); subtraction operator (–)
. (period). *See* selected name
/* */. *See* comment
/. *See* division operator (/)
/=. *See* inequality operator (/=)
:=. *See* variable assignment
<>. *See* box symbol (<>)
<. *See* less than operator (<)
<=. *See* less than or equal operator (<=)
<=. *See* signal assignment
=. *See* equality operator (=)
=>. *See* choice
>. *See* greater than operator (>)
>=. *See* greater than or equal operator (>=)
?. *See* matching case statement; matching selected signal assignment; matching selected variable assignment
?/=. *See* matching inequality operator (?/=)
?<. *See* matching less than operator (?<)
?<=. *See* matching less than or equal operator (?<=)
?=. *See* matching equality operator (?=)
?>. *See* matching greater than operator (?>)
?>=. *See* matching greater than or equal operator (?>=)

[ ]. *See* signature
\. *See* extended identifier
––. *See* comment

A

abs operator, 36, 38, 41, 58, 294, 300, 308, 309
abstract data type (ADT), 244
abstraction, 3, 153
access type
 synthesis, 378
active, 142
active attribute, 147
adder
 behavioral example, 139, 149
 entity example, 136
 exercise, 196, 198, 199, 332, 333, 355, 357, 373
 function example, 318
 functional example, 170, 301
 generic example, 331
 procedure example, 209
 structural example, 367
 synthesis example, 380
addition instruction, 415
addition operator (+), 36, 38, 41, 58, 294, 300, 307
address alignment, exercise, 236
address decoder
 exercise, 197
 functional example, 118, 240
ADT. *See* abstract data type
aggregate
 array, **99**, 105, 111, 170
  memory initialization, 399
  read only memory, 399
  target of assignment, 102, 170
 as a choice, 124
 choice, 99, 130
 multidimensional array, 100
 record, **130**
 sub-array, 101, 102, 103
alarm clock, **425**
 architecture example, 427
 entity example, 427

structural example, 346
synthesis, **433**
synthesis exercise, 435
alias, **315**
 array, 317
 data object, **315**
 declaration, 315, 320
 non-data item, **320**, 323
 slice, 317
 subtype indication, 317, 320
 unconstrained array parameter, 318, 319
all
 configuration declaration, 341
 process sensitivity list, 163, 214
  synthesis, 383
 use clause, 188, 252
alternative
 case generate, 370
 case statement, 69
ALU. *See* arithmetic/logic unit
analysis, 14, **184**, 342
 order, 185, 248
and gate
 behavioral example, 11, 111, 160
 functional example, 326
 instantiation example, 179, 183, 327
and operator, 46, 58, 59, 114, 229, 296, 301, 307, 308
and-or-invert gate
 behavioral example, 112
 entity example, 137
 exercise, 134
 instantiation example, 182
 structural example, 140
arbiter
 behavioral example, 126
 exercise, 198, 284
 functional example, 146, 170
arccos function, 291
arccosh function, 292
architecture, 8, **135**, 184
 component instantiation statement, 175
 declarative part, 138, 202, 249
 most recently analyzed, 175, 341

499